The
LOW-FAT
WAY TO COOK

The LOW-FAT WAY TO COOK

Oxmoor House®

Copyright 1993 by Oxmoor House, Inc.
Book Division of Southern Progress Corporation
P.O. Box 2463, Birmingham, Alabama 35201

Library of Congress Catalog Number: 93-084154
ISBN: 0-8487-1125-4

Manufactured in the United States of America
First Printing 1993

Editor-in-Chief: Nancy J. Fitzpatrick
Senior Foods Editor: Susan Carlisle Payne
Senior Editor, Editorial Services: Olivia Kindig Wells
Director of Manufacturing: Jerry R. Higdon
Art Director: James Boone

The Low-Fat Way To Cook

Editor: Lisa A. Hooper
Assistant Editor: Anne C. Chappell, M.S., R.D.
Foods Editor: Cathy A. Wesler, R.D.
Assistant Copy Editor: Holly Ensor
Editorial Assistant: Rebecca Meng Sommers
Director, Test Kitchens: Vanessa Taylor Johnson
Assistant Director, Test Kitchens: Gayle Hays Sadler
Test Kitchen Home Economists: Michele Brown Fuller, Telia Johnson,
    Elizabeth Luckett, Christina A. Pieroni, Kathleen Royal,
    Angie Neskaug Sinclair, Jan A. Smith
Assistant Art Director: Cynthia R. Cooper
Senior Photographer: Jim Bathie
Photographer: Ralph Anderson
Senior Photo Stylist: Kay E. Clarke
Photo Stylist: Virginia R. Cravens
Production Manager: Rick Litton
Associate Production Manager: Theresa L. Beste
Production Assistant: Marianne Jordan
Text and Recipe Coordinator: Helen Anne Dorrough, M.S., R.D.

Cover: *Santa Fe-Style Grilled Turkey Tenderloins (page 163)*
Frontispiece: *Grilled Pesto Lamb Chops (page 141) and Pasta and Red Peppers (page 115)*

CONTENTS

LOW-FAT BASICS

Low-fat eating is not just for people who are trying to lose weight. Everyone can benefit from keeping dietary fat to 30 percent or less of total calories. Not only does a low-fat diet help prevent obesity but studies show that it also reduces the risk of heart disease, diabetes, and some types of cancer.

The Low-Fat Way To Cook is a realistic approach to trimming fat from your diet. This cookbook can help you develop an enjoyable, nutritious eating style to follow for a lifetime. If you want to eat healthier foods but don't want to sacrifice taste, this book is for you. All of the recipes are lower in total fat than similar traditional recipes, with the majority having less than 30 percent of calories from fat and less than 10 percent of calories from saturated fat.

The current dietary recommendation to reduce fat intake to no more than 30 percent of total calories refers to the fat intake for the entire day. So if you have one high-fat item during a meal, you can balance it out with low-fat choices for the rest of the day and still remain within the recommended percentage.

The nutrient grid following each recipe lists the grams of total fat per serving, as well as the grams of saturated, polyunsaturated, and monounsaturated fat per serving. Also, the grid lists the grams of protein, carbohydrate, and fiber and the milligrams of cholesterol and sodium per serving. Calories per serving and the percentage of calories from fat follow the recipe yield.

The percentage of calories from fat per serving can sometimes be misleading, so note the total grams of fat per serving as well as the percentage. For example, a salad dressing may have 68 percent of calories from fat, yet still have less than one gram of fat per serving.

The calorie and nutrient breakdown for each recipe is derived from a computer analysis based on information from the U.S. Department of Agriculture (USDA). The nutrient values are as accurate as possible and are based on these assumptions:

• All meats are trimmed of fat and skin before cooking.
• When a range is given for an ingredient, the lesser amount is calculated.
• A percentage of alcohol calories evaporates when heated; this reduction is reflected in the calculations.
• When a marinade is used, only the amount absorbed is calculated.
• Garnishes and optional ingredients are not calculated.

As you become familiar with the equipment, techniques, and methods for cooking with less fat, preparing nutritious recipes will become second nature. The following pages are filled with information to help make low-fat cooking a part of your lifestyle.

Oriental Chicken Stir-Fry (page 154) captures the essence of low-fat cooking. This main-dish recipe features stir-frying, a fast and flavorful low-fat technique, and it is filled with tender chunks of chicken, fresh vegetables, and savory spices.

7

Facts About Fats

How Much Fat Do You Need?

The advice to eat less fat has become familiar, but exactly how much less fat and which foods are lower in fat are not always clear. To get started with a low-fat lifestyle, it's important to know how much fat your body actually needs and to be aware of the different types of dietary fats.

Although it's true that some fat is necessary each day for fat-soluble vitamin transport, the amount needed is minimal. In fact, about a tablespoon of fat is all that is required, and you can easily get that amount in lean meats and low-fat dairy products. The goal, however, need not be to eliminate fat from your diet. You can significantly reduce your risk of disease simply by lowering fat intake from the current U.S. average of 37 percent of total calories to 30 percent of total calories.

Here's an easy way to keep track of the percentage of fat you eat. Instead of calculating fat percentages for each individual food, translate the 30 percent figure into grams of total fat and set a fat budget for the day based on the number of calories you plan to consume. Then simply add up your fat grams at the end of the day.

You can calculate your recommended fat allowance by multiplying your total daily calorie requirement by .30 and dividing by 9. (Fat contains nine calories per gram, while carbohydrate and protein each contain four calories per gram.) See the "Daily Fat Limits" chart above to determine the maximum amount of fat grams allowed each day for you to stay within the recommended percentages for fat. For example, if you are consuming 1,500 calories per day, you should eat no more than 50 grams of fat per day.

DAILY FAT LIMITS		
Calories Per Day	**30 Percent of Calories**	**Grams of Fat**
1,200	360	40
1,500	450	50
1,800	540	60
2,000	600	67
2,200	660	73
2,500	750	83
2,800	840	93

Types of Fats

All dietary fats consist of three basic types of fatty acids and are classified as either saturated or unsaturated, depending on the type of fatty acid that is present in the greatest amount. Saturated fats can raise blood cholesterol levels more than anything else in the diet and should be limited to 10 percent or less of total calories per day.

Saturated fats are easily identified because most of them are solid at room temperature. These fats are found primarily in animal products such as whole milk, cream, butter, lard, whole milk cheese, ice cream, red meat, and poultry skin. Skinned poultry products, fish, and shellfish contain very little saturated fat.

Saturated fats are found in some vegetable products as well. The vegetable fats that are highly saturated — commonly called tropical oils — are cocoa butter and coconut oil, palm oil, and palm kernel oil. Tropical oils are used in many convenience products and confectioneries.

Unsaturated fats are classified as either polyunsaturated or monounsaturated, depending on which type of fatty acid is predominant. These fats come from plants and are usually liquid at room temperature.

Unsaturated fats become more saturated when changed from their natural liquid state to a solid form by a process called hydrogenation. Shortening and margarine are made this way. Hydrogenated or partially hydrogenated fats are saturated and have the same cholesterol-raising abilities as other saturated fats. The more hydrogenation these products undergo, the more solid and saturated they become.

Polyunsaturated fats include vegetable oils such as corn, safflower, soybean, and sunflower oils. Monounsaturated fats include canola, olive, and peanut oils. These fats have been shown to help lower blood cholesterol levels, but that doesn't mean they should be eaten in unlimited amounts. Each should account for no more than 10 percent of total calories per day.

Putting together all of this information to create delicious, low-fat meals isn't hard. Simply emphasize breads, cereals, rice, pasta, vegetables, and fruits; choose fish, poultry, or lean meats; limit added fat; and avoid high-fat foods.

Cutting Techniques

Cutting ingredients correctly is important for successful recipes. Mastering the techniques described and pictured below will ensure that cut foods added to a recipe cook in the time specified. To make cutting easier, begin with a sharp set of knives and a cutting board.

Mince. Cut the food into very small, irregular-shaped pieces.

Dice. Cut the food into cubes that are ⅛ to ¼ inch on each side.

Chop. Cut the food into ¼-inch irregular-shaped pieces (about the size of a green pea).

Cube. Cut the food into small blocks that are ½ inch or larger on each side.

Slice. Hold the food with fingers away from the blade at a distance that equals one slice. Slice; then move fingers back the width of another slice.

Diagonally slice. Cut the food by holding the knife at a 45-degree angle to the food. Diagonal slicing exposes more surface area of the food and promotes faster cooking.

Julienne. Cut the food into ⅛-inch-thick slices; stack slices, and cut into ⅛-inch-thick strips. Cut strips to desired length.

Grate. Push the food across a grating surface to make very fine pieces.

Shred. Cut the food into long, narrow strips or push the food across a shredding surface.

Mince

Dice

Chop

Cube

Slice

Diagonally slice

Julienne

Grate

Shred

Low-Fat Cooking Tools

The right tools will make low-fat cooking easier. You can add pieces gradually as you become more familiar with your cooking needs.

Blender. A blender can be used to puree foods, make breadcrumbs, and blend beverages, sauces, and salad dressings. Although a food processor can perform the same functions, the tall, narrow container of a blender works better for some procedures.

For instance, the shape of a blender makes it ideal for processing small batches.

Colander. A colander or strainer allows you to drain fat from cooked ground meats as well as drain water from pasta or other foods. Spoon cooked ground meat into the colander; let the fat drain, and discard.

Egg separator. An egg separator easily separates the low-fat egg white

from the higher-fat yolk. It traps the thick yolk in the saucer and allows the white to slide through the slots.

Fat-off ladle. The design of this ladle allows fat to be skimmed from meat stocks, soups, and stews. When the ladle is lowered into the liquid, the fat flows through slots around the edge of the ladle and collects in the bowl. When the ladle is full, the fat is poured off from the opposite end.

The right tools make any task easier, and low-fat cooking can be a pleasure with a few key pieces of cooking equipment.

Food processor. A processor can chop, slice, shred, grind, puree, and mix food quickly and easily. Processors vary in capacity and power from compact models to machines designed for large-scale food preparation. Determine how often you will be using the processor and how much food you will be preparing before deciding which model to purchase.

Grater. A grater does many of the same things a food processor does, and it is also useful for small jobs such as shredding cheese or grating orange peel. An upright stainless steel grater with several sizes of grating holes is the best choice.

Gravy strainer or fat-separating cup. A gravy strainer looks like a measuring cup with a spout. The spout is attached near the bottom of the cup,

Skim fat from liquids with a gravy strainer. The fat rises to the top; then the low-fat liquid can be poured from the bottom.

allowing liquid to be poured out while the fat floats to the top.

Hot-air popper. A hot-air popper is a must for popcorn lovers because it pops kernels without the use of fat. Prepackaged popcorn as well as microwave popcorn (even some of the "light" ones) may be loaded with fat. If you don't have a hot-air popper, you can brush a large saucepan with a small amount of vegetable oil before adding the popcorn. Although this method is not fat-free, the popped

corn is much lower in fat than many commercial varieties.

Kitchen shears. Use shears to make easy work of trimming excess fat from meats and poultry, cutting fins off fish, cutting poultry into pieces, snipping fresh herbs, and performing a variety of other kitchen tasks.

Meat thermometer. A meat thermometer helps prevent overcooking and is helpful for cooking lean meats.

Nonstick baking pans, baking sheets, and muffin pans. Nonstick pans allow baking without having to heavily grease the pan, thus decreasing the amount of fat.

Nonstick skillet. A nonstick skillet helps keep fat to a minimum because foods that already contain fat, such as meat and poultry, can be cooked without adding additional fat. And foods that have almost no fat, such as fruits and vegetables, can be cooked successfully with just a little vegetable cooking spray.

Pasta portioner. A pasta portioner helps ensure the correct yield for pasta recipes. Fill the opening for the desired measure with enough pasta to fit snugly in the opening.

Pressure cooker. Today's pressure cooker is safe and easy to use. It can reduce cooking time by one-half to one-third for foods that require long, moist-heat cooking such as less tender, low-fat cuts of meat. A pressure cooker also helps foods retain nutrients that are often lost in conventional cooking.

Ruler. A ruler is helpful for measuring the dimensions and thicknesses of foods that are called for in some recipes.

Scales. Portion sizes are important in healthy cooking, and the cooked weight of a food can be very different from its uncooked weight. Scales reflect those differences and can help you prepare recipes accurately. Look for a model that has a sturdy base,

gives measurements in ounces, and is easy to read and clean.

Spoons. Wooden and plastic spoons should be used when cooking in nonstick pans because metal spoons can mar the nonstick coating. Use metal spoons for general mixing.

Steam basket or steamer. Steaming allows foods to cook without the addition of fat and, because the food is not cooked in the water, vitamin loss

Preserve flavor, texture, and nutrients by cooking fresh vegetables in a steamer.

is minimal. Many varieties of steamers are available, from metal baskets to stackable bamboo baskets. A simple rack or folding steam basket that prevents food from touching the water will work for most recipes.

Wire grilling basket. A grilling basket prevents tender fish steaks, fillets, and vegetables from falling through the grill rack. To prevent sticking and to aid in clean up, coat the basket with vegetable cooking spray before adding the food.

Wok. A wok is the favored cooking utensil for stir-frying because its sloping sides allow for even distribution of heat, quick cooking, and the use of very little oil. The traditional wok has a round bottom for cooking over a gas flame. Flat-bottomed woks and stir-fry pans are for cooking on electric ranges. Nonstick woks and stir-fry pans can eliminate the need for added fat.

Low-Fat Techniques

Described and pictured on these pages are many of the techniques used throughout *The Low-Fat Way To Cook* to lower the fat content of the recipes. By applying these techniques to your own recipes, you can turn high-fat standbys into healthy favorites.

• When purchasing meat, buy only the leanest cuts of beef, pork, lamb, and veal. Select cuts such as beef tenderloin, eye of round, top round, round tip, top loin, and sirloin; pork tenderloin, center loin, leg (fresh ham), and shoulder; leg of lamb, shoulder, and loin; or veal cutlets, sirloin, shoulder, and loin. Be sure to trim all visible fat from the meat before cooking.

• Roast meats and poultry on a rack in a broiler pan to allow fat to drip away. For easy cleanup, coat the broiler pan with vegetable cooking spray before cooking.

• Remove the skin from poultry before cooking. To prevent poultry from drying out, reduce heat and cook just until done.

• Make soups, stews, and stocks or broths ahead of time and chill overnight in the refrigerator. After the soup has chilled, skim off the hardened fat with a spoon, discard the fat, and then reheat.

• If there is no time to chill the soup, stock, or broth overnight, skim off as much fat as possible and add several ice cubes to the warm liquid. The fat

Adding ice cubes to soup

will cling to the ice cubes, which can then be removed and discarded.

• Use a fat-skimmer to remove fat from meat drippings. For further fat reduction, chill the meat drippings in the refrigerator, and then skim off any solidified fat.

• Brown ground meat in a nonstick skillet without added fat or in a skillet coated with vegetable cooking spray. In addition to lean ground beef, try ground turkey or ground chicken. After cooking, spoon the cooked ground meat into a colander

Draining meat in a colander

to drain excess fat.

• To further reduce the fat content of cooked ground meat, pat meat dry with paper towels after draining. If other ingredients are to be added back to the skillet, wipe drippings from skillet with a paper towel.

Skimming fat from soup

Using a fat skimmer

Draining meat on paper towels

• Sauté in a nonstick skillet and use little or no added fat. Coat the skillet with vegetable cooking spray, and stir often to prevent sticking.

Sautéing in a nonstick skillet

Spraying skillet with cooking spray

• Coat baking dishes, baking pans, and casseroles with vegetable cooking spray instead of greasing the dishes with butter, oil, or shortening. You can flour a baking pan that has been coated with vegetable cooking spray just as you would flour a pan that has been coated in the traditional manner with shortening or butter.

• To add more flavor to foods, spray the pan or skillet with olive oil-flavored or butter-flavored vegetable cooking spray.

• Marinate lean meats, fish, and poultry in fat-free or low-fat marinades to enhance their flavors. Reduce or omit oil from marinade recipes by substituting water or broth. Other low-fat ingredients for marinades include citrus juices, wines, and flavored vinegars.

• Use herbs, spices, and salt-free seasoning blends to flavor vegetables, meats, fish, and poultry. Citrus juices, flavored vinegars, and wines can also help bring out the natural flavor of the foods. To substitute dried herbs for fresh, use approximately one-third of the fresh amount.

• Use egg whites or an egg substitute in place of whole eggs. Instead of one whole egg, use two egg whites or one-fourth cup egg substitute. Egg whites and egg substitutes should be cooked over low to medium heat or they will toughen and become dry.

• Use whipped evaporated skimmed milk in place of fat-laden whipping cream or whipped topping mixes. Place evaporated skimmed milk in a mixing bowl; place the mixing bowl and the beaters in the freezer for 30 minutes or until small ice crystals form around the top of the bowl. Remove the bowl and the beaters from the freezer and beat milk at high speed until soft peaks form.

Whipping evaporated skimmed milk

• Cook with wines and other spirits to add flavor but no fat. Experiment with different wines and liqueurs. Most of the alcohol and calories will evaporate during cooking, leaving only the flavor behind. Small amounts of extracts, such as vanilla and almond, also add flavor without adding fat.

• Make nonfat yogurt cheese to use as an alternative to cream cheese and sour cream. Place nonfat yogurt in a yogurt funnel, refrigerate, and let drain for at least 12 hours. Spoon yogurt cheese into a bowl and discard liquid. You can also spoon the yogurt into a colander lined with cheesecloth. Cover and refrigerate 12 hours. Use nonfat yogurt without added

Making yogurt cheese in a funnel

gelatin. One (16-ounce) carton of yogurt will yield about one cup of yogurt cheese.

• Use flavored mustards — either the mild or hot and spicy varieties — as low-fat condiments for sandwiches. But remember that even though mustards are low in fat, they do contain fairly high amounts of sodium.

• Add a sweet touch to bagels, toast, and muffins with jams and jellies; they are essentially fat-free. Try low-sugar jams and all-fruit spreads if you are trying to reduce sugar intake.

Low-Fat Cooking Methods

As you become familiar with *The Low-Fat Way To Cook,* you will see that the cooking methods we use achieve the fullest flavor possible while keeping the fat content low. Cooking methods you'll want to try are described below.

Bake or roast. Cooking in an oven where the food is surrounded by dry heat is known as baking or roasting. Meats and poultry that are baked are generally covered and may have liquid added to help keep them moist. Roasted meats and poultry are cooked uncovered, without the addition of liquid, until they have a well-browned exterior and moist interior.

To prevent lean meats from drying out, marinate in a low-fat marinade before roasting or baste with a low-fat liquid while cooking. Baking works well for lean meats and poultry, and roasting requires fairly tender cuts of meat or poultry.

Braise or stew. Cooking food slowly in a small amount of liquid in a tightly covered pot is known as braising or stewing. Use either of these methods to develop the flavor of the food and to tenderize tough cuts of meat. Unlike stewing, braising requires that meat be browned before it is covered with liquid and simmered. Coat the pot with cooking spray or a small amount of vegetable oil when browning meat. Stewing usually requires more liquid than braising and uses smaller pieces of meat. Refrigerate braised and stewed dishes overnight to allow the fat to congeal on the top; skim off and discard the hardened fat before reheating.

En papillote. Food baked inside a wrapping of parchment paper is referred to as en papillote. As the food bakes and creates steam, the parchment puffs into a dome. The food

cooks in its own juices without the need for added fat. Fish, boned poultry, and other delicate cuts of meat are well-suited for this method of low-fat cooking.

Grill or broil. Cooking food directly over or under a heat source is known as grilling or broiling. The cooking temperature is regulated by the distance between the food and the heat source. For broiling, meats, fish, and poultry should be placed on a rack in a broiler pan to allow fat to drip away from the food. When grilling, coat the grill rack with vegetable cooking spray before placing over the coals. The cooking spray will help keep the food from sticking.

Microwave. A microwave oven cooks food with high-frequency radio waves that vibrate the food molecules and create friction to produce heat and cook the food. Foods cook quickly with little or no liquid in a microwave oven. Microwaving helps preserve flavor, texture, color, and nutrients and requires little or no fat. The foods most suitable for microwaving are those that are conventionally cooked by a moist-heat cooking method. Foods with a high moisture content, such as vegetables, fruits, fish, and sauces, are especially suited for microwaving.

Oven-fry. Baking foods on a rack to give all sides equal exposure to the heat is known as oven-frying. The food is often breaded, and the result is a crisp outer coating and juicy interior similar to that of deep-fat fried foods. Oven-frying is a low-fat cooking method often used for pork chops, chicken, and fish.

Pan-broil. Cooking meats, poultry, or fish quickly in a heavy, ungreased skillet over high heat is known as pan-broiling. Any drippings from the

food are poured off as they form and then discarded.

Poach. Cooking food gently in water or other liquid held just below the boiling point is called poaching. No added fat is required, and the food retains its flavor, shape, and texture. Poultry, firm fish, and firm fruits such as pears and apples are examples of foods suitable for poaching.

Pressure cook. Steaming food under pressure in a tightly sealed pot that has a valve system to control the amount of pressure is known as pressure cooking. Excess steam is released through a series of openings in the cover. This method of cooking eliminates the need for added fat, tenderizes tough cuts of meat, and retains nutrients. New designs in pressure cookers have made them safe and easy to use.

Sauté or stir-fry. Cooking food quickly in a wok or skillet over high heat in a small amount of fat is known as sautéing or stir-frying. Coating a nonstick skillet or wok with vegetable cooking spray or cooking in a small amount of broth, wine, vinegar, or water can eliminate the need for added fat. The ingredients are stirred in the pan constantly during cooking so that they cook evenly. Because it is deep and has sloping sides, a wok requires less fat than does a skillet.

Steam. Cooking food over, not in, boiling water is called steaming. Food is placed on a rack or in a steamer basket and covered. If you don't have a steamer basket, you can place a colander or strainer in a large saucepan and cover it tightly. No added fat is needed for steaming, and the food retains its shape, texture, and flavor. Fish, shellfish, poultry, and vegetables are ideal foods for steaming.

What's on the Label?

As more information about the relationship between diet and disease prevention becomes available, health-conscious shoppers are looking at their grocery lists with a new perspective. The number of low-fat and nonfat items on grocery store shelves has noticeably increased in direct response to consumer demand for healthier foods. Before your next trip to the supermarket, read the following sections on food labeling so you'll be armed with the latest information for making healthy food choices.

In 1990, the Nutrition Labeling and Education Act was passed, which mandated that the Food and Drug Administration (FDA) revise its food-labeling guidelines. The final guidelines were approved in December 1992, and these guidelines reflect the most comprehensive changes in food labeling in 50 years. The purpose of food-label reform is to clear up confusion and to help consumers choose more healthful diets. Two parts of the new food label address the health concerns of today's consumers — the "Nutrition Facts" panel and the ingredient label.

From breads, cereals, and pastas to low-fat cheeses and salad dressings, the grocery store shelves abound with healthy food choices. Read labels carefully when you are making low-fat selections.

Nutrition Facts Panel

Under the new FDA rules, a nutrition facts panel must be displayed on almost all processed foods. The label must list the following information per serving:

Serving size
Servings per container
Calories
Calories from fat
Total fat (grams and percent daily value)
Saturated fat (grams and percent daily value)
Cholesterol (milligrams and percent daily value)
Sodium (milligrams and percent daily value)
Total carbohydrate (grams and percent daily value)
Dietary fiber (grams and percent daily value)
Sugars (grams)
Protein (grams)
Vitamin A (percent daily value)
Vitamin C (percent daily value)
Calcium (percent daily value)
Iron (percent daily value)

The percent daily value is based on a 2,000-calorie diet. The daily value may vary depending on individual calorie needs.

Listing a product's percent of calories from fat will be optional on nutrition labels. If it's not on the label, calculate this percentage by dividing the calories from fat by the total calories and multiplying this number by 100. For example,

Nutrition Facts
Calories 90
Calories from Fat 30
$$30 \div 90 = .33$$
$$.33 \times 100 = 33\%$$

Therefore, approximately 33 percent of the calories per serving of this food are from fat.

The label will also list nutrient intake recommendations for total fat, saturated fat, cholesterol, sodium, carbohydrate, and fiber for a 2,000-calorie diet as well as a 2,500-calorie diet. See the sample label below for an example.

Nutrition Facts

Serving Size ½ cup (114g)
Servings Per Container 4

Amount Per Serving

Calories 90	Calories from Fat 30

	% Daily Value*
Total Fat 3g	**5%**
Saturated Fat 0g	**0%**
Cholesterol 0mg	**0%**
Sodium 300mg	**13%**
Total Carbohydrate 13g	**4%**
Dietary Fiber 3g	**12%**
Sugars 3g	
Protein 3g	

Vitamin A 80%	•	Vitamin C 60%
Calcium 4%	•	Iron 4%

*Percent Daily Values are based on a 2,000 calorie diet. Your daily values may be higher or lower depending on your calorie needs:

	Calories:	2,000	2,500
Total Fat	Less than	65g	80g
Sat Fat	Less than	20g	25g
Cholesterol	Less than	300mg	300mg
Sodium	Less than	2,400mg	2,400mg
Total Carbohydrate		300g	375g
Dietary Fiber		25g	30g

Calories per gram:

Fat 9 • Carbohydrate 4 • Protein 4

Ingredient Label

An ingredient label must appear on all processed foods that contain more than one ingredient. It should list ingredients in descending order by weight. For example, if a product contains macaroni, cheese sauce, and salt, the ingredient that contributes the most weight should be listed first. Unfortunately, it's impossible to determine the percentage of each ingredient from this list. However, by checking the number of fats and fat-containing ingredients in a product, you can tell where the fat comes from and whether it is saturated.

Spotting Saturated Fat

By looking at the ingredient list on the label of a product, you can tell whether the product contains highly saturated fats such as animal fats, tropical oils, or hydrogenated oils. All of the fats and food items listed below are highly saturated and should be avoided:

Beef fat
Beef tallow
Butter
Cocoa butter
Coconut oil
Cream
Hydrogenated vegetable oil
Lard
Palm oil
Palm kernel oil
Shortening
Sour cream
Suet
Whole milk
Whole milk cheese

Instead of buying products made with these saturated fats, choose products that are made with polyunsaturated fats such as corn, safflower, sesame, soybean, or sunflower oils. Or select products with monounsaturated fats such as canola oil, olive oil, or peanut oil.

Claims About Fat

The FDA now has strict guidelines regulating the fat-related claims that can be stated on the labels of packaged products. Listed below are the approved fat-related terms and their definitions.

Fat-free. A product labeled fat-free must contain less than 0.5 gram of fat per serving, and it must not have any added fat or oil. A product that meets this requirement can also be labeled "zero fat" or "no fat."

Low-fat. A low-fat product must contain 3 grams or less of fat per serving or per 100 grams (3½ ounces) of the food.

(Percent) Fat-free. A percent fat-free claim may describe only foods that meet the FDA definitions of low-fat or fat-free that are listed previously.

Reduced-fat. A product that is labeled reduced-fat must contain no more than half the fat of an identified comparison, and the reduction must exceed 3 grams of fat per serving.

Low saturated fat. The product must contain 1 gram or less of saturated fat per serving and no more than 15 percent of calories from fat.

Cholesterol-free. The product must contain less than 2 milligrams of cholesterol per serving and 2 grams or less of saturated fat per serving.

Low-cholesterol. Products labeled low-cholesterol must contain 20 milligrams or less of cholesterol per serving and 2 grams or less of saturated fat per serving.

Lean and extra lean. The terms lean and extra lean on product labels can describe the fat content of meat, poultry, and seafood. A meat labeled lean must have less than 10 grams of fat, less than 4 grams of saturated fat, and less than 95 milligrams of cholesterol per serving. Extra lean products must have less than 5 grams of fat, less than 2 grams of saturated fat, and less than 95 milligrams of cholesterol per serving.

WHAT'S A SERVING?

Under the new FDA labeling regulations, serving sizes on nutrition information labels will be standardized. Serving size will be based on the portion customarily consumed by an average person over the age of 4 years, and it will appear in common household as well as metric measures. Refer to the list of portions below that count as 1 serving.

Breads, Cereals, Rice, and Pasta	Vegetables	Fruits	Milk, Yogurt, and Cheese	Meats, Poultry, Fish, Dried Beans, Eggs, and Nuts
1 slice bread	1 cup raw leafy vegetables	½ cup chopped fresh fruit	1 cup skim milk	2 to 3 ounces cooked lean meat, poultry, or fish
½ bagel	½ cup chopped raw vegetables	½ cup canned fruit	1 cup nonfat or low-fat yogurt	½ cup cooked dried beans
1 English muffin	½ cup cooked vegetables	½ cup cooked fruit	1½ ounces reduced-fat cheese	1 egg
1 hamburger or hot dog bun	¾ cup vegetable juice	1 medium-size piece fresh fruit	2 ounces reduced-fat process cheese	¼ cup egg substitute
1 ounce ready-to-eat cereal		¾ cup fruit juice		2 tablespoons peanut butter
½ cup cooked cereal				
½ cup cooked pasta				
½ cup cooked rice				

Supermarket Selections

Careful reading of product labels when you shop will allow you to choose a variety of low-fat foods that provide the nutrients you and your family need. As you become familiar with the labels of staples and other often-purchased items, shopping for low-fat products will become easier and less time-consuming.

The next time you go to the supermarket, concentrate first on reading the labels of items on your shopping list. Then, if you have time, read the labels of some of the products on one aisle or in one section of the store. Breaking the supermarket into small areas will make the task manageable.

The information on the following pages will guide you down the grocery aisles and help you make healthy, low-fat choices.

Breads and Cereals

Breads and cereals are excellent sources of complex carbohydrates, fiber, vitamins, and minerals. Although generally low in fat, these products become high in fat with the addition of fats and oils during processing. But by choosing wisely, you can make carbohydrate foods the base of a low-fat diet. According to the current U.S. Dietary Guidelines, adults should eat six to 11 servings of carbohydrate-rich foods each day.

Breads. Many varieties of sliced or loaf breads are low in fat. French bread, Italian bread, bagels, English muffins, pita bread, sourdough bread, corn tortillas, and flour tortillas made without oil are also good low-fat choices. Commercial biscuits and muffins are higher in fat than plain breads. Read labels carefully, and choose the breads that are lowest in fat. If you purchase breads that do not have nutrition information labels, select plain breads instead of those that contain cheese, nuts, or seeds.

Cereals. The number of ready-to-eat cereals on the shelves is staggering. Check labels, choosing products that have two grams or less of fat and at least two grams of fiber per serving. Examine the ingredient list for saturated fats, and make sure the first ingredient is a grain instead of a sugar.

Grains, Legumes, and Pastas

Grains, legumes, and pastas are all low-fat sources of complex carbohydrates. In addition to being rich in fiber, vitamins, and minerals, these foods offer a variety of textures and flavors that can keep the excitement in low-fat eating.

Grains. Don't shortchange yourself on grains. Include rice, but also try barley, buckwheat, bulgur, oats, and quinoa. Brown rice has more fiber than white, but both are good low-fat choices. Prepackaged rice mixes usually have added fat and salt, but several are available in reduced-fat, reduced-salt versions. If you are using a regular rice mix, you can cut the amount of fat called for in half.

Legumes. Fat-free and rich in carbohydrate, protein, and fiber, beans are probably the best nutritional buy in the supermarket. You can buy dried beans and rehydrate them yourself, or you can buy canned beans that are ready to heat and eat.

Pastas. Pastas generally contain very little fat. It is the toppings made of butter, cheese, cream, and oil that can turn pasta into a high-fat food. Check the nutrition labels on pasta sauces to determine which are lowest in fat. When preparing creamy sauce mixes, reduce the amount of fat called for and substitute skim milk for whole milk. Most forms of uncooked pasta contain about the same amount of fat, so experiment with different shapes and sizes. Egg noodles contain slightly more fat and cholesterol than other types of pastas, but not enough to make them a high-fat product.

Fruits and Vegetables

Fruits and vegetables are naturally low in fat and high in fiber. They are also good sources of vitamins A and C, iron, magnesium, potassium, and folic acid. Include three to five servings of vegetables and two to four servings of fruit in your meal plan each day.

Fruits. Load up your shopping cart in the fruit section. Buy fresh fruits often and leave the peel on when feasible. Unsweetened canned and frozen fruits provide the same nutrients as fresh fruits, but they usually have less fiber. Choose canned juices that are 100 percent juice. Although fruit drinks and fruit-flavored sodas have little or no fat, they usually have a high sugar content and are not good sources of vitamins and minerals.

Vegetables. Fresh, frozen, and canned vegetables are a mainstay of low-fat cooking. If you are purchasing frozen vegetables, plain ones are best because they contain no added fat. Read the labels of boil-in-bag products, international-style vegetables, and vegetable medleys to choose those that are low in fat.

The wider the variety of vegetables you eat, the better off you will be because different vegetables provide different nutrients. Dark green leafy vegetables and deep yellow-orange vegetables such as spinach, turnip greens, carrots, yellow squash, and sweet potatoes should be eaten several times a week because they are good sources of beta carotene, which converts to vitamin A. Cauliflower, broccoli, and green peppers are good sources of vitamin C; asparagus, turnip greens, and spinach are good sources of folic acid.

Dairy Products

Dairy products are the best food sources of calcium, and they are rich in protein, vitamins, and minerals. Most adults should include at least two servings of dairy products each day. Teenagers, young adults (to age 24), and women who are pregnant or breast-feeding need at least three servings a day. Whole milk dairy products are high in saturated fat, so choose dairy products labeled nonfat, skim, or reduced-fat.

Milk. Skim, ½ percent, or 1 percent milk is the best low-fat choice for people over two years of age. (Children below the age of two do not need low-fat milk.) Two percent milk is not a good low-fat choice because it has about 35 percent of calories from fat. If you prefer the taste of whole milk, try mixing nonfat dry milk powder with skim milk to give it a richer color and texture. The dry milk will also add extra calcium.

Yogurt and sour cream. Nonfat and low-fat yogurt are available in plain and fruit-flavored varieties. Plain yogurt is a good low-fat substitute for sour cream or mayonnaise in many recipes. Also, low-fat or nonfat sour cream alternative can be used in place of regular sour cream.

Cheese. The last few years have brought significant changes in the availability of reduced-fat and nonfat cheese products. Most of these new cheeses are made with either skim or low-fat milk, but some of the "light" cheeses are made by replacing the butterfat in the milk with vegetable oil. This process reduces the saturated fat content of the cheese but not the overall fat content.

FAT PERCENTAGES OF CHEESES

Percent Calories from Fat	Type of Cheese
0 to 9%	Nonfat cottage cheese Nonfat process cream cheese product Nonfat process cheese slices
10 to 29%	1% low-fat cottage cheese 2% low-fat cottage cheese

30 to 39%	Low-fat process American
	  cheese slices
	Low-fat process Swiss
	  cheese slices

40 to 49%	Creamed small-curd cottage cheese Lite ricotta cheese
50 to 59%	Reduced-fat mild Cheddar Reduced-fat sharp Cheddar Reduced-fat colby Reduced-fat Monterey Jack Monterey Jack Part-skim mozzarella Parmesan Part-skim ricotta
60 to 69%	Process American cheese slices Light process cream cheese product Gouda Mozzarella Muenster Provolone Ricotta Romano Swiss
70 to 79%	Blue Brick Brie Camembert Cheddar Colby Edam Feta Fontina Gruyère
80 to 90%	Cream cheese Neufchâtel cheese

Choose nonfat or 1 percent low-fat cottage cheese instead of regular cottage cheese and select nonfat, part-skim, or lite ricotta cheese instead of whole milk ricotta cheese. Nonfat cream cheese product, light process cream cheese product, and Neufchâtel cheese are all suitable substitutes for regular cream cheese.

When buying cheeses such as American, Cheddar, Swiss, Monterey Jack, or mozzarella, choose nonfat or reduced-fat versions that contain five grams or less fat per ounce. Look for reduced-fat cheeses in a variety of forms, including shredded, blocks, processed slices, or spreads.

Meats and Poultry

Meats and poultry are good sources of complete proteins, but they can also be significant sources of fat. Skinned poultry is a low-fat meat, but lean cuts of beef, pork, and lamb can also be included in a low-fat eating plan. Nutrition experts recommend two to three servings of cooked lean meat or poultry each day. Choose meats that are low in fat, and make sure portion sizes are about three ounces of cooked meat.

Meats. Currently, nutrition information labels are not required for fresh meats. Until this type of labeling is mandatory, look for lean cuts that have the least amount of trimmable fat and the least marbling. The chart on page 147 lists the leanest cuts of beef, veal, lamb, and pork.

Consider not only the cut of meat but also the grade. USDA Select is lower in fat than USDA Choice, for example. Low-fat ground meat products are now on the market, and their packages often have labels displaying fat information per serving.

For sandwiches, choose lean deli-sliced ham or turkey, or chicken- or turkey-based cold cuts instead of bologna, salami, or high-fat ham.

Poultry. Poultry is the low-fat star of the meat counter. White poultry meat has less fat than dark, but that doesn't mean dark meat should be avoided; it's comparable in fat content to some lean cuts of red meat.

To choose the bird lowest in fat, remember that smaller chickens (fryers and broilers) are leaner than larger chickens (roasters), and larger chickens are leaner than hens and capons. Most of the fat in poultry comes from the skin or pockets of fat just under the skin, so the skin should be removed either before cooking or just before eating.

Ground turkey is readily available at most supermarkets and is often substituted for ground beef or ground pork in recipes. Most prepackaged ground turkey is a mixture of white and dark meat, unless the label specifically states ground turkey breast. If you prefer white meat only, you can ask the store's butcher to grind turkey breast for you.

When buying a whole turkey, avoid purchasing the self-basting type because commercial basting solutions are high in fat. Baste the turkey with fat-free chicken broth instead.

Fish and Shellfish

Fish and shellfish are good choices for low-fat eating — it's the breading and cooking methods that can make these foods high in fat. Check the labels of frozen commercial products such as breaded fish fillets and fish sticks to make sure they meet the standards for a low-fat food and can be baked instead of fried. Canned tuna, salmon, and sardines are all healthy choices when packed in water instead of oil.

Although shrimp and lobster have more cholesterol than fish and other shellfish, they are low in saturated fat. People who are concerned about cholesterol intake should note that the American Heart Association approves a three-ounce serving of cooked shrimp or lobster per week.

Eggs and Egg Substitutes

One egg contains about five grams of fat and 213 milligrams of cholesterol. To reduce fat and cholesterol in your favorite recipes, substitute two egg whites or one-fourth cup egg substitute for one whole egg. (Two large eggs will generally yield one-fourth cup of egg whites.)

Commercial reduced-cholesterol egg products and egg substitutes are available in the refrigerator and freezer sections of the supermarket. Read labels to find the one lowest in fat because many commercial products contain vegetable oil. Reduced-cholesterol liquid whole egg products are available with 80 percent less cholesterol than shell eggs, but they have the same amount of fat.

Fats and Oils

A healthy diet includes fats and oils in limited amounts. When choosing fats, remember that some are better choices than others. Butter, regular margarine, shortening, and vegetable oils are all 100 percent fat, but the difference lies in whether the fat is saturated, polyunsaturated, monounsaturated, or a combination of these three fatty acids. Choose fats and oils that contain the least amount of saturated fat per serving.

Canola, olive, and peanut oils are highest in monounsaturated fats; corn, safflower, soybean, and sunflower oils are higher in polyunsaturated fats. (See the chart, "Comparison of Fatty Acid Percentages in Fats and Oils," on page 21.)

To reduce saturated fat intake, use margarine instead of butter and choose a margarine that lists water or canola, corn, safflower, soybean, or sunflower oil as the first ingredient.

COMPARISON OF FATTY ACID PERCENTAGES IN FATS AND OILS

All dietary fats contain three basic types of fatty acids. Fats and oils are generally classified as saturated, monounsaturated, or polyunsaturated, depending on which fatty acid is present in the greatest amount. See the graph below for a comparison of the fatty acid contents of various fats and oils.

Type of Fat	Percentages		
Canola oil	7%	58%	35%
Safflower oil	10%	13%	77%
Sunflower oil	11%	20%	69%
Corn oil	13%	25%	62%
Olive oil	14%	77%	9%
Soybean oil	15%	24%	61%
Sesame oil	18%	40%	40%
Peanut oil	18%	49%	33%
Margarine	19%	49%	32%
Cottonseed oil	26%	18%	52%
Vegetable shortening	28%	44%	28%
Lard	41%	47%	12%
Palm oil	49%	37%	9%
Butter	66%	30%	4%
Palm kernel oil	80%	10%	2%
Coconut oil	87%	6%	2%

■ Saturated Fatty Acids

■ Monounsaturated Fatty Acids

□ Polyunsaturated Fatty Acids

Source: *Composition of Foods*, Agriculture Handbook No. 8-4. Washington, D.C., USDA, 1990.

All margarines are mostly fat, but make sure that the saturated fat content is two grams or less per serving.

Reduced-calorie margarines and spreads usually meet the requirement for a low amount of saturated fat. Often, the first ingredient in these products is water, which has been whipped into the margarine to increase the volume without adding fat. Reduced-calorie margarine is available in tubs, squeeze bottles, and sticks.

Nonfat mayonnaise and salad dressings can be used in place of regular mayonnaise and salad dressings in most recipes. Experiment with nonfat salad dressings because some brands have a better taste and texture than others. If you can't quite make the switch to nonfat mayonnaise or fat-free salad dressings, try one of the reduced-fat products; they usually contain about half the fat of regular salad dressings.

Sweets

Although sugars such as granulated, powdered, or brown sugar contain no fat, many dessert products containing these sugars are very high in fat. Most cakes, pies, cookies, and candies are primarily a combination of fat and sugar. The high fat content is one reason that rich desserts should be eaten only occasionally and in small portions.

There are more commercial low-fat dessert items on the market than ever before. Read product labels carefully to determine whether the dessert item is truly low-fat, or whether it simply contains slightly less fat than the original product. Sherbets, sorbets, fruit ices, most ice milks, frozen nonfat and low-fat yogurts, and frozen fruit and juice bars are all good dessert choices. But remember that not all low-fat desserts are low in calories. A product may have less fat but more sugar, making it higher in calories than the original product.

Recipe Modification

Once you are familiar with the low-fat ingredient substitutions and the low-fat cooking techniques in this book, you may want to modify some of your own recipes. Before you start, answer the following questions about your recipe:
- Are all the high-fat ingredients essential?
- Are there nonfat or low-fat versions of any of the ingredients?
- Can a low-fat cooking technique or method be substituted?
- Will the recipe work if some of the high-fat ingredients are reduced or omitted?

For a quick lesson in modifying recipes to lower fat content as well as calories, compare the ingredient lists on the right for the traditional and the low-fat versions of Chocolate Swirl Cheesecake. (The complete recipe for the low-fat cheesecake appears on page 62.) For more suggestions on making low-fat ingredient substitutions, see the chart on page 23.

TRADITIONAL

2 cups graham cracker crumbs
½ cup margarine, melted
¼ cup sugar
1 (15-ounce) carton ricotta cheese, drained
1 (8-ounce) package cream cheese, softened
1 (8-ounce) carton sour cream
1½ cups sugar
2½ tablespoons all-purpose flour
1 teaspoon vanilla extract
3 large eggs
2 (1-ounce) squares semisweet chocolate, melted
¼ cup whipped cream
1 tablespoon grated semisweet chocolate

Yield: 16 servings (365 calories [53% from fat] per serving).

FAT 21.5g (SAT 10.3g, MONO 6.1g, POLY 2.8g)
PROTEIN 7.4g   CARBOHYDRATE 37g
FIBER 0.5g   CHOLESTEROL 79mg   SODIUM 234mg

LOW-FAT

1 cup graham cracker crumbs
¼ cup reduced-calorie margarine
2 tablespoons sugar
1 (15-ounce) carton part-skim ricotta cheese, drained
1 (8-ounce) carton nonfat cream cheese product, softened
1 (8-ounce) carton plain nonfat yogurt
1 cup sugar
2½ tablespoons all-purpose flour
2½ teaspoons vanilla extract
½ cup egg substitute, thawed
2 egg whites
2 tablespoons unsweetened cocoa
1½ tablespoons reduced-calorie margarine

Yield: 16 servings (167 calories [27% from fat] per serving).

FAT 5.0g (SAT 1.6g, MONO 1.5g, POLY 1.1g)
PROTEIN 7.3g   CARBOHYDRATE 22.8g
FIBER 0.2g   CHOLESTEROL 10mg   SODIUM 218mg

Rich, creamy, and luscious — this low-fat version of Chocolate Swirl Cheesecake meets all the standards of a traditional cheesecake, but with only one-fourth the fat and less than half the calories.

LOW-FAT INGREDIENT SUBSTITUTIONS

Recipe calls for:	Substitute:
Fats and Oils	
Butter	Reduced-calorie margarine or margarine with liquid polyunsaturated or monounsaturated oil listed as the first ingredient; also, polyunsaturated or monounsaturated oil
Margarine	Reduced-calorie margarine or margarine with liquid polyunsaturated or monounsaturated oil listed as the first ingredient; also, polyunsaturated or monounsaturated oil
Mayonnaise	Nonfat or reduced-calorie mayonnaise
Oil	Polyunsaturated or monounsaturated oil in reduced amount
Salad dressing	Nonfat or oil-free salad dressing
Shortening	Polyunsaturated or monounsaturated oil in amount reduced by one-third
Dairy Products	
Sour cream	Nonfat sour cream alternative, light sour cream, low-fat or nonfat yogurt
Whipping cream	Chilled evaporated skimmed milk, whipped
American, Cheddar, colby, edam, Monterey Jack, mozzarella, and Swiss cheeses	Cheeses with 5 grams of fat or less per ounce
Cottage cheese	Nonfat or 1% low-fat cottage cheese
Cream cheese	Nonfat or light process cream cheese product, Neufchâtel cheese
Ricotta cheese	Nonfat, lite, or part-skim ricotta cheese
Milk, whole or 2%	Skim milk, ½% milk, 1% milk, evaporated skimmed milk diluted equally with water
Ice cream	Nonfat or low-fat frozen yogurt, low-fat frozen dairy dessert, ice milk, sherbet, sorbet
Meats, Poultry, and Eggs	
Bacon	Canadian bacon, turkey bacon, lean ham
Beef, veal, lamb, pork, high-fat cuts	Chicken, turkey, or lean cuts of meat trimmed of all visible fat
Ground beef	Extra-lean ground beef, ground turkey
Luncheon meat	Skinned, sliced turkey or chicken breast, lean cooked ham, lean roast beef
Poultry	Skinned poultry
Tuna packed in oil	Tuna packed in spring water
Turkey, self-basting	Turkey basted with fat-free broth
Egg, whole	2 egg whites or ¼ cup egg substitute
Miscellaneous	
Soups, canned, condensed cream	99% fat-free condensed cream soups
Chocolate, unsweetened	3 tablespoons unsweetened cocoa plus 1 tablespoon polyunsaturated oil or margarine
Fudge sauce	Chocolate syrup
Nuts	Reduced amount; use one-third to one-half less

APPETIZERS AND BEVERAGES

From simple nibbles to elaborate appetite teasers, these mouth-watering recipes will delight your guests as well as your family. While the fat and calories have been trimmed, the myriad of flavors and variety of textures guarantee satisfaction.

APPETIZERS

Appetizers made with mayonnaise, cream cheese, sour cream, butter, and a variety of aged cheeses have always been popular party fare, but these ingredients can also make a recipe high in fat and cholesterol. Fortunately for healthy eaters, most of these products are now available in reduced-fat or nonfat forms. By simply substituting low-fat ingredients for their higher fat counterparts, you can significantly decrease the amount of total fat, saturated fat, cholesterol, and calories in a recipe.

Although appetizers are not generally considered to be the foundation of a meal, they often incorporate items that make a nutritional contribution. For example, trays of attractively arranged fruits and vegetables served with low-fat or nonfat dips and spreads can boost your intake of vitamins and minerals without fattening consequences.

Appetizers served before the meal should complement the menu. Serve a light appetizer before a hearty meal and a robust appetizer before a meal with milder flavors. The same considerations apply to the texture of the food; if one course is crunchy or chewy, the other should be softer.

The most difficult decision a party planner may face is how many appetizers to serve. First, consider whether the appetizer will be followed by a meal. If so, plan on serving about four bites per person. For a two-hour party for 20 to 40 people that will not be followed by a meal, such as a reception or a cocktail buffet, serve six to eight different appetizers, allowing 10 to 15 bites for each guest.

Serving several cold or room temperature hors d'oeuvres and only two or three hot ones will allow the cook to spend less time in the kitchen and more time visiting with guests.

When casual elegance is the order of the evening, serve Herb-Crusted Beef Tenderloin Appetizers (page 30) and Party Antipasto (page 29).

Dips and Spreads

Flavorful dips and spreads stay in great demand as party fare because they are easy to make and convenient to transport. When served with low-fat crackers or chips and beautifully arranged trays of fresh fruits and vegetables, these types of appetizers are the perfect healthy beginning to a dinner party.

Firm-textured fresh fruits and vegetables make excellent containers for serving dips and spreads. Offer your favorite vegetable dip in an eggplant shell or a head of cabbage that has been hollowed out. Creamy fruit dips are especially appealing when they are presented in a pineapple boat or cantaloupe shell.

Slices of raw zucchini, turnips, squash, and steamed new potatoes are healthy alternatives for canapé bases. Serve your favorite canapé-type appetizers on these low-fat vegetable bases rather than on high-fat crackers and pastries.

CREAMY AMARETTO DIP

2 cups 1% low-fat cottage cheese
¾ cup sifted powdered sugar
¾ cup light process cream cheese
  product
¼ cup amaretto or other almond-
  flavored liqueur

Position knife blade in food processor bowl; add all ingredients, and process until smooth, scraping sides of processor bowl once. Cover and chill thoroughly. Serve with sliced fresh fruit. Yield: 3 cups (26 calories [24% from fat] per tablespoon).

FAT 0.7g (SAT 0.4g, MONO 0.0g, POLY 0.0g)
PROTEIN 1.5g CARBOHYDRATE 2.7g
FIBER 0.0g CHOLESTEROL 2mg SODIUM 58mg

QUICK HUMMUS DIP

1 (15-ounce) can garbanzo beans,
  undrained
2 cloves garlic
1 green onion, cut into pieces
¼ cup lemon juice
2 tablespoons sesame seeds
2 tablespoons plain nonfat yogurt
½ teaspoon ground cumin
½ teaspoon sesame oil
¼ teaspoon ground red pepper

Drain beans, reserving 2 tablespoons liquid; set aside. Position knife blade in food processor bowl; top with cover. Drop garlic through food chute with processor running; process 3 seconds or until garlic is minced. Add beans, reserved liquid, green onion, and remaining ingredients. Process until smooth, scraping sides of processor bowl once.

Transfer mixture to a serving bowl; cover and chill at least 2 hours. Serve dip with toasted pita triangles. Yield: 1¾ cups (31 calories [23% from fat] per tablespoon).

FAT 0.8g (SAT 0.1g, MONO 0.3g, POLY 0.4g)
PROTEIN 1.6g CARBOHYDRATE 4.8g
FIBER 0.6g CHOLESTEROL 0mg SODIUM 32mg

SMOKED SALMON SPREAD

1 (15½-ounce) can red salmon,
  drained and flaked
1 (8-ounce) carton nonfat process
  cream cheese product, softened
1 tablespoon prepared horseradish
1 tablespoon grated onion
1 tablespoon lemon juice
⅛ teaspoon liquid smoke
1 tablespoon chopped fresh
  parsley
48 whole wheat Melba rounds

Combine first 6 ingredients in a medium bowl; stir well. Transfer mixture to a serving bowl; cover and chill thoroughly. Sprinkle with chopped parsley before serving. Serve spread with Melba rounds. Yield: 16 appetizer servings (86 calories [20% from fat] per 2 tablespoons spread and 3 Melba rounds).

FAT 1.9g (SAT 0.5g, MONO 0.8g, POLY 0.6g)
PROTEIN 7.5g CARBOHYDRATE 8.6g
FIBER 0.5g CHOLESTEROL 11mg SODIUM 211mg

HOT ARTICHOKE AND PARMESAN SPREAD

1 cup 1% low-fat cottage cheese
½ cup grated Parmesan cheese
2 tablespoons nonfat mayonnaise
2 tablespoons plain nonfat yogurt
1 clove garlic, minced
⅛ teaspoon hot sauce
1 (14-ounce) can artichoke hearts,
  drained and finely chopped
Vegetable cooking spray
48 whole wheat Melba rounds

Position knife blade in food processor bowl; add first 6 ingredients. Process until mixture is smooth, scraping sides of processor bowl once. Transfer mixture to a bowl; stir in artichokes.

Spoon artichoke mixture into a 1-quart baking dish coated with cooking spray. Bake at 350° for 20 minutes or until thoroughly heated. Serve with Melba rounds. Yield: 16 appetizer servings (73 calories [17% from fat] per 2 tablespoons spread and 3 Melba rounds).

FAT 1.4g (SAT 0.8g, MONO 0.3g, POLY 0.2g)
PROTEIN 4.7g CARBOHYDRATE 10.3g
FIBER 0.6g CHOLESTEROL 3mg SODIUM 158mg

Layered Diablo Dip, packed with Tex-Mex flavors, deserves crisp Corn Tortilla Chips (page 33), which are lower in fat and calories than most commercial chips.

Choose a Healthy Dipper

A little imagination can add new dimensions to dips. Choose an assortment of fresh vegetables or fruits with different textures and colors to serve as dippers. Here are some ideas:

Apple wedges
Asparagus spears
Banana slices
Broccoli flowerets
Cantaloupe cubes
Carrot sticks
Cauliflower flowerets
Celery sticks
Cherry tomatoes
Cucumber slices
Grapes
Green beans (blanched)
Green onions
Green or sweet red pepper strips
Honeydew cubes
Jicama strips
Mushrooms
Peach slices
Pear slices
Pineapple chunks
Radish roses
Snow peas
Strawberries
Sugar snap peas
Turnip strips
Yellow squash slices
Zucchini slices

LAYERED DIABLO DIP

Vegetable cooking spray
6 ounces freshly ground raw turkey
6 ounces ground round
½ cup chopped onion
1 (16-ounce) can pinto beans, drained and mashed
1 teaspoon chili powder
½ teaspoon ground cumin
1 (4-ounce) can chopped green chiles, undrained
½ cup (2 ounces) shredded reduced-fat Monterey Jack cheese
½ cup (2 ounces) shredded 40% less-fat Cheddar cheese
¾ cup no-salt-added commercial picante sauce
½ cup nonfat sour cream alternative
¼ cup sliced green onions
Corn Tortilla Chips (page 33)

Coat a nonstick skillet with cooking spray; place over medium-high heat until hot. Add turkey, ground round, and chopped onion; cook until meat is browned, stirring until it crumbles. Drain and pat dry with paper towels. Set aside.

Combine beans, chili powder, and cumin; stir well. Spread bean mixture in a shallow 1½-quart baking dish coated with cooking spray; layer meat mixture, green chiles, cheeses, and picante sauce over bean mixture. Bake, uncovered, at 350° for 20 minutes or until cheese melts and mixture is thoroughly heated.

Top dip evenly with sour cream and green onions. Serve with Corn Tortilla Chips. Yield: 24 appetizer servings (90 calories [29% from fat] per 3 tablespoons dip and 3 chips).

FAT 2.9g (SAT 1.1g, MONO 0.9g, POLY 0.4g)
PROTEIN 6.2g CARBOHYDRATE 10.2g
FIBER 1.3g CHOLESTEROL 11mg SODIUM 182mg

Cold Appetizers

Cold appetizers are a favorite choice of many cooks because they are easy to prepare and convenient to serve. As an added bonus, they can be made ahead of time and served straight from the refrigerator or at room temperature.

FRUIT KABOBS WITH YOGURT-PINEAPPLE DIP

2 medium-size red apples
2 medium pears
2 tablespoons lemon juice
42 unsweetened pineapple chunks
42 seedless red or green grapes (about ½ pound)
42 fresh strawberries, hulled
Yogurt-Pineapple Dip

Cut apples into 42 bite-size pieces; set aside. Repeat procedure with pears. Combine apple, pear, and lemon juice, tossing gently.

Thread apple, pear, pineapple, grapes, and strawberries alternately on 42 (6-inch) skewers. Serve kabobs with Yogurt-Pineapple Dip. Yield: 42 appetizer servings (42 calories [26% from fat] per serving).

Yogurt-Pineapple Dip
1 (8-ounce) package light process cream cheese product, softened
2 (8-ounce) cartons vanilla low-fat yogurt
1 teaspoon lemon juice
½ teaspoon grated orange rind
⅛ teaspoon coconut extract
1 (8-ounce) can unsweetened crushed pineapple, drained

Beat cream cheese at medium speed of an electric mixer until light and fluffy; add yogurt, lemon juice, orange rind, and coconut extract. Beat until smooth. Stir in pineapple. Cover dip, and chill thoroughly. Yield: 3½ cups.

FAT 1.2g (SAT 0.7g, MONO 0.1g, POLY 0.1g)
PROTEIN 1.3g CARBOHYDRATE 7.3g
FIBER 1.0g CHOLESTEROL 4mg SODIUM 38mg

MUSHROOM-ALMOND PASTRY CUPS

3 sheets commercial frozen phyllo pastry, thawed
Butter-flavored vegetable cooking spray
2 tablespoons blanched slivered almonds, toasted
2½ cups chopped fresh mushrooms
1 clove garlic, crushed
2 tablespoons nonfat mayonnaise
¼ teaspoon dried whole thyme
Dash of ground white pepper
1 tablespoon minced green onions

Place 1 sheet of phyllo on a damp towel (keep remaining phyllo covered). Lightly coat phyllo with cooking spray. Layer 2 remaining sheets of phyllo on first sheet, lightly coating each with cooking spray. Cut stack of phyllo into 18 (3-inch) squares with a sharp knife.

Coat miniature (1½-inch) muffin pans with cooking spray. Gently press 1 stack of phyllo into each of 18 muffin cups to form a shell. Bake at 350° for 8 minutes or until phyllo is lightly browned. Gently remove pastry cups from pans; cool on wire racks.

Place almonds in container of an electric blender. Top with cover, and process 30 seconds or until almonds are ground; set aside.

Coat a large nonstick skillet with cooking spray; place over medium-high heat until hot. Add mushrooms and garlic; sauté 4 to 5 minutes or until mushrooms are tender and liquid evaporates. Add mayonnaise, thyme, white pepper, and ground almonds to mushroom mixture; stir well.

Spoon about 2 teaspoons mushroom mixture into each pastry cup; top evenly with minced green onions. Yield: 18 appetizers (20 calories [32% from fat] each).

FAT 0.7g (SAT 0.1g, MONO 0.3g, POLY 0.2g)
PROTEIN 0.7g CARBOHYDRATE 3.1g
FIBER 0.2g CHOLESTEROL 0mg SODIUM 22mg

CRABMEAT-STUFFED CHERRY TOMATOES

32 cherry tomatoes
¼ cup nonfat cottage cheese
½ pound fresh crabmeat, drained and flaked
¼ cup minced celery
1 tablespoon minced green onions
1 tablespoon minced green pepper
1½ teaspoons lemon juice
1 teaspoon prepared horseradish
⅛ teaspoon garlic powder

Cut top off each cherry tomato. Scoop out and discard pulp, leaving shells intact. Invert tomato shells on paper towels to drain.

Place cottage cheese in container of an electric blender; top with cover, and process until smooth. Transfer cottage cheese to a medium bowl; stir in crabmeat and remaining ingredients. Spoon crabmeat mixture evenly into tomato shells. Cover and chill thoroughly. Yield: 32 appetizers (11 calories [16% from fat] each).

FAT 0.2g (SAT 0.0g, MONO 0.0g, POLY 0.1g)
PROTEIN 1.8g CARBOHYDRATE 0.7g
FIBER 0.2g CHOLESTEROL 7mg SODIUM 29mg

PARTY ANTIPASTO

1 (9-ounce) package fresh cheese
    tortellini, uncooked
1 (15-ounce) can garbanzo beans,
    drained
1 (14-ounce) can artichoke hearts,
    drained and quartered
1 (11½-ounce) jar pepperoncini
    peppers, drained
1 pint small cherry tomatoes
½ pound small fresh mushrooms
1 cup julienne-cut carrot
1 cup julienne-cut celery
1 cup julienne-cut green pepper
1 cup julienne-cut yellow squash
½ cup whole ripe olives
Antipasto Vinaigrette

Cook tortellini according to package directions, omitting salt and fat; drain well.

Combine cooked tortellini, garbanzo beans, and next 9 ingredients in a large bowl. Pour Antipasto Vinaigrette over vegetable mixture; toss gently to coat. Cover and chill mixture at least 4 hours.

Transfer mixture to a large serving bowl, using a slotted spoon. Yield: 24 appetizer servings (75 calories [22% from fat] per ½-cup serving).

Antipasto Vinaigrette
⅔ cup canned low-sodium chicken
    broth, undiluted
¼ cup white wine vinegar
1 (2-ounce) jar diced pimiento,
    drained
1 tablespoon dried Italian
    seasoning
2 tablespoons lemon juice
2 teaspoons sugar
2 teaspoons Dijon mustard
2 teaspoons olive oil
½ teaspoon garlic powder
½ teaspoon salt

Combine all ingredients in a jar; cover tightly, and shake vigorously to blend. Shake vinaigrette well before serving. Yield: 1⅓ cups.

FAT 1.8g (SAT 0.4g, MONO 0.7g, POLY 0.5g)
PROTEIN 3.4g CARBOHYDRATE 12.0g
FIBER 1.4g CHOLESTEROL 5mg SODIUM 213mg

LEMON-DIJON MARINATED SHRIMP

1 quart water
36 unpeeled medium-size fresh
    shrimp (about 1½ pounds)
1 cup water
⅓ cup lemon juice
2 tablespoons Dijon mustard
2 cloves garlic, minced
¾ teaspoon dried whole dillweed
½ teaspoon peeled, minced
    gingerroot
¼ teaspoon crushed red pepper
36 fresh snow pea pods, trimmed

Bring 1 quart water to a boil in a Dutch oven; add shrimp, and cook 3 to 5 minutes or until shrimp are done. Drain shrimp well; rinse with cold water. Chill. Peel and devein shrimp, and place in a shallow baking dish; set aside.

Combine 1 cup water and next 6 ingredients in a small bowl; stir well. Pour over shrimp; toss gently. Cover and marinate in refrigerator 4 to 6 hours, stirring occasionally.

Arrange snow peas in a vegetable steamer over boiling water. Cover and steam 3 to 5 minutes or until crisp-tender. Remove snow peas from steamer, and chill.

Wrap a snow pea around each shrimp; secure with a wooden pick, and arrange on a serving platter. Yield: 3 dozen appetizers (13 calories [14% from fat] each).

FAT 0.2g (SAT 0.0g, MONO 0.1g, POLY 0.1g)
PROTEIN 2.1g CARBOHYDRATE 0.6g
FIBER 0.1g CHOLESTEROL 18mg SODIUM 46mg

SHRIMP AND CRABMEAT CANAPÉS

3 cups water
1 teaspoon liquid shrimp and crab
    boil seasoning
1 pound unpeeled small fresh
    shrimp
½ pound fresh lump crabmeat,
    drained
1 cup finely chopped celery
⅓ cup soft breadcrumbs
⅓ cup nonfat mayonnaise
¼ cup plain nonfat yogurt
1 tablespoon chopped pimiento
1 teaspoon lemon juice
¾ teaspoon low-sodium
    Worcestershire sauce
⅛ teaspoon dry mustard
⅛ teaspoon ground red pepper
72 Melba rounds

Bring water and seasoning to a boil in a medium saucepan; add shrimp, and cook 3 to 5 minutes or until shrimp are done. Drain shrimp well; rinse with cold water. Chill. Peel and devein shrimp; coarsely chop.

Combine shrimp, crabmeat, and next 9 ingredients in a large bowl; stir well. Top each Melba round with 2 teaspoons shrimp mixture. Serve immediately. Yield: 6 dozen appetizers (30 calories [6% from fat] each).

FAT 0.2g (SAT 0.0g, MONO 0.0g, POLY 0.1g)
PROTEIN 2.2g CARBOHYDRATE 4.0g
FIBER 0.3g CHOLESTEROL 11mg SODIUM 75mg

Timesaver for Shrimp

If you are serving shrimp at your next party, purchase peeled and deveined shrimp, and have them steamed at the supermarket. Two pounds unpeeled fresh shrimp equals 1 pound cooked, peeled, and deveined shrimp.

Hot Appetizers

Most hot appetizers need to be prepared at the last minute, requiring additional planning and scheduling. Typically, hot appetizers are creamy seafood dips, savory sausage balls, or other high-fat choices. This section of recipes includes low-fat alternatives that use vegetable mixtures, lean meats, low-fat cheeses, phyllo pastry, and yogurt-based sauces.

HERBED ZUCCHINI CANAPÉS

2 medium zucchini, cut into
 ½-inch slices
Vegetable cooking spray
2 tablespoons minced green onions
2 tablespoons nonfat mayonnaise
1 tablespoon Dijon mustard
¼ teaspoon dried whole marjoram
¼ teaspoon dried whole thyme
½ cup plus 2 tablespoons soft
 breadcrumbs
2 tablespoons grated Parmesan
 cheese
½ teaspoon paprika
1 tablespoon reduced-calorie
 margarine, melted

Arrange zucchini slices on a baking sheet coated with cooking spray. Combine green onions and next 4 ingredients; stir well. Spread mixture evenly over zucchini slices.

Combine breadcrumbs, Parmesan cheese, paprika, and margarine in a small bowl; stir well. Sprinkle mixture evenly over zucchini slices. Bake at 450° for 5 minutes or until lightly browned. Serve immediately. Yield: 30 appetizers (10 calories [45% from fat] each).

FAT 0.5g (SAT 0.1g, MONO 0.0g, POLY 0.0g)
PROTEIN 0.4g CARBOHYDRATE 1.3g
FIBER 0.2g CHOLESTEROL 0mg SODIUM 43mg

APPETIZER CRABMEAT CAKES

Vegetable cooking spray
⅓ cup minced onion
¼ cup minced sweet red pepper
¾ cup plus 2 tablespoons fine, dry
 breadcrumbs, divided
2 egg whites
1½ tablespoons chopped fresh
 parsley
1¼ teaspoons Old Bay Seasoning
¼ teaspoon salt
¼ teaspoon ground red pepper
2½ tablespoons nonfat mayonnaise
1 tablespoon plus 1 teaspoon lemon
 juice
1¼ teaspoons low-sodium
 Worcestershire sauce
1¼ pounds fresh crabmeat, drained
 and flaked

Coat a nonstick skillet with cooking spray; place over medium-high heat until hot. Add onion and sweet red pepper; sauté until tender. Transfer vegetable mixture to a large bowl. Stir in ½ cup plus 2 tablespoons breadcrumbs, reserving ¼ cup breadcrumbs. Stir in egg whites and remaining ingredients.

Shape crabmeat mixture into 48 (1-inch-diameter) patties, using 1 tablespoon mixture per patty. Dredge patties in reserved breadcrumbs. Cover and chill 30 minutes.

Coat a nonstick skillet or griddle with cooking spray; place over medium heat until hot. Add crabmeat patties, in batches, and cook 3 minutes on each side or until golden. Serve warm. Yield: 4 dozen appetizers (19 calories [14% from fat] each).

FAT 0.3g (SAT 0.0g, MONO 0.1g, POLY 0.1g)
PROTEIN 2.0g CARBOHYDRATE 1.9g
FIBER 0.1g CHOLESTEROL 8mg SODIUM 123mg

HERB-CRUSTED BEEF TENDERLOIN APPETIZERS

1½ tablespoons dried parsley flakes
1½ teaspoons crushed black
 peppercorns
¾ teaspoon dried whole thyme
½ teaspoon salt
¼ teaspoon garlic powder
1 (3-pound) beef tenderloin
Vegetable cooking spray
Fluted mushrooms (optional)
Fresh watercress sprigs (optional)
24 (1-ounce) French rolls
Horseradish Spread (page 190)

Combine first 5 ingredients in a small bowl; set aside. Trim fat from tenderloin. Place tenderloin on a rack in a roasting pan coated with vegetable cooking spray. Rub tenderloin with herb mixture. Insert meat thermometer into thickest part of tenderloin, if desired.

Heat oven to 500°; place tenderloin in oven. Reduce heat to 350°, and bake for 50 to 55 minutes or until thermometer registers 140° (rare) or 160° (medium).

Let tenderloin stand 10 minutes; slice diagonally across grain into thin slices, and arrange on a serving platter. If desired, garnish with fluted mushrooms and fresh watercress sprigs. Serve tenderloin with French rolls and Horseradish Spread. Yield: 24 appetizer servings (189 calories [22% from fat] per serving).

FAT 4.9g (SAT 1.8g, MONO 2.0g, POLY 0.6g)
PROTEIN 18.5g CARBOHYDRATE 25.1g
FIBER 0.8g CHOLESTEROL 37mg SODIUM 398mg

SPINACH-RICOTTA PHYLLO TRIANGLES

2 (10-ounce) packages frozen
  chopped spinach, thawed
Butter-flavored vegetable cooking
  spray
1 cup minced onion
⅔ cup crumbled feta cheese
⅔ cup part-skim ricotta cheese
2 tablespoons dry sherry
1 teaspoon dried whole oregano
½ teaspoon garlic powder
½ teaspoon salt
½ teaspoon freshly ground pepper
14 sheets commercial frozen phyllo
  pastry, thawed
Fresh oregano sprigs (optional)

Drain spinach, and press between paper towels until barely moist. Set spinach aside.

Coat a large nonstick skillet with cooking spray; place over medium-high heat until hot. Add onion; sauté until tender. Remove from heat, and stir in spinach, feta cheese, and next 6 ingredients.

Place 1 sheet of phyllo on a damp towel (keep remaining phyllo sheets covered). Lightly coat phyllo with cooking spray. Layer another phyllo sheet on first sheet, lightly coating with cooking spray. Cut stack of phyllo crosswise into 7 strips (each about 2⅓ inches wide) with scissors or a sharp knife.

Working with one strip at a time, place about 2 teaspoons spinach mixture at base of strip (keep remaining strips covered). Fold the right bottom corner over to form a triangle. Continue folding the triangle back and forth to end of strip. Repeat procedure with vegetable cooking spray, remaining phyllo sheets, and remaining spinach mixture.

Place triangles, seam side down, on baking sheets coated with vegetable cooking spray. Lightly spray top of each triangle with vegetable cooking spray. Bake at 350° for 35 minutes or until golden. Transfer triangles to a serving platter, and garnish with fresh oregano sprigs, if desired. Serve warm. Yield: 49 appetizers (37 calories [24% from fat] each).

FAT 1.0g (SAT 0.5g, MONO 0.2g, POLY 0.2g)
PROTEIN 1.7g   CARBOHYDRATE 5.4g
FIBER 0.4g   CHOLESTEROL 2mg   SODIUM 54mg

Press thawed spinach firmly between several layers of paper towels to remove excess moisture and to prevent the filling from becoming soggy.

Fold the narrow strips of phyllo pastry back and forth to form triangles that encase the spinach and cheese filling in neat little packets.

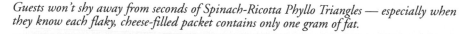

Guests won't shy away from seconds of Spinach-Ricotta Phyllo Triangles — especially when they know each flaky, cheese-filled packet contains only one gram of fat.

Spray Spinach-Ricotta Phyllo Triangles with butter-flavored vegetable cooking spray before baking to give them a golden brown appearance.

31

Lamb Meatballs with Herbed Cheese Dip

2 pounds lean ground lamb
½ cup finely minced onion
¼ cup soft breadcrumbs
2 tablespoons chopped fresh mint
2 tablespoons peeled, minced
  gingerroot
1 teaspoon ground cumin
½ teaspoon salt
¼ teaspoon pepper
¼ teaspoon ground cinnamon
Vegetable cooking spray
2 tablespoons lemon juice
Herbed Cheese Dip

Combine first 9 ingredients in a large bowl; stir well. Shape mixture into 60 (1¼-inch) meatballs. Cover and chill 1 hour.

Arrange meatballs on rack of a broiler pan coated with cooking spray. Broil 8 to 10 minutes or until done, turning once.

Sprinkle meatballs with lemon juice. Serve warm with Herbed Cheese Dip. Yield: 30 appetizer servings (57 calories [36% from fat] per 2 meatballs and 2 teaspoons dip).

Herbed Cheese Dip

1 cup nonfat cottage cheese
1 tablespoon minced green onions
1 tablespoon skim milk
1 tablespoon plain nonfat yogurt
½ teaspoon dried whole dillweed
¼ teaspoon salt
⅛ teaspoon garlic powder
⅛ teaspoon white wine
  Worcestershire sauce

Combine all ingredients in container of an electric blender; top with cover, and process until smooth. Cover and chill. Yield: 1¼ cups.

FAT 2.3g (SAT 0.8g, MONO 1.0g, POLY 0.2g)
PROTEIN 8.0g CARBOHYDRATE 0.9g
FIBER 0.1g CHOLESTEROL 22mg SODIUM 111mg

Strawberry Yogurt Pops and Crispy Snack Mix are healthy after-school snacks.

Snacks

Eating between meals used to be frowned upon, but not anymore. Small snacks throughout the day can give a boost to nutrient intake and add variety to the diet.

Although commercial crackers and other snacks tend to be high in fat, baked snack products that are lower in fat are available.

Strawberry Yogurt Pops

1 (16-ounce) package frozen
  unsweetened strawberries,
  thawed and crushed
1 (8-ounce) carton strawberry
  low-fat yogurt
⅔ cup cranberry juice cocktail
1 tablespoon sugar
10 (3-ounce) paper cups
10 wooden sticks

Combine first 4 ingredients in a medium bowl, stirring well. Spoon mixture evenly into paper cups. Insert a wooden stick into center of each cup, and freeze until firm. To serve, peel cup from pop. Yield: 10 servings (53 calories [5% from fat] each).

FAT 0.3g (SAT 0.2g, MONO 0.1g, POLY 0.0g)
PROTEIN 1.1g CARBOHYDRATE 12.2g
FIBER 0.4g CHOLESTEROL 1mg SODIUM 14mg

Sesame Pita Triangles

3 (6-inch) whole wheat pita bread
  rounds
1 tablespoon low-sodium soy sauce
2½ teaspoons dark sesame oil
¾ teaspoon water
¼ teaspoon garlic powder
2 tablespoons sesame seeds

Separate each pita bread crosswise into 2 rounds; cut each round into 8 wedges. Place wedges, cut side down, on ungreased baking sheets.

Combine soy sauce, oil, water, and garlic powder; brush mixture evenly over wedges. Sprinkle evenly with sesame seeds. Bake at 350° for 10 minutes or until lightly browned. Let cool on wire racks. Store in airtight containers. Yield: 4 dozen (16 calories [28% from fat] each).

FAT 0.5g (SAT 0.1g, MONO 0.2g, POLY 0.2g)
PROTEIN 0.3g CARBOHYDRATE 2.4g
FIBER 0.5g CHOLESTEROL 0mg SODIUM 8mg

CRISPY SNACK MIX

1½ cups small unsalted pretzels
1 cup bite-size shredded whole wheat cereal biscuits
1 cup bite-size corn-and-rice cereal
1 cup commercial plain croutons
¾ cup bite-size crispy bran squares
2 tablespoons reduced-calorie margarine
1 tablespoon low-sodium Worcestershire sauce
2 teaspoons dried Italian seasoning
¼ teaspoon pepper
⅛ teaspoon salt
⅛ teaspoon garlic powder
2 tablespoons grated Parmesan cheese

Combine first 5 ingredients in a large bowl. Toss well, and set aside.

Combine margarine and next 5 ingredients in a small saucepan; cook over medium heat, stirring frequently, until margarine melts. Pour margarine mixture over cereal mixture. Sprinkle with cheese; toss well.

Spread mixture in a 13- x 9- x 2-inch baking dish. Bake at 275° for 45 minutes or until crisp, stirring occasionally. Cool completely. Store in an airtight container. Yield: 5 cups (103 calories [24% from fat] per ½-cup serving).

FAT 2.7g (SAT 0.4g, MONO 0.4g, POLY 0.4g)
PROTEIN 2.7g CARBOHYDRATE 18.0g
FIBER 1.9g CHOLESTEROL 1mg SODIUM 219mg

CORN TORTILLA CHIPS

2 cups water
9 (6-inch) corn tortillas

Pour water into a shallow baking dish. Working with 1 tortilla at a time, dip tortilla into water for 2 seconds. Drain and cut tortilla into 8 wedges. Repeat procedure with remaining tortillas and water.

Place one-third of tortilla wedges in a single layer on an ungreased baking sheet. Bake at 350° for 15 minutes or until crisp and lightly browned. Remove chips from baking sheet; let cool on wire racks. Repeat procedure 2 more times with remaining tortillas. Yield: 6 dozen chips (8 calories [11% from fat] each).

FAT 0.1g (SAT 0.0g, MONO 0.0g, POLY 0.1g)
PROTEIN 0.3g CARBOHYDRATE 1.6g
FIBER 0.2g CHOLESTEROL 0mg SODIUM 7mg

PARMESAN CRACKERS

1½ cups quick-cooking oats, uncooked
1 cup all-purpose flour
¼ cup wheat germ
¾ teaspoon baking powder
¼ teaspoon salt
1½ tablespoons sugar
¼ cup reduced-calorie margarine
⅓ cup plus 2 tablespoons water
Vegetable cooking spray
2 tablespoons grated Parmesan cheese

Combine first 6 ingredients in a large bowl; stir well. Cut in margarine with a pastry blender until mixture resembles coarse crumbs. Add water, stirring just until dry ingredients are moistened.

Place dough on a large baking sheet coated with cooking spray; roll dough to a 12½- x 12-inch rectangle.

Cut dough into 60 (2½- x 1-inch) rectangles; pierce rectangles with a fork, and sprinkle with cheese. Bake at 350° for 22 to 24 minutes or until crisp and lightly browned.

Remove crackers from baking sheet; let cool on wire racks. Store in an airtight container. Yield: 5 dozen (23 calories [28% from fat] each).

FAT 0.7g (SAT 0.1g, MONO 0.2g, POLY 0.3g)
PROTEIN 0.7g CARBOHYDRATE 3.5g
FIBER 0.3g CHOLESTEROL 0mg SODIUM 24mg

Use a ruler and sharp knife to score Parmesan Crackers before baking. During baking, the crackers will pull apart into separate pieces.

Smart Snacks

Instead of high-fat snacks, offer these low-fat alternatives, each with less than 5 grams of total fat:

1 apple
1 banana
1 bagel
8 carrot or celery sticks
½ cup dried fruit
1 English muffin
2 fig bars
3 gingersnaps
1 orange
20 pretzel sticks
2 rice cakes
5 vanilla wafers

BEVERAGES

Offering a refreshing drink to guests has long been a symbol of hospitality. Drinking cool beverages is also a good way to quench thirsts and replace fluids after exercise. For tasty sippers that are satisfying yet low in fat and calories, offer a beverage in this section to family and friends.

Although many beverage recipes have little or no fat, creamier ones tend to be higher in fat. To lower the fat content in your favorite beverage recipe, substitute low-fat or nonfat dairy products for whole milk products. For example, substitute skim milk for half-and-half or whole milk,

and ice milk or low-fat or nonfat frozen yogurt for ice cream.

Many of the beverages in this chapter can be made ahead and stored in the refrigerator until serving time. If the recipe calls for a carbonated beverage or alcohol, wait until just before serving to add it to the recipe.

Cold and Hot Beverages

Most of the recipes featured in this section are easy to put together. And although the recipes are simple to prepare, their flavors are much more sophisticated than that of a can of soda or a bottle of fruit juice.

Most of these beverage recipes make enough to serve several people. However, if you are looking for a recipe to serve a crowd, many can easily be doubled or tripled.

ORANGE JUICY

1 (12-ounce) can frozen orange
  juice concentrate, thawed and
  undiluted
2 cups water
2 cups skim milk
½ cup sugar
2 teaspoons vanilla extract
¼ teaspoon almond extract
8 cups ice cubes

Combine half of each of the first 6 ingredients in container of an electric blender; top with cover, and process 30 seconds. Gradually add 4 cups ice cubes, and process until mixture is smooth.

Transfer mixture to a large pitcher. Repeat procedure with remaining half

of ingredients. Serve immediately. Yield: 3 quarts (94 calories [1% from fat] per 1-cup serving).

FAT 0.1g (SAT 0.1g, MONO 0.0g, POLY 0.0g)
PROTEIN 2.1g CARBOHYDRATE 21.3g
FIBER 0.2g CHOLESTEROL 1mg SODIUM 22mg

SPARKLING RASPBERRY SPRITZER

1 (16-ounce) package frozen
  unsweetened raspberries, thawed
1 (24-ounce) bottle white grape
  juice, chilled
1¾ cups club soda, chilled

Place raspberries in container of an electric blender; top with cover, and process until smooth. Strain raspberry puree, and discard seeds.

Combine raspberry puree and grape juice in a medium pitcher, stirring well. Stir in club soda just before serving. Serve immediately. Yield: 1½ quarts (112 calories [3% from fat] per 1-cup serving).

FAT 0.4g (SAT 0.0g, MONO 0.0g, POLY 0.2g)
PROTEIN 0.7g CARBOHYDRATE 28.0g
FIBER 5.6g CHOLESTEROL 0mg SODIUM 18mg

RUBY REFRESHER

1 (16-ounce) bag unsweetened
  frozen strawberries
1 (12-ounce) can frozen cranberry
  juice cocktail concentrate,
  thawed and undiluted
1 cup unsweetened pineapple juice,
  chilled
¼ cup lemon juice, chilled
2½ cups club soda, chilled

Combine strawberries and cranberry juice concentrate in container of an electric blender or food processor; top with cover, and process until smooth. Transfer mixture to a large pitcher; stir in pineapple juice and lemon juice. Stir in club soda just before serving. Serve immediately. Yield: 2 quarts (189 calories [1% from fat] per 1-cup serving).

FAT 0.2g (SAT 0.0g, MONO 0.0g, POLY 0.1g)
PROTEIN 0.4g CARBOHYDRATE 48.6g
FIBER 0.5g CHOLESTEROL 0mg SODIUM 27mg

These refreshing sippers are low in fat and high in flavor. Clockwise from top right: Tropical Mango Cooler, Sparkling Raspberry Spritzer, and Banana Split Smoothie.

BANANA SPLIT SMOOTHIE

1¼ cups peeled, sliced ripe banana
  (about 2 medium)
1 (8-ounce) can crushed pineapple
  in juice, undrained
1 cup crushed ice
½ cup unsweetened orange juice
1 teaspoon sugar
1 (8-ounce) carton vanilla low-fat
  yogurt

    Combine first 5 ingredients in container of an electric blender. Top with cover; process until smooth. Add yogurt; process until blended. Serve immediately. Yield: 4 cups (138 calories [7% from fat] per 1-cup serving).

FAT 1.0g (SAT 0.5g, MONO 0.2g, POLY 0.2g)
PROTEIN 3.7g CARBOHYDRATE 30.7g
FIBER 1.7g CHOLESTEROL 3mg SODIUM 39mg

VANILLA MILKSHAKE

4 cups vanilla nonfat frozen yogurt
1¾ cups skim milk
½ teaspoon vanilla extract

    Combine all ingredients in container of an electric blender. Top with cover; process until smooth. Serve immediately. Yield: 5 cups (162 calories [1% from fat] per 1-cup serving).

FAT 0.1g (SAT 0.1g, MONO 0.0g, POLY 0.0g)
PROTEIN 8.4g CARBOHYDRATE 33.2g
FIBER 0.0g CHOLESTEROL 2mg SODIUM 141mg

Chocolate Milkshake: Substitute 4½ cups chocolate nonfat frozen yogurt for vanilla nonfat frozen yogurt; add ⅓ cup chocolate syrup. Omit vanilla. Yield: 6 cups (196 calories [1% from fat] per 1-cup serving).

FAT 0.3g (SAT 0.1g, MONO 0.0g, POLY 0.0g)
PROTEIN 8.4g CARBOHYDRATE 41.6g
FIBER 0g CHOLESTEROL 1mg SODIUM 142mg

TROPICAL MANGO COOLER

1 cup cubed ripe mango
1 cup apricot nectar
¼ cup frozen tangerine juice
  concentrate, thawed and
  undiluted
1 tablespoon fresh lime juice
2 teaspoons sugar
¼ teaspoon almond extract
¼ teaspoon vanilla extract
¼ teaspoon rum flavoring
2 cups club soda, chilled

    Combine first 8 ingredients in container of an electric blender; top with cover, and process until smooth. Transfer mixture to a pitcher. Stir in club soda just before serving. Serve over ice. Yield: 4 cups (106 calories [2% from fat] per 1-cup serving).

FAT 0.2g (SAT 0.0g, MONO 0.1g, POLY 0.0g)
PROTEIN 0.7g CARBOHYDRATE 26.3g
FIBER 1.1g CHOLESTEROL 0mg SODIUM 27mg

LEMON-MINT TEA

10 lemon-flavored tea bags
3 tablespoons crushed fresh
  mint leaves
2 cups boiling water
1¼ cups fresh orange juice
1 (6-ounce) can frozen lemonade
  concentrate, thawed and
  undiluted
¼ cup sugar
8¼ cups water

Place tea bags and mint leaves in a pitcher; add boiling water. Cover and steep 5 minutes. Remove and discard tea bags; stir in orange juice, lemonade concentrate, sugar, and 8¼ cups water. Cover; chill at least 8 hours.

Strain mixture; discard mint. Serve over ice. Yield: 3 quarts (54 calories [0% from fat] per 1-cup serving).

FAT 0.0g (SAT 0.0g, MONO 0.0g, POLY 0.0g)
PROTEIN 0.2g   CARBOHYDRATE 13.7g
FIBER 0.1g   CHOLESTEROL 0mg   SODIUM 2mg

SPICED TEA MIX

3 cups orange-flavored breakfast
  beverage crystals
2 cups sugar
½ cup instant tea
1 (.31-ounce) package unsweetened
  lemon-flavored drink mix
1½ teaspoons ground cinnamon
1 teaspoon ground cloves

Combine all ingredients in a large bowl; stir well. Store mix in an airtight container at room temperature.

For each serving, place 2 tablespoons mix in a cup; stir in ¾ cup hot water. Yield: 40 servings (148 calories [0% from fat] per serving).

FAT 0.0g (SAT 0.0g, MONO 0.0g, POLY 0.0g)
PROTEIN 0.1g   CARBOHYDRATE 37g
FIBER 0.1g   CHOLESTEROL 0mg   SODIUM 3mg

SPICED COFFEE

¾ cup ground Colombian coffee
¾ teaspoon ground cinnamon
¼ teaspoon ground nutmeg
2 teaspoons vanilla extract
8½ cups water

Place coffee in filter basket; sprinkle with cinnamon, nutmeg, and vanilla. Add water to coffee maker; brew according to manufacturer's directions. Yield: 2 quarts (9 calories [0% from fat] per 1-cup serving).

FAT 0.0g (SAT 0.0g, MONO 0.0g, POLY 0.0g)
PROTEIN 0.2g   CARBOHYDRATE 1.5g
FIBER 0.1g   CHOLESTEROL 0mg   SODIUM 5mg

CHILLED COFFEE PUNCH

4 cups strong brewed coffee
2 tablespoons sugar
4 cups skim milk
1 tablespoon brandy extract
1 teaspoon vanilla extract

Combine coffee and sugar in a pitcher. Chill thoroughly. Stir in milk and remaining ingredients. Serve over ice. Yield: 2 quarts (67 calories [3% from fat] per 1-cup serving).

FAT 0.2g (SAT 0.1g, MONO 0.1g, POLY 0.0g)
PROTEIN 4.3g   CARBOHYDRATE 9.7g
FIBER 0.0g   CHOLESTEROL 2mg   SODIUM 66mg

DELUXE HOT CHOCOLATE

⅓ cup firmly packed brown sugar
⅓ cup unsweetened cocoa
1 cup water
5 cups skim milk
1 teaspoon vanilla extract

Combine brown sugar and cocoa in a saucepan; stir in water. Bring to a boil over medium heat, stirring occasionally; reduce heat, and slowly stir in milk. Cook until thoroughly heated, stirring constantly. Remove from heat; stir in vanilla. Serve immediately. Yield: 1½ quarts (105 calories [7% from fat] per ¾-cup serving).

FAT 0.8g (SAT 0.5g, MONO 0.1g, POLY 0.0g)
PROTEIN 6.3g   CARBOHYDRATE 18.2g
FIBER 0.0g   CHOLESTEROL 3mg   SODIUM 84mg

A LITTLE CREAM IN YOUR COFFEE?

Adding a little cream, half-and-half, or nondairy creamer to a cup of coffee can add more fat than you may think. Note the amount of fat and calories in 2 tablespoons of each of the following products.

Product	Fat (grams)	Calories
Heavy cream	11.2	104
Powdered nondairy creamer	4.2	66
Half-and-half	3.4	40
Liquid nondairy creamer	3.2	44
Whole milk	1.0	19
2% milk	0.6	15
Skim milk	0.1	11

If you are partial to nondairy creamers, be sure to read the labels. These products vary in the type of fat used, and some are high in saturated fats. Look for nondairy creamers made with polyunsaturated fats.

Spirited Beverages

The recipes featured here are favorites that your guests are sure to enjoy. Chances are you won't be able to tell the difference between the low-fat and original versions of Creamy Piña Coladas or Holiday Nog, a delightful low-cholesterol version of the traditional holiday favorite.

HOT SPICED WINE

1 cup water
1 cup unsweetened apple juice
1 cup unsweetened orange juice
⅓ cup sugar
2 teaspoons whole cloves
4 (3-inch) sticks cinnamon
6 lemon slices
6 orange slices
5 cups Burgundy or other dry
    red wine
Cinnamon sticks (optional)

Combine first 4 ingredients in a large nonaluminum saucepan; stir well. Place cloves and cinnamon sticks on a small piece of cheesecloth; tie ends of cheesecloth together. Add cheesecloth bag to juice mixture. Bring mixture to a boil; reduce heat, and simmer 10 minutes, stirring occasionally. Remove from heat; add lemon and orange slices. Cover; let stand 15 minutes.

Add wine to juice mixture; stir well. Bring mixture almost to a boil (do not boil). Remove and discard cheesecloth bag and fruit slices. Pour hot beverage into mugs, and garnish with cinnamon sticks, if desired. Yield: 7½ cups (55 calories [0% from fat] per ¾-cup serving).

FAT 0.0g (SAT 0.0g, MONO 0.0g, POLY 0.0g)
PROTEIN 0.4g   CARBOHYDRATE 13.8g
FIBER 0.1g   CHOLESTEROL 0mg   SODIUM 10mg

SUNSHINE MARGARITAS

1⅔ cups fresh orange juice
1 cup frozen limeade concentrate,
    thawed and undiluted
⅔ cup tequila
4 cups ice cubes
2 cups club soda, chilled
Lime slices (optional)
Orange slices (optional)

Combine first 3 ingredients in container of an electric blender; top with cover, and process 30 seconds. Gradually add ice cubes; process until smooth. Transfer mixture to a large pitcher.

Just before serving, add club soda to orange juice mixture; stir gently. Pour beverage into glasses. If desired, garnish each glass with lime slices and orange slices; serve immediately. Yield: 2 quarts (135 calories [1% from fat] per 1-cup serving).

FAT 0.1g (SAT 0.0g, MONO 0.0g, POLY 0.0g)
PROTEIN 0.4g   CARBOHYDRATE 23.6g
FIBER 0.1g   CHOLESTEROL 0mg   SODIUM 13mg

HOLIDAY NOG

2 (12-ounce) cans evaporated
    skimmed milk
3 cups skim milk
1½ cups frozen egg substitute,
    thawed
¾ cup sifted powdered sugar
2 cups vanilla nonfat frozen yogurt,
    softened
⅔ cup bourbon
2 tablespoons vanilla extract
Freshly grated nutmeg (optional)

Combine first 4 ingredients in a large pitcher, stirring well. Chill mixture thoroughly.

To serve, transfer chilled mixture to a large punch bowl. Stir in softened frozen yogurt, bourbon, and vanilla. Sprinkle with freshly grated nutmeg, if desired. Serve immediately. Yield: 2½ quarts (105 calories [2% from fat] per ½-cup serving).

FAT 0.2g (SAT 0.1g, MONO 0.0g, POLY 0.0g)
PROTEIN 6.3g   CARBOHYDRATE 14.5g
FIBER 0.0g   CHOLESTEROL 2mg   SODIUM 97mg

CREAMY PIÑA COLADAS

1 (8-ounce) can pineapple chunks
    in juice, undrained
1 large ripe banana, peeled and
    sliced
1 (12-ounce) can evaporated
    skimmed milk, chilled
¼ cup light rum
½ teaspoon coconut extract
Ice cubes

Combine half of each of first 5 ingredients in container of an electric blender; top with cover, and process until smooth. Gradually add enough ice cubes to bring mixture to 3-cup level; process until smooth.

Transfer mixture to a pitcher. Repeat procedure with remaining half of ingredients. Serve immediately. Yield: 1½ quarts (115 calories [2% from fat] per 1-cup serving).

FAT 0.3g (SAT 0.1g, MONO 0.0g, POLY 0.0g)
PROTEIN 4.7g   CARBOHYDRATE 17.4g
FIBER 0.8g   CHOLESTEROL 2mg   SODIUM 66mg

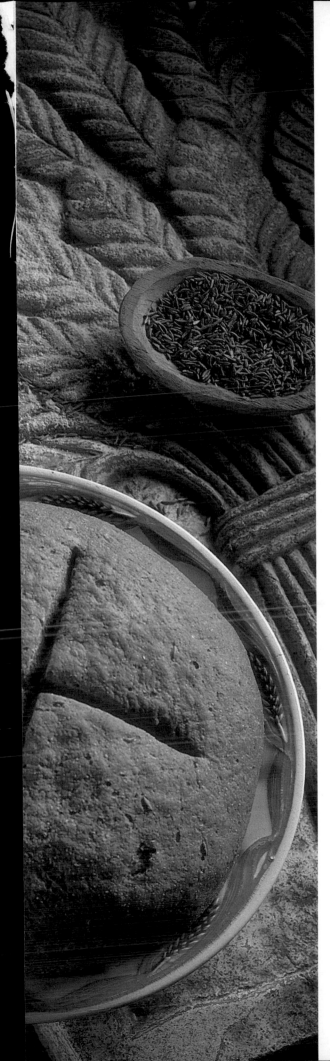

BREADS

Nothing quite compares with the enticing aroma of homemade bread baking in the oven, and those who bake their own breads can attest to the fact that it is a rewarding and satisfying experience. Breads are also a good source of complex carbohydrates, fiber, B vitamins, and iron.

Breads are little more than flour mixed with a liquid, a leavening agent, and a fat, with a few other ingredients added for flavor and variety. With some simple ingredient adjustments, most breads can fit easily into a low-fat lifestyle.

The fat content in a bread recipe increases with the addition of shortening, butter, margarine, oil, whole milk, eggs, sour cream, and cheese. Thus to decrease the fat content, our recipes have been modified to use reduced-calorie margarine, egg substitute, skim milk, yogurt, reduced-fat cheeses, and smaller amounts of regular margarine and vegetable oil. Whenever possible, the number of whole eggs has been reduced, and egg whites have been added to make up the difference in volume.

If you are new to bread baking, start with some easy quick breads such as Orange Biscuits or Granola Muffins. Once you are comfortable with quick breads, move on to a basic yeast bread such as Whole Wheat Rolls. Then you'll be ready to tackle fun variations such as Apple Danish or Cinnamon-Almond Sweet Rolls.

The texture of a bread depends a great deal on the type of flour used. Most flours contain varying amounts of a protein called gluten. Kneading the dough develops the gluten, which gives the bread its structure and helps hold in gas bubbles formed by the leavening agent.

Bread flour is a high-protein, hard wheat flour with a high gluten content, making it ideal for yeast breads that require an elastic framework developed by a long kneading process.

All-purpose flour is a combination of hard and soft wheat flours and works well for most baked products. Self-rising flour is simply all-purpose flour that has had a leavening agent and salt blended in before packaging.

Whole wheat flour contains wheat germ, which gives it not only a higher fiber content but also a slightly higher fat content due to the oils found in the germ. Whole wheat flour should be refrigerated to prevent the oils from turning rancid.

Whole wheat flour has a low gluten content, so it works best when used with all-purpose flour or bread flour. This combination provides a better texture by strengthening the framework of the bread.

All-purpose flour may be stored for up to 12 months, while self rising flour retains its leavening ability for about six months. Store all-purpose and self-rising flour in airtight containers in a cool, dry place.

Whole wheat flour, rye flour, and caraway seeds are the key ingredients in these hearty loaves of Molasses Rye Loaf and Pumpernickel Bread (page 52).

Quick breads are just that — quick! They require no rising time and little, if any, kneading. They are usually leavened by baking powder or baking soda that starts the rising process when a liquid is added. Eggs may also be used as a leavener.

Quick breads fall into two categories — batter and dough breads.

Batter breads include muffins, cornbreads, loaf breads, pancakes, and waffles. For most, the dry ingredients are combined, then the liquid ingredients are combined and added to the dry ingredients. The batter is stirred just until the dry ingredients are moistened. Overmixing will create tunnels, peaks, and a coarse texture.

Dough breads include biscuits, scones, and some coffee cakes. Quick dough breads are made by cutting a solid fat into the dry ingredients, then gently stirring in a liquid. The dough is kneaded several times on a lightly floured surface to help blend the ingredients and improve the texture of the bread.

Biscuits

Traditionally, vegetable shortening or lard has been used as the fat in biscuits. However, these products are almost never used in low-fat recipes because of their extremely high saturated fat content. Vegetable oil may sometimes be used in place of shortening, and reduced-calorie and regular margarines are often substituted.

Although most biscuits use baking powder or baking soda for leavening, Whole Wheat Yeast Biscuits contains yeast in addition to the traditional leavening ingredients.

A good biscuit should double in height during baking. The top crust should be golden brown and the sides lighter in color. The inside of a biscuit should be flaky and tender.

EASY DROP BISCUITS

1½ cups all-purpose flour
2 teaspoons baking powder
½ teaspoon baking soda
¼ teaspoon salt
1 cup plain low-fat yogurt
¼ cup frozen egg substitute, thawed
1 tablespoon vegetable oil
Vegetable cooking spray

Combine first 4 ingredients; make a well in center of mixture. Combine yogurt, egg substitute, and oil; add to flour mixture, stirring just until dry ingredients are moistened.

Drop dough by rounded tablespoonfuls, 2 inches apart, onto a baking sheet coating with cooking spray. Bake at 400° for 15 minutes or until golden. Yield: 1 dozen (82 calories [18% from fat] each).

FAT 1.6g (SAT 0.4g, MONO 0.4g, POLY 0.6g)
PROTEIN 3.1g · CARBOHYDRATE 13.5g
FIBER 0.4g CHOLESTEROL 1mg SODIUM 154mg

ORANGE DROP BISCUITS

1¼ cups all-purpose flour
1½ teaspoons baking powder
¼ teaspoon baking soda
1 tablespoon sugar
3 tablespoons reduced-calorie margarine
⅓ cup 1% low-fat cottage cheese
¼ cup frozen egg substitute, thawed
3 tablespoons low-sugar orange marmalade
¾ teaspoon grated orange rind
Vegetable cooking spray

Combine first 4 ingredients; cut in margarine with a pastry blender until mixture resembles coarse meal. Combine cottage cheese, egg substitute, orange marmalade, and orange rind; add to flour mixture, stirring just until dry ingredients are moistened.

Drop dough by tablespoonfuls onto a baking sheet coated with cooking spray. Bake at 400° for 8 minutes or until golden. Yield: 20 biscuits (45 calories [24% from fat] each).

FAT 1.2g (SAT 0.2g, MONO 0.4g, POLY 0.5g)
PROTEIN 1.6g CARBOHYDRATE 7.0g
FIBER 0.2g CHOLESTEROL 0mg SODIUM 70mg

Preparing drop biscuits is easy — just combine the ingredients, and drop the dough by spoonfuls onto a baking sheet.

Even the busiest person will stop for breakfast when it includes Whole Wheat Yeast Biscuits.

CHEESE AND BASIL BISCUITS

1 cup plus 1 tablespoon all-purpose flour
¼ cup white cornmeal
1¾ teaspoons baking powder
¼ teaspoon salt
2 tablespoons unsalted margarine
½ cup skim milk
¼ cup (1 ounce) shredded reduced-fat sharp Cheddar cheese
2½ tablespoons chopped fresh basil
1 tablespoon all-purpose flour
Vegetable cooking spray

Combine first 4 ingredients in a medium bowl; cut in margarine with a pastry blender until mixture resembles coarse meal. Combine milk, cheese, and basil; add to flour mixture, stirring just until dry ingredients are moistened.

Sprinkle 1 tablespoon flour over work surface. Turn dough out onto surface; knead 3 or 4 times. Roll dough to ½-inch thickness; cut with a 2-inch biscuit cutter. Place rounds on a baking sheet coated with cooking spray. Bake at 425° for 12 minutes or until golden. Yield: 1 dozen (82 calories [29% from fat] each).

FAT 2.6g (SAT 0.7g, MONO 1.0g, POLY 0.7g)
PROTEIN 2.5g CARBOHYDRATE 12.0g
FIBER 0.5g CHOLESTEROL 2mg SODIUM 115mg

WHOLE WHEAT YEAST BISCUITS

1 package dry yeast
¼ cup warm water (105° to 115°)
1¾ cups plus 2 tablespoons all-purpose flour
¾ cup whole wheat flour
1 teaspoon baking powder
½ teaspoon baking soda
¼ teaspoon salt
1 tablespoon sugar
3 tablespoons reduced-calorie margarine
⅔ cup nonfat buttermilk
2 tablespoons all-purpose flour
Vegetable cooking spray

Dissolve yeast in warm water in a small bowl; let stand 5 minutes.

Combine all-purpose flour and next 5 ingredients in a medium bowl; cut in margarine with a pastry blender until mixture resembles coarse meal. Add yeast mixture and buttermilk to flour mixture, stirring just until dry ingredients are moistened. Cover and refrigerate 8 hours.

Sprinkle 2 tablespoons all-purpose flour evenly over work surface. Turn dough out onto floured surface, and knead for 1 minute. Roll dough to ½-inch thickness on floured surface; cut into rounds with a 2-inch biscuit cutter. Place rounds on a baking sheet coated with cooking spray. Bake at 425° for 10 to 12 minutes or until golden. Yield: 16 biscuits (82 calories [19% from fat] each).

FAT 1.7g (SAT 0.3g, MONO 0.5g, POLY 0.7g)
PROTEIN 2.5g CARBOHYDRATE 14.5g
FIBER 1.2g CHOLESTEROL 0mg SODIUM 113mg

The Proper Measure

To measure flour accurately, stir lightly, then spoon the flour into a dry-ingredient measuring cup. Use the straight edge of a knife or spatula to level, and avoid shaking the cup as this packs the flour.

Muffins are a favorite bread for breakfast, lunch, dinner, and snacks. Baking them is easy, and you can control how much fat is added, making homemade muffins a healthier choice than most commercial brands.

To achieve the best texture in muffins, mix ingredients properly. Combine the dry ingredients; make a well in the center of the mixture. Combine the liquid ingredients, and pour into the well, stirring just until the dry ingredients are moistened. If the batter is stirred until all the lumps are removed, the muffins will form pointed tops and tunnels will develop throughout. Although the taste won't be affected if this happens, the muffins may be tough.

Unless the recipe states otherwise, remove muffins from pans immediately after baking to prevent them from getting moist on the bottom.

APPLE AND SPICE MUFFINS

1 cup all-purpose flour
1 cup whole wheat flour
1½ teaspoons baking powder
½ teaspoon baking soda
¼ teaspoon salt
⅓ cup toasted wheat germ
¼ cup firmly packed brown sugar
1 teaspoon ground cinnamon
¼ teaspoon ground nutmeg
½ cup skim milk
2 tablespoons vegetable oil
1 egg, lightly beaten
2 egg whites, lightly beaten
2 cups peeled, shredded cooking apple
1 teaspoon grated lemon rind
Vegetable cooking spray

Combine first 9 ingredients in a large bowl; make a well in center of mixture. Combine milk, oil, egg, and egg whites; stir in apple and lemon rind. Add apple mixture to flour mixture, stirring just until dry ingredients are moistened.

Spoon batter into muffin pans coated with vegetable cooking spray, filling two-thirds full. Bake at 400° for 10 to 12 minutes or until lightly browned. Yield: 16 muffins (111 calories [23% from fat] each).

FAT 2.8g (SAT 0.6g, MONO 0.8g, POLY 1.2g)
PROTEIN 3.5g CARBOHYDRATE 18.7g
FIBER 1.9g CHOLESTEROL 14mg SODIUM 107mg

THREE-BRAN MUFFINS

1 cup shreds of wheat bran cereal
½ cup morsels of bran cereal
½ cup boiling water
¾ cup nonfat buttermilk
½ cup honey
3 tablespoons vegetable oil
1 teaspoon baking soda
4 egg whites, lightly beaten
1 cup all-purpose flour
1 teaspoon baking powder
¼ teaspoon salt
1 cup unprocessed wheat bran
¾ cup chopped dates
Vegetable cooking spray

Combine cereals and water in a medium bowl; let stand 3 minutes. Add buttermilk, honey, oil, baking soda, and egg whites, stirring well.

Combine flour and next 3 ingredients in a large bowl; make a well in center of mixture. Add cereal mixture to flour mixture, stirring just until dry ingredients are moistened. Fold in chopped dates.

Spoon batter into muffin pans coated with cooking spray, filling three-fourths full. Bake at 350° for 20 to 25 minutes or until a wooden pick inserted in center comes out clean. Yield: 1½ dozen (123 calories [21% from fat] each).

FAT 2.9g (SAT 0.5g, MONO 0.8g, POLY 1.3g)
PROTEIN 3.3g CARBOHYDRATE 25.3g
FIBER 4.0g CHOLESTEROL 0mg SODIUM 161mg

CHEESE AND PEPPER MUFFINS

2 cups all-purpose flour
¾ cup yellow cornmeal
1½ tablespoons baking powder
½ teaspoon salt
3 tablespoons sugar
¼ teaspoon ground red pepper
½ cup (2 ounces) shredded reduced-fat sharp Cheddar cheese
¼ cup finely chopped onion
¼ cup finely chopped sweet red pepper
1 (8-ounce) carton plain nonfat yogurt
⅔ cup skim milk
½ cup frozen egg substitute, thawed
2 tablespoons vegetable oil
Vegetable cooking spray

Combine first 9 ingredients; make a well in center of mixture. Combine yogurt, milk, egg substitute, and oil; add to flour mixture, stirring just until dry ingredients are moistened.

Spoon batter into muffin pans coated with cooking spray, filling two-thirds full. Bake at 400° for 20 minutes or until lightly browned. Yield: 1½ dozen (120 calories [20% from fat] each).

FAT 2.6g (SAT 0.7g, MONO 0.7g, POLY 1.0g)
PROTEIN 4.6g CARBOHYDRATE 19.3g
FIBER 0.8g CHOLESTEROL 3mg SODIUM 188mg

Cornbreads

Cornbread is a type of quick bread that substitutes cornmeal for most, if not all, of the flour. A variety of low-fat ingredients can be added to basic cornbread batter including reduced-fat cheeses, chopped onion, chopped pepper, and herbs. Old-fashioned cornbreads are often made with bacon drippings and baked in a cast-iron skillet coated with additional bacon drippings. But concern about the amount of fat in this otherwise healthy bread has yielded delicious low-fat recipes for cornbread.

GRANOLA MUFFINS

3 cups low-fat granola with raisins
1 cup boiling water
2⅓ cups all-purpose flour
2 teaspoons baking soda
¼ teaspoon salt
⅔ cup firmly packed brown sugar
2 cups nonfat buttermilk
⅓ cup vegetable oil
1 egg, lightly beaten
2 egg whites, lightly beaten
Vegetable cooking spray

Combine granola and water in a medium bowl; let stand 10 minutes.

Combine flour and next 3 ingredients in a bowl; make a well in center of mixture. Combine buttermilk, oil, egg, and egg whites, stirring well. Add buttermilk mixture and granola mixture to flour mixture, stirring just until dry ingredients are moistened.

Spoon batter into muffin pans coated with cooking spray, filling three-fourths full. Bake at 350° for 20 to 22 minutes or until a wooden pick inserted in center comes out clean. Yield: 28 muffins (138 calories [25% from fat] each).

FAT 3.9g (SAT 0.6g, MONO 1.3g, POLY 1.8g)
PROTEIN 3.3g CARBOHYDRATE 23.3g
FIBER 1.0g CHOLESTEROL 8mg SODIUM 128mg

BUTTERMILK CORN MUFFINS

1 cup yellow cornmeal
1 cup all-purpose flour
2 teaspoons baking powder
½ teaspoon salt
¼ teaspoon baking soda
1 tablespoon sugar
1½ cups nonfat buttermilk
3 tablespoons vegetable oil
2 egg whites, lightly beaten
Vegetable cooking spray

Combine first 6 ingredients in a medium bowl; make a well in center of mixture. Combine buttermilk, oil, and egg whites; add to cornmeal mixture, stirring just until dry ingredients are moistened.

Spoon batter into muffin pans coated with cooking spray, filling three-fourths full. Bake at 425° for 12 to 14 minutes or until golden. Remove from pans immediately. Yield: 15 muffins (105 calories [28% from fat] each).

FAT 3.3g (SAT 0.6g, MONO 0.9g, POLY 1.5g)
PROTEIN 3.0g CARBOHYDRATE 15.7g
FIBER 0.7g CHOLESTEROL 1mg SODIUM 165mg

BASIC SKILLET CORNBREAD

1½ cups yellow cornmeal
¾ cup all-purpose flour
2 teaspoons baking powder
1 teaspoon baking soda
½ teaspoon salt
2 cups nonfat buttermilk
1½ tablespoons vegetable oil
1 egg, lightly beaten
2 egg whites, lightly beaten
Vegetable cooking spray

Combine first 5 ingredients in a large bowl; make a well in center of mixture. Combine buttermilk, oil, egg, and egg whites; add to cornmeal mixture, stirring just until dry ingredients are moistened.

Coat a 10-inch cast-iron skillet with vegetable cooking spray. Heat skillet at 450° for 4 to 5 minutes or until hot. Remove skillet from oven; pour batter into hot skillet. Bake at 450° for 20 to 25 minutes or until lightly browned. Remove cornbread from skillet immediately. Yield: 10 servings (158 calories [18% from fat] per serving).

FAT 3.2g (SAT 0.7g, MONO 0.9g, POLY 1.2g)
PROTEIN 5.8g CARBOHYDRATE 26.0g
FIBER 1.3g CHOLESTEROL 24mg SODIUM 329mg

CRISPY OVEN-BAKED HUSH PUPPIES

⅔ cup yellow cornmeal
⅔ cup all-purpose flour
2 teaspoons baking powder
½ teaspoon salt
½ teaspoon sugar
¼ teaspoon onion powder
¼ teaspoon garlic powder
⅛ teaspoon ground red pepper
½ cup evaporated skimmed milk
2 tablespoons vegetable oil
3 egg whites, lightly beaten
Vegetable cooking spray

Combine first 8 ingredients in a medium bowl; make a well in center of mixture. Combine milk, oil, and egg whites in a small bowl; stir well. Add milk mixture to cornmeal mixture, stirring just until dry ingredients are moistened.

Spoon batter evenly into miniature (1¾-inch) muffin pans coated with vegetable cooking spray, filling three-fourths full. Bake at 425° for 13 to 15 minutes or until hush puppies are lightly browned. Remove from pans immediately. Yield: 2 dozen (46 calories [29% from fat] each).

FAT 1.5g (SAT 0.3g, MONO 0.4g, POLY 0.7g)
PROTEIN 1.5g   CARBOHYDRATE 6.5g
FIBER 0.3g   CHOLESTEROL 0mg   SODIUM 87mg

Serve Crispy Oven-Baked Hush Puppies as a low-fat accompaniment to a healthy fish dinner. These little muffins taste just like the fried version, but they have much less fat.

After combining the dry ingredients for Crispy Oven-Baked Hush Puppies, make a "well" in the center of the mixture to hold the combined liquid ingredients.

Add the combined liquid ingredients to the dry ingredients, stirring just until moistened. Overmixing will cause tunnels and peaks to form in the hush puppies.

Coat the miniature muffin pans with cooking spray to prevent the hush puppies from sticking. Fill the pans three-fourths full with batter.

Quick Loaves and Breakfast Breads

Most of these quick breads are prepared using the same procedure for combining the ingredients in muffins. Some loaves may develop a crack down the center of the loaf during baking, which is characteristic of this type of bread.

Breakfast breads such as coffee cakes, pancakes, and waffles are easy to prepare and add a special touch to any breakfast or brunch. Most commercial frozen pancakes, waffles, coffee cakes, muffins, loaves, and the packaged mixes for making these favorites are too high in fat to be included in a low-fat eating plan.

SPICED BRAN LOAF

½ cup shreds of wheat bran cereal
1 cup nonfat buttermilk
1 cup whole wheat flour
1 cup all-purpose flour
1 teaspoon baking powder
1 teaspoon baking soda
¼ teaspoon salt
1 teaspoon ground cinnamon
¼ teaspoon ground nutmeg
¼ cup honey
3 tablespoons vegetable oil
1 egg, lightly beaten
Vegetable cooking spray

Combine cereal and buttermilk in a medium bowl; let stand 5 minutes.

Combine whole wheat flour and next 6 ingredients in a large bowl; make a well in center of mixture. Combine honey, oil, and egg, stirring well. Add honey mixture and cereal mixture to flour mixture, stirring just until dry ingredients are moistened.

Spoon batter into an 8½- x 4½- x 3-inch loafpan coated with cooking spray. Bake at 350° for 35 to 40 minutes or until a wooden pick inserted in center comes out clean. Cool in pan 10 minutes; remove from pan, and let cool completely on a wire rack. Yield: 16 servings (111 calories [27% from fat] per ½-inch slice).

FAT 3.3g (SAT 0.7g, MONO 0.9g, POLY 1.4g)
PROTEIN 3.2g   CARBOHYDRATE 18.8g
FIBER 2.1g   CHOLESTEROL 14mg   SODIUM 152mg

PUMPKIN-PECAN BREAD

1¾ cups all-purpose flour
1 teaspoon baking powder
½ teaspoon baking soda
¼ teaspoon salt
½ cup sugar
¾ teaspoon ground cinnamon
½ teaspoon ground nutmeg
1 cup cooked, mashed pumpkin
½ cup frozen egg substitute, thawed
2½ tablespoons vegetable oil
¼ cup chopped pecans
Vegetable cooking spray

Combine first 7 ingredients in a large bowl; make a well in center of mixture. Combine pumpkin, egg substitute, and oil, stirring well; add to flour mixture, stirring just until dry ingredients are moistened. Fold in chopped pecans.

Spoon batter into an 8½- x 4½- x 3-inch loafpan coated with cooking spray. Bake at 350° for 40 to 45 minutes or until a wooden pick inserted in center comes out clean. Cool in pan 10 minutes; remove from pan, and let cool completely on a wire rack. Yield: 16 servings (113 calories [28% from fat] per ½-inch slice).

FAT 3.5g (SAT 0.5g, MONO 1.4g, POLY 1.4g)
PROTEIN 2.4g   CARBOHYDRATE 18.0g
FIBER 0.6g   CHOLESTEROL 0mg   SODIUM 93mg

DATE AND PECAN COFFEE CAKE

Vegetable cooking spray
⅓ cup sugar
⅓ cup firmly packed brown sugar
2 tablespoons margarine, softened
1 egg
1 cup all-purpose flour
½ teaspoon baking powder
½ teaspoon baking soda
1 teaspoon ground cinnamon
¾ teaspoon ground ginger
¼ teaspoon ground allspice
½ cup plain nonfat yogurt
½ cup chopped dates
⅓ cup chopped pecans
1 tablespoon powdered sugar

Coat a 9-inch round cakepan with cooking spray. Line bottom of pan with wax paper; coat paper with cooking spray. Set aside.

Combine ⅓ cup sugar, brown sugar, margarine, and egg in a large bowl; beat at medium speed of an electric mixer until blended.

Combine flour and next 5 ingredients in a small bowl; add flour mixture to creamed mixture alternately with yogurt, beginning and ending with flour mixture. Mix just until blended after each addition. Stir in dates and pecans.

Spoon batter into prepared pan. Bake at 350° for 25 to 30 minutes or until a wooden pick inserted in center comes out clean. Cool in pan 10 minutes. Remove cake from pan, and peel off wax paper; let cool on a wire rack. Sift powdered sugar over top of cooled cake. Yield: 12 servings (150 calories [25% from fat] per serving).

FAT 4.2g (SAT 0.7g, MONO 2.1g, POLY 1.1g)
PROTEIN 2.5g   CARBOHYDRATE 26.6g
FIBER 1.1g   CHOLESTEROL 19mg   SODIUM 84mg

Packed with fresh berries and whole grain goodness, Raspberry Coffee Ring is perfect for breakfast or brunch.

RASPBERRY COFFEE RING

1 cup all-purpose flour
⅔ cup unprocessed oat bran
½ cup whole wheat flour
1 teaspoon baking soda
1 cup firmly packed brown sugar
1¼ cups vanilla low-fat yogurt
½ teaspoon grated lemon rind
1 egg, lightly beaten
1 egg white, lightly beaten
1 cup fresh raspberries
1 tablespoon all-purpose flour
Vegetable cooking spray
½ cup sifted powdered sugar
2 teaspoons skim milk

Combine first 5 ingredients in a large bowl; make a well in center of mixture. Combine yogurt, grated lemon rind, egg, and egg white; add to flour mixture, stirring just until dry ingredients are moistened. Toss berries with 1 tablespoon all-purpose flour; fold berries into batter. Spoon batter into a 6-cup Bundt pan coated with cooking spray. Bake at 350° for 45 minutes or until a wooden pick inserted in center comes out clean. Cool in pan 10 minutes; remove from pan. Cool on a wire rack.

Combine sifted powdered sugar and milk, stirring well; let stand 2 minutes. Drizzle glaze over cooled cake. Yield: 14 servings (169 calories [6% from fat] per serving).

FAT 1.2g (SAT 0.3g, MONO 0.3g, POLY 0.2g)
PROTEIN 4.2g   CARBOHYDRATE 36.2g
FIBER 2.2g   CHOLESTEROL 17mg   SODIUM 86mg

Pancakes and Waffles for Dessert

For a change of pace, top pancakes or waffles with nonfat vanilla yogurt and fresh fruit and serve as dessert. To keep the pancakes or waffles warm until serving time, place them on an ovenproof platter in a 200° oven. Or prepare the pancakes or waffles ahead, let cool completely, and store in an airtight container at room temperature for up to 2 days. Reheat on a wire rack at 350° just until warm.

WHOLE WHEAT-APPLE PANCAKES

1 cup all-purpose flour
1 cup whole wheat flour
1 tablespoon baking powder
½ teaspoon baking soda
½ teaspoon salt
2 tablespoons brown sugar
½ teaspoon ground cinnamon
1½ cups nonfat buttermilk
¾ cup unsweetened apple juice
3 tablespoons reduced-calorie
  margarine, melted
1 egg, lightly beaten
2 egg whites, lightly beaten
1 cup grated cooking apple
Vegetable cooking spray

Combine first 7 ingredients in a large bowl; make a well in center of mixture. Combine buttermilk, apple juice, margarine, egg, and egg whites; add to flour mixture, stirring just until dry ingredients are moistened. Fold in grated apple.

For each pancake, spread ¼ cup batter onto a hot griddle or skillet coated with vegetable cooking spray, spreading batter to a 4-inch circle. Cook pancakes until tops are covered with bubbles and edges look cooked; turn pancakes, and cook other side. Yield: 19 (4-inch) pancakes (81 calories [20% from fat] each).

FAT 1.8g (SAT 0.3g, MONO 0.6g, POLY 0.7g)
PROTEIN 3.0g CARBOHYDRATE 13.7g
FIBER 1.2g CHOLESTEROL 12mg SODIUM 178mg

GINGERBREAD WAFFLES

¼ cup reduced-calorie margarine,
  softened
¼ cup molasses
1 egg
2 egg whites
1¼ cups all-purpose flour
1 cup whole wheat flour
2 teaspoons baking powder
½ teaspoon baking soda
¼ teaspoon salt
2 teaspoons ground ginger
1 teaspoon ground cinnamon
¼ teaspoon ground cloves
1¾ cups boiling water
Vegetable cooking spray

Beat margarine at medium speed of an electric mixer until fluffy; gradually add molasses, beating well. Add egg and egg whites, one at a time, beating after each addition.

Combine all-purpose flour and next 7 ingredients, stirring well. Add flour mixture to creamed mixture alternately with water, beginning and ending with flour mixture. Beat just until blended after each addition.

Coat an 8-inch square waffle iron with vegetable cooking spray; allow waffle iron to preheat. Pour 1¼ cups batter onto hot waffle iron, spreading batter to edges. Bake 7 to 8 minutes or until steaming stops. Repeat procedure 2 more times with remaining batter. Yield: 12 (4-inch) waffles (129 calories [22% from fat] each).

FAT 3.2g (SAT 0.5g, MONO 1.1g, POLY 1.2g)
PROTEIN 3.9g CARBOHYDRATE 21.9g
FIBER 1.7g CHOLESTEROL 18mg SODIUM 187mg

OVEN-BAKED AMARETTO FRENCH TOAST

2 egg whites
⅓ cup skim milk
2 tablespoons brown sugar
3 tablespoons frozen egg substitute,
  thawed
2 tablespoons amaretto
¼ teaspoon salt
¼ teaspoon ground cinnamon
8 (¾-inch-thick) slices French bread
Vegetable cooking spray
Maple syrup (optional)
Powdered sugar (optional)

Beat egg whites at high speed of an electric mixer until stiff peaks form. Set aside.

Combine milk and next 5 ingredients in a medium bowl, beating at high speed of an electric mixer until sugar dissolves. Gently fold one-third of egg whites into milk mixture; fold in remaining egg whites.

Dip bread slices in milk mixture, coating well. Place in a 13- x 9- x 2-inch baking pan coated with cooking spray. Bake at 425° for 7 minutes; turn and bake an additional 3 minutes or until golden. Serve immediately. If desired, serve French toast with maple syrup or powdered sugar. Yield: 8 servings (114 calories [6% from fat] per serving).

FAT 0.7g (SAT 0.2g, MONO 0.3g, POLY 0.3g)
PROTEIN 4.3g CARBOHYDRATE 19.7g
FIBER 0.7g CHOLESTEROL 1mg SODIUM 265mg

Specialty Quick Breads

Specialty quick breads such as crêpes and popovers don't fall into any particular category of quick breads, but these were too good to pass up. And the garlic bread is especially quick to prepare.

BASIC CRÊPES

1⅓ cups all-purpose flour
¼ teaspoon salt
1½ cups plus 2 tablespoons skim milk
2 teaspoons vegetable oil
2 eggs, lightly beaten
2 egg whites, lightly beaten
Vegetable cooking spray

Combine flour and salt, stirring well. Combine milk, oil, eggs, and egg whites, stirring well. Gradually add milk mixture to flour mixture, beating well with wire whisk until batter is smooth. Refrigerate batter at least 2 hours.

Coat a 6-inch nonstick crêpe pan or skillet with vegetable cooking spray. Place over medium heat just until hot, not smoking. Pour 2 tablespoons batter into pan; quickly tilt pan in all directions so batter covers bottom of pan in a thin film. Cook 1 minute or until crêpe can be shaken loose from pan. Flip crêpe, and cook about 30 seconds. (Place filling on spotted side of crêpe.)

Place crêpes on a towel to cool. Stack cooled crêpes between layers of wax paper to prevent sticking. Repeat procedure until all batter is used. Yield: 2 dozen (43 calories [21% from fat] each).

FAT 1.0g (SAT 0.3g, MONO 0.3g, POLY 0.3g)
PROTEIN 2.1g CARBOHYDRATE 6.2g
FIBER 0.2g CHOLESTEROL 19mg SODIUM 43mg

CHEDDAR POPOVERS

3 egg whites
½ cup skim milk
1 tablespoon reduced-calorie margarine, melted
⅓ cup bread flour
2 tablespoons whole wheat flour
⅛ teaspoon salt
Vegetable cooking spray
2 tablespoons shredded reduced-fat sharp Cheddar cheese

Beat egg whites at high speed of an electric mixer until foamy. Add milk and margarine; beat at medium speed until mixture is well blended. Gradually add bread flour, whole wheat flour, and salt, beating until mixture is smooth.

Coat muffin pans with cooking spray. Heat at 450° for 2 to 3 minutes or until hot. Remove pan from oven. Pour 1 tablespoon batter into each cup; sprinkle each with 1 teaspoon cheese. Fill cups three-fourths full with remaining batter. Bake at 375° for 45 minutes. Cut a small slit in top of each popover, and bake an additional 5 minutes. Serve immediately. Yield: 6 popovers (70 calories [27% from fat] each).

FAT 2.1g (SAT 0.5g, MONO 0.7g, POLY 0.7g)
PROTEIN 4.3g CARBOHYDRATE 8.5g
FIBER 0.5g CHOLESTEROL 2mg SODIUM 120mg

CHEESY GARLIC BREAD

1 (1-pound) loaf Italian bread
Butter-flavored vegetable cooking spray
¼ cup grated Parmesan cheese
1 tablespoon minced fresh parsley
¼ teaspoon garlic powder

Slice bread in half horizontally; coat cut surface of each half with cooking spray. Combine cheese, parsley, and garlic powder; sprinkle over cut surface of one half of bread. Top with other half of bread.

Wrap loaf in heavy-duty aluminum foil; bake at 350° for 20 to 22 minutes or until bread is thoroughly heated. Yield: 20 servings (69 calories [8% from fat] per ½-inch slice).

FAT 0.6g (SAT 0.4g, MONO 0.3g, POLY 0.3g)
PROTEIN 2.6g CARBOHYDRATE 12.9g
FIBER 0.6g CHOLESTEROL 1mg SODIUM 156mg

High-Altitude Baking

High altitudes (above 3,500 feet) have a pronounced effect on baked goods. The atmospheric pressure at high altitudes is lower due to a thinner blanket of air. This decrease in air pressure means that adjustments need to be made in some ingredients, baking times, and baking temperatures. For example:
• If sugar is used, decrease the amount by approximately 1 teaspoon per tablespoon used.
• Oven temperature may be decreased by 25°F to avoid adjusting baking time.
• Decrease the amount of yeast called for in the recipe by ½ teaspoon per tablespoon.
• As altitude increases, atmospheric pressure decreases, causing yeast breads to rise more rapidly. To extend the rising time and develop the characteristic flavor in yeast breads, allow the dough to rise twice, punching down the dough after each rising.

YEAST BREADS

Yeast breads that are high in fat, especially coffee cakes and specialty breads, have had butter or margarine added for flavor and tenderness. The recipes in this section offer a variety of low-fat yeast breads so flavorful and tender that it's hard to believe they are good for you.

All About Yeast

Although the bread recipes that follow were tested with active dry yeast, quick-rising yeast can usually be substituted in equal amounts (except for the Apple Danish recipe) following the package directions. One package of active dry yeast contains about 1 tablespoon of yeast.

All yeast should be stored in a cool, dry place. It may also be stored in the refrigerator or freezer; just bring the yeast to room temperature before using it in a recipe.

Most recipes require that you activate the regular form of active dry yeast by dissolving it in a small amount of warm liquid (105° to 115°) before adding to other ingredients. If the liquid is too hot, it will kill the yeast; if the liquid is too cool, it will slow the rising process. Recipes that combine the dry yeast with the dry ingredients before the liquid ingredients are added require the liquid mixture to be very warm (120° to 130°F) to activate the yeast.

Two Types of Yeast Bread

Although most of these recipes are for yeast breads that are kneaded, batter yeast breads that don't require kneading are included as well. Kneading the dough develops the gluten in the flour, which gives structure to the bread and creates a better texture and greater volume.

In batter breads, the yeast is usually mixed with the dry ingredients. The liquid ingredients are then added, and the mixture is beaten with an electric mixer to develop the gluten. Additional flour is also stirred in. The dough is stickier than that for kneaded breads, and it produces a bread that has a coarser texture.

Yeast Rolls

Homemade yeast rolls, fresh from the oven, deserve a special place on any menu. Take your experience with baking bread one step further and try one of these yeast roll recipes. Their great taste and textures will have your family eating healthier without even knowing it.

BOWKNOT ROLLS

1 package dry yeast
1 tablespoon plus 1 teaspoon sugar, divided
½ cup warm water (105° to 115°)
2 cups skim milk
2 tablespoons unsalted margarine
7¼ cups all-purpose flour, divided
1 teaspoon salt
2 tablespoons all-purpose flour
Vegetable cooking spray

Dissolve yeast and 2 teaspoons sugar in warm water in a large bowl; let stand 5 minutes.

Combine milk and margarine in a small saucepan. Cook over medium heat, stirring occasionally, until margarine melts. Let milk mixture cool to 105° to 115°.

Combine 4 cups all-purpose flour, salt, and remaining 2 teaspoons sugar. Add flour mixture and milk mixture to yeast mixture; beat at medium speed of an electric mixer until mixture is well blended. Gradually stir in enough of the remaining 3¼ cups all-purpose flour to make a soft dough.

Sprinkle 2 tablespoons all-purpose flour evenly over work surface. Turn dough out onto floured surface, and knead until dough is smooth and elastic (about 8 to 10 minutes). Place dough in a large bowl coated with vegetable cooking spray, turning to coat top of dough. Cover and let rise in a warm place (85°), free from drafts, 1 hour or until dough is doubled in bulk.

Punch dough down, and divide into 24 equal portions; shape each portion of dough into a 10-inch rope. Tie each rope into a loose knot, and place on 2 large baking sheets coated with vegetable cooking spray. Cover and let rise in a warm place, free from drafts, 15 to 20 minutes or until dough is doubled in bulk.

Bake at 425° for 12 to 14 minutes or until golden. Remove rolls from baking sheets, and let cool on wire racks. Yield: 2 dozen (159 calories [8% from fat] each).

FAT 1.4g (SAT 0.3g, MONO 0.5g, POLY 0.4g)
PROTEIN 4.0g CARBOHYDRATE 31.1g
FIBER 1.1g CHOLESTEROL 0mg SODIUM 109mg

Spiced Pumpkin Rolls is fitting for holiday feasts but may become a year-round favorite.

SPICED PUMPKIN ROLLS

1 package dry yeast
⅓ cup sugar, divided
¾ cup warm water (105° to 115°)
1 cup cooked, mashed pumpkin
1 tablespoon pumpkin pie spice
¾ teaspoon salt
1 egg, lightly beaten
3¾ cups bread flour
1 cup whole wheat flour
2 tablespoons bread flour
Vegetable cooking spray

Dissolve yeast and ½ teaspoon sugar in warm water in a large bowl; let stand 5 minutes. Stir in remaining sugar, pumpkin, and next 3 ingredients. Gradually stir in 3¾ cups bread flour and whole wheat flour to make a soft dough.

Sprinkle 2 tablespoons bread flour evenly over work surface. Turn dough out onto floured surface, and knead until smooth and elastic (about 8 to 10 minutes). Place dough in a large bowl coated with cooking spray, turning to coat top. Cover and let rise in a warm place (85°), free from drafts, 1 hour and 15 minutes or until dough is doubled in bulk.

Punch dough down, and divide into 24 equal portions; shape each portion into a 10-inch rope. Tie each rope into a loose knot, and place on baking sheets coated with cooking spray. Cover and let rise in a warm place, free from drafts, 30 to 35 minutes or until doubled in bulk.

Bake at 425° for 12 minutes or until lightly browned. Remove rolls from baking sheets, and let cool on wire racks. Yield: 2 dozen (115 calories [6% from fat] each).

FAT 0.8g (SAT 0.2g, MONO 0.2g, POLY 0.3g)
PROTEIN 3.8g CARBOHYDRATE 23.1g
FIBER 0.8g CHOLESTEROL 9mg SODIUM 77mg

WHOLE WHEAT ROLLS

1 package dry yeast
1 cup warm water (105° to 115°)
1 tablespoon honey
1½ cups whole wheat flour
1½ cups all-purpose flour
2 tablespoons vegetable oil
¾ teaspoon salt
1 tablespoon all-purpose flour
Vegetable cooking spray

Dissolve yeast in warm water in a large bowl; stir in honey, and let stand 5 minutes.

Combine 1½ cups whole wheat flour and 1½ cups all-purpose flour. Add 1½ cups flour mixture, oil, and salt to yeast mixture; beat at medium speed of an electric mixer until blended. Gradually stir in 1 cup flour mixture; cover and let rest 5 minutes.

Sprinkle 1 tablespoon all-purpose flour evenly over work surface. Turn dough out onto floured surface, and knead until smooth and elastic (about 8 to 10 minutes). Work in enough of the remaining ½ cup flour mixture, 1 tablespoon at a time, to prevent dough from sticking to hands.

Place dough in a large bowl coated with cooking spray, turning to coat top. Cover and let rise in a warm place (85°), free from drafts, 45 minutes or until doubled in bulk.

Punch dough down, and divide into 24 equal portions. Shape each portion into a ball, and place 3 inches apart on baking sheets coated with cooking spray. Cover and let rise in a warm place, free from drafts, 30 minutes or until doubled in bulk.

Bake at 375° for 12 to 14 minutes or until lightly browned. Let cool on wire racks. Yield: 2 dozen (69 calories [18% from fat] each).

FAT 1.4g (SAT 0.2g, MONO 0.4g, POLY 0.6g)
PROTEIN 2.0g CARBOHYDRATE 12.5g
FIBER 1.3g CHOLESTEROL 0mg SODIUM 74mg

OVERNIGHT CRESCENT ROLLS

1 package dry yeast
¼ cup warm water (105° to 115°)
3¾ cups all-purpose flour, divided
½ cup plain nonfat yogurt
¼ cup sugar
2½ tablespoons vegetable oil
¾ teaspoon salt
2 egg whites
2 tablespoons all-purpose flour,
   divided
Butter-flavored vegetable cooking
   spray

Dissolve yeast in warm water in a large bowl; let stand 5 minutes. Add 2 cups flour, yogurt, and next 4 ingredients; beat at medium speed of an electric mixer until blended. Gradually stir in enough of the remaining 1¾ cups flour to make a soft dough. Cover and refrigerate 8 hours.

Sprinkle 1 tablespoon flour evenly over work surface. Turn dough out onto floured surface, and knead until smooth and elastic (about 8 to 10 minutes). Divide dough in half. Roll 1 portion to a 10-inch circle; coat with cooking spray, and cut into 12 wedges. Roll up wedges, beginning at wide end; seal points. Place rolls, point side down, on a baking sheet coated with cooking spray; curve rolls into crescents.

Repeat procedure with remaining 1 tablespoon flour and dough. Cover and let rise in a warm place (85°), free from drafts, 45 minutes or until dough is doubled in bulk.

Bake at 375° for 10 to 12 minutes or until golden. Remove rolls from baking sheets, and let cool on wire racks. Yield: 2 dozen (100 calories [15% from fat] each).

FAT 1.7g (SAT 0.4g, MONO 0.5g, POLY 0.8g)
PROTEIN 2.7g CARBOHYDRATE 18.0g
FIBER 0.6g CHOLESTEROL 0mg SODIUM 82mg

Yeast Bread Loaves

Preparing yeast bread loaves gives you a sense of accomplishment and the pleasure of savoring the flavor, aroma, and texture of the "staff of life." If you've never made yeast bread loaves, follow the directions, being careful not to destroy the yeast by adding water that is too warm.

It is important to bake bread in the correct size loafpan; otherwise, the shape of the loaf will not be as attractive and the baking time may not be correct. For a crisp, glossy crust, brush the loaf with water, skim milk, or a beaten egg white before baking.

Bake bread in the center of a preheated oven. If baking more than one loaf at a time, allow room around each pan so the heat can circulate. When a loaf is done, it should pull slightly away from the edge of the pan and sound hollow when tapped.

BASIC WHITE BREAD

2 packages dry yeast
2 teaspoons sugar
2 cups warm water (105° to 115°)
4¾ cups bread flour, divided
⅓ cup instant nonfat dry milk
   powder
2 tablespoons vegetable oil
1½ teaspoons salt
3 tablespoons bread flour, divided
Vegetable cooking spray

Dissolve yeast and sugar in warm water in a bowl; let stand 5 minutes. Add 2 cups flour and next 3 ingredients; beat at medium speed of an electric mixer until blended. Stir in remaining 2¾ cups flour to make a soft dough; cover and let rest 15 minutes.

Sprinkle 1 tablespoon flour over work surface. Turn dough out onto floured surface; knead until smooth and elastic (about 8 to 10 minutes). Place dough in a large bowl coated with cooking spray, turning to coat top. Cover and let rise in a warm place (85°), free from drafts, 1 hour or until doubled in bulk.

Sprinkle 1 tablespoon flour evenly over work surface. Punch dough down; divide in half. Turn 1 portion out onto work surface, and roll to a 10- x 6-inch rectangle. Roll up dough, jellyroll fashion, starting at short side, pressing firmly to eliminate air pockets. Pinch ends to seal. Place dough, seam side down, in an 8½- x 4½- x 3-inch loafpan coated with cooking spray. Repeat procedure with remaining 1 tablespoon flour and dough. Cover and let rise in a warm place, free from drafts, 45 minutes or until doubled in bulk.

Bake at 375° for 25 minutes or until loaves sound hollow when tapped. Remove from pans; cool on wire racks. Yield: 32 servings (91 calories [13% from fat] per ½-inch slice).

FAT 1.2g (SAT 0.2g, MONO 0.3g, POLY 0.6g)
PROTEIN 3.1g CARBOHYDRATE 16.4g
FIBER 0.6g CHOLESTEROL 0mg SODIUM 117mg

As you roll up dough for loaves, press firmly to eliminate air pockets, which would cause holes or tunnels to form in the loaf.

FRENCH BREAD

1 package dry yeast
1 teaspoon sugar
¼ cup warm water (105° to 115°)
¾ cup water
¼ cup skim milk
1 tablespoon reduced-calorie
    margarine
1 tablespoon sugar
1 teaspoon salt
3½ cups all-purpose flour,
    divided
2 teaspoons all-purpose flour
Vegetable cooking spray
1 egg white, lightly beaten
1 tablespoon water
1 teaspoon sesame seeds

Dissolve yeast and 1 teaspoon sugar in warm water in a large bowl; let stand 5 minutes.

Combine ¾ cup water, milk, and margarine in a small saucepan. Cook over medium heat, stirring occasionally, until margarine melts. Let cool to 105° to 115°.

Add milk mixture, 1 tablespoon sugar, salt, and 1¼ cups flour to yeast mixture; beat at medium speed of an electric mixer until well blended. Gradually stir in enough of the remaining 2¼ cups flour to make a soft dough. Cover and let stand in a warm place (85°), free from drafts, for 10 minutes. Stir gently; cover. Repeat stirring procedure every 10 minutes for 40 minutes.

Sprinkle 2 teaspoons flour evenly over work surface. Turn dough out onto floured surface; divide dough in half. Shape each portion into a 17-inch rope; tuck ends under to seal. Place ropes in 2 French bread loafpans coated with cooking spray. Cover and let rise in a warm place, free from drafts, 40 minutes or until dough is doubled in bulk.

Gently make 3 or 4 slits, about ¼ inch deep, diagonally across each loaf, using a sharp knife. Combine egg white and 1 tablespoon water; brush loaves with egg white mixture, and sprinkle with sesame seeds. Bake at 400° for 20 minutes or until loaves sound hollow when tapped. Remove from pans, and let cool on wire racks. Yield: 36 servings (50 calories [7% from fat] per 1-inch slice).

FAT 0.4g (SAT 0.1g, MONO 0.1g, POLY 0.1g)
PROTEIN 1.5g CARBOHYDRATE 10.0g
FIBER 0.4g CHOLESTEROL 0mg SODIUM 71mg

MOLASSES RYE LOAF

1 package dry yeast
¼ cup warm water (105° to 115°)
3 tablespoons molasses, divided
2 cups medium rye flour
3¾ cups all-purpose flour, divided
1½ teaspoons caraway seeds
1 teaspoon salt
1¾ cups skim milk
¼ cup unsalted margarine
3 tablespoons all-purpose flour
Vegetable cooking spray

Dissolve yeast in warm water in a small bowl. Stir in 1 tablespoon molasses; let stand 5 minutes.

Combine 2 cups rye flour, ¾ cup all-purpose flour, caraway seeds, and salt in a large bowl; stir well. Set aside.

Combine milk, margarine, and remaining 2 tablespoons molasses in a saucepan. Cook over medium heat, stirring occasionally, until margarine melts. Let cool to 105° to 115°.

Add milk mixture and yeast mixture to flour mixture. Beat at low speed of an electric mixer just until blended; beat at medium speed an additional 3 minutes. Gradually stir in enough of the remaining 3 cups all-purpose flour to make a stiff dough.

Sprinkle 3 tablespoons all-purpose flour evenly over work surface. Turn dough out onto surface, and knead until smooth and elastic (about 5 to 7 minutes). Place dough in a large bowl coated with cooking spray, turning to coat top. Cover and let rise in a warm place (85°), free from drafts, 1 hour or until doubled in bulk.

Punch dough down, and divide in half. Divide each half into 17 equal portions; roll each portion into a ball. Place 6 balls along each long side of 2 (9- x 5- x 3-inch) loafpans coated with cooking spray; place a row of 5 balls down the center of each pan. Cover and let rise in a warm place, free from drafts, 45 minutes or until doubled in bulk.

Bake at 375° for 20 to 25 minutes or until golden. Remove from pans, and let cool on wire racks. Yield: 36 servings (91 calories [15% from fat] per ½-inch slice).

FAT 1.5g (SAT 0.3g, MONO 0.6g, POLY 0.5g)
PROTEIN 2.4g CARBOHYDRATE 16.8g
FIBER 1.3g CHOLESTEROL 0mg SODIUM 72mg

PUMPERNICKEL BREAD

2 packages dry yeast
½ cup warm water (105° to 115°)
2¼ cups medium rye flour, divided
2 cups all-purpose flour, divided
1 cup whole wheat flour
¼ cup shreds of wheat bran cereal,
    crushed
¼ cup yellow cornmeal
2 tablespoons unsweetened cocoa
¾ teaspoon salt
1½ cups warm water (105° to 115°)
¼ cup molasses
1 tablespoon vegetable oil
2 teaspoons caraway seeds
2½ tablespoons all-purpose flour
Vegetable cooking spray

Dissolve yeast in ½ cup warm water in a bowl; let stand 5 minutes.

Combine 1 cup rye flour, 1 cup all-purpose flour, whole wheat flour, and

You'll relish the fragrant aroma of fresh parsley, dillweed, and rosemary in Savory Herb Bread.

next 4 ingredients in a large bowl. Add yeast mixture, 1½ cups warm water, molasses, and oil to flour mixture; beat at low speed of an electric mixer just until blended. Add remaining 1¼ cups rye flour; beat at medium speed 3 minutes. Stir in caraway seeds and enough of the remaining 1 cup all-purpose flour to make a stiff dough. (Dough will be sticky.)

Sprinkle work surface evenly with 2½ tablespoons all-purpose flour. Turn dough out onto floured surface, and knead 1 minute. Cover and let rest 10 minutes.

Knead dough until smooth and elastic (about 8 to 10 minutes). Place dough in a large bowl coated with vegetable cooking spray, turning to coat top. Cover and let rise in a warm place (85°), free from drafts, 1 hour or until doubled in bulk.

Punch dough down, and divide in half. Shape each half into a round loaf, place loaves on a baking sheet coated with vegetable cooking spray. Cover and let rise in a warm place, free from drafts, 30 to 35 minutes or until dough is doubled in bulk.

Using a sharp knife, gently cut an X, ¼ inch deep, in top of each loaf. Cut a piece of aluminum foil long enough to fit around one loaf, allowing a 1-inch overlap; fold foil lengthwise into thirds. Wrap foil around loaf; secure foil with freezer tape. Repeat procedure with second loaf.

Bake at 375° for 35 minutes or until loaves sound hollow when tapped. Remove foil, and let cool on wire racks. Yield: 32 servings (89 calories [8% from fat] per wedge).

FAT 0.8g (SAT 0.2g, MONO 0.2g, POLY 0.3g)
PROTEIN 2.5g CARBOHYDRATE 18.3g
FIBER 2.2g CHOLESTEROL 0mg SODIUM 62mg

SAVORY HERB BREAD

2 cups whole wheat flour
2 tablespoons instant nonfat dry
  milk powder
1 package dry yeast
2 tablespoons minced fresh parsley
1 tablespoon minced fresh dillweed
¾ teaspoon minced fresh rosemary
¾ teaspoon salt
¼ teaspoon ground white pepper
1¼ cups skim milk
½ cup minced onion
¼ cup margarine
2 tablespoons honey
2¼ cups all-purpose flour
2 tablespoons all-purpose flour,
  divided
Vegetable cooking spray

Combine first 8 ingredients in a large bowl; stir well. Set aside.

Combine milk, onion, margarine, and honey in a small saucepan. Cook over medium heat until margarine melts. Let cool to 120° to 130°. Add milk mixture to whole wheat flour mixture. Beat at low speed of an electric mixer just until blended; beat at high speed 3 minutes. Gradually stir in 2¼ cups all-purpose flour to make a soft dough.

Sprinkle 1 tablespoon all-purpose flour evenly over work surface. Turn dough out onto floured surface, and knead until smooth and elastic (about 8 to 10 minutes). Place in a large bowl coated with cooking spray, turning to coat top. Cover and let rise in a warm place (85°), free from drafts, 1 hour or until doubled in bulk.

Sprinkle remaining 1 tablespoon all-purpose flour evenly over work surface. Punch dough down; turn out onto a floured surface. Roll dough to a 10- x 6-inch rectangle. Roll up dough, jellyroll fashion, starting at short side, pressing to eliminate air pockets. Pinch ends to seal. Place seam side down in a 9- x 5- x 3-inch loafpan coated with cooking spray. Cover and let rise in a warm place, free from drafts, 40 minutes or until dough is doubled in bulk.

Bake at 350° for 50 to 55 minutes or until loaf sounds hollow when tapped. (Cover with aluminum foil the last 15 minutes of baking to prevent excess browning, if necessary.) Remove from pan; let cool on a wire rack. Yield: 18 servings (147 calories [18% from fat] per ½-inch slice).

FAT 3.0g (SAT 0.6g, MONO 1.2g, POLY 1.0g)
PROTEIN 4.7g CARBOHYDRATE 26.1g
FIBER 2.4g CHOLESTEROL 1mg SODIUM 142mg

Sweet Yeast Breads

If you look at the labels on commercial sweet rolls and coffee cakes, you will see that most are high in fat and cholesterol. With a little extra effort, you can serve your family and friends delicious sweet rolls and coffee cakes that you know are healthy. For convenience, double the recipe, and freeze one batch. You'll be a step ahead the next time you want a special breakfast treat.

CINNAMON-ALMOND SWEET ROLLS

4 cups all-purpose flour, divided
1 package dry yeast
¼ teaspoon salt
1 cup skim milk
¼ cup honey
3 tablespoons reduced-calorie margarine
2 egg whites
2 tablespoons all-purpose flour, divided
Vegetable cooking spray
2 tablespoons reduced-calorie margarine, melted
⅓ cup chopped almonds
2½ tablespoons brown sugar
½ teaspoon ground cinnamon
¾ cup sifted powdered sugar
½ teaspoon ground cinnamon
¼ teaspoon ground nutmeg
1½ tablespoons skim milk
¼ teaspoon almond extract

Combine 1 cup flour, yeast, and salt in a large bowl; stir well. Set aside.

Combine 1 cup milk, honey, and 3 tablespoons margarine in a small saucepan. Cook over medium heat, stirring occasionally, until margarine melts. Let cool to 120° to 130°.

Add milk mixture to flour mixture. Beat at low speed of an electric mixer just until blended; beat at medium speed an additional 3 minutes. Add egg whites and 1 cup flour; beat at medium speed an additional 2 minutes. Stir in enough of remaining 2 cups flour to make a soft dough.

Sprinkle 1 tablespoon flour evenly over work surface. Turn dough out onto floured surface, and knead until smooth and elastic (about 8 to 10 minutes). Place dough in a large bowl coated with cooking spray, turning to coat top. Cover and let rise in a warm place (85°), free from drafts, 1 hour or until doubled in bulk.

Sprinkle remaining 1 tablespoon flour evenly over work surface. Punch dough down; turn out onto floured surface. Roll dough to an 18- x 12-inch rectangle; brush with melted margarine. Combine almonds, brown sugar, and ½ teaspoon cinnamon; sprinkle evenly over dough.

Roll up dough, jellyroll fashion, starting at long side. Pinch seam to seal. Cut roll into ½-inch slices. Place slices, cut side down, in two 13- x 9- x 2-inch baking pans coated with cooking spray. Cover and let rise in a warm place, free from drafts, 45 minutes or until doubled in bulk.

Bake at 375° for 18 minutes or until golden. Combine powdered sugar and remaining ingredients; drizzle glaze over hot rolls. Yield: 3 dozen (97 calories [22% from fat] each).

FAT 2.4g (SAT 0.3g, MONO 1.1g, POLY 0.8g)
PROTEIN 2.4g CARBOHYDRATE 16.9g
FIBER 0.7g CHOLESTEROL 0mg SODIUM 39mg

Kids will love a breakfast that includes Cinnamon-Almond Sweet Rolls and Orange Juicy (page 34) during Saturday-morning cartoons.

APPLE DANISH

½ cup sliced almonds
4¾ cups all-purpose flour
½ teaspoon salt
½ teaspoon ground cinnamon
½ cup skim milk
½ cup unsweetened apple juice,
    divided
¼ cup plus 2 tablespoons honey,
    divided
¼ cup unsalted margarine
1 package dry yeast
1 cup grated cooking apple
½ teaspoon almond extract
1 egg
2 egg whites
2 tablespoons all-purpose flour,
    divided
Vegetable cooking spray
Baked Apple Filling
1 egg white, lightly beaten

Place almonds in container of an electric blender or food processor; top with cover, and process until almonds are finely ground. Combine ground almonds, 4¾ cups flour, salt, and cinnamon; stir well. Reserve 2 cups flour mixture, and set aside; set remaining flour mixture aside.

Combine milk, ¼ cup apple juice, ¼ cup honey, and margarine in a small saucepan. Cook over medium heat, stirring occasionally, until margarine melts. Let milk mixture cool to 120° to 130°.

Combine 2 cups reserved flour mixture, milk mixture, yeast, and next 4 ingredients in a large bowl. Beat at low speed of an electric mixer just until blended; beat at medium speed an additional 3 minutes. Gradually stir in enough of remaining flour mixture to make a soft dough.

Sprinkle 1 tablespoon flour evenly over work surface. Turn dough out onto floured surface, and knead until dough is smooth and elastic (about 8 to 10 minutes). Place dough in a large bowl coated with cooking spray, turning to coat top. Cover and let rise in a warm place (85°), free from drafts, 1 hour or until doubled in bulk.

Sprinkle remaining 1 tablespoon flour evenly over work surface. Punch dough down; turn out onto a floured surface. Roll dough to a 24- x 16-inch rectangle, and cut into 24 (4-inch) squares. Spoon about 2 tablespoons Baked Apple Filling into center of each square, and fold corners toward center, overlapping slightly; pinch corners and edges to seal.

Place pastries, seam side up, on baking sheets coated with cooking spray. Cover and let rise in a warm place, free from drafts, 45 minutes or until dough is doubled in bulk.

Brush pastries with egg white. Bake at 350° for 20 to 22 minutes or until golden. Combine remaining ¼ cup apple juice and 2 tablespoons honey; brush apple juice mixture over warm pastries. Serve warm.

Leftover pastries may be placed in an airtight container and frozen up to 1 month. Thaw at room temperature. Yield: 2 dozen (172 calories [19% from fat] each).

Baked Apple Filling

6½ cups peeled, sliced cooking
    apple
Vegetable cooking spray
1½ tablespoons brown sugar
1 teaspoon ground cinnamon
2½ teaspoons vanilla extract

Arrange apple in a 13- x 9- x 2-inch baking dish coated with vegetable cooking spray. Combine brown sugar, cinnamon, and vanilla; drizzle over apple, and toss gently. Cover and bake at 350° for 30 to 35 minutes or until apple is tender. Yield: 2¾ cups.

FAT 3.6g (SAT 0.6g, MONO 1.7g, POLY 0.9g)
PROTEIN 4.2g CARBOHYDRATE 31.1g
FIBER 2.0g CHOLESTEROL 9mg SODIUM 62mg

GERMAN SWEET BREAD

1 package dry yeast
¼ cup sugar, divided
¾ cup warm water (105° to 115°)
2½ cups bread flour, divided
½ cup currants
⅓ cup instant nonfat dry milk
    powder
1 teaspoon grated lemon rind
½ teaspoon salt
¼ cup margarine, melted
1 egg
2 egg whites
Vegetable cooking spray
½ cup sifted powdered sugar
1½ teaspoons skim milk
¼ teaspoon vanilla extract
1 tablespoon sliced almonds,
    toasted

Dissolve yeast and 1 tablespoon sugar in warm water in a large bowl; let stand 5 minutes. Add remaining 3 tablespoons sugar, 1¼ cups flour, and next 7 ingredients; beat at medium speed of an electric mixer until blended. Gradually stir in remaining 1¼ cups flour.

Coat a 1½-quart soufflé dish with cooking spray; spoon batter into dish. Cover and let rise in a warm place (85°), free from drafts, 25 to 30 minutes or until batter is ½ inch from top of soufflé dish.

Bake at 350° for 25 to 30 minutes or until a wooden pick inserted in center comes out clean. Cool in dish 10 minutes; remove from dish, and let cool on a wire rack.

Combine powdered sugar, milk, and vanilla in a small bowl; stir well. Drizzle glaze mixture over top of cooled bread; sprinkle with almonds. Yield: 22 servings (119 calories [22% from fat] per serving).

FAT 2.9g (SAT 0.5g, MONO 1.1g, POLY 0.8g)
PROTEIN 3.5g CARBOHYDRATE 20.1g
FIBER 0.5g CHOLESTEROL 10mg SODIUM 97mg

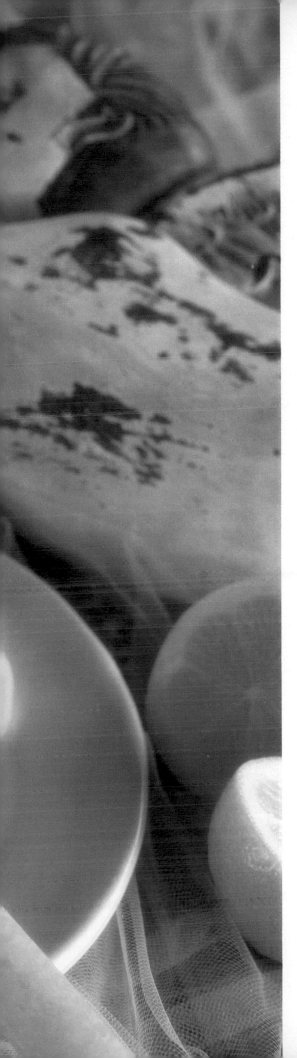

DESSERTS

Desserts are one of life's simple pleasures — one you don't have to give up when cutting back on fat. These cakes, cheesecakes, cookies, and pies prove that healthy desserts can satisfy a sweet tooth without sacrificing flavor. So go ahead and treat yourself to a little something sweet.

After trying some of the desserts on the following pages, you may find that you don't crave the heavy, fat-laden versions nearly as much as you once did. Many of your favorite dessert recipes can be lightened by simply substituting low-fat and nonfat dairy products for their higher fat counterparts. And often you can reduce the number of eggs to just one, substituting two egg whites for each additional egg called for in the recipe.

Substituting reduced-calorie margarine for butter or regular margarine is not a good idea for most desserts; use this product only in recipes that have been tested with it. Because water has been whipped into it, reduced-calorie margarine may yield a wetter product than desired. Switching from butter to regular margarine does not lower the total fat in a recipe, but it does decrease the saturated fat without altering the recipe.

Fresh fruit is always a good choice for dessert. Many of our dessert recipes incorporate fruit because it is virtually fat-free and loaded with vitamins, minerals, and fiber. Many supermarkets — even small ones — now carry a wide selection of fresh fruit throughout the year.

Desserts in this chapter that contain primarily fresh fruit or dairy products should be stored in the refrigerator. We do not recommend that you prepare any of these types of desserts ahead and freeze. Freezing would change the texture of a fruit dish, and puddings and custards have a tendency to break down and become watery after being frozen.

Although it is fine to freeze the cakes and cookies prepared from the featured recipes, we recommend freezing the cakes without frostings or glazes. If you add the frosting or glaze just before serving, the cake will taste fresher and no one will guess that you did the lengthy part ahead of time.

Some of these desert recipes call for special pieces of cooking equipment such as springform pans, soufflé dishes, molds, and crêpe pans. Before beginning the preparation, read through the recipe carefully to make sure you have the required pieces of equipment or suitable substitutes.

A low-fat diet calls for desserts that satisfy a sweet tooth without being too filling. A slice of Lemon Meringue Pie (page 71) fills that order perfectly.

Cakes

Cakes are generally divided into two categories — shortening (or butter) cakes and foam cakes. Shortening cakes include basic layer cakes, pound cakes, fruitcakes, and others typically made with shortening, butter, or stick-type margarine.

The wonderful thing about the shortening-type cakes featured in this section is that none actually contain shortening or butter. These recipes use vegetable oil, regular margarine, or reduced-calorie margarine. This substitution drastically lowers the saturated fat content of these established favorites without affecting their moist textures and rich flavors.

Foam cakes include angel, sponge, and chiffon cakes. (Angel cakes, also known as angel food cakes, contain no fat and are a smart selection for healthy eating.) Foam cakes are leavened by air beaten into the egg whites, which also gives the cakes their characteristic texture.

Mix and match the layer cakes in this section with the frostings and fillings that follow for some flavorful combinations that will delight friends and family. And unless you tell them the dessert is low in fat, they'll probably never know.

Turn Cake Into Cupcakes

Most cake batters can be baked in paper-lined muffin pans for cupcakes. Fill the cups two-thirds full, and bake at 350° for 15 to 20 minutes or until a wooden pick inserted in center comes out clean. Remove cupcakes from pans immediately, and let cool completely on wire racks. Most 2-layer cake recipes yield 24 to 30 cupcakes.

BASIC WHITE CAKE LAYERS

Vegetable cooking spray
2 teaspoons cake flour
1¾ cups sifted cake flour
1 cup superfine sugar
2 teaspoons baking powder
½ cup skim milk
⅓ cup vegetable oil
1 teaspoon vanilla extract
6 egg whites
1 teaspoon cream of tartar

Coat 2 (9-inch) round cakepans or 2 (8-inch) square cakepans with vegetable cooking spray; line bottom of each pan with wax paper. Coat wax paper with vegetable cooking spray, and dust with 2 teaspoons flour. Set pans aside.

Combine 1¾ cups flour, sugar, and baking powder in a large bowl, stirring well. Combine milk, oil, and vanilla in a small bowl, stirring well. Add milk mixture to flour mixture, stirring well.

Beat egg whites at high speed of an electric mixer just until egg whites are foamy. Add cream of tartar, and beat until stiff peaks form. Gently fold one-third of beaten egg whites into batter; gently fold in remaining beaten egg whites.

Pour batter evenly into prepared pans. Bake at 350° for 20 to 22 minutes or until a wooden pick inserted in center comes out clean. Cool in pans 10 minutes; remove from pans, and peel off wax paper. Cool layers completely on wire racks. Yield: 12 servings (191 calories [29% from fat] per serving).

FAT 6.2g (SAT 1.1g, MONO 1.8g, POLY 3.0g)
PROTEIN 3.4g   CARBOHYDRATE 30.3g
FIBER 0.5g   CHOLESTEROL 0mg   SODIUM 99mg

CHOCOLATE CAKE LAYERS

Vegetable cooking spray
2 teaspoons all-purpose flour
1 cup water
½ cup margarine
¼ cup unsweetened cocoa
2 cups all-purpose flour
1½ cups sugar
¼ teaspoon salt
½ cup nonfat buttermilk
1 teaspoon baking soda
2 egg whites
1 egg

Coat 2 (9-inch) round cakepans or 2 (8-inch) square cakepans with cooking spray; line bottom of each pan with wax paper. Coat wax paper with cooking spray, and dust with 2 teaspoons flour. Set aside.

Combine water, margarine, and cocoa in a saucepan; cook over medium heat until margarine melts.

Combine 2 cups flour, sugar, and salt in a large bowl; stir well. Add margarine mixture to flour mixture; beat at low speed of an electric mixer 1 minute or until well blended.

Combine buttermilk and baking soda. Add buttermilk mixture, egg whites, and egg to flour mixture; beat at medium speed of an electric mixer 2 minutes or until mixture is smooth.

Pour batter evenly into prepared pans. Bake at 350° for 22 to 25 minutes or until a wooden pick inserted in center comes out clean. Cool in pans 10 minutes; remove from pans, and peel off wax paper. Cool layers completely on wire racks. Yield: 12 servings (262 calories [29% from fat] per serving).

FAT 8.5g (SAT 1.8g, MONO 3.5g, POLY 2.5g)
PROTEIN 4.3g   CARBOHYDRATE 42.7g
FIBER 0.6g   CHOLESTEROL 19mg   SODIUM 232mg

Old-Fashioned Gingerbread

⅓ cup margarine, softened
½ cup sugar
1 cup molasses
1 egg
2½ cups all-purpose flour
1½ teaspoons baking soda
½ teaspoon salt
1 teaspoon ground ginger
1 teaspoon ground cinnamon
½ teaspoon ground cloves
1 cup hot water
Vegetable cooking spray
Warm Lemon Glaze

Beat margarine at medium speed of an electric mixer until fluffy; gradually add sugar, beating well. Add molasses and egg; beat well.

Combine flour and next 5 ingredients; add flour mixture to creamed mixture alternately with water, beginning and ending with flour mixture. Mix after each addition.

Pour batter into a 9-inch square baking pan coated with cooking spray. Bake at 350° for 40 minutes or until a wooden pick inserted in center comes out clean. Cool in pan 10 minutes; pour Warm Lemon Glaze over cake. Cut into squares; serve immediately. Yield: 12 servings (289 calories [18% from fat] per serving).

Warm Lemon Glaze
1 cup sifted powdered sugar
¼ teaspoon grated lemon rind
1½ tablespoons fresh lemon juice
1½ teaspoons water
½ teaspoon vanilla extract

Combine all ingredients in a saucepan; cook over low heat, stirring frequently, until warm. Yield: ⅓ cup.

FAT 5.8g (SAT 1.2g, MONO 2.4g, POLY 1.8g)
PROTEIN 3.3g CARBOHYDRATE 56.6g
FIBER 0.8g CHOLESTEROL 18mg SODIUM 270mg

Orange Pound Cake Loaf

Vegetable cooking spray
1 teaspoon all-purpose flour
1¾ cups all-purpose flour
2 teaspoons baking powder
¼ teaspoon salt
¾ cup sugar
1 tablespoon grated orange rind
⅔ cup fresh orange juice
¼ cup vegetable oil
4 egg whites

Coat bottom of an 8½- x 4½- x 3-inch loafpan with vegetable cooking spray; dust pan with 1 teaspoon flour. Set aside.

Combine 1¾ cups flour and next 3 ingredients in a large bowl. Combine orange rind, juice, and oil; add to flour mixture. Beat at medium speed of an electric mixer just until smooth (batter will be thick).

Beat egg whites at high speed of an electric mixer until stiff peaks form. Fold one-third of beaten egg whites into batter; gently fold in remaining beaten egg whites.

Pour batter into prepared pan. Bake at 350° for 55 minutes or until a wooden pick inserted in center comes out clean. Cool in pan 10 minutes; remove from pan, and let cool on a wire rack. Yield: 16 servings (126 calories [26% from fat] per ½-inch slice).

FAT 3.6g (SAT 0.6g, MONO 1.0g, POLY 1.7g)
PROTEIN 2.4g CARBOHYDRATE 21.3g
FIBER 0.4g CHOLESTEROL 0mg SODIUM 88mg

Chocolate Angel Food Cake

1¼ cups sugar, divided
1 cup sifted cake flour
¼ cup unsweetened cocoa
12 egg whites
1½ teaspoons cream of tartar
¼ teaspoon salt
1 teaspoon vanilla extract
½ teaspoon almond extract
1 teaspoon powdered sugar

Sift ¼ cup sugar, flour, and cocoa together in a small bowl; set aside.

Beat egg whites in an extra-large bowl at high speed of an electric mixer until foamy. Add cream of tartar and next 3 ingredients; beat until soft peaks form. Gradually add remaining 1 cup sugar, 2 tablespoons at a time, beating until stiff peaks form. Sift flour mixture over egg white mixture, ¼ cup at a time, folding in carefully after each addition.

Spoon batter into an ungreased 10-inch tube pan; spread evenly with a spatula. Break large air pockets by cutting through batter with a knife. Bake at 375° for 30 minutes or until cake springs back when lightly touched.

Remove cake from oven; invert pan, and cool completely. Loosen cake from sides of pan, using a narrow metal spatula; remove from pan. Sift powdered sugar over cooled cake. Yield: 12 servings (140 calories [2% from fat] per serving).

FAT 0.3g (SAT 0.2g, MONO 0.0g, POLY 0.0g)
PROTEIN 4.6g CARBOHYDRATE 29.4g
FIBER 0.0g CHOLESTEROL 0mg SODIUM 128mg

Frostings, Fillings, and Glazes

Cakes, cupcakes, and cookies become something special when you add a frosting, filling, or glaze. Several of these recipes contain no fat, and those that do are much lower in fat than their original versions.

FLUFFY WHITE FROSTING

2 teaspoons unflavored gelatin
2½ tablespoons cold water
¾ cup light-colored corn syrup
1 tablespoon vanilla extract
2 egg whites
½ teaspoon cream of tartar

Sprinkle gelatin over cold water in a saucepan; let stand 1 minute. Add corn syrup; cook over medium heat, stirring constantly, just until mixture comes to a boil and gelatin dissolves. Remove from heat; add vanilla.

Beat egg whites and cream of tartar in a medium bowl at high speed of an electric mixer until foamy. Slowly add corn syrup mixture, and continue beating until stiff peaks form and frosting is of spreading consistency (about 10 minutes). To serve, spread frosting over cake layers or cupcakes. Yield: 2¼ cups (23 calories [0% from fat] per tablespoon).

FAT 0.0g (SAT 0.0g, MONO 0.0g, POLY 0.0g)
PROTEIN 0.3g CARBOHYDRATE 5.2g
FIBER 0.0g CHOLESTEROL 0mg SODIUM 14mg

CREAMY CHOCOLATE FROSTING

3 cups sifted powdered sugar
¼ cup unsweetened cocoa
¼ teaspoon salt
¼ cup skim milk
1½ teaspoons vanilla extract

Combine all ingredients; stir until frosting is of spreading consistency. Spread over cake layers, cupcakes, or brownies. Yield: 1¼ cups (77 calories [2% from fat] per tablespoon).

FAT 0.2g (SAT 0.1g, MONO 0.0g, POLY 0.0g)
PROTEIN 0.4g CARBOHYDRATE 18.7g
FIBER 0.0g CHOLESTEROL 0mg SODIUM 32mg

TART LEMON FILLING

3 tablespoons sugar
2 tablespoons plus ¾ teaspoon cornstarch
½ cup plus 2 tablespoons water
1½ tablespoons fresh lemon juice
1 tablespoon frozen egg substitute, thawed
1 teaspoon grated lemon rind

Combine first 5 ingredients in a saucepan. Cook over medium heat, stirring constantly, until mixture comes to a boil; boil 1 minute. Remove from heat; stir in lemon rind, and let cool. Cover and chill.

To serve, spread filling between cake layers. Yield: ¾ cup plus 2 tablespoons (16 calories [0% from fat] per tablespoon).

FAT 0.0g (SAT 0.0g, MONO 0.0g, POLY 0.0g)
PROTEIN 0.1g CARBOHYDRATE 4.0g
FIBER 0.0g CHOLESTEROL 0mg SODIUM 2mg

CHOCOLATE GLAZE

3 cups sifted powdered sugar
¼ cup unsweetened cocoa
¼ cup plus 1½ tablespoons hot water

Combine all ingredients in a small bowl, stirring until smooth. To serve, drizzle glaze over cakes, cupcakes, or cookies. Yield: 1 cup (93 calories [2% from fat] per tablespoon).

FAT 0.2g (SAT 0.1g, MONO 0.0g, POLY 0.0g)
PROTEIN 0.4g CARBOHYDRATE 23.0g
FIBER 0.0g CHOLESTEROL 0mg SODIUM 1mg

POWDERED SUGAR GLAZE

1½ cups sifted powdered sugar
2 tablespoons skim milk
½ teaspoon vanilla extract

Combine all ingredients in a small bowl, stirring well. To serve, drizzle glaze over cake layers or cupcakes. Yield: ½ cup (89 calories [0% from fat] per tablespoon).

FAT 0.0g (SAT 0.0g, MONO 0.0g, POLY 0.0g)
PROTEIN 0.1g CARBOHYDRATE 22.7g
FIBER 0.0g CHOLESTEROL 0mg SODIUM 2mg

Lemon Glaze: Substitute lemon juice for milk. Yield: ½ cup (89 calories [0% from fat] per tablespoon).

FAT 0.0g (SAT 0.0g, MONO 0.0g, POLY 0.0g)
PROTEIN 0.0g CARBOHYDRATE 22.8g
FIBER 0.0g CHOLESTEROL 0mg SODIUM 0mg

Tips for Frosting Cakes
• Cool cake layers completely before frosting.
• Brush crumbs from tops and sides of cake layers before frosting.
• Keep frosting off the serving plate by placing several strips of wax paper around the edges of the plate before stacking the layers. Simply remove the wax paper strips after frosting to reveal a clean serving plate.

Cheesecakes

Even the most conscientious dieter may have a weakness when it comes to cheesecake. As the name implies, cheesecakes begin with cheese — usually cream cheese, cottage cheese, or ricotta cheese. Fortunately, low-fat and nonfat versions of these dairy products are available. All it takes is a simple ingredient substitution in a recipe to considerably reduce the fat content of a cheesecake.

For additional information and hints on substituting lower fat ingredients for their higher fat counterparts in your favorite cheesecake recipe, see the chart on page 23.

KEY LIME CHEESECAKE

¾ cup graham cracker crumbs
3 tablespoons reduced-calorie
  margarine, melted
2 tablespoons sugar
3 cups plain nonfat yogurt
1 tablespoon plus 1 teaspoon
  unflavored gelatin
⅓ cup Key lime juice
¾ cup sugar
1½ cups 1% low-fat cottage cheese
½ cup light process cream cheese
  product
2 teaspoons grated lime rind
Lime rind curls (optional)

Combine crumbs, margarine, and 2 tablespoons sugar; stir well. Press mixture evenly into bottom of a 9-inch springform pan. Bake at 350° for 8 minutes. Cool completely.

Line a large colander or sieve with a double layer of cheesecloth that has been rinsed out and squeezed dry; allow cheesecloth to extend over the edge of the colander.

Stir yogurt until smooth; pour into colander. Fold edges of cheesecloth over to cover yogurt. Place colander in a large bowl; refrigerate at least 8 hours. Remove yogurt from colander; discard liquid. Remove cheesecloth from yogurt, and set aside.

Sprinkle gelatin over lime juice in a small nonaluminum saucepan; let stand 1 minute. Add ¾ cup sugar; cook over low heat, stirring constantly, until gelatin dissolves. Remove from heat, and let cool.

Position knife blade in food processor bowl. Add cottage cheese, cream cheese, and gelatin mixture; process just until smooth. Add yogurt cheese, and process until smooth. Stir in lime rind.

Pour mixture into prepared crust. Cover and chill at least 8 hours. Garnish with lime rind curls, if desired. Yield: 16 servings (118 calories [24% from fat] per serving).

FAT 3.2g (SAT 1.1g, MONO 0.7g, POLY 0.7g)
PROTEIN 5.5g CARBOHYDRATE 17.3g
FIBER 0.0g CHOLESTEROL 5mg SODIUM 191mg

STRAWBERRY-AMARETTO CHEESECAKE

Vegetable cooking spray
¼ cup chocolate wafer cookie
  crumbs
1 (24-ounce) carton 1% low-fat
  cottage cheese
2 (8-ounce) cartons light process
  cream cheese product
¾ cup plus 2 tablespoons sugar,
  divided
¼ cup amaretto
1 teaspoon vanilla extract
½ cup frozen egg substitute, thawed
2 egg whites
⅛ teaspoon cream of tartar
2 cups fresh strawberry halves
⅓ cup apple jelly, melted

Coat the bottom of a 10-inch springform pan with cooking spray; dust with cookie crumbs. Set aside.

Position knife blade in food processor bowl. Add cottage cheese and cream cheese; process until smooth. Add ¾ cup sugar, amaretto, and vanilla; process until smooth. Add egg substitute; process just until blended. Transfer cheese mixture to a large bowl; set aside.

Beat egg whites and cream of tartar at high speed of an electric mixer until soft peaks form. Gradually add remaining 2 tablespoons sugar, beating until stiff peaks form. Gently fold one-third of egg white mixture into cheese mixture; gently fold in remaining egg white mixture.

Pour mixture into prepared pan. Bake at 400° for 12 minutes; reduce oven temperature to 200°, and bake for 25 to 30 minutes or until set. Turn off oven, and partially open oven door; leave cheesecake in oven for 1 hour. Remove from oven, and let cool on wire rack to room temperature. Cover and chill at least 8 hours. Arrange strawberry halves over cheesecake, and brush with jelly. Yield: 16 servings (182 calories [29% from fat] per serving).

FAT 5.8g (SAT 3.3g, MONO 0.3g, POLY 0.3g)
PROTEIN 9.7g CARBOHYDRATE 23.1g
FIBER 0.5g CHOLESTEROL 20mg SODIUM 362mg

Chocolate Swirl Cheesecake

1 cup graham cracker crumbs
¼ cup reduced-calorie margarine, melted
2 tablespoons sugar
1 (15-ounce) carton part-skim ricotta cheese, drained
1 (8-ounce) carton nonfat process cream cheese product, softened
1 (8-ounce) carton plain nonfat yogurt
1 cup sugar
2½ tablespoons all-purpose flour
2½ teaspoons vanilla extract
½ cup frozen egg substitute, thawed
2 egg whites
2 tablespoons unsweetened cocoa
1½ tablespoons reduced-calorie margarine, melted

Combine first 3 ingredients; press mixture into bottom of a 9-inch springform pan. Bake at 350° for 8 minutes. Cool completely.

Position knife blade in food processor bowl. Add ricotta cheese and next 5 ingredients; process until smooth. Add egg substitute and egg whites; process just until blended. Reserve ½ cup mixture; pour remaining mixture into prepared crust.

Combine reserved cheese mixture, cocoa, and 1½ tablespoons margarine; drizzle over mixture in pan. Swirl with a knife. Place pan in a shallow baking dish. Add hot water to dish to depth of 1 inch. Bake at 325° for 1 hour or until almost set. Turn off oven; partially open oven door. Leave cheesecake in oven for 1 hour. Remove from oven; let cool. Cover and chill. Yield: 16 servings (167 calories [27% from fat] per serving).

FAT 5.0g (SAT 1.6g, MONO 1.5g, POLY 1.1g)
PROTEIN 7.3g CARBOHYDRATE 22.8g
FIBER 0.0g CHOLESTEROL 10mg SODIUM 218mg

Cookies

Cookies come in all shapes and sizes, and they are classified by the way they are formed. In this section, you will find drop cookies as well as hand-shaped and refrigerated cookies. Bar cookies are also included; they travel well in a lunch box, and also are an easy dessert to transport to picnics or parties.

These low-fat cookies are made with regular or reduced-calorie margarine. Whether you are using regular or reduced-calorie, be sure to use stick-type margarine, not a spread. If you are using 100 percent corn oil margarine, the dough may be softer than with other margarines and may need to be chilled if the cookies will be shaped or sliced.

Applesauce-Date Oatmeal Cookies

⅓ cup margarine, softened
1 cup firmly packed brown sugar
4 egg whites
1 cup all-purpose flour
½ teaspoon baking powder
½ teaspoon baking soda
1½ teaspoons ground allspice
½ cup unsweetened applesauce
2 cups quick-cooking oats, uncooked
1 cup chopped unsweetened dates
Vegetable cooking spray

Beat margarine at medium speed of an electric mixer until fluffy; gradually add sugar, and beat well. Add egg whites; beat well.

Combine flour and next 3 ingredients in a small bowl; add to creamed mixture alternately with applesauce, beginning and ending with flour mixture. Mix after each addition. Stir in oats and dates.

Drop dough by level tablespoonfuls, 2 inches apart, onto cookie sheets coated with vegetable cooking spray. Bake at 375° for 8 to 10 minutes or until cookies are lightly browned. Cool slightly on cookie sheets. Remove from cookie sheets, and cool completely on wire racks. Yield: 4 dozen (61 calories [22% from fat] each).

FAT 1.5g (SAT 0.3g, MONO 0.6g, POLY 0.5g)
PROTEIN 1.2g CARBOHYDRATE 11.0g
FIBER 0.7g CHOLESTEROL 0mg SODIUM 32mg

Chewy Lemon Wafers

2 egg whites
1½ cups all-purpose flour
½ teaspoon baking soda
¼ teaspoon salt
1 cup sugar
½ teaspoon ground cinnamon
⅓ cup margarine, melted
2 teaspoons grated lemon rind
1 teaspoon lemon extract
Vegetable cooking spray

Beat egg whites with a wire whisk until foamy. Add flour and next 7 ingredients; stir until mixture is smooth (dough will be soft).

Shape dough into 48 (1-inch) balls; place balls, 2 inches apart, on cookie sheets coated with vegetable cooking spray. Bake at 350° for 7 to 8 minutes or until cookies are lightly browned. Cool slightly on cookie sheets. Remove cookies from cookie sheets, and cool completely on wire racks. Yield: 4 dozen (43 calories [27% from fat] each).

FAT 1.3g (SAT 0.3g, MONO 0.6g, POLY 0.4g)
PROTEIN 0.6g CARBOHYDRATE 7.2g
FIBER 0.1g CHOLESTEROL 0mg SODIUM 38mg

Peanut Butter and Jelly Sandwich Cookies combines two kid-pleasing foods into one sweet treat.

SNICKERDOODLES

¾ cup reduced-calorie margarine,
  softened
1½ cups sugar
2 eggs
1 teaspoon vanilla extract
4 cups all-purpose flour
1 teaspoon baking soda
½ teaspoon salt
2 teaspoons cream of tartar
2 tablespoons sugar
1½ teaspoons ground cinnamon
Vegetable cooking spray

Beat margarine at medium speed of an electric mixer until fluffy; gradually add 1½ cups sugar, beating well. Add eggs and vanilla; beat well.

Combine flour and next 3 ingredients in a bowl, stirring well. Gradually add flour mixture to creamed mixture, mixing well. Cover and chill 2 hours.

Combine 2 tablespoons sugar and cinnamon in a small bowl; set aside.

Shape dough into 1-inch balls; roll balls in sugar mixture. Place balls, 2 inches apart, on cookie sheets coated with cooking spray. Bake at 400° for 8 minutes or until cookies are very lightly browned. Cool slightly on cookie sheets. Remove from cookie sheets, and cool completely on wire racks. Yield: 6 dozen (55 calories [23% from fat] each).

FAT 1.4g (SAT 0.2g, MONO 0.5g, POLY 0.6g)
PROTEIN 0.9g CARBOHYDRATE 9.9g
FIBER 0.2g CHOLESTEROL 6mg SODIUM 54mg

PEANUT BUTTER AND JELLY SANDWICH COOKIES

⅓ cup reduced-calorie margarine,
  softened
¼ cup creamy peanut butter
¾ cup granulated brown sugar
¼ cup frozen egg substitute, thawed
1 teaspoon vanilla extract
1¾ cups all-purpose flour
½ teaspoon baking soda
½ cup plus 1½ tablespoons grape
  jelly or strawberry jam

Beat margarine and peanut butter at medium speed of an electric mixer until fluffy; gradually add sugar; beat well. Add egg substitute and vanilla; beat well.

Combine flour and soda in a small bowl, stirring well. Gradually add flour mixture to creamed mixture, mixing well.

Shape dough into 56 (1-inch) balls. Place balls, 2 inches apart, on ungreased cookie sheets; flatten cookies in a crisscross pattern with a fork. Bake at 350° for 9 minutes or until lightly browned. Cool slightly on cookie sheets. Remove from cookie sheets; cool completely on wire racks.

Place about 1 teaspoon jelly on bottoms of half the cooled cookies; top with remaining cookies. Yield: 28 cookies (88 calories [27% fat] each).

FAT 2.6g (SAT 0.4g, MONO 1.1g, POLY 1.0g)
PROTEIN 1.7g CARBOHYDRATE 14.9g
FIBER 0.4g CHOLESTEROL 0mg SODIUM 52mg

Transfer cookies to wire racks after baking to allow air to circulate and prevent the bottoms of the cookies from becoming soggy.

FROSTED CHOCOLATE BROWNIES

½ cup plus 3 tablespoons reduced-calorie margarine, softened
1⅓ cups sugar
8 egg whites
½ cup nonfat sour cream alternative
⅓ cup evaporated skimmed milk
2 teaspoons vanilla extract
1⅓ cups all-purpose flour
1 teaspoon baking powder
½ teaspoon salt
⅔ cup unsweetened cocoa
Vegetable cooking spray
Creamy Chocolate Frosting (page 60)

Beat margarine at medium speed of an electric mixer until fluffy; gradually add sugar and beat well. Add egg whites, sour cream, milk, and vanilla; beat well.

Combine flour and next 3 ingredients in a small bowl; stir well. Add flour mixture to creamed mixture, mixing well. Pour batter into a 13- x 9- x 2-inch baking pan coated with vegetable cooking spray. Bake at 350° for 25 minutes or until a wooden pick inserted in center comes out clean. Cool in pan on a wire rack. Spread Creamy Chocolate Frosting over cooled brownies; cut into squares. Yield: 24 servings (183 calories [19% from fat] per serving).

FAT 3.9g (SAT 0.8g, MONO 1.3g, POLY 1.5g)
PROTEIN 3.5g CARBOHYDRATE 34.1g
FIBER 0.2g CHOLESTEROL 0mg SODIUM 164mg

RASPBERRY-OATMEAL SQUARES

1 (10-ounce) package frozen raspberries in light syrup, thawed
2 tablespoons sugar
2 tablespoons cornstarch
¼ teaspoon almond extract
⅓ cup margarine, softened
⅔ cup firmly packed brown sugar
1 teaspoon vanilla extract
1 cup quick-cooking oats, uncooked
¾ cup all-purpose flour
¼ cup whole wheat flour
½ teaspoon baking soda
⅛ teaspoon salt
Vegetable cooking spray

Combine raspberries, sugar, and cornstarch in a saucepan; stir until smooth. Bring to a boil, stirring constantly, and cook 1 minute or until thickened. Remove from heat, and stir in almond extract. Set aside.

Beat margarine at medium speed of an electric mixer until fluffy; add brown sugar, beating well. Add vanilla; beat well.

Combine oats and next 4 ingredients in a small bowl; stir well. Add to creamed mixture, stirring until mixture resembles coarse meal.

Press 2 cups oat mixture evenly into bottom of a 9-inch square baking pan coated with cooking spray; set remaining oat mixture aside. Bake at 375° for 6 to 8 minutes or until crust looks puffed.

Spread raspberry mixture evenly over prepared crust; top raspberry mixture with remaining oat mixture, gently pressing into raspberry mixture. Bake at 375° for 15 to 17 minutes or until golden. Cool completely in pan on a wire rack. Cut into squares. Yield: 16 servings (144 calories [26% from fat] per serving).

FAT 4.2g (SAT 0.8g, MONO 1.8g, POLY 1.4g)
PROTEIN 1.8g CARBOHYDRATE 25.3g
FIBER 2.2g CHOLESTEROL 0mg SODIUM 92mg

Fruit Desserts

Fruit is a naturally low-fat dessert. It satisfies a sweet tooth without adding fat and extra sugar, and is loaded with vitamins, minerals, and fiber.

Choosing high-quality, flavorful fruit is the key to a delectable dessert. Purchasing fresh fruit in season increases your chances of getting the best quality at the lowest price.

Many fruits are available year-round. If a certain variety of a fresh fruit is not available, frozen fruits and those canned in their own juice are suitable alternatives. Fresh frozen fruits without syrup are the most similar to fresh.

SUGAR-AND-SPICE BAKED APPLES

6 medium cooking apples
¼ cup plus 2 tablespoons raisins
¼ cup firmly packed brown sugar
½ teaspoon ground cinnamon
½ teaspoon ground nutmeg
2 tablespoons reduced-calorie margarine
1 cup unsweetened apple juice

Core apples to within ½ inch from bottom; peel top third of each apple. Combine raisins and next 3 ingredients in a small bowl; spoon mixture evenly into cavity of each apple. Place apples in a 10- x 6- x 2-inch baking dish. Top each apple with 1 teaspoon margarine; pour apple juice evenly over apples.

Cover and bake at 350° for 35 to 40 minutes or until apples are tender, basting occasionally with juice. Yield: 6 servings (206 calories [14% from fat] per serving).

Microwave Directions: Core apples to within ½ inch from bottom; peel top third of each apple. Combine raisins and next 3 ingredients; spoon mixture evenly into cavity of each apple. Place apples in a 10- x 6- x 2-inch baking dish. Top each apple with 1 teaspoon margarine; pour apple juice evenly over apples.

Cover with heavy-duty plastic wrap, and vent. Microwave at HIGH 10 to 12 minutes or until apples are tender, basting with juice and rotating dish a quarter-turn every 2 minutes. Let stand, covered, 5 minutes before serving.

FAT 3.2g (SAT 0.5g, MONO 0.9g, POLY 1.3g)
PROTEIN 0.6g CARBOHYDRATE 47.8g
FIBER 6.1g CHOLESTEROL 0mg SODIUM 42mg

CINNAMON-RAISIN APPLE TURNOVERS

2½ cups peeled, chopped cooking apple
2 tablespoons lemon juice
¼ cup chopped dried apricot
¼ cup raisins
3 tablespoons brown sugar
1 tablespoon reduced-calorie margarine, melted
¾ teaspoon ground cinnamon
¼ teaspoon ground nutmeg
⅛ teaspoon ground ginger
8 sheets commercial frozen phyllo pastry, thawed
Butter-flavored vegetable cooking spray
2 teaspoons powdered sugar

Combine apple and lemon juice in a large bowl; toss well. Add dried apricot and next 6 ingredients; stir gently, and set aside.

Place 1 sheet of phyllo on a damp towel (keep remaining phyllo covered). Lightly coat phyllo sheet with cooking spray. Fold phyllo in half lengthwise, and spray again. Place about ⅓ cup apple mixture at base of phyllo strip. Fold the right bottom corner over to form a triangle; continue folding back and forth to end of strip. Repeat entire procedure with remaining sheets of phyllo and apple mixture.

Place triangles, seam side down, on a baking sheet coated with cooking spray. Lightly spray tops of triangles with cooking spray. Bake at 400° for 12 to 15 minutes or until golden. Remove baking sheet from oven, and cool 5 minutes on a wire rack. Sift powdered sugar over turnovers, and serve warm. Yield: 8 servings (148 calories [11% from fat] each).

FAT 2.0g (SAT 0.3g, MONO 0.5g, POLY 0.7g)
PROTEIN 2.6g CARBOHYDRATE 31.6g
FIBER 1.5g CHOLESTEROL 0mg SODIUM 21mg

SUMMER FRUIT IN SPARKLING CIDER

1 cup cubed fresh pineapple
1 cup sliced nectarines
¾ cup pitted fresh cherries
¾ cup seedless green grapes
½ cup sliced plums
1 cup sparkling apple cider, chilled

Combine first 5 ingredients in a medium glass bowl; toss gently. Cover and freeze 1 hour or until fruit mixture is partially frozen. To serve, pour cider over fruit mixture, and toss gently. Serve immediately. Yield: 4 servings (111 calories [7% from fat] per serving).

FAT 0.9g (SAT 0.2g, MONO 0.2g, POLY 0.3g)
PROTEIN 1.0g CARBOHYDRATE 27.1g
FIBER 2.8g CHOLESTEROL 0mg SODIUM 3mg

Fresh Fruit Ambrosia

2 medium oranges
1 medium-size Red Delicious apple,
    cored and cubed
1 cup fresh pineapple chunks
½ cup seedless green grapes, halved
½ cup unsweetened orange juice
2 tablespoons sugar
1 tablespoon Grand Marnier or
    other orange-flavored liqueur
1 cup sliced fresh strawberries
3 tablespoons flaked coconut

Peel oranges, and slice crosswise; cut each slice into quarters. Combine orange, apple, pineapple, and grapes in a medium bowl; toss gently. Combine orange juice, sugar, and liqueur; stir until sugar dissolves. Pour orange juice mixture over fruit; toss gently. Cover and chill 2 to 3 hours.

To serve, add strawberries, and toss gently. Spoon fruit mixture evenly into individual dessert bowls, and sprinkle evenly with coconut. Yield: 10 servings (71 calories [13% from fat] per ½-cup serving).

FAT 1.0g (SAT 0.7g, MONO 0.1g, POLY 0.1g)
PROTEIN 0.6g CARBOHYDRATE 15.4g
FIBER 2.5g CHOLESTEROL 0mg SODIUM 6mg

Minted Melon in Honeyed Tulip Cups

1 cup cantaloupe balls
1 cup honeydew balls
1 cup watermelon balls
1 teaspoon finely chopped
    fresh mint
2 tablespoons brown sugar
1 tablespoon plus 1 teaspoon honey
2 teaspoons margarine
¼ cup all-purpose flour
¼ teaspoon vanilla extract
⅛ teaspoon ground cinnamon
Vegetable cooking spray
Fresh mint sprigs (optional)

Combine melon balls and mint; toss gently. Cover and chill.

Combine brown sugar, honey, and margarine in a saucepan. Cook over medium heat, stirring until margarine melts. Remove from heat; stir in flour, vanilla, and cinnamon.

Working quickly, spoon mixture into 4 circles on a baking sheet coated with cooking spray. Using fingers coated with cooking spray, spread mixture to 4½-inch circles. Bake at 325° for 9 minutes or until golden.

Remove baking sheet from oven; let cool 30 seconds. Remove cookies from baking sheet, and place each cookie over an inverted 6-ounce custard cup. Shape cookies around cups to form tulip-shaped cups; let cool completely over custard cups.

Spoon mixture evenly into cookie cups. Garnish with mint sprigs, if desired. Yield: 4 servings (133 calories [16% from fat] per serving).

FAT 2.4g (SAT 0.6g, MONO 0.9g, POLY 0.7g)
PROTEIN 1.8g CARBOHYDRATE 27.7g
FIBER 1.5g CHOLESTEROL 0mg SODIUM 34mg

Strawberries à l'Orange

1 tablespoon grated orange rind
2 tablespoons fresh orange juice
1 tablespoon Cointreau or other
    orange-flavored liqueur
1 teaspoon sugar
2¼ cups fresh strawberries, halved

Combine first 4 ingredients. Pour mixture over strawberries; toss gently. Cover and chill.

To serve, toss gently, and spoon evenly into individual dessert dishes. Yield: 4 servings (46 calories [6% from fat] per serving).

FAT 0.3g (SAT 0.0g, MONO 0.1g, POLY 0.2g)
PROTEIN 0.6g CARBOHYDRATE 9.6g
FIBER 2.3g CHOLESTEROL 0mg SODIUM 1mg

Tropical Fruit in Custard Sauce

1 (10½-ounce) loaf commercial
    angel food cake
¼ cup sugar
3 tablespoons cornstarch
¼ teaspoon salt
1¾ cups skim milk
2 tablespoons frozen egg substitute,
    thawed
3 tablespoons cream sherry
1 (8-ounce) can pineapple chunks
    in juice, drained
1 medium mango, peeled, seeded,
    and cubed
1 kiwifruit, peeled and sliced
1 carambola (starfruit), sliced
½ cup sliced fresh strawberries
Fresh mint sprigs (optional)

Cut cake into 1-inch cubes; set aside. Combine sugar, cornstarch, and salt in a saucepan; gradually stir in milk. Cook over medium heat, stirring constantly, until mixture comes to a boil. Cook 1 minute, stirring constantly. Remove from heat.

Gradually stir one-fourth of hot milk mixture into egg substitute; add to remaining hot mixture, stirring constantly with a wire whisk. Cook over low heat, stirring constantly, 1 minute or until mixture is thickened. Remove from heat. Cool slightly; add cream sherry, stirring well. Cover and chill thoroughly.

Combine custard mixture, cake cubes, pineapple chunks, and next 4 ingredients in a large bowl; toss gently. Cover and chill thoroughly.

To serve, spoon custard mixture evenly into individual dessert bowls. Garnish with fresh mint sprigs, if desired. Yield: 6 servings (218 calories [2% from fat] per serving).

FAT 0.5g (SAT 0.1g, MONO 0.1g, POLY 0.1g)
PROTEIN 5.1g CARBOHYDRATE 47.5g
FIBER 1.7g CHOLESTEROL 1mg SODIUM 187mg

Frozen Desserts

Frozen desserts such as ice cream are sure to be enjoyed on hot summer days. But as cool and refreshing as a bowl of ice cream may be, it's sure to add not only calories to the diet but fat and saturated fat as well.

The frozen treats featured in this section will satisfy your craving for ice cream without adding excess fat and calories to your diet. Low-fat dairy products such as skim milk and yogurt have replaced the traditional whipping cream and whole milk usually found in ice creams. This change yields an array of frozen desserts, each containing less than 8 percent of total calories from fat.

REFRESHING PINEAPPLE SHERBET

1 envelope unflavored gelatin
¼ cup unsweetened pineapple juice
1 cup skim milk
¾ cup sugar
¼ cup instant nonfat dry milk powder
2 (15½-ounce) cans crushed pineapple in juice, undrained
1 tablespoon lemon juice
Lemon rind curls (optional)

Sprinkle gelatin over pineapple juice in a saucepan; let stand 1 minute. Cook over low heat, stirring constantly, until gelatin dissolves. Remove from heat; add milk, sugar, and milk powder, stirring until sugar dissolves. Stir in pineapple and lemon juice. Pour mixture into a 9-inch square pan; freeze until almost firm.

Position knife blade in food processor bowl. Add half of frozen mixture; process until smooth. Transfer mixture to pan. Repeat procedure with remaining half of frozen mixture. Cover and freeze until firm.

Let sherbet stand at room temperature 10 minutes. Scoop into individual dessert bowls. Garnish with lemon rind curls, if desired. Serve immediately. Yield: 7 cups (97 calories [1% from fat] per ½-cup serving).

FAT 0.1g (SAT 0.0g, MONO 0.0g, POLY 0.2g)
PROTEIN 2.1g CARBOHYDRATE 23.2g
FIBER 0.5g CHOLESTEROL 1mg SODIUM 22mg

RASPBERRY-CHAMPAGNE SORBET

6½ cups fresh raspberries
1 cup sugar
1½ cups brut champagne, chilled
½ cup unsweetened orange juice
Fresh raspberries (optional)

Position knife blade in food processor bowl. Add raspberries and sugar; process until smooth. Strain raspberry mixture through a sieve, and discard seeds. Transfer mixture to a large bowl; add champagne and orange juice, stirring well.

Pour raspberry mixture into freezer can of a 1-gallon hand-turned or electric freezer. Freeze according to manufacturer's instructions. (Mixture may take longer to freeze due to addition of champagne.) Pack freezer with additional ice and salt, and let stand 1 hour, if desired.

Scoop sorbet into individual dessert bowls. Garnish with fresh raspberries, if desired. Serve immediately. Yield: 6 cups (126 calories [3% from fat] per ½-cup serving).

FAT 0.4g (SAT 0.0g, MONO 0.0g, POLY 0.2g)
PROTEIN 0.0g CARBOHYDRATE 26.2g
FIBER 5.3g CHOLESTEROL 0mg SODIUM 1mg

CRANBERRY-PINEAPPLE ICE

4½ cups water, divided
2¼ cups fresh cranberries
1¼ cups sugar, divided
1 cup unsweetened pineapple juice
3 tablespoons unsweetened orange juice
Fresh mint sprigs (optional)

Combine ¾ cup water, fresh cranberries, and ½ cup sugar in a small saucepan; stir well. Bring cranberry mixture to a boil over medium heat; cook 8 minutes or until cranberries pop, stirring frequently. Remove from heat, and let cool.

Position knife blade in food processor bowl. Add cranberry mixture; process until smooth. Strain puree through a sieve; discard pulp.

Combine cranberry puree, remaining 3¾ cups water, remaining ¾ cup sugar, pineapple juice, and orange juice in a large bowl; stir well.

Pour cranberry mixture into freezer can of a 1-gallon hand-turned or electric freezer. Freeze according to manufacturer's instructions. Pack freezer with additional ice and salt; let stand 1 hour, if desired.

Scoop mixture into individual dessert bowls. Garnish with fresh mint sprigs, if desired. Serve immediately. Yield: 10 cups (63 calories [0% from fat] per ½-cup serving).

FAT 0.0g (SAT 0.0g, MONO 0.0g, POLY 0.0g)
PROTEIN 0.1g CARBOHYDRATE 16.1g
FIBER 0.2g CHOLESTEROL 0mg SODIUM 0mg

VANILLA FROZEN YOGURT

2 envelopes unflavored gelatin
2 cups skim milk
1 cup sugar
Dash of salt
5 cups vanilla low-fat yogurt
1 tablespoon plus 1 teaspoon
  vanilla extract

Sprinkle gelatin over milk in a saucepan; let stand 1 minute. Cook over low heat, stirring constantly, until gelatin dissolves. Remove from heat; add sugar and salt, stirring until sugar dissolves. Stir in yogurt and vanilla. Cover and chill 1 hour.

Pour yogurt mixture into freezer can of a 1-gallon hand-turned or electric freezer; freeze according to manufacturer's instructions. Scoop yogurt into individual bowls. Serve immediately. Yield: 11 cups (92 calories [7% from fat] per ½-cup serving).

FAT 0.7g (SAT 0.4g, MONO 0.2g, POLY 0.0g)
PROTEIN 3.9g CARBOHYDRATE 17.5g
FIBER 0.0g CHOLESTEROL 3mg SODIUM 53mg

Peach Frozen Yogurt: Add 3 pounds fresh peaches, peeled, pitted, and pureed, to yogurt mixture before chilling. Pour into freezer can of a 5-quart hand-turned or electric freezer. Yield: 15 cups (80 calories [6% from fat] per ½-cup serving).

FAT 0.5g (SAT 0.3g, MONO 0.2g, POLY 0.0g)
PROTEIN 3.0g CARBOHYDRATE 16.2g
FIBER 0.5g CHOLESTEROL 2mg SODIUM 39mg

Strawberry Frozen Yogurt: Add 6 cups fresh strawberries, hulled and pureed, to yogurt mixture before chilling. Yield: 13 cups (87 calories [7% from fat] per ½-cup serving).

FAT 0.7g (SAT 0.4g, MONO 0.2g, POLY 0.1g)
PROTEIN 3.4g CARBOHYDRATE 17.0g
FIBER 0.8g CHOLESTEROL 3mg SODIUM 45mg

Puddings and Custards

The smooth, creamy goodness of puddings and custards appeals to young and old alike. This favorite comfort food is simply a cooked mixture of milk, eggs, and sugar.

These recipes taste like the ones you remember from childhood, but the fat content has been greatly reduced. Low-fat and nonfat dairy products such as skim milk, reduced-calorie margarine, egg substitute, and nonfat sour cream alternative have been used to keep the fat content low without changing the traditional tastes and textures. Some whole eggs are used, but the number has been reduced, and cornstarch and egg substitute have been added to thicken the mixtures.

Constant stirring during the cooking process helps the mixture remain smooth and not scorch. Cook the custard over medium heat; high heat may cause the mixture to curdle.

OLD-FASHIONED BANANA PUDDING

⅓ cup firmly packed brown sugar
1½ tablespoons cornstarch
1⅔ cups skim milk
⅓ cup frozen egg substitute, thawed
1 tablespoon margarine
1 teaspoon vanilla extract
26 vanilla wafers
3 medium bananas, peeled and
  sliced (about 2 cups)
3 egg whites
2 tablespoons sugar

Combine brown sugar and cornstarch in a saucepan; gradually stir in milk. Cook over medium heat, stirring constantly, until mixture comes to a boil. Cook 1 minute, stirring constantly. Remove from heat.

Gradually stir about one-fourth of hot milk mixture into egg substitute; add to remaining hot mixture, stirring constantly. Cook over medium heat, stirring constantly, 3 minutes or until mixture is thickened. Remove from heat; stir in margarine and vanilla. Cool completely.

Arrange half of vanilla wafers in bottom of a 2-quart casserole; top with half of banana slices and half of custard. Repeat layering procedure with remaining vanilla wafers, banana slices, and custard.

Beat egg whites at high speed of an electric mixer until soft peaks form. Gradually add 2 tablespoons sugar, beating until stiff peaks form. Spread meringue over custard, sealing to edge of dish. Bake at 325° for 25 minutes or until golden. Yield: 6 servings (273 calories [22% from fat] per serving).

FAT 6.6g (SAT 1.2g, MONO 2.1g, POLY 1.4g)
PROTEIN 6.9g CARBOHYDRATE 47.2g
FIBER 1.7g CHOLESTEROL 1mg SODIUM 190mg

RASPBERRY CUSTARD BRÛLÉE

2 cups fresh raspberries
3 tablespoons sugar
1 tablespoon cornstarch
1½ cups skim milk
1 egg, lightly beaten
3 tablespoons nonfat sour cream
  alternative
¾ teaspoon vanilla extract
2 tablespoons brown sugar

Divide raspberries evenly among 6 (4-ounce) ovenproof ramekins or custard cups. Set aside.

Combine sugar and cornstarch in a small saucepan; stir well. Combine milk and egg in a small bowl, stirring well; add to dry ingredients. Cook over medium heat, stirring constantly, until mixture comes to a boil. Remove from heat; let cool 5 minutes. Stir in sour cream and vanilla.

Spoon custard mixture evenly over raspberries. Place ramekins on a baking sheet. Sprinkle each with 1 teaspoon brown sugar. Broil 5½ inches from heat 2 minutes or until sugar melts. Serve immediately. Yield: 6 servings (101 calories [11% from fat] per serving).

FAT 1.2g (SAT 0.3g, MONO 0.4g, POLY 0.2g)
PROTEIN 4.0g CARBOHYDRATE 18.8g
FIBER 3.0g CHOLESTEROL 38mg SODIUM 49mg

CREAMY VANILLA-ALMOND CUSTARD

2½ cups skim milk
1 cup frozen egg substitute, thawed
⅓ cup sugar
1 teaspoon vanilla extract
⅛ teaspoon almond extract
Vegetable cooking spray
2 tablespoons sliced almonds, toasted

Combine first 5 ingredients in a large bowl; stir well. Pour mixture evenly into 6 (6-ounce) custard cups coated with cooking spray.

Place cups in a large shallow baking pan; add hot water to pan to a depth of 1 inch. Bake at 300° for 1 hour and 25 minutes or until a knife inserted in center comes out clean. Remove cups from water; cool slightly. Cover and chill thoroughly.

Sprinkle evenly with almonds just before serving. Yield: 6 servings (128 calories [18% from fat] per serving).

FAT 2.6g (SAT 0.4g, MONO 1.5g, POLY 0.6g)
PROTEIN 8.3g CARBOHYDRATE 17.8g
FIBER 0.5g CHOLESTEROL 2mg SODIUM 114mg

PUMPKIN FLAN

½ cup sugar
Vegetable cooking spray
1 (12-ounce) can evaporated skimmed milk
½ cup skim milk
¼ cup sugar
¾ cup frozen egg substitute, thawed
1½ cups cooked, mashed pumpkin
1¼ teaspoons pumpkin pie spice

Sprinkle ½ cup sugar in a small heavy skillet. Cook over medium heat, stirring constantly with a wooden spoon, until sugar melts and turns light brown. Pour caramel syrup into an 8-inch round cakepan coated with cooking spray, tilting pan to coat evenly; set aside. (Caramel syrup will harden.)

Combine milks and ¼ cup sugar in a medium saucepan; heat just until bubbles form around edge of saucepan, stirring until sugar dissolves. Remove from heat.

Gradually stir one-fourth of hot milk mixture into egg substitute; add to remaining hot mixture, stirring constantly. Add pumpkin and pumpkin pie spice; stir well.

Place prepared cakepan in a large shallow baking pan on oven rack; pour pumpkin mixture into prepared cakepan (cakepan will be very full). Pour hot water to a depth of 1 inch into large pan. Cover and bake at 325° for 1 hour or until a knife inserted near center comes out clean.

Remove cakepan from water; let cool on a wire rack. Cover and chill at least 4 hours. To serve, loosen edges of flan with a spatula; invert onto a serving plate. Drizzle any remaining sauce over flan. Yield: 6 servings (185 calories [2% from fat] per serving).

FAT 0.4g (SAT 0.2g, MONO 0.1g, POLY 0.1g)
PROTEIN 8.7g CARBOHYDRATE 38.0g
FIBER 1.1g CHOLESTEROL 3mg SODIUM 124mg

Creamy Vanilla-Almond Custard makes an elegant dessert when served in pretty baking cups. It's simple to prepare and uses ingredients that are probably in your cupboard.

Pastry and Crumb Crusts

Traditional pastry is made by cutting shortening into flour, sprinkling the mixture with cold water, and stirring gently to form a dough. Basic pastry can still be yours — the only difference is that shortening, which is high in saturated fat, should be replaced with regular margarine in slightly reduced amounts. The recipe for Basic Pastry Shell featured in this section bakes and tastes remarkably like the higher fat version.

Although these recipes are more than 30 percent total fat per serving of crust only, adding a low-fat filling lowers the fat percentage to 30 percent or less of total calories.

It doesn't take any special equipment to prepare basic pastry — just a pastry blender or two knives to cut the margarine into the flour, a rolling pin, and a pie plate. To minimize stickiness when rolling out pastry, roll the dough between two sheets of heavy-duty plastic wrap or on a floured pastry cloth, using a floured rolling pin cover on the rolling pin. It's important to avoid overworking pastry dough. The more the dough is handled, the more gluten will develop, making the pastry tough.

For best results, use an ovenproof glass pieplate or a dull metal piepan. Shiny metal pans reflect heat and prevent the crust from browning.

Crumb crusts work well for pies that have cold fillings. To keep total fat low in these types of crusts, the amount of fat has been reduced significantly — from the usual six tablespoons of margarine in a traditional crumb crust to three tablespoons. Instead of butter, regular margarine and reduced-calorie margarine have been used with no noticeable difference in texture or flavor. Before being filled, the crusts are baked to set the crumbs.

BASIC PASTRY SHELL

1¼ cups all-purpose flour
⅓ cup margarine
2 to 3 tablespoons cold water

Place flour in a medium bowl; cut in margarine with a pastry blender until mixture resembles coarse meal. Sprinkle cold water, 1 tablespoon at a time, evenly over surface; stir with a fork until dry ingredients are moistened. Shape dough into a ball.

Place dough between 2 sheets of heavy-duty plastic wrap, and gently press to a 4-inch circle. Chill 20 minutes. Roll dough to a 12-inch circle. Place in freezer 5 minutes or until plastic wrap can be removed easily. Remove top sheet of plastic wrap. Invert and fit pastry into a 9-inch pieplate; remove remaining sheet of plastic wrap. Fold edges of pastry under and flute; seal to edge of pieplate.

For baked pastry shell, prick bottom and sides of pastry with a fork. Bake at 450° for 10 minutes or until lightly browned. Cool on a wire rack. Yield: 8 servings (139 calories [51% from fat] per serving).

FAT 7.8g (SAT 1.5g, MONO 3.4g, POLY 2.5g)
PROTEIN 2.1g   CARBOHYDRATE 15.0g
FIBER 0.5g   CHOLESTEROL 0mg   SODIUM 89mg

CINNAMON-GINGERSNAP CRUST

1½ cups gingersnap cookie crumbs
1½ tablespoons sugar
½ teaspoon ground cinnamon
3 tablespoons margarine, melted
Vegetable cooking spray

Combine first 4 ingredients in a small bowl; stir well. Press mixture evenly into bottom and up sides of a 9-inch pieplate coated with cooking spray. Bake at 350° for 8 minutes. Cool completely on a wire rack. Yield: 8 servings (142 calories [49% from fat] per serving).

FAT 7.8g (SAT 1.7g, MONO 3.4g, POLY 2.3g)
PROTEIN 1.4g   CARBOHYDRATE 16.8g
FIBER 0.1g   CHOLESTEROL 8mg   SODIUM 78mg

GRAHAM CRACKER CRUST

¾ cup graham cracker crumbs
¼ cup sugar
3 tablespoons reduced-calorie margarine, melted
Vegetable cooking spray

Combine first 3 ingredients; stir well. Press mixture evenly into bottom and up sides of a 9-inch pieplate coated with cooking spray. Bake at 350° for 8 minutes. Cool on a wire rack. Yield: 8 servings (86 calories [39% from fat] per serving).

FAT 3.7g (SAT 0.4g, MONO 1.0g, POLY 3.1g)
PROTEIN 0.6g   CARBOHYDRATE 13.2g
FIBER 0.2g   CHOLESTEROL 0mg   SODIUM 101mg

Press graham cracker crumbs into a pieplate using a dry-ingredient measuring cup. This allows you to press the crust firmly into the plate while creating a rim around the crust.

Pies, Tarts, and Cobblers

Fruit fillings such as those used in pies, tarts, cobblers, and crisps are easy to adjust because fat is seldom used in their preparation. For cream fillings, substitute skim milk for whole milk and egg substitute for whole eggs.

In this section, meringue toppings have been used in place of whipped cream to reduce fat. Cornstarch, rather than egg yolks, thickens the fillings for the pies and tarts. The fillings will thicken as they cool.

VANILLA CREAM PIE

½ cup sugar
¼ cup cornstarch
¼ teaspoon salt
2½ cups skim milk
¼ cup frozen egg substitute, thawed
1 tablespoon vanilla extract
1 baked Basic Pastry Shell (page 70)
3 egg whites
3 tablespoons sugar

Combine ½ cup sugar, cornstarch, and salt in a saucepan; gradually stir in milk. Cook over medium heat, stirring constantly, until mixture comes to a boil. Cook 1 minute, stirring constantly. Remove from heat.

Gradually stir one-fourth of hot mixture into egg substitute; add to remaining hot mixture, stirring constantly. Cook over medium heat, stirring constantly, 2 minutes or until mixture is thickened. Remove from heat; stir in vanilla. Spoon mixture into pastry shell.

Beat egg whites at high speed of an electric mixer until foamy. Gradually add 3 tablespoons sugar, 1 tablespoon at a time, beating until stiff peaks form. Spread meringue over hot filling, sealing to edge of crust. Bake at 325° for 25 minutes or until golden. Cool completely on a wire rack. Yield: 8 servings (262 calories [27% from fat] per serving).

FAT 7.8g (SAT 1.6g, MONO 3.4g, POLY 2.4g)
PROTEIN 6.7g   CARBOHYDRATE 40.3g
FIBER 0.6g   CHOLESTEROL 2mg   SODIUM 233mg

Chocolate Cream Pie: Add 3 tablespoons unsweetened cocoa to dry ingredients in saucepan. Decrease vanilla to 1½ teaspoons. Yield: 8 servings (268 calories [27% from fat] per serving).

FAT 8.1g (SAT 1.8g, MONO 3.4g, POLY 2.5g)
PROTEIN 7.3g   CARBOHYDRATE 41.0g
FIBER 0.6g   CHOLESTEROL 2mg   SODIUM 234mg

LEMON MERINGUE PIE

⅔ cup sugar
⅓ cup cornstarch
2 cups skim milk
½ cup frozen egg substitute, thawed
2 teaspoons grated lemon rind
⅓ cup fresh lemon juice
1 baked Basic Pastry Shell (page 70)
4 egg whites
½ teaspoon cream of tartar
½ teaspoon vanilla extract
2 tablespoons sugar

Combine ⅔ cup sugar and cornstarch in a saucepan; gradually stir in milk. Cook over medium heat, stirring constantly, until mixture comes to a boil. Cook 1 minute, stirring constantly. Remove from heat.

Gradually stir one-fourth of hot mixture into egg substitute; add to remaining hot mixture, stirring constantly. Cook over medium heat, stirring constantly, 2 minutes or until thickened. Remove from heat; stir in lemon rind and juice. Spoon mixture into pastry shell.

Beat egg whites, cream of tartar, and vanilla at high speed of an electric mixer until foamy. Gradually add 2 tablespoons sugar, beating until stiff peaks form. Spread meringue over hot filling, sealing to edge of crust. Bake at 325° for 25 minutes or until golden. Cool completely on a wire rack. Yield: 8 servings (276 calories [26% from fat] per serving).

FAT 7.9g (SAT 1.6g, MONO 3.4g, POLY 2.5g)
PROTEIN 7.4g   CARBOHYDRATE 44.0g
FIBER 0.6g   CHOLESTEROL 1mg   SODIUM 183mg

APPLE-BERRY CRISP

2 medium cooking apples, peeled, cored, and thinly sliced
1 tablespoon lemon juice
Vegetable cooking spray
1 (10-ounce) package frozen raspberries in light syrup, thawed
1 cup regular oats, uncooked
3 tablespoons reduced-calorie margarine, melted
2 tablespoons honey
1 teaspoon ground cinnamon
½ teaspoon ground nutmeg

Combine apple and lemon juice; toss gently. Place apple in a 10- x 6- x 2-inch baking dish coated with cooking spray; top with raspberries.

Combine oats and remaining ingredients; sprinkle evenly over raspberries. Bake at 375° for 30 minutes or until lightly browned and apple is tender. Yield: 8 servings (139 calories [24% from fat] per serving).

FAT 3.7g (SAT 0.5g, MONO 1.2g, POLY 1.5g)
PROTEIN 2.0g   CARBOHYDRATE 26.7g
FIBER 4.6g   CHOLESTEROL 0mg   SODIUM 42mg

Two-Berry Holiday Tart

⅔ cup all-purpose flour
⅔ cup whole wheat flour
⅛ teaspoon salt
⅓ cup vegetable oil
3 tablespoons water
½ teaspoon almond extract
2 cups fresh cranberries
1 (10-ounce) package frozen
    raspberries in light syrup, thawed
½ cup sugar
½ cup low-sugar raspberry spread
2 tablespoons cornstarch
2 tablespoons water
½ teaspoon almond extract

Combine flours and salt; stir well. Combine oil, water, and ½ teaspoon almond extract; add to flour mixture, stirring just until dry ingredients are moistened. Shape dough into a ball. Roll dough between 2 sheets of heavy-duty plastic wrap to an 11-inch circle. Remove top sheet of plastic wrap. Invert and fit pastry into a 9-inch tart pan. Remove remaining sheet of plastic wrap. Prick bottom and sides of pastry with a fork. Bake at 425° for 12 minutes or until lightly browned. Remove from oven; cool completely on a wire rack.

Combine cranberries and next 3 ingredients in a saucepan. Cook over medium heat 15 minutes, stirring frequently. Combine cornstarch and 2 tablespoons water, stirring until smooth. Add cornstarch mixture to cranberry mixture. Cook, stirring constantly, until mixture is thickened and bubbly. Remove from heat; stir in ½ teaspoon almond extract.

Spoon filling into tart shell. Cover and chill 4 hours or until set. Yield: 10 servings (225 calories [30% from fat] per serving).

FAT 7.5g (SAT 1.3g, MONO 2.2g, POLY 3.6g)
PROTEIN 2.2g CARBOHYDRATE 38.4g
FIBER 3.5g CHOLESTEROL 0mg SODIUM 29mg

72

Summer Blackberry Cobbler

8 cups fresh blackberries, divided
1 cup sugar
⅓ cup cornstarch
2 tablespoons reduced-calorie
    margarine
½ teaspoon ground cinnamon
½ teaspoon almond extract
Vegetable cooking spray
Dough for Basic Pastry Shell
    (page 70)
2 teaspoons skim milk
1 tablespoon sugar

Combine 6 cups blackberries and next 5 ingredients in a large saucepan. Bring to a boil over medium heat, stirring occasionally; cook 1 minute or until thickened. Remove from heat; let cool slightly.

Gently stir in remaining 2 cups blackberries. Pour blackberry mixture into an 8-inch square baking dish coated with vegetable cooking spray. Let cool completely.

Place dough for Basic Pastry Shell between 2 sheets of heavy-duty plastic wrap; gently press to a 4-inch square. Chill 20 minutes. Roll dough to an 8-inch square. Place in freezer 5 minutes or until plastic wrap can be removed easily. Remove top sheet of plastic wrap. Cut pastry into ½-inch strips. Arrange strips lattice-style over blackberry mixture; seal strips to edge of dish. Brush strips with milk, and sprinkle with 1 tablespoon sugar.

Bake at 375° for 45 to 50 minutes or until pastry is golden and filling is bubbly. Yield: 8 servings (348 calories [26% from fat] per serving).

FAT 10.1g (SAT 1.8g, MONO 4.1g, POLY 3.5g)
PROTEIN 3.1g CARBOHYDRATE 63.6g
FIBER 10.5g CHOLESTEROL 0mg SODIUM 118mg

Brimming with fresh berries, Summer Blackberry Cobbler seals a meal with natural sweetness.

Specialty Desserts

Some occasions call for an exciting dessert — one that may take more effort to prepare but whose results will be worth the work. These recipes for mousse, crêpes, meringues, and soufflés make appropriate desserts for any important event.

The fact that these recipes are low-fat makes them even more appealing. Even though traditional preparation methods are used, low-fat ingredient substitutions have been made to keep these delightful specialties as guilt-free as possible.

CREAMY VANILLA MOUSSE WITH BLUEBERRY SAUCE

2½ cups fresh blueberries
¼ cup sugar
¼ cup water
1 teaspoon cornstarch
1 envelope unflavored gelatin
¾ cup plus 2 tablespoons skim milk
1 (8-ounce) carton vanilla low-fat yogurt
4 ounces Neufchâtel cheese, softened
2½ tablespoons sugar
Vegetable cooking spray

Combine blueberries, ¼ cup sugar, water, and cornstarch in a medium saucepan. Cook over medium heat, stirring constantly, 5 minutes or until sugar dissolves and mixture is thickened. Remove from heat, and let cool slightly. Cover blueberry mixture, and chill thoroughly.

Sprinkle gelatin over milk in a small saucepan; let stand 1 minute. Cook mixture over low heat, stirring constantly, until gelatin dissolves. Remove pan from heat; set aside, and let cool.

Position knife blade in food processor bowl. Add yogurt, cheese, and 2½ tablespoons sugar; process 1 minute. Add gelatin mixture to yogurt mixture, and process 1 minute or until mixture is smooth. Spoon yogurt mixture into a 3-cup mold coated with vegetable cooking spray. Cover and chill until firm.

Unmold mousse onto a serving plate. Serve with blueberry sauce. Yield: 6 servings (189 calories [25% from fat] per serving).

FAT 5.3g (SAT 3.2g, MONO 1.5g, POLY 0.3g)
PROTEIN 6.4g CARBOHYDRATE 30.6g
FIBER 3.0g CHOLESTEROL 17mg SODIUM 124mg

TROPICAL CHOCOLATE CRÊPES

½ cup all-purpose flour
1 tablespoon sugar
1 tablespoon unsweetened cocoa
½ cup evaporated skimmed milk
1 egg
1 tablespoon reduced-calorie margarine, melted
Vegetable cooking spray
⅔ cup chopped fresh pineapple
½ cup chopped fresh papaya
2 medium kiwifruit, peeled and sliced
Chocolate Glaze
2 tablespoons sliced almonds, toasted

Combine first 6 ingredients in container of an electric blender; top with cover, and process until smooth. Refrigerate batter at least 2 hours.

Coat a 6-inch crêpe pan or non-stick skillet with vegetable cooking spray; place over medium heat until just hot, not smoking. Pour 2 tablespoons batter into pan; quickly tilt pan in all directions so batter covers pan in a thin film. Cook 1 minute or until crêpe can be shaken loose. Flip crêpe, and cook about 30 seconds. (Place filling on spotted side.)

Place crêpes on a towel to cool. Stack crêpes between layers of wax paper to prevent sticking. Repeat procedure until all batter is used.

Arrange fresh pineapple, papaya, and kiwifruit down center of each crêpe. Roll up crêpes, and place seam side down on individual dessert plates; drizzle each crêpe with 1 tablespoon Chocolate Glaze. Sprinkle evenly with almonds. Yield: 8 servings (177 calories [25% from fat] per serving).

Chocolate Glaze

2 tablespoons reduced-calorie margarine
2 tablespoons unsweetened cocoa
2 tablespoons water
½ teaspoon vanilla extract
1 cup sifted powdered sugar

Melt margarine in a small saucepan. Add cocoa and water, stirring until smooth. Cook over medium-low heat, stirring constantly, until mixture begins to thicken (do not boil). Remove saucepan from heat, and add vanilla and powdered sugar, stirring until smooth. Yield: ½ cup.

FAT 4.9g (SAT 0.9g, MONO 1.9g, POLY 1.5g)
PROTEIN 4.1g CARBOHYDRATE 30.3g
FIBER 1.3g CHOLESTEROL 28mg SODIUM 70mg

Draw circles on parchment paper using a biscuit cutter or the edge of a bowl. Turn the paper over to prevent the meringues from coming in contact with pencil lead.

The peaks of stiffly beaten egg whites should just hold their shape and not fall over. If overbeaten, the egg whites will be dry and won't expand properly during baking.

Pipe the meringue onto the parchment, using the traced circles as a guide. Pipe a circle with the meringue; then fill in the circle to form the bottom of the shell.

Strawberry-Filled Meringues is a sophisticated dessert that is virtually fat-free. It's the perfect finale to a formal dinner.

STRAWBERRY-FILLED MERINGUES

6 egg whites
¾ teaspoon cream of tartar
¾ cup superfine sugar
¾ teaspoon vanilla extract
¼ teaspoon almond extract
Glazed Strawberry Filling

Line 2 baking sheets with parchment paper. Draw 4 (4-inch) circles on each sheet of paper; turn paper over. Set aside.

Beat egg whites and cream of tartar at high speed of an electric mixer until soft peaks form. Gradually add sugar, 1 tablespoon at a time, beating until stiff peaks form. Gently fold in flavorings.

Pipe meringue onto circles on paper, building up sides to form a shell. Bake at 225° for 1 hour and 20 minutes. Turn oven off. Cool completely in oven at least 2 hours or overnight with oven door closed. (Empty baked meringue shells may be stored in an airtight container for up to 3 days.)

Fill shells with Glazed Strawberry Filling. Yield: 8 servings (157 calories [2% from fat] per serving).

Glazed Strawberry Filling

3 cups fresh strawberry halves
2 tablespoons sugar
1 (10-ounce) package frozen
  raspberries in light syrup,
  thawed
2 teaspoons cornstarch
2 teaspoons Cointreau or other
  orange-flavored liqueur
1½ teaspoons lemon juice

Combine strawberry halves and sugar, tossing gently. Set aside.

Place raspberries in container of an electric blender or food processor; top with cover, and process until smooth. Press raspberries through a sieve; set puree aside, and discard seeds.

Combine strained raspberries and cornstarch in a small saucepan; stir until smooth. Bring to a boil over medium heat, stirring constantly, and cook 1 minute or until mixture is thickened. Remove sauce from heat; stir in liqueur and lemon juice.

Pour raspberry sauce over strawberry halves; toss gently to coat. Cover and chill 2 to 3 hours. Toss gently before spooning into baked meringue shells. Yield: 2½ cups.

FAT 0.3g (SAT 0.0g, MONO 0.0g, POLY 0.1g)
PROTEIN 3.1g CARBOHYDRATE 36.3g
FIBER 3.9g CHOLESTEROL 0mg SODIUM 60mg

GRAND MARNIER SOUFFLÉS

Butter-flavored vegetable cooking
  spray
2 teaspoons sugar
Bittersweet Chocolate Sauce
¼ cup reduced-calorie margarine
¼ cup all-purpose flour
¾ cup skim milk
¼ cup Grand Marnier or other
  orange-flavored liqueur
2 tablespoons sugar
2 egg yolks, beaten
1 teaspoon vanilla extract
6 egg whites
⅛ teaspoon cream of tartar
3 tablespoons sugar

Coat 8 (6-ounce) soufflé dishes with vegetable cooking spray; sprinkle bottom of each soufflé dish evenly with ¼ teaspoon sugar. Spoon 1 tablespoon plus 1 teaspoon Bittersweet Chocolate Sauce into each soufflé dish. Set aside.

Melt margarine in a medium saucepan over medium heat. Add flour, stirring until mixture is smooth. Cook mixture 1 minute, stirring constantly. Gradually add milk, liqueur, and 2 tablespoons

sugar, stirring constantly. Cook sauce, stirring constantly, until mixture is thickened and bubbly.

Gradually stir about one-fourth of hot mixture into egg yolks; add to remaining hot mixture, stirring constantly. Cook over low heat 1 to 2 minutes, stirring constantly. Remove mixture from heat, and stir in vanilla. Let cool 5 minutes.

Beat egg whites and cream of tartar at high speed of an electric mixer until foamy. Gradually add 3 tablespoons sugar, 1 tablespoon at a time, beating until stiff peaks form. Fold about one-fourth of beaten egg white into custard mixture; gently fold in remaining beaten egg white. Spoon ¾ cup egg white mixture into each prepared soufflé dish.

Place soufflé dishes in 2 (9-inch) square baking pans; pour hot water into pans to a depth of ½ inch. Bake at 350° for 25 minutes or until soufflés are puffed and golden. Remove dishes from water, and serve immediately. Yield: 8 servings (203 calories [26% from fat] per serving).

Bittersweet Chocolate Sauce

¼ cup plus 2 tablespoons
  unsweetened cocoa
¼ cup sugar
¼ cup hot water
3 tablespoons light corn syrup
2 tablespoons Grand Marnier or
  other orange-flavored liqueur

Combine cocoa and sugar in a small saucepan; stir well. Gradually add water, stirring until mixture is smooth. Stir in corn syrup and liqueur. Bring mixture to a boil over medium heat; boil 2 minutes or until thickened, stirring constantly. Cool completely. Yield: ⅔ cup.

FAT 5.8g (SAT 1.3g, MONO 1.9g, POLY 1.9g)
PROTEIN 5.6g CARBOHYDRATE 32.5g
FIBER 0.1g CHOLESTEROL 55mg SODIUM 123mg

EGGS AND CHEESE

Because eggs contain a high amount of cholesterol, and cheese contains a high amount of saturated fat, these foods are often excluded from healthy eating plans. The recipes in this chapter use egg whites or egg substitutes as well as reduced-fat cheeses so that egg and cheese dishes can return to their rightful place on your menus.

EGGS

At one time, eggs were thought to be a nearly perfect food — low in calories yet packed with protein, vitamins, and minerals. But as more has been learned about the role cholesterol plays in causing heart disease, the egg has toppled from its pedestal.

One egg yolk contains about 213 milligrams of cholesterol — a significant amount when compared with the American Heart Association's (AHA) recommendation of no more than 300 milligrams of cholesterol per day for adults. The AHA suggests limiting egg consumption to four per week to help keep cholesterol intake to a minimum.

Thirty-five percent of the cholesterol in American diets comes from egg yolks, with half of that amount in "visible" forms such as scrambled eggs, omelets, and hard-cooked eggs. The "invisible" half turns up in breads, pancakes, cakes, and cookies. Many recipes work well when two egg whites are substituted for a whole egg. (Egg whites contain no cholesterol.) And recipes that call for two whole eggs can yield good results when two egg whites are substituted for one of the whole eggs. These changes substantially decrease the cholesterol content in a recipe.

Egg substitutes can be used in place of whole eggs in many recipes. They are a liquid blend of egg whites, corn oil, food starch, skim milk powder, and artificial coloring. Although these products contain no cholesterol, they are higher in sodium than a whole egg. (One-fourth cup egg substitute is equivalent to one whole egg.) Egg substitutes are found in either the freezer section or dairy case of the grocery store.

Although some recipes work fine with egg whites, others do not; keep both egg whites and egg substitute on hand. If you don't want to buy one of the commercial egg substitutes, you can make your own using the recipe on page 78. Cook egg substitutes slowly over medium heat; they are lower in fat than whole eggs and can become tough and dry if cooked over heat that is too high.

Strawberry Cheese Blintzes (page 82) have a low-fat filling tucked inside delicate crêpes.

EGG SUBSTITUTE

8 egg whites
⅓ cup instant nonfat dry milk
   powder
2 tablespoons water
2 teaspoons vegetable oil
3 drops yellow food coloring
   (optional)

Combine all ingredients in container of an electric blender or food processor; top with cover, and process 30 seconds.

To store, refrigerate mixture in a covered container up to 1 week, or freeze in an airtight container up to 1 month. Yield: 1 cup (88 calories [24% from fat] per ¼-cup serving).

FAT 2.3g (SAT 0.5g, MONO 0.7g, POLY 1.1g)
PROTEIN 10.3g   CARBOHYDRATE 5.9g
FIBER 0.0g   CHOLESTEROL 2mg   SODIUM 158mg

BREAKFAST BURRITOS

6 (6-inch) flour tortillas
2 cups frozen egg substitute,
   thawed
¼ cup water
¾ cup plus 2 tablespoons
   commercial taco sauce, divided
2 tablespoons canned chopped
   green chiles, drained
¼ teaspoon salt
Dash of pepper
Vegetable cooking spray
½ cup plus 1 tablespoon shredded
   reduced-fat sharp Cheddar
   cheese, divided

Wrap tortillas in aluminum foil. Bake at 350° for 7 minutes. Set tortillas aside, and keep warm.

Combine egg substitute, water, 2 tablespoons taco sauce, and next 3 ingredients in a medium bowl; stir well. Coat a large nonstick skillet with cooking spray; place over medium

heat until hot. Add egg substitute mixture; cook, stirring frequently, until mixture is softly set.

Spoon mixture evenly over each tortilla; top each with 1 tablespoon taco sauce and 1 tablespoon cheese. Roll up tortillas; place, seam side down, on a serving platter. Top evenly with remaining taco sauce and cheese. Yield: 6 servings (232 calories [17% from fat] per serving).

FAT 4.3g (SAT 1.7g, MONO 1.5g, POLY 0.6g)
PROTEIN 13.5g   CARBOHYDRATE 34.9g
FIBER 0.9g   CHOLESTEROL 7mg   SODIUM 498mg

MEXICAN BREAKFAST CASSEROLE

4 cups ½-inch French bread cubes
Vegetable cooking spray
1 cup diced lean cooked ham
¼ cup chopped sweet red pepper
1 (4-ounce) can chopped green
   chiles, drained
1¼ cups (5 ounces) shredded
   reduced-fat sharp Cheddar cheese
1¼ cups frozen egg substitute,
   thawed
1 cup skim milk
¼ teaspoon onion powder
¼ teaspoon ground cumin
¼ teaspoon dry mustard
¼ teaspoon ground red pepper
Paprika
2 cups Santa Fe Salsa (page 190)

Place bread cubes in a 9-inch square baking dish coated with vegetable cooking spray; top evenly with ham, chopped pepper, green chiles, and cheese. Set aside.

Combine egg substitute and next 5 ingredients, stirring well; pour over ham mixture. Sprinkle with paprika. Cover and refrigerate 8 hours.

Remove from refrigerator, and let stand, covered, at room temperature 30 minutes. Bake, uncovered, at 350°

for 35 minutes or until golden. Top each serving with ¼ cup Santa Fe Salsa. Yield: 8 servings (192 calories [28% from fat] per serving).

FAT 6.0g (SAT 2.8g, MONO 2.2g, POLY 0.6g)
PROTEIN 15.8g   CARBOHYDRATE 18.1g
FIBER 1.5g   CHOLESTEROL 24mg   SODIUM 594mg

WEST INDIES FRITTATA

½ pound fresh crabmeat, drained
   and flaked
¼ cup finely chopped celery
2 tablespoons finely chopped
   purple onion
2 tablespoons cider vinegar
¼ teaspoon pepper
¼ cup chopped sweet red pepper
1 cup frozen egg substitute, thawed
¼ teaspoon salt
⅛ teaspoon garlic powder
⅛ teaspoon pepper
Vegetable cooking spray
¼ cup alfalfa sprouts

Combine first 5 ingredients in a small bowl; toss gently. Cover and chill at least 2 hours.

Transfer crabmeat mixture to a small nonstick skillet. Add sweet red pepper, and cook over low heat until thoroughly heated, stirring occasionally. Drain well, and set aside.

Combine egg substitute, salt, garlic powder, and ⅛ teaspoon pepper in a medium bowl; stir well. Coat a medium nonstick skillet with cooking spray; place over medium heat. Add egg substitute mixture; cover and cook 8 to 10 minutes or until set. Top evenly with crabmeat mixture and alfalfa sprouts. Cut frittata into wedges. Yield: 4 servings (93 calories [12% from fat] per serving).

FAT 1.2g (SAT 0.1g, MONO 0.2g, POLY 0.4g)
PROTEIN 17.1g   CARBOHYDRATE 2.7g
FIBER 0.4g   CHOLESTEROL 53mg   SODIUM 388mg

NO-YOLK DEVILED EGGS

¾ cup 1% low-fat cottage cheese
1 tablespoon sweet pickle relish
2 teaspoons prepared mustard
½ teaspoon low-sodium
   Worcestershire sauce
⅛ teaspoon garlic powder
6 hard-cooked eggs
Paprika
Fresh parsley sprigs (optional)

Spoon cottage cheese onto several layers of paper towels; spread to ½-inch thickness. Cover with additional paper towels; let stand 5 minutes. Scrape cottage cheese from paper towel, using a rubber spatula.

Position knife blade in food processor bowl; add cottage cheese, pickle relish, and next 4 ingredients. Top with cover, and process until mixture is smooth.

Peel eggs; slice in half lengthwise, and carefully remove yolks. Reserve egg yolks for another use. Spoon filling mixture into a decorating bag fitted with a large star tip. Pipe filling mixture into egg whites. Sprinkle with paprika, and garnish with fresh parsley sprigs, if desired. Yield: 12 servings (17 calories [5% from fat] per serving).

FAT 0.1g (SAT 0.1g, MONO 0.1g, POLY 0.0g)
PROTEIN 3.0g   CARBOHYDRATE 0.9g
FIBER 0.0g   CHOLESTEROL 0mg   SODIUM 83mg

Perfect for picnics or potluck dinners, No-Yolk Deviled Eggs lacks the saturated fat and cholesterol of the traditional version, but it still has all the flavor.

Spread the cottage cheese in a thin layer on several thicknesses of paper towels, which will absorb the excess moisture.

Spoon the cheese mixture into a decorating bag fitted with a star tip. For less mess, turn down the top third of the bag before filling.

Pipe the cheese mixture into the egg whites. Sprinkle with paprika, and garnish with fresh parsley for a pretty presentation.

BAKED EGG CUPS

4 (1-ounce) slices whole wheat
  bread
Vegetable cooking spray
1 tablespoon grated Parmesan
  cheese
⅛ teaspoon garlic powder
⅛ teaspoon ground red pepper
1 cup frozen egg substitute, thawed

Remove crusts from bread slices. Press 1 slice into each of 4 (6-ounce) custard cups coated with cooking spray. Bake at 425° for 8 minutes.

Combine cheese, garlic powder, and pepper; stir well. Pour ¼ cup egg substitute into each cup; sprinkle with cheese mixture. Bake at 350° for 15 to 17 minutes or until set. Serve immediately. Yield: 4 servings (81 calories [12% from fat] per serving).

FAT 1.1g (SAT 0.3g, MONO 0.2g, POLY 0.2g)
PROTEIN 8.4g CARBOHYDRATE 9.6g
FIBER 0.6g CHOLESTEROL 2mg SODIUM 207mg

CHICKEN FOO YONG

Vegetable cooking spray
¼ teaspoon peeled, minced
  gingerroot
1 cup fresh bean sprouts
¼ cup sliced green onions
¼ cup chopped fresh mushrooms
2 tablespoons diced celery
2 tablespoons diced carrot
1 cup frozen egg substitute, thawed
½ cup diced cooked chicken breast
  (skinned before cooking and
  cooked without salt)
Foo Yong Sauce

Coat a nonstick skillet with cooking spray; place over medium heat until hot. Add gingerroot; sauté 2 minutes. Add bean sprouts and next 4 ingredients; sauté until tender. Transfer mixture to a bowl; let cool.

Add egg substitute and chicken to vegetable mixture; stir well. Let stand 10 minutes; stir well.

Coat skillet with cooking spray; place over medium heat until hot. Pour ½ cup chicken mixture into skillet, spreading to a 5-inch circle. Cook until browned on both sides. Repeat procedure 3 times with remaining mixture. Serve with Foo Yong Sauce. Yield: 4 servings (101 calories [18% from fat] per serving).

Foo Yong Sauce

1½ teaspoons cornstarch
1 teaspoon sugar
½ cup canned low-sodium chicken
  broth, undiluted
1 tablespoon low-sodium soy sauce
1 teaspoon white vinegar
¼ cup frozen English peas, thawed
2 tablespoons sliced green onions

Combine cornstarch and sugar in a saucepan; stir in broth, soy sauce, and vinegar. Cook over medium heat, stirring constantly, until mixture comes to a boil. Stir in peas and green onions; boil 2 minutes. Yield: ⅔ cup.

FAT 2.0g (SAT 0.4g, MONO 0.5g, POLY 0.4g)
PROTEIN 13.2g CARBOHYDRATE 7.0g
FIBER 1.1g CHOLESTEROL 17mg SODIUM 231mg

OMELET FOR ONE

¼ cup julienne-cut carrot
¼ cup julienne-cut zucchini
1½ teaspoons chopped fresh chives
¾ teaspoon chopped fresh dillweed
2 tablespoons part-skim ricotta
  cheese
2 tablespoons nonfat sour cream
  alternative
½ cup frozen egg substitute,
  thawed
2 teaspoons water
⅛ teaspoon salt
Vegetable cooking spray

Arrange carrot and zucchini in a vegetable steamer over boiling water. Cover and steam 2 to 3 minutes or until crisp-tender; drain well.

Combine steamed vegetable mixture, chives, and next 3 ingredients in a medium bowl; stir well. Set aside. Combine egg substitute, water, and salt in a small bowl; stir well.

Coat a small nonstick skillet with cooking spray; place over medium heat until hot. Pour egg substitute mixture into skillet. As mixture begins to cook, gently lift edges of omelet with a spatula, and tilt pan to allow uncooked portion to flow underneath. When set, spoon vegetable mixture over half of omelet. Loosen omelet with a spatula, and carefully fold in half. Slide omelet onto a warm serving plate. Yield: 1 serving (143 calories [18% from fat] per serving).

FAT 2.8g (SAT 1.5g, MONO 0.7g, POLY 0.1g)
PROTEIN 18.3g CARBOHYDRATE 9.8g
FIBER 1.2g CHOLESTEROL 10mg SODIUM 543mg

GARDEN-FRESH PUFFY OMELET

½ cup frozen egg substitute,
  thawed
2 tablespoons skim milk
1½ teaspoons minced fresh
  dillweed
⅛ teaspoon pepper
4 egg whites
1 tablespoon all-purpose flour
Vegetable cooking spray
½ cup alfalfa sprouts
1 medium tomato, thinly sliced
1½ tablespoons grated Parmesan
  cheese

Combine first 4 ingredients in a small bowl; stir well, and set aside.

Beat egg whites at high speed of an electric mixer until soft peaks form; add flour, beating until stiff peaks form. Fold egg white mixture into egg substitute mixture.

Coat a small nonstick skillet with cooking spray; place over medium heat until hot. Pour half of egg white mixture into skillet, spreading evenly. Cover and cook 5 minutes or until center is set. Arrange half of sprouts, tomato, and cheese over one half of omelet. Loosen omelet with a spatula, and fold in half. Slide omelet onto a warm serving plate. Repeat procedure with remaining half of egg white mixture, sprouts, tomato, and cheese. Yield: 2 servings (122 calories [12% from fat] per serving).

FAT 1.7g (SAT 0.8g, MONO 0.4g, POLY 0.2g)
PROTEIN 16.4g   CARBOHYDRATE 10.3g
FIBER 1.5g   CHOLESTEROL 3mg   SODIUM 283mg

SUNSHINE SCRAMBLE

1 cup frozen egg substitute, thawed
¼ cup skim milk
¼ cup nonfat sour cream alternative
¼ teaspoon salt
⅛ teaspoon pepper
¼ cup chopped green onions
Vegetable cooking spray

Combine first 5 ingredients in container of an electric blender or food processor; top with cover, and process 10 seconds or until frothy. Transfer mixture to a medium bowl; stir in green onions.

Coat a large nonstick skillet with cooking spray; place over medium heat until hot. Add egg substitute mixture; cook, stirring frequently, until mixture is firm but still moist. Yield: 4 servings (48 calories [4% from fat] per serving).

FAT 0.2g (SAT 0.0g, MONO 0.0g, POLY 0.0g)
PROTEIN 7.6g   CARBOHYDRATE 3.0g
FIBER 0.1g   CHOLESTEROL 0mg   SODIUM 255mg

SHRIMP AND ARTICHOKE QUICHE

3 cups water
1 teaspoon liquid shrimp and crab boil seasoning
1 pound unpeeled medium-size fresh shrimp
Vegetable cooking spray
⅓ cup Italian-seasoned breadcrumbs
¾ cup frozen egg substitute, thawed
¼ cup all-purpose flour
½ teaspoon baking powder
¼ teaspoon salt
1 (14-ounce) can artichoke hearts, drained and chopped
¾ cup nonfat cottage cheese
½ cup (2 ounces) shredded reduced-fat Monterey Jack cheese
⅓ cup sliced green onions
¼ cup (1 ounce) shredded reduced-fat sharp Cheddar cheese
½ teaspoon hot sauce

Bring water and seasoning to a boil in a medium saucepan; add shrimp, and cook 3 to 5 minutes or until shrimp are done. Drain well; rinse with cold water. Chill shrimp. Peel and devein shrimp; coarsely chop, and set aside.

Coat a 10-inch quiche dish or pie-plate with vegetable cooking spray. Coat bottom and sides of quiche dish evenly with toasted breadcrumbs. Set quiche dish aside.

Combine egg substitute, flour, baking powder, and salt in a large bowl; stir well. Stir in shrimp, artichoke hearts, and remaining ingredients. Pour artichoke mixture into prepared quiche dish. Bake at 350° for 35 to 40 minutes or until set. Let quiche stand 10 minutes before serving. Yield: 8 servings (142 calories [18% from fat] per serving).

FAT 2.8g (SAT 1.4g, MONO 0.3g, POLY 0.3g)
PROTEIN 18.0g   CARBOHYDRATE 11.4g
FIBER 0.6g   CHOLESTEROL 79mg   SODIUM 520mg

FAT AND CHOLESTEROL CONTENT OF EGGS AND EGG SUBSTITUTES
(Based on ¼-cup portions)

Product	Calories	Fat (grams)	Cholesterol (milligrams)
Large whole egg	75	5.0	213
Egg white	33	0.0	0
Frozen egg substitute, thawed	30	0.0	0
Frozen egg substitute with cheese, thawed	65	3.0	2
Refrigerated egg substitute	53	2.0	1
Egg Substitute (page 78)	89	2.3	2

The main ingredient in most cheese is whole milk or cream. It takes about eight pounds of milk to produce one pound of cheese, making cheese very concentrated in total fat, saturated fat, cholesterol, and sodium. In fact, some cheeses have up to 90 percent of calories from fat.

Manufacturers have responded to consumer demands for cheeses that contain less fat. However, many of the new products still have 50 percent or more of their calories from fat. Nutrition labeling is not required on cheese made from whole milk. But reduced-fat and nonfat cheeses and processed cheese products are labeled, making it possible for you to calculate their fat content.

To reduce the amount of cheese you use, try shredding or grating the cheese to make it go further. If you substitute a more strongly flavored cheese for a milder one, you can reduce the amount of cheese called for in a recipe by one-third to one-half.

When cooking with cheeses that are lower in fat, you will notice differences in texture and melting quality. Lower fat cheeses tend to be less smooth and satiny in texture than higher fat ones, and lower fat products melt less quickly. Becoming accustomed to these characteristics will be easy once you're enjoying the healthy benefits of cheese products that are lower in fat.

Most cheeses react quickly to heat; therefore, it is best to cook cheese slowly over low heat. High heat or overcooking can make cheese tough and stringy. For cheese to melt evenly, it should be shredded, grated, or chopped before being added to a recipe. Add it to sauces and other hot mixtures in small batches so that it will not clump. For best results, top casseroles and other baked dishes with shredded cheese at the last minute; then return the casserole to the oven just long enough for the cheese to melt.

STRAWBERRY CHEESE BLINTZES

1½ cups nonfat cottage cheese
½ cup light process cream cheese product, softened
2 egg whites, lightly beaten
2 tablespoons honey
1 teaspoon grated lemon rind
½ teaspoon vanilla extract
12 Basic Crêpes (page 48)
Vegetable cooking spray
⅓ cup nonfat sour cream alternative
⅓ cup low-sugar strawberry spread
Fresh strawberries (optional)

Combine first 6 ingredients; stir well. Spoon 3 tablespoons cheese mixture in center of each Basic Crêpe. Fold right and left sides of crêpe over filling; fold bottom and top of crêpe over filling, forming a square.

Place blintzes, seam side down, on a large baking sheet coated with vegetable cooking spray. Bake at 350° for 12 minutes or until blintzes are thoroughly heated. Top evenly with sour cream alternative and strawberry spread. Garnish with fresh strawberries, if desired. Serve immediately. Yield: 12 servings (103 calories [23% from fat] per serving).

FAT 2.6g (SAT 1.2g, MONO 0.3g, POLY 0.4g)
PROTEIN 8.2g CARBOHYDRATE 12.4g
FIBER 0.2g CHOLESTEROL 26mg SODIUM 225mg

CHEESE AND VEGETABLE PHYLLO PIE

½ pound fresh asparagus
Butter-flavored vegetable cooking spray
½ cup thinly sliced leeks
2 cloves garlic, minced
1 (10-ounce) package frozen chopped spinach, thawed and drained
1 cup part-skim ricotta cheese
4 ounces goat cheese
¾ cup frozen egg substitute, thawed
¼ cup freshly grated Parmesan cheese
½ teaspoon dried whole thyme
⅛ teaspoon ground white pepper
13 sheets commercial frozen phyllo pastry, thawed

Snap off tough ends of asparagus. Remove scales from spears with a knife or vegetable peeler, if desired. Cut asparagus into 1-inch pieces.

Coat a large nonstick skillet with cooking spray; place over medium-high heat until hot. Add asparagus, leeks, and garlic; sauté until tender. Remove from heat; stir in spinach and next 6 ingredients. Set aside.

Coat a 10-inch springform pan with cooking spray; set aside. Place 1 sheet of phyllo on a damp towel (keep remaining phyllo covered). Lightly coat phyllo with cooking spray. Layer 7 more sheets of phyllo on first sheet, lightly coating each layer with cooking spray, and fanning each layer slightly to the right. Gently press the stack of phyllo into prepared pan, pressing gently in center to form a pastry shell. (The overhanging edges of phyllo will form a circle around the edge of the pan.)

Pour vegetable mixture into pan. Top with 5 more sheets of phyllo, lightly coating each layer with cooking spray, and fanning each layer slightly to the right. Press top sheets down over filling; fold overhanging edges over top to enclose filling. Bake, uncovered, at 400° for 25 minutes. Cover and bake an additional 35 minutes or until golden. Let stand 15 minutes. Remove sides from pan, and transfer to a serving platter. Serve warm. Yield: 8 servings (229 calories [29% from fat] per serving).

FAT 7.3g (SAT 4.4g, MONO 1.8g, POLY 0.5g)
PROTEIN 14.1g CARBOHYDRATE 27.7g
FIBER 1.7g CHOLESTEROL 25mg SODIUM 315mg

WELSH RAREBIT

¾ cup evaporated skimmed milk
1 cup (4 ounces) shredded reduced-fat sharp Cheddar cheese
1 teaspoon Dijon mustard
½ teaspoon low-sodium Worcestershire sauce
⅛ teaspoon lemon juice
Dash of ground red pepper
8 (¾-inch-thick) slices French bread, toasted

Pour milk into a small saucepan; place over medium heat. Cook, stirring constantly, until mixture is thoroughly heated (do not boil). Add cheese and next 4 ingredients, stirring until cheese melts and mixture is smooth. Reduce heat to low, and cook 2 minutes, stirring frequently.

To serve, place bread on individual serving plates, and top each slice with 2 tablespoons cheese sauce. Serve immediately. Yield: 8 servings (159 calories [22% from fat] per serving).

FAT 3.8g (SAT 1.8g, MONO 1.1g, POLY 0.4g)
PROTEIN 9.0g CARBOHYDRATE 21.7g
FIBER 0.5g CHOLESTEROL 12mg SODIUM 341mg

CHEESY RICE SOUFFLÉ

Vegetable cooking spray
1½ tablespoons reduced-calorie margarine
3 tablespoons all-purpose flour
¾ cup skim milk
½ cup (2 ounces) shredded reduced-fat sharp Cheddar cheese
¼ teaspoon dry mustard
⅛ teaspoon ground red pepper
⅓ cup frozen egg substitute, thawed
1 cup cooked brown rice (cooked without salt or fat)
4 egg whites

Cut a piece of aluminum foil long enough to fit around a 1½-quart soufflé dish, allowing a 1-inch overlap; fold lengthwise into thirds. Coat one side of foil and bottom of dish with cooking spray; wrap foil around dish, coated side against dish, allowing it to extend 3 inches above rim to form a collar; secure with string.

Melt margarine in a small heavy saucepan over medium heat. Add flour; stir until smooth. Cook 1 minute, stirring constantly. Gradually add milk; cook, stirring constantly, until thickened and bubbly. Remove from heat; add cheese, mustard, and red pepper, stirring until cheese melts. Gradually stir one-fourth of hot mixture into egg substitute; add to remaining hot mixture, stirring constantly. Stir in rice.

Beat egg whites at high speed of an electric mixer until stiff peaks form. Fold one-third of egg whites into cheese mixture; fold in remaining egg whites. Spoon mixture into prepared dish. Bake at 325° for 55 minutes or until set. Serve immediately. Yield: 6 servings (123 calories [30% from fat] per serving).

FAT 4.1g (SAT 1.4g, MONO 0.8g, POLY 1.0g)
PROTEIN 8.8g CARBOHYDRATE 12.7g
FIBER 0.7g CHOLESTEROL 7mg SODIUM 171mg

A Nonfat Cheese Option

Yogurt cheese is similar in taste and appearance to higher fat items such as cream cheese and sour cream. But yogurt cheese made with nonfat yogurt contains no fat. For best results, start with nonfat yogurt made without gelatin.

To make yogurt cheese, line a colander or sieve with a double layer of cheesecloth that has been rinsed out and squeezed dry; allow the cheesecloth to extend over the edge of the colander. Spoon plain nonfat yogurt into the colander, and fold the edges of the cheesecloth over to cover the yogurt. Place the colander in a large bowl; refrigerate for at least 8 hours. Remove the yogurt cheese from the colander, and discard the liquid. Place the cheese in an airtight container, and store in the refrigerator. (It takes 16 ounces of yogurt to yield 1 cup of yogurt cheese.)

Use yogurt cheese to top baked potatoes or to spread on bagels. Fold in fresh or dried herbs, and use the cheese as a savory spread for crackers. Or stir in orange juice concentrate and fresh fruit to top pancakes, waffles, or French toast.

Place the yogurt in a cheesecloth-lined colander; place the colander in a bowl to catch the liquid that drains. The finished product is yogurt cheese.

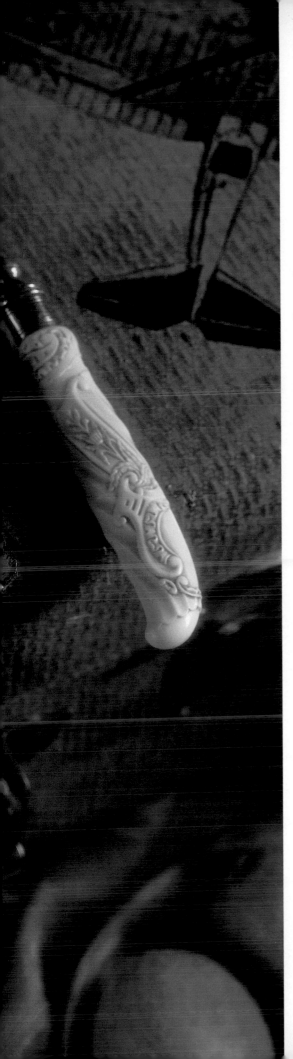

FISH AND SHELLFISH

Fish and shellfish offer an array of healthy choices to feature on your menus. Most contain relatively little cholesterol, and the fats they contain are mainly monounsaturated and polyunsaturated. The best things about fish and shellfish are that they're easy to prepare and they cook in a flash.

FISH

When it comes to choosing a great-tasting entrée that's relatively low in calories, fat, and saturated fat, fish is hard to beat. Furthermore, fish is a superior protein source that is rich in essential vitamins and minerals. Fish also contains omega-3 fatty acids (the polyunsaturated fat that may help reduce the risk of heart disease).

As you scan the nutrient analyses for the recipes in this section, you will notice that a few of the recipes derive more than 30 percent of total calories per serving from fat. These recipes use fish that are high in omega-3 fatty acids, so every effort has been made to add very little, if any, extra fat.

Selecting Fish

Fresh fish should be purchased from a reputable store that has quick turnover, regularly replenished stock, and refrigerated storage cases. The term "fresh" associated with fish means that it has never been frozen, not that it was caught just hours ago. Fresh fish should have a clean smell, not an offensive or "fishy" odor. The eyes should be clean, clear, and full, almost bulging. As fish loses freshness, the eyes become cloudy, pink, and sunken in appearance.

The flesh should be firm and should spring back when pressed lightly; if an indentation remains, do not buy the fish. Fresh fish should have shiny skin with the scales firmly attached. The gills should be bright pinkish-red and not slimy. Brown, slimy gills are a good indication that the fish has begun to deteriorate.

Fish steaks and fillets should be firm to the touch. They should appear moist and freshly cut with no yellowing or browning around the edges. Frozen fish should be wrapped in moisture- and vapor-resistant packaging and should be solidly frozen with no discoloration or freezer burn. There should be little or no air within the wrapping.

Market Forms of Fish

You can purchase fish in a variety of market forms. Described below are those called for in our recipes.

Whole or round. A whole or round fish is exactly as it comes from the water. It may or may not need to be scaled, but it will need to be eviscerated, or gutted, before cooking.

Drawn. A whole fish that has been eviscerated and scaled is referred to as a drawn fish.

Grouper with Fruit and Pepper Salsa (page 87) brings a taste of the tropics to your table.

85

Dressed or pan-dressed. A drawn fish that has had the head and fins removed is referred to as a dressed fish. The tail may or may not have been previously removed on a dressed fish. Smaller fish that have been dressed are called pan-dressed.

Fillets. The boneless sides of a dressed fish that have been cut lengthwise away from the backbone are known as fillets.

Steaks. Cross-sectional slices cut from large, dressed fish are called steaks. The slices usually measure ¾ to 1 inch thick. The only bones in a fish steak are a cross-section of the backbone and ribs.

Storing Fish

Fresh fish is best when cooked the day of purchase. But it may be stored in the original wrapping in the coldest part of the refrigerator for up to two days if the wrapping is moisture- and vapor-resistant. If it is not, wrap the fish tightly in heavy-duty plastic wrap or freezer paper before storing. A damp cloth placed over the fish, inside the wrapping, will prevent the fish from drying out. Fresh fish should be frozen within two days of purchase, and it may be stored in the freezer for up to three months.

Following purchase, commercially frozen fish products should be returned to the freezer to maintain quality. Store at 0°F or below to prevent loss of flavor, texture, and nutrients. Avoid packaging that is soft or covered with ice crystals. This condition indicates that the product has been partially thawed and refrozen.

Thaw commercially frozen fish products as you would frozen fresh fish. Frozen breaded fish products should not be thawed before cooking; prepare these products according to package directions. Cooked fish can be stored for two or three days in the refrigerator.

BLACKENED AMBERJACK

1 (1-pound) amberjack fillet
1 tablespoon paprika
2 teaspoons onion powder
2 teaspoons garlic powder
1 teaspoon dried whole thyme
1 teaspoon dried whole oregano
1 teaspoon black pepper
½ teaspoon ground red pepper
Vegetable cooking spray

Cut fillet into 4 equal pieces. Combine paprika and next 6 ingredients in a small bowl; stir well. Dredge fish in spice mixture; let stand 5 minutes.

Coat a large cast-iron skillet with cooking spray; place over high heat until very hot. Add fish, and cook 3 minutes. Turn fish, and cook an additional 3 to 4 minutes or until fish flakes easily when tested with a fork. Fish should look charred. (You may prefer to do this procedure outside due to the small amount of smoke that is created.) Yield: 4 servings (182 calories [30% from fat] per serving).

FAT 6.0g (SAT 1.5g, MONO 1.6g, POLY 2.1g)
PROTEIN 27.2g   CARBOHYDRATE 3.8g
FIBER 0.8g   CHOLESTEROL 43mg   SODIUM 46mg

PECAN CATFISH

6 (4-ounce) farm-raised catfish fillets
1 cup soft whole wheat breadcrumbs
Vegetable cooking spray
¼ cup nonfat sour cream alternative
1 tablespoon lemon juice
1 tablespoon Dijon mustard
3 tablespoons chopped pecans, toasted

Dredge fillets in breadcrumbs, and place fillets on rack of a broiler pan coated with cooking spray. Bake at

500° for 10 minutes or until fish flakes easily when tested with a fork. Arrange fillets on a serving platter; set aside, and keep warm.

Combine sour cream, lemon juice, and mustard in a saucepan; cook over medium-low heat, stirring constantly, until heated (do not boil). Spoon evenly over fillets; sprinkle evenly with pecans. Yield: 6 servings (190 calories [37% from fat] per serving).

FAT 7.8g (SAT 1.4g, MONO 3.4g, POLY 1.9g)
PROTEIN 22.6g   CARBOHYDRATE 6.2g
FIBER 0.6g   CHOLESTEROL 66mg   SODIUM 202mg

OVEN-FRIED CATFISH

1 egg white, lightly beaten
2 tablespoons malt vinegar
¼ cup instant nonfat dry milk powder
¼ cup yellow cornmeal
¼ cup toasted wheat germ
1 teaspoon dried parsley flakes
1 teaspoon dried celery flakes
1 teaspoon paprika
½ teaspoon salt
½ teaspoon onion powder
½ teaspoon dry mustard
½ teaspoon dried whole basil
⅛ teaspoon garlic powder
8 (6-ounce) dressed catfish
Vegetable cooking spray

Combine egg white and vinegar; stir well. Combine milk powder and next 10 ingredients; dip fish into egg white mixture, and dredge in cornmeal mixture. Place fish on rack of a broiler pan coated with cooking spray. Bake at 400° for 20 minutes or until fish flakes easily when tested with a fork. Yield: 8 servings (177 calories [28% from fat] per serving).

FAT 5.5g (SAT 1.2g, MONO 1.9g, POLY 1.4g)
PROTEIN 23.7g   CARBOHYDRATE 7.4g
FIBER 1.1g   CHOLESTEROL 67mg   SODIUM 247mg

Team Vegetable-Topped Flounder with a tossed salad and crusty roll for a light, quick meal that's perfect following a workout at the gym.

GROUPER WITH FRUIT AND PEPPER SALSA

½ cup chopped fresh pineapple
⅓ cup chopped green pepper
⅓ cup chopped sweet red pepper
⅓ cup chopped sweet yellow pepper
1 kiwifruit, peeled and thinly sliced
1 tablespoon white wine vinegar
1½ teaspoons water
1 teaspoon brown sugar
1 teaspoon peeled, grated gingerroot
⅛ teaspoon crushed red pepper
2 tablespoons lemon juice
¼ teaspoon curry powder
⅛ teaspoon salt
3 (8-ounce) grouper fillets, halved
Vegetable cooking spray

Combine first 10 ingredients; cover and chill at least 2 hours.

Combine lemon juice, curry powder, and salt. Place fillets on rack of a broiler pan coated with cooking spray; brush with lemon juice mixture. Broil 5½ inches from heat 8 minutes or until fish flakes easily when tested with a fork. Transfer fillets to a serving platter; top evenly with pineapple mixture. Yield: 6 servings (140 calories [10% from fat] per serving).

FAT 1.6g (SAT 0.3g, MONO 0.3g, POLY 0.5g)
PROTEIN 24.6g CARBOHYDRATE 5.8g
FIBER 1.1g CHOLESTEROL 46mg SODIUM 102mg

Low-Fat Cooking Methods for Fish and Shellfish

Bake
Broil
En papillote
Grill
Microwave
Oven-fry
Poach
Sauté or pan-fry
Steam

VEGETABLE-TOPPED FLOUNDER

8 (4-ounce) flounder fillets
Vegetable cooking spray
1 teaspoon lemon juice
¼ teaspoon pepper
¼ cup frozen apple juice
    concentrate, thawed
½ cup diced onion
½ cup diced celery
¼ cup diced green pepper
¼ cup diced sweet red pepper
2 teaspoons sesame seeds, toasted

Place fillets in a 13- x 9- x 2-inch baking dish coated with cooking spray. Drizzle with lemon juice, and sprinkle with pepper.

Combine apple juice concentrate and next 4 ingredients in a nonstick skillet. Bring to a boil, reduce heat, and simmer until vegetables are crisp-tender. Spoon mixture evenly over fillets. Bake at 350° for 20 minutes or until fish flakes easily when tested with a fork. Transfer fillets and vegetables to a serving platter, using a slotted spoon; sprinkle with sesame seeds. Yield: 8 servings (130 calories [13% from fat] per serving).

FAT 1.9g (SAT 0.4g, MONO 0.4g, POLY 0.6g)
PROTEIN 21.9g CARBOHYDRATE 5.4g
FIBER 0.5g CHOLESTEROL 60mg SODIUM 104mg

Vietnamese-Style Steamed Halibut

4 (4-ounce) halibut fillets
2 tablespoons low-sodium soy
    sauce
2 tablespoons dry sherry
1 tablespoon peeled, minced
    gingerroot
2 cloves garlic, minced
4 large Chinese cabbage leaves
¼ cup sliced green onions
1 tablespoon minced fresh
    cilantro
¼ teaspoon salt
⅛ teaspoon ground white pepper
2 tablespoons lemon juice

Place fillets in a shallow baking dish. Combine soy sauce, sherry, gingerroot, and garlic in a small bowl, stirring well; pour over fillets. Cover and marinate in refrigerator 30 minutes.

Cook cabbage leaves in boiling water 30 seconds. Rinse leaves under cold water; drain well.

Remove fillets from marinade; discard marinade. Combine green onions, cilantro, salt, and ground white pepper in a small bowl, stirring well. Place one fillet at the base of a cabbage leaf; sprinkle with one-fourth of green onion mixture. Fold sides of cabbage leaf over fillet, wrapping fillet like a package. Repeat procedure with remaining fillets, cabbage leaves, and green onion mixture.

Arrange fish packets in a vegetable steamer over boiling water. Cover and steam 10 to 12 minutes or until fish flakes easily when tested with a fork. Arrange packets on a serving platter, and brush with lemon juice. Yield: 4 servings (144 calories [17% from fat] per serving).

FAT 2.7g (SAT 0.4g, MONO 0.8g, POLY 1.0g)
PROTEIN 24.6g CARBOHYDRATE 3.0g
FIBER 0.7g CHOLESTEROL 53mg SODIUM 339mg

Ginger-Lime Mahimahi

2 (12-ounce) mahimahi fillets
¼ cup lime juice
1 tablespoon honey
1 clove garlic, minced
1 (⅛-inch-thick) slice peeled
    gingerroot
Vegetable cooking spray

Cut each fillet into 3 equal pieces; place fish in a shallow baking dish. Combine lime juice and next 3 ingredients in a small bowl, stirring well; pour over fish. Cover and marinate in refrigerator 1 hour.

Remove fish from marinade, reserving marinade. Remove and discard gingerroot. Coat grill rack with vegetable cooking spray; place on grill over medium-hot coals. Place fish on rack, and cook 8 minutes on each side or until fish flakes easily when tested with a fork, basting frequently with marinade. Yield: 6 servings (109 calories [7% from fat] per serving).

FAT 0.9g (SAT 0.2g, MONO 0.1g, POLY 0.3g)
PROTEIN 20.3g CARBOHYDRATE 4.1g
FIBER 0.0g CHOLESTEROL 49mg SODIUM 70mg

What Are Omega-3 Fatty Acids?

An omega-3 fatty acid is a type of polyunsaturated fat found in fish that have dark, moist flesh. These fatty acids may help lessen the chance of a heart attack by making blood platelets less likely to clump together and attach to blood vessel walls. Fish that have the highest amount of omega-3 fatty acids include the following:

Anchovy	Salmon
Herring	Sardine
Mackerel	Trout, lake
Pompano	Tuna
Sablefish	Whitefish

Florentine Orange Roughy en Papillote

18 cherry tomatoes, halved
½ cup chopped green onions
¼ cup lemon juice
1 (10-ounce) package frozen
    chopped spinach, thawed
Vegetable cooking spray
¾ pound fresh mushrooms, sliced
2 cloves garlic, minced
¼ teaspoon salt
6 (4-ounce) orange roughy fillets
12 lemon slices

Combine first 3 ingredients. Cover and chill at least 1 hour.

Drain spinach, and press between paper towels. Set aside.

Cut 6 (15- x 12-inch) rectangles of parchment paper; fold in half lengthwise. Trim each into a heart shape. Place on baking sheets; open out flat.

Coat a large nonstick skillet with cooking spray; place over medium-high heat until hot. Add mushrooms and garlic; sauté 3 to 4 minutes or until tender. Stir in spinach and salt. Place one-sixth of spinach mixture on one half of each parchment heart near the crease; place fillets on spinach mixture. Spoon tomato mixture evenly over fillets; top each with 2 lemon slices.

Fold paper edges over to seal. Starting with rounded edges of hearts, pleat and crimp edges of parchment to make an airtight seal. Bake at 450° for 10 minutes or until bags are puffed and lightly browned.

Place packets on individual serving plates. Cut an opening in the top of each packet, and fold paper back. Serve immediately. Yield: 6 servings (120 calories [10% from fat] per serving).

FAT 1.4g (SAT 0.1g, MONO 0.6g, POLY 0.2g)
PROTEIN 19.8g CARBOHYDRATE 8.3g
FIBER 3.0g CHOLESTEROL 23mg SODIUM 212mg

Layer the ingredients for Florentine Orange Roughy en Papillote near the crease of the parchment-paper heart. This leaves enough room for sealing the edges.

Pleat and crimp the edges of the parchment heart firmly to form a tight seal. As the fish bakes in the airtight bag, it will remain flavorful and moist.

To serve, use scissors to cut a large opening in the top of the bag, then fold back the corners to reveal a colorful entrée that should be served immediately.

Florentine Orange Roughy en Papillote requires a little extra preparation, but the results prove worth the effort when you open the steaming packet.

GINGERED POACHED SALMON

2 cups Chablis or other dry white
    wine
½ cup water
8 green onions, cut into 1-inch
    pieces
1 small lemon, sliced
¼ cup peeled, minced gingerroot
¼ teaspoon salt
4 (4-ounce) salmon steaks (½ inch
    thick)
Green onion fans (optional)

Combine first 6 ingredients in a large nonstick skillet. Bring to a boil; cover, reduce heat, and simmer 10 minutes, stirring occasionally.

Add salmon steaks to skillet. Bring to a boil; reduce heat, and simmer 8 minutes or until fish flakes easily when tested with a fork. Transfer salmon steaks to a serving platter. Garnish with green onion fans, if desired. Yield: 4 servings (222 calories [40% from fat] per serving).

FAT 9.9g (SAT 1.7g, MONO 4.7g, POLY 2.2g)
PROTEIN 25.6g   CARBOHYDRATE 8.5g
FIBER 1.1g   CHOLESTEROL 77mg   SODIUM 222mg

Drain canned salmon thoroughly. Using your fingers, remove and discard the skin and bones. Flake the fish with a fork before using it in a recipe.

SALMON CROQUETTES WITH MUSTARD SAUCE

Vegetable cooking spray
½ cup finely chopped celery
½ cup finely chopped onion
1 (15½-ounce) can red salmon,
    drained and flaked
½ cup fat-free saltine cracker
    crumbs
¼ cup frozen egg substitute,
    thawed
2 egg whites, lightly beaten
3 tablespoons lemon juice
¼ teaspoon pepper
Mustard Sauce

Coat a medium nonstick skillet with vegetable cooking spray; place over medium-high heat until hot. Add celery and onion; sauté until tender. Combine vegetable mixture, salmon, and next 5 ingredients in a medium bowl; stir well. Shape mixture into 8 (½-inch-thick) patties.

Coat a large nonstick skillet with cooking spray; place over medium-high heat until hot. Add patties, and cook 4 to 6 minutes or until lightly browned, turning once. Serve with Mustard Sauce. Yield: 4 servings (230 calories [31% from fat] per 2 croquettes and 2 tablespoons sauce).

Mustard Sauce

1½ teaspoons reduced-calorie
    margarine
2¼ teaspoons all-purpose flour
½ cup skim milk
1½ teaspoons spicy brown mustard
½ teaspoon lemon juice

Melt margarine in small saucepan over medium heat; add flour, stirring until smooth. Cook 1 minute, stirring constantly. Gradually add milk; cook, stirring constantly, until thickened. Remove from heat; stir in mustard and lemon juice. Yield: ½ cup.

FAT 7.9g (SAT 1.5g, MONO 2.5g, POLY 2.1g)
PROTEIN 23.9g   CARBOHYDRATE 15.5g
FIBER 0.7g   CHOLESTEROL 40mg   SODIUM 275mg

TANGY BROILED SCAMP

3 tablespoons lemon juice
1 teaspoon dried whole oregano
½ teaspoon garlic powder
½ teaspoon dry mustard
½ teaspoon paprika
¼ teaspoon dried whole tarragon
1 pound scamp fillets
1 cup soft breadcrumbs
Vegetable cooking spray
1 tablespoon reduced-calorie
    margarine, melted

Combine first 6 ingredients in a shallow dish; stir well. Dip fillets in lemon juice mixture; dredge evenly in breadcrumbs.

Place fillets on rack of a broiler pan coated with cooking spray. Drizzle margarine over fillets. Broil 5½ inches from heat 7 to 9 minutes or until fish flakes easily when tested with a fork. Yield: 4 servings (199 calories [34% from fat] per serving).

FAT 7.5g (SAT 1.2g, MONO 2.4g, POLY 2.6g)
PROTEIN 23.1g   CARBOHYDRATE 8.8g
FIBER 0.4g   CHOLESTEROL 68mg   SODIUM 130mg

SNAPPER VERACRUZ

4 (4-ounce) red snapper fillets
  (¾ inch thick)
Vegetable cooking spray
1½ tablespoons fresh lime juice
1 medium onion, thinly sliced
3 cloves garlic, minced
2½ cups peeled, chopped plum
  tomato
2 tablespoons chopped fresh
  cilantro
2 teaspoons seeded, minced serrano
  chile pepper
¼ teaspoon salt
⅓ cup sliced ripe olives
Lime slices (optional)
Fresh cilantro sprigs (optional)

Place fillets in an 11- x 7- x 2-inch baking dish coated with cooking spray. Brush with lime juice; set aside.

Coat a nonstick skillet with cooking spray; place over medium-high heat until hot. Add onion and garlic; sauté 3 minutes. Stir in tomato and next 3 ingredients; cook 5 minutes. Stir in olives. Spoon mixture over fillets. Cover and bake at 400° for 25 minutes or until fish flakes easily when tested with a fork.

Arrange lime slices on individual plates, if desired. Using a slotted spoon, place a fillet on each plate; spoon tomato mixture evenly over fillets. Garnish with cilantro sprigs, if desired. Yield: 4 servings (173 calories [18% from fat] per serving).

FAT 3.4g (SAT 0.6g, MONO 1.2g, POLY 0.9g)
PROTEIN 25.1g CARBOHYDRATE 10.9g
FIBER 2.7g CHOLESTEROL 42mg SODIUM 303mg

Plain baked fish becomes a memorable dish when topped with fresh vegetables and herbs. Snapper Veracruz gets its flavor kick from tomato, onion, chile peppers, and cilantro.

CRABMEAT-STUFFED SOLE

Vegetable cooking spray
1½ teaspoons reduced-calorie
  margarine
¼ cup minced celery
3 tablespoons minced onion
3 tablespoons chopped fresh parsley
1½ tablespoons minced shallot
1½ tablespoons minced green
  pepper
1 small clove garlic, minced
1 teaspoon all-purpose flour
3 tablespoons skim milk
3 tablespoons Chablis or other dry
  white wine
3 ounces fresh lump crabmeat,
  drained
½ cup fine, dry breadcrumbs
½ teaspoon dried Italian seasoning
⅛ teaspoon salt
Dash of pepper
6 (4-ounce) sole fillets
Creamy Dill Sauce (page 184)

Coat a large nonstick skillet with cooking spray; add margarine. Place over medium-high heat until margarine melts. Add celery and next 5 ingredients; sauté until tender. Add flour; cook 1 minute, stirring constantly. Gradually add milk and wine; cook over medium heat, stirring constantly, until slightly thickened. Stir in crabmeat, breadcrumbs, Italian seasoning, salt, and pepper.

Spoon even amounts of crabmeat mixture onto each fillet; roll up, and secure with a wooden pick. Place in an 11- x 7- x 1½-inch baking dish coated with cooking spray; spoon Creamy Dill Sauce over rolls. Bake, uncovered, at 425° for 15 minutes or until fish flakes easily when tested with a fork. Yield: 6 servings (218 calories [17% from fat] per serving).

FAT 4.1g (SAT 0.8g, MONO 1.2g, POLY 1.4g)
PROTEIN 29.3g CARBOHYDRATE 14.5g
FIBER 0.7g CHOLESTEROL 71mg SODIUM 425mg

Sole Véronique

4 (4-ounce) sole fillets
Vegetable cooking spray
¼ teaspoon salt
⅛ teaspoon ground white pepper
⅔ cup Chablis or other dry white
  wine
2 teaspoons lemon juice
1 medium carrot, cut into julienne
  strips
1½ tablespoons reduced-calorie
  margarine
2 tablespoons sliced green onions
1½ tablespoons all-purpose flour
1 cup skim milk
½ cup seedless green grapes,
  halved

Place fillets in a 13- x 9- x 2-inch baking dish coated with vegetable cooking spray; sprinkle evenly with salt and pepper. Combine wine and lemon juice, stirring well; pour over fillets. Bake, uncovered, at 350° for 18 to 20 minutes or until fish flakes easily when tested with a fork. Transfer fillets to a serving platter; set aside, and keep warm.

Arrange carrot strips in a vegetable steamer over boiling water. Cover and steam 6 to 8 minutes or until crisp-tender. Set aside.

Coat a small saucepan with cooking spray; add margarine. Place over medium heat until margarine melts. Add green onions; sauté until tender. Add flour, stirring until smooth. Cook 1 minute, stirring constantly. Gradually add milk; cook over medium heat, stirring constantly, until mixture is thickened and bubbly. Pour sauce evenly over fillets; top evenly with carrot strips and grapes. Yield: 4 servings (193 calories [21% from fat] per serving).

FAT 4.6g (SAT 0.8g, MONO 1.3g, POLY 1.6g)
PROTEIN 24.4g CARBOHYDRATE 13.4g
FIBER 1.4g CHOLESTEROL 61mg SODIUM 326mg

Hickory-Smoked Trout

Hickory chips
8 (4-ounce) trout fillets
1½ cups water
½ cup firmly packed dark brown
  sugar
⅓ cup lemon juice
¼ teaspoon ground red pepper
Vegetable cooking spray
¼ teaspoon salt

Soak hickory chips in water for at least 30 minutes.

Place trout in a zip-top heavy-duty plastic bag. Combine water and next 3 ingredients. Pour over trout; seal bag, and shake gently until fillets are well coated. Marinate in refrigerator 2 hours, turning bag occasionally.

Remove trout from marinade, reserving marinade; set fillets and marinade aside.

Prepare charcoal fire in smoker; let burn 20 minutes. Place hickory chips on coals. Place water pan in smoker; add hot water and reserved marinade to fill line on pan. Place trout, skin side down, on smoker rack coated with cooking spray; sprinkle with salt. Cover with lid; cook 1 hour or until fish flakes easily when tested with a fork. Yield: 8 servings (189 calories [19% from fat] per serving).

FAT 3.9g (SAT 0.7g, MONO 1.2g, POLY 1.4g)
PROTEIN 23.4g CARBOHYDRATE 14.2g
FIBER 0.0g CHOLESTEROL 65mg SODIUM 108mg

Oriental Grilled Tuna Steaks

6 (4-ounce) tuna steaks (¾ inch
  thick)
1 cup thinly sliced green onions
¼ cup plus 2 tablespoons rice wine
  vinegar
¼ cup plus 2 tablespoons low-
  sodium soy sauce
1 tablespoon sesame oil
1 tablespoon peeled, grated
  gingerroot
¼ teaspoon ground red pepper
Vegetable cooking spray

Place tuna steaks in a shallow baking dish. Combine green onions and next 5 ingredients in a small bowl, stirring well; reserve ¼ cup mixture, and set aside. Pour remaining mixture over steaks. Cover and marinate in refrigerator 2 hours.

Remove steaks from marinade; discard marinade. Coat grill rack with cooking spray; place on grill over medium coals. Place steaks on rack, and cook 4 minutes on each side or until fish flakes easily when tested with a fork, basting frequently with reserved green onion mixture. Yield: 6 servings (198 calories [35% from fat] per serving).

FAT 7.6g (SAT 1.7g, MONO 2.6g, POLY 2.4g)
PROTEIN 28.5g CARBOHYDRATE 1.0g
FIBER 0.3g CHOLESTEROL 46mg SODIUM 310mg

Low in fat and calories and rich in protein, shellfish is perfect for a low-fat eating plan. A popular misconception about shellfish is that it is high in cholesterol, but analyses show that most types (except shrimp) are quite low in cholesterol. And shellfish is especially low in total fat and saturated fat — that is, if it's not battered and deep-fat fried.

Selecting Shellfish

Freshness is critical when buying shellfish. Once removed from the water, it begins to deteriorate quickly. Although many types of shellfish are kept alive in water tanks or on beds of ice until purchased, most are also available fresh, frozen, cooked, or frozen cooked.

Whole lobsters and crabs should be purchased alive and kept alive until ready to cook. Lobsters should be moving and should curl their tails when lifted from the water. Crabs should also move energetically.

Fresh raw shrimp vary in color from greenish gray to pink, indicating the type of water the shrimp came from, not their quality. All shrimp will turn pale pink during cooking. The flesh should feel firm and slippery, and fresh shrimp should have a mild, sweet smell. An odor of ammonia indicates deterioration.

Fresh oysters, mussels, and hard-shelled clams are displayed on beds of crushed ice. They should keep their shells closed once harvested from the water, so tap the shell if it is slightly open. If alive, the shell will close immediately. If it does not close, it should be discarded. Scallops are shucked immediately after harvest because they never close their shells once removed from the water.

Storing Shellfish

Store live clams, mussels, and oysters in their shells in the refrigerator. Place them in a large container, and cover with a damp cloth. Stored in this manner, they will remain fresh three to four days. If any shells open during storage, tap them and discard any that don't close quickly.

Store shucked clams, mussels, oysters, and scallops covered in their own juices in the refrigerator for up to two days. You can also freeze them for up to three months.

Crabs and lobsters are best cooked the day of purchase. To store until cooking time, place the crabs or lobsters on a tray, cover with a damp towel or newspaper, and place in the refrigerator or an ice-filled cooler. Use the cooked meat within two days, or freeze the meat in a tightly covered container for up to one month.

Rinse fresh raw shrimp under cold running water; drain well. Store in a tightly covered container in the refrigerator for up to two days. Store cooked shrimp in the refrigerator for up to three days.

How Much To Buy

Deciding how much fresh seafood to purchase can be confusing. The following amounts to buy per serving are appropriate for low-fat eating.

Crabs. Serve three blue crabs per person, while allowing about three ounces of lump crabmeat or three stone crab claws for each serving.

Lobsters. Count on about one serving from a one-pound lobster.

Clams, mussels, and oysters. Allow six to nine live clams or oysters, or 10 to 12 live mussels in the shell per serving or serve four ounces of each, shucked, for each serving.

Scallops. Allow four ounces of shucked scallops per person, whether they are bay scallops or sea scallops.

Shrimp. One pound of headless shrimp in the shell will yield about one-half pound after peeling. Allow about one-fourth pound of peeled shrimp per serving.

EAST COAST CRABMEAT CAKES

2 pounds fresh lump crabmeat, drained
1 cup soft whole wheat breadcrumbs
⅔ cup minced onion
⅔ cup minced celery
¼ cup nonfat mayonnaise
1 egg white, lightly beaten
2 teaspoons Old Bay seasoning
2 teaspoons Dijon mustard
2 teaspoons low-sodium Worcestershire sauce
¼ teaspoon ground red pepper
Vegetable cooking spray
¾ cup Tangy Lemon Sauce (page 185)

Combine first 10 ingredients; shape mixture into 12 (½-inch-thick) patties. Cover and chill 1 hour.

Coat a griddle or large nonstick skillet with cooking spray; place over medium heat until hot. Add crabmeat cakes, in batches, and cook 4 to 5 minutes on each side or until golden. Serve crabmeat cakes with Tangy Lemon Sauce. Yield: 6 servings (156 calories [15% from fat] per 2 cakes and 2 tablespoons sauce).

FAT 2.6g (SAT 0.3g, MONO 0.4g, POLY 0.9g)
PROTEIN 22.7g CARBOHYDRATE 9.9g
FIBER 1.0g CHOLESTEROL 102mg SODIUM 938mg

CRABMEAT AU GRATIN

Vegetable cooking spray
½ cup chopped green onions
2 cups skim milk
¼ cup all-purpose flour
1¼ pounds fresh lump crabmeat, drained
¼ cup grated Parmesan cheese
2½ tablespoons chopped fresh parsley
¾ teaspoon dry mustard
¾ teaspoon low-sodium Worcestershire sauce
¼ teaspoon ground red pepper
¼ teaspoon paprika
⅛ teaspoon ground white pepper
½ cup (2 ounces) shredded reduced-fat Cheddar cheese

Coat a small nonstick skillet with cooking spray; place over medium-high heat until hot. Add green onions; sauté until tender. Remove from heat, and set aside.

Combine milk and flour in container of an electric blender; top with cover, and process until smooth. Pour flour mixture into a large saucepan; cook over medium heat, stirring constantly, about 10 minutes or until thickened and bubbly. Add green onions, crabmeat, and next 7 ingredients; stir well. Pour mixture into a 1-quart casserole coated with cooking spray. Bake at 350° for 20 to 25 minutes or until thoroughly heated. Sprinkle with cheese, and bake an additional 5 minutes or until cheese melts. Yield: 4 servings (256 calories [24% from fat] per serving).

FAT 6.7g (SAT 2.9g, MONO 0.8g, POLY 0.9g)
PROTEIN 33.6g CARBOHYDRATE 13.7g
FIBER 0.6g CHOLESTEROL 124mg SODIUM 571mg

CRABMEAT IMPERIAL

Vegetable cooking spray
¼ cup chopped celery
¼ cup chopped green pepper
¼ cup chopped sweet red pepper
1 egg, lightly beaten
¼ cup plus 1 tablespoon nonfat mayonnaise, divided
1 tablespoon chopped fresh parsley
1½ tablespoons lemon juice
1½ tablespoons low-sodium soy sauce
½ teaspoon Dijon mustard
⅛ teaspoon ground red pepper
⅛ teaspoon hot sauce
1 pound fresh lump crabmeat, drained
Pimiento strips (optional)
Celery leaves (optional)

Coat a small nonstick skillet with vegetable cooking spray; place over medium-high heat until hot. Add celery, green pepper, and sweet red pepper; sauté until tender. Combine egg and 3 tablespoons mayonnaise in a medium bowl; add pepper mixture, parsley, and next 5 ingredients, stirring well. Add crabmeat; stir gently just until blended.

Spoon crabmeat mixture evenly into 4 baking shells. Place shells on a baking sheet. Bake at 375° for 20 minutes or until golden. Remove from oven, and top evenly with remaining 2 tablespoons mayonnaise. If desired, garnish with pimiento strips and celery leaves. Yield: 4 servings (149 calories [21% from fat] per serving).

FAT 3.5g (SAT 0.7g, MONO 0.8g, POLY 1.0g)
PROTEIN 24.0g CARBOHYDRATE 3.7g
FIBER 0.4g CHOLESTEROL 165mg SODIUM 541mg

COLORFUL CRABMEAT AND LINGUINE

8 ounces linguine, uncooked
½ pound fresh mushrooms, sliced
½ cup chopped green onions
½ cup chopped sweet red pepper
⅓ cup cream sherry
1 pound fresh lump crabmeat, drained
¼ cup chopped fresh parsley
2 teaspoons lemon juice

Cook linguine according to package directions, omitting salt and fat. Drain well, and set aside.

Combine mushrooms, green onions, pepper, and sherry in a large skillet. Cook over medium heat, stirring frequently, until vegetables are tender. Stir in crabmeat, parsley, and lemon juice; cook until heated.

Divide linguine evenly among 4 individual serving plates; top evenly with crabmeat mixture. Yield: 4 servings (347 calories [8% from fat] per serving).

FAT 3.1g (SAT 0.4g, MONO 0.4g, POLY 1.3g)
PROTEIN 30.4g CARBOHYDRATE 48.1g
FIBER 2.8g CHOLESTEROL 106mg SODIUM 309mg

To open clam shells that will not be steamed open, use a clam or oyster knife with a protective glove or towel. Insert the blade of the knife between the shell halves opposite the hinge, and twist the blade to force the shell halves apart.

LOBSTER THERMIDOR

5 (6-ounce) fresh or frozen lobster tails, thawed
Vegetable cooking spray
1½ cups sliced fresh mushrooms
¼ cup chopped shallot
1 clove garlic, minced
½ cup instant nonfat dry milk powder
1½ cups skim milk
2 tablespoons reduced-calorie margarine
3 tablespoons all-purpose flour
2 tablespoons dry sherry
1 teaspoon dry mustard
¼ teaspoon salt
¼ teaspoon ground white pepper
2½ tablespoons freshly grated Parmesan cheese
¼ teaspoon paprika

Cook lobster tails in boiling water 5 to 6 minutes or until done; drain. Rinse with cold water. Split and clean tails. Cut lobster tail meat into ½-inch pieces; set aside.

Coat a large nonstick skillet with vegetable cooking spray; place over medium-high heat until hot. Add mushrooms, shallot, and garlic; sauté until tender. Set aside.

Combine milk powder and skim milk in a small bowl; stir well. Melt margarine in a medium saucepan over medium heat; add flour, stirring until smooth. Cook 1 minute, stirring constantly. Gradually add milk mixture to flour mixture; cook, stirring constantly, until mixture is thickened and bubbly. Stir in sherry, mustard, salt, and pepper. Add cooked lobster and mushroom mixture; cook, stirring constantly, just until mixture is thoroughly heated.

Spoon lobster mixture evenly into 6 (6-ounce) ovenproof ramekins or custard cups; sprinkle evenly with Parmesan cheese and paprika. Bake at 400° for 12 to 14 minutes or until bubbly. Yield: 6 servings (186 calories [20% from fat] per serving).

FAT 4.1g (SAT 1.0g, MONO 1.3g, POLY 1.2g)
PROTEIN 22.4g CARBOHYDRATE 14.5g
FIBER 0.4g CHOLESTEROL 56mg SODIUM 530mg

STEAMED CLAMS

3 dozen cherrystone clams
¾ cup water
⅓ cup Chablis or other dry white wine
1½ tablespoons Old Bay seasoning
½ teaspoon ground white pepper
Lemon wedges (optional)

Scrub clams thoroughly, discarding any that are cracked or open.

Combine water and next 3 ingredients in a large Dutch oven; bring to a boil. Add clams; cover, reduce heat, and simmer 10 to 12 minutes or until clams open. Remove and discard any unopened clams.

Remove remaining clams with a slotted spoon, reserving liquid, if desired. Serve clams immediately with reserved liquid and lemon wedges, if desired. Yield: 4 servings (88 calories [12% from fat] per serving).

FAT 1.2g (SAT 0.1g, MONO 0.1g, POLY 0.4g)
PROTEIN 14.6g CARBOHYDRATE 3.6g
FIBER 0.2g CHOLESTEROL 39mg SODIUM 846mg

CLAMS IN RED SAUCE

3 dozen littleneck clams
2 tablespoons cornmeal
Vegetable cooking spray
1 tablespoon olive oil
½ cup finely chopped onion
1 clove garlic, minced
1 cup Chablis or other dry white
   wine
2 (14-ounce) cans plum tomatoes
   with basil, undrained and
   chopped
2 (8-ounce) cans no-salt-added
   tomato sauce
1 tablespoon dried whole basil
½ teaspoon crushed red pepper
6 cups cooked linguine (cooked
   without salt or fat)
¼ cup chopped fresh parsley

Scrub clams thoroughly, discarding any that are cracked or open. Place remaining clams in a large bowl; cover with cold water, and sprinkle with cornmeal. Let stand 30 minutes. Drain and rinse clams; set aside. Discard cornmeal.

Coat a Dutch oven with cooking spray; add oil. Place over medium heat until hot. Add onion and garlic; sauté until tender. Add wine; bring to a boil, and cook 5 minutes. Add tomato and next 3 ingredients; reduce heat, and simmer, uncovered, 10 minutes, stirring occasionally.

Place clams on top of tomato mixture. Cover and cook 8 to 10 minutes or until clams open. Remove and discard any unopened clams.

Divide linguine evenly among 6 large soup bowls; top linguine evenly with clam mixture, and sprinkle evenly with chopped fresh parsley. Yield: 6 servings (333 calories [11% from fat] per serving).

FAT 4.1g (SAT 0.6g, MONO 1.9g, POLY 0.9g)
PROTEIN 16.6g CARBOHYDRATE 57.3g
FIBER 4.9g CHOLESTEROL 19mg SODIUM 271mg

WINE-POACHED MUSSELS

2 dozen mussels
½ cup Chablis or other dry white
   wine
¼ cup sliced green onions
2 tablespoons chopped fresh parsley
2 tablespoons shredded carrot
2 teaspoons lemon juice
⅛ teaspoon pepper
¼ cup canned low-sodium chicken
   broth, undiluted
⅛ teaspoon butter flavoring

Remove beards on mussels, and scrub shells thoroughly. Discard any open or cracked mussels or heavy ones (they're filled with sand).

Bring wine to a boil in a Dutch oven. Add mussels; cover and simmer 8 to 10 minutes or until shells open, shaking pan several times. Transfer mussels to a bowl using a slotted spoon, reserving cooking liquid in pan. Let mussels cool slightly. Remove and discard halves of shells to which mussels are not attached. Loosen mussels remaining in shells, and arrange shells, open sides up, on individual serving plates.

Strain reserved cooking liquid into a small skillet; add green onions and next 4 ingredients. Cook over high heat until liquid is reduced to about ½ cup. Stir in chicken broth and butter flavoring; cook just until thoroughly heated. Spoon sauce evenly over mussels, and serve immediately. Yield: 2 servings (159 calories [23% from fat] per serving).

FAT 4.1g (SAT 0.7g, MONO 0.9g, POLY 1.0g)
PROTEIN 20.9g CARBOHYDRATE 8.8g
FIBER 0.4g CHOLESTEROL 48mg SODIUM 332mg

OYSTERS MÉLANGE

Vegetable cooking spray
1 cup sliced fresh mushrooms
½ cup chopped sweet red pepper
¼ cup chopped shallot
¼ cup sliced green onions
¼ cup chopped celery
½ cup Chablis or other dry white
   wine
2 teaspoons cornstarch
1 teaspoon chicken-flavored
   bouillon granules
½ teaspoon salt
¼ teaspoon black pepper
⅛ teaspoon ground red pepper
2 (12-ounce) containers Select
   oysters, drained
5 cups cooked rice (cooked without
   salt or fat)
2 tablespoons chopped fresh parsley

Coat a large nonstick skillet with cooking spray; place over medium-high heat until hot. Add mushrooms and next 4 ingredients; sauté 3 to 4 minutes or until tender.

Combine wine and cornstarch; stir in bouillon granules, salt, black pepper, and ground red pepper. Add to vegetable mixture; bring to a boil. Add oysters; reduce heat, and simmer 5 minutes or until oyster edges curl.

Spoon rice onto a serving platter; top with oyster mixture. Sprinkle with parsley. Yield: 5 servings (333 calories [11% from fat] per serving).

FAT 4.0g (SAT 1.0g, MONO 0.4g, POLY 1.1g)
PROTEIN 14.6g CARBOHYDRATE 58.1g
FIBER 1.8g CHOLESTEROL 75mg SODIUM 562mg

SCALLOP AND PASTA TOSS

Vegetable cooking spray
1 tablespoon reduced-calorie
   margarine
2 cups diagonally sliced celery
1 cup sliced fresh mushrooms
½ cup sliced green onions
½ cup sliced carrot
2 cloves garlic, minced
¾ pound fresh bay scallops
2 tablespoons water
2 teaspoons white wine
   Worcestershire sauce
½ teaspoon ground ginger
¼ teaspoon salt
⅛ teaspoon pepper
4 cups cooked spinach linguine
   (cooked without salt or fat)

Coat a large nonstick skillet with cooking spray; add margarine. Place over medium-high heat until margarine melts. Add celery, mushrooms, green onions, carrot, and garlic; sauté until crisp-tender. Add scallops and next 5 ingredients; cook 5 to 7 minutes or until scallops are opaque, stirring occasionally.

Place linguine in a large serving bowl; add scallop mixture, and toss gently. Yield: 4 servings (323 calories [14% from fat] per serving).

FAT 5.0g (SAT 0.7g, MONO 1.8g, POLY 1.5g)
PROTEIN 23.3g   CARBOHYDRATE 46.8g
FIBER 4.9g   CHOLESTEROL 28mg   SODIUM 444mg

CURRIED SCALLOPS AND VEGETABLES

Vegetable cooking spray
1½ cups shredded carrot
1 cup diced celery
¼ teaspoon pepper
2 teaspoons reduced-calorie
   margarine
1 pound fresh bay scallops
1 tablespoon Chablis or other dry
   white wine
½ teaspoon curry powder
¼ teaspoon salt
Chopped fresh chives (optional)

Coat a large nonstick skillet with cooking spray; place over medium-high heat until hot. Add carrot, celery, and pepper; sauté until vegetables are crisp-tender. Set mixture aside, and keep warm.

Coat skillet with cooking spray; add margarine. Place over medium-high heat until margarine melts. Add scallops; sauté 1 minute. Add wine, curry powder, and salt; cook an additional 4 to 5 minutes or until scallops are opaque.

Spoon carrot mixture evenly onto 4 individual serving plates; top evenly with scallop mixture. Garnish with chopped fresh chives, if desired. Yield: 4 servings (133 calories [17% from fat] per serving).

FAT 2.5g (SAT 0.3g, MONO 0.6g, POLY 1.0g)
PROTEIN 19.6g   CARBOHYDRATE 7.4g
FIBER 1.7g   CHOLESTEROL 37mg   SODIUM 387mg

The chef in the house will like Scallop and Pasta Toss because it's quick to prepare. Family members will love this colorful seafood dish for its varied flavors.

Shrimp Monterey contains fresh cilantro, Monterey Jack cheese, and jalapeño pepper — ingredients that add zest without masking the shrimp's delicate flavor.

LEMON-SAUCED SCALLOPS

¾ cup all-purpose flour
¼ teaspoon ground white pepper
1½ pounds fresh bay scallops
3 egg whites, lightly beaten
Vegetable cooking spray
1 tablespoon plus 1 teaspoon
   reduced-calorie margarine,
   divided
⅔ cup Chablis or other dry
   white wine
½ cup sliced green onions
¼ cup lemon juice
⅛ teaspoon salt

Combine flour and white pepper in a small shallow dish; stir well. Dredge scallops in flour mixture. Dip scallops in egg white; dredge in flour mixture again.

Coat a large nonstick skillet with cooking spray; add 2 teaspoons margarine. Place over medium-high heat until margarine melts. Add half of scallops; cook 6 to 8 minutes or until scallops are lightly browned, turning to brown all sides. Remove scallops from skillet; set aside, and keep warm. Repeat procedure with remaining 2 teaspoons margarine and scallops. Wipe drippings from skillet with a paper towel.

Add wine and remaining ingredients to skillet; cook 3 minutes or until mixture reduces to ¼ cup. Arrange scallops on a large serving platter; spoon sauce evenly over scallops. Yield: 6 servings (185 calories [14% from fat] per serving).

FAT 2.8g (SAT 0.3g, MONO 0.7g, POLY 1.0g)
PROTEIN 22.5g CARBOHYDRATE 16.5g
FIBER 0.6g CHOLESTEROL 37mg SODIUM 285mg

SHRIMP MONTEREY

2¼ pounds unpeeled medium-size
   fresh shrimp
Vegetable cooking spray
1½ tablespoons chopped fresh
   cilantro
3 tablespoons all-purpose flour
1¼ cups skim milk, divided
1½ tablespoons reduced-calorie
   margarine
½ cup (2 ounces) shredded
   reduced-fat Monterey Jack cheese
1 jalapeño pepper, seeded and
   chopped
1 tablespoon grated Parmesan
   cheese
Fresh cilantro sprigs (optional)

Peel and devein shrimp; arrange shrimp in a steamer basket over boiling water. Cover and steam 3 to 5 minutes or until shrimp are done. Divide shrimp evenly among 6 (1½-cup) baking dishes coated with vegetable cooking spray. Sprinkle with cilantro, and set aside.

Combine flour and ¼ cup milk in a small bowl; stir until smooth. Combine flour mixture, remaining 1 cup milk, and margarine in a small saucepan. Cook over medium heat, stirring constantly, until mixture is thickened and bubbly. Remove from heat; add shredded Monterey Jack cheese and chopped jalapeño pepper, stirring until cheese melts.

Pour sauce evenly over shrimp; sprinkle evenly with Parmesan cheese. Broil 5½ inches from heat 3 to 5 minutes or until lightly browned. Garnish with fresh cilantro sprigs, if desired. Yield: 6 servings (161 calories [29% from fat] per serving).

FAT 5.1g (SAT 1.8g, MONO 1.0g, POLY 1.3g)
PROTEIN 22.1g CARBOHYDRATE 5.1g
FIBER 0.1g CHOLESTEROL 165mg SODIUM 310mg

LEMON-GARLIC SHRIMP

2¼ pounds unpeeled large fresh
  shrimp
Vegetable cooking spray
3 tablespoons minced onion
3 tablespoons minced fresh parsley
3 cloves garlic, minced
½ cup lemon juice
¼ cup commercial oil-free Italian
  dressing
¼ cup water
¼ cup low-sodium soy sauce
½ teaspoon freshly ground pepper

Peel and devein shrimp, leaving tails intact. Place shrimp in a large, shallow baking dish. Set aside.

Coat a nonstick skillet with cooking spray; place over medium-high heat until hot. Add onion, parsley, and garlic; sauté until tender. Stir in lemon juice and remaining ingredients. Pour mixture over shrimp. Cover and marinate in refrigerator 1 to 2 hours, stirring occasionally.

Uncover shrimp; broil 5½ inches from heat 5 minutes or until done, basting with marinade. Serve with a slotted spoon. Yield: 6 servings (88 calories [10% from fat] per serving).

FAT 1.0g (SAT 0.2g, MONO 0.2g, POLY 0.4g)
PROTEIN 17.1g CARBOHYDRATE 1.7g
FIBER 0.2g CHOLESTEROL 157mg SODIUM 289mg

SESAME SHRIMP KABOBS

32 unpeeled large fresh shrimp
1 (6-ounce) can unsweetened
  pineapple juice
2 tablespoons lime juice
1 tablespoon low-sodium soy sauce
1 tablespoon honey
½ teaspoon sesame oil
¼ teaspoon peeled, minced
  gingerroot
Vegetable cooking spray
2 tablespoons sesame seeds, toasted

Peel and devein shrimp, leaving tails intact. Place shrimp in a zip-top heavy-duty plastic bag. Combine pineapple juice and next 5 ingredients; pour over shrimp. Seal bag, and shake until shrimp are well coated. Marinate in refrigerator 3 to 4 hours, turning bag occasionally.

Remove shrimp from marinade, reserving marinade. Thread shrimp on 4 (15-inch) skewers. Coat grill rack with cooking spray; place on grill over medium-hot coals. Place kabobs on rack, and cook 6 minutes or until done, turning and basting frequently with marinade. Sprinkle sesame seeds over shrimp, gently pressing seeds onto shrimp. Yield: 4 servings (157 calories [22% from fat] per serving).

FAT 3.8g (SAT 0.6g, MONO 1.2g, POLY 1.6g)
PROTEIN 19.0g CARBOHYDRATE 11.3g
FIBER 0.2g CHOLESTEROL 166mg SODIUM 290mg

SHRIMP SCAMPI

2 pounds unpeeled large fresh
  shrimp
Vegetable cooking spray
2 teaspoons olive oil
8 cloves garlic, coarsely chopped
1 teaspoon seeded, minced red chile
  pepper
1 tablespoon lime juice

Peel and devein shrimp. Coat a large nonstick skillet with cooking spray; add oil and garlic. Place over medium-high heat 1 minute. Add shrimp and pepper; cook 4 minutes, stirring constantly. Add lime juice, and cook an additional 3 minutes or until shrimp turn pink. Yield: 4 servings (149 calories [27% from fat] per serving).

FAT 4.4g (SAT 0.7g, MONO 2.0g, POLY 1.0g)
PROTEIN 23.3g CARBOHYDRATE 2.8g
FIBER 0.2g CHOLESTEROL 172mg SODIUM 170mg

NEW ORLEANS-STYLE BARBECUE SHRIMP

Vegetable cooking spray
1 tablespoon olive oil
1 cup sliced green onions
6 cloves garlic, minced
1 cup canned no-salt-added
  chicken broth, undiluted
½ cup fresh lemon juice
1½ tablespoons paprika
1 teaspoon dried whole
  rosemary
1 teaspoon dried whole basil
1 teaspoon dried whole oregano
¾ teaspoon salt
½ teaspoon ground red pepper
½ teaspoon black pepper
6 bay leaves
2¼ pounds unpeeled medium-size
  fresh shrimp

Coat a large nonstick skillet with vegetable cooking spray; add oil. Place over medium-high heat until hot. Add green onions and garlic; sauté until tender. Add broth and next 9 ingredients, stirring well. Bring to a boil; cover, reduce heat, and simmer 10 minutes, stirring occasionally. Uncover and simmer an additional 5 minutes, stirring frequently. Remove from heat; cover and let stand at room temperature 2 to 3 hours, stirring occasionally.

Peel and devein shrimp. Uncover sauce; bring sauce to a boil over medium heat, stirring occasionally. Add peeled and deveined shrimp to sauce; cook 5 minutes or until shrimp are done, stirring occasionally. Remove and discard bay leaves. If desired, serve shrimp mixture over cooked rice or toasted French bread slices. Yield: 6 servings (204 calories [24% from fat] per serving).

FAT 5.5g (SAT 0.8g, MONO 2.1g, POLY 1.3g)
PROTEIN 30.2g CARBOHYDRATE 7.8g
FIBER 0.9g CHOLESTEROL 215mg SODIUM 529mg

CREAMY SEAFOOD OVER TOAST POINTS

½ pound unpeeled medium-size
   fresh shrimp
3 cups water
Vegetable cooking spray
½ cup sliced green onions
2 cups sliced fresh mushrooms
⅓ cup all-purpose flour
2 teaspoons chicken-flavored
   bouillon granules
2 cups skim milk
¼ cup dry sherry
¼ teaspoon ground white pepper
½ pound fresh lump crabmeat,
   drained
½ pound fresh bay scallops
2 cups frozen broccoli flowerets,
   thawed
1 cup frozen sliced carrot, thawed
8 (1-ounce) slices whole wheat
   bread, toasted and quartered

Peel and devein shrimp. Bring water to a boil in a medium saucepan; add shrimp, and cook 3 to 5 minutes or until shrimp are done. Drain well, and set aside.

Coat a large nonstick skillet with cooking spray; place over medium-high heat until hot. Add green onions and mushrooms; sauté 3 to 4 minutes or until tender. Combine flour, bouillon granules, milk, sherry, and pepper; stir well. Add to mushroom mixture; bring to a boil, stirring constantly. Reduce heat, and simmer 3 to 4 minutes or until thickened. Add shrimp, crabmeat, and next 3 ingredients; cook 5 minutes or until scallops are opaque.

Arrange toast points on individual serving plates; top evenly with seafood mixture. Yield: 8 servings (205 calories [11% from fat] per serving).

FAT 2.4g (SAT 0.5g, MONO 0.4g, POLY 0.8g)
PROTEIN 21.0g CARBOHYDRATE 26.2g
FIBER 2.1g CHOLESTEROL 67mg SODIUM 562mg

SEAFOOD NEWBURG

2 (8-ounce) fresh or frozen lobster
   tails, thawed
3 ounces Neufchâtel cheese
Vegetable cooking spray
1 teaspoon vegetable oil
⅔ cup sliced fresh mushrooms
½ cup chopped onion
⅓ cup all-purpose flour
3 cups skim milk
2 tablespoons frozen egg substitute,
   thawed
3 tablespoons dry sherry
1 tablespoon lemon juice
¼ teaspoon salt
¼ teaspoon black pepper
⅛ teaspoon dry mustard
⅛ teaspoon paprika
Dash of ground red pepper
½ pound fresh lump crabmeat,
   drained
6 cups cooked long-grain rice
   (cooked without salt or fat)
Paprika

Cook lobster tails in boiling water 6 to 8 minutes or until done; drain. Rinse tails with cold water. Split and clean tails. Coarsely chop meat, and set aside.

Freeze cheese 15 minutes or until firm; cut cheese into ¼-inch cubes, and set aside.

Coat a large nonstick skillet with vegetable cooking spray; add oil. Place over medium heat until hot. Add mushrooms and onion; sauté until tender. Add flour; cook 1 minute, stirring constantly (mixture will be dry and crumbly).

Combine milk and egg substitute; stir well. Gradually add milk mixture to flour mixture; cook, stirring constantly, until mixture is thickened.

Add cheese, stirring until cheese melts. Stir in sherry and next 7 ingredients; cook, stirring constantly, 2 to 3 minutes or until heated. Place rice on a serving platter. Spoon seafood mixture over rice, and sprinkle with paprika. Yield: 6 servings (305 calories [17% from fat] per serving).

FAT 5.7g (SAT 2.6g, MONO 1.5g, POLY 0.9g)
PROTEIN 26.4g CARBOHYDRATE 35.3g
FIBER 1.0g CHOLESTEROL 100mg SODIUM 333mg

SEAFOOD KABOBS

16 unpeeled large fresh shrimp
16 fresh sea scallops
¾ pound amberjack fillets, cut into
   16 pieces
½ cup unsweetened pineapple juice
¼ cup low-sodium soy sauce
2 tablespoons white wine
   Worcestershire sauce
1½ teaspoons vegetable oil
¼ teaspoon salt
¼ teaspoon ground ginger
⅛ teaspoon onion powder
1 clove garlic, crushed
32 snow pea pods
32 fresh pineapple chunks
Vegetable cooking spray

Peel and devein shrimp. Place seafood in a zip-top plastic bag. Combine pineapple juice and next 7 ingredients. Pour half of mixture over seafood. Reserve remaining half of mixture; set aside. Seal bag, and toss gently until seafood is well coated. Marinate in refrigerator 2 hours.

Remove seafood from marinade; discard marinade. Thread seafood, pea pods, and pineapple chunks on 16 (8-inch) skewers. Coat grill rack with cooking spray; place on grill over medium-hot coals. Place kabobs on rack; cook 6 minutes or until done, turning and basting with reserved juice mixture. Yield: 8 servings (177 calories [18% from fat] per serving).

FAT 3.6g (SAT 0.8g, MONO 0.9g, POLY 1.2g)
PROTEIN 22.9g CARBOHYDRATE 12.5g
FIBER 1.6g CHOLESTEROL 89mg SODIUM 292mg

Mixed Seafood Grill in Cornhusks

19 dried cornhusks
¾ pound unpeeled medium-size fresh shrimp
1 (8-ounce) salmon fillet
½ pound fresh sea scallops
3 tablespoons Chablis or other dry white wine
2 tablespoons reduced-calorie margarine, melted
2 teaspoons salt-free lemon-pepper seasoning
Vegetable cooking spray

Cover dried cornhusks with hot water; let stand 1 hour or until softened. Drain well; pat cornhusks with paper towels to remove excess water.

Peel and devein shrimp. Remove skin from salmon, and cut salmon into 1-inch cubes. Place shrimp, salmon, and scallops in a medium bowl. Combine wine, margarine, and lemon-pepper seasoning; stir well. Pour over seafood, and toss gently.

Tear 3 cornhusks into 32 (¼-inch) strips. Tie 2 strips together at ends, making 16 strips; set aside.

Overlap 2 cornhusks; place one-eighth of seafood mixture in center of cornhusks. Fold bottom and top of cornhusks over mixture; tie with a cornhusk strip. Fold right and left sides of cornhusk over fillet, forming a square; tie with another cornhusk strip. Repeat procedure, using remaining cornhusks, strips, and seafood mixture.

Coat grill rack with cooking spray; place on grill over medium coals. Place packets on rack, and cook 5 minutes on each side or until done. Yield: 8 servings (107 calories [35% from fat] per serving).

FAT 4.2g (SAT 0.7g, MONO 1.3g, POLY 1.5g)
PROTEIN 15.3g CARBOHYDRATE 1.3g
FIBER 0.1g CHOLESTEROL 53mg SODIUM 118mg

CALORIE, FAT, AND CHOLESTEROL CONTENT OF FISH AND SHELLFISH

Fish or Shellfish (3 ounces cooked)	Calories	Fat (grams)	Cholesterol (milligrams)
Fish			
Bass, striped	105	2.5	88
Catfish, freshwater	132	4.8	66
Cod	89	0.7	47
Flounder	100	1.3	58
Grouper	100	1.1	40
Haddock	95	0.8	63
Halibut	119	2.5	35
Mackerel, Spanish	134	5.4	62
Mahimahi	93	0.8	80
Monkfish	82	1.7	27
Orange roughy	76	0.8	22
Perch	100	1.0	98
Pollack	100	1.1	77
Pompano	179	10.3	54
Red snapper	109	1.5	40
Salmon			
Coho	157	6.4	42
Sockeye	184	9.3	74
Scamp	100	1.1	40
Sole	100	1.3	58
Swordfish	132	4.4	43
Trout, rainbow	128	3.7	62
Tuna			
White, canned in water, drained	116	2.1	36
Yellowfin	118	1.0	49
Whitefish	146	6.4	65
Shellfish			
Clams	126	1.7	57
Crabs			
Alaskan king	82	1.3	45
Blue	87	1.5	85
Dungeness	94	1.1	65
Crawfish	97	1.1	151
Lobsters	83	0.5	61
Mussels	146	3.8	48
Oysters	117	4.2	93
Scallops	100	0.9	37
Shrimp	84	0.9	166

GRAINS, LEGUMES, AND PASTAS

The variety of ways in which you can serve grains, legumes, and pastas is endless. Not only are they perfect for combining with fresh vegetables and low-fat sauces but they also are high in soluble and insoluble fiber, low in fat, and rich in vitamins and minerals.

GRAINS

Remember when grains and pastas were considered fattening because they were high in carbohydrate? Now we know that complex carbohydrates are allies in the crusade for healthy eating. The desire for healthier, low-fat foods has moved grains into a prominent place in the everyday diet. Popular grains have always included barley, corn, oats, and rice. Now lesser known grains such as bulgur wheat, cracked wheat, couscous, and quinoa are making their way into America's cupboards as a welcome change from pasta and rice.

Rice — The Most Popular Grain

Rice is classified according to its size — long-, medium-, or short-grain. Long-grain rice is four to five times as long as it is wide and when cooked, the grains are separate and fluffy. Long-grain rice is used in salads, pilafs, curries, or other dishes where a separate and more distinct grain is preferred.

Medium- and short-grain varieties of rice are short, plump, and very moist when cooked. They stick together more than long-grain varieties. Short-grain rice is often preferred for Oriental food because it's easiest to eat with chopsticks. Medium- and short-grain varieties are a good choice for rice puddings and molds.

In the United States, white rice is often enriched so that the vitamin and mineral content will be similar to that of unprocessed rice. If the product label states that the rice is enriched, do not rinse it before cooking. Rinsing washes away the important nutrients that have been added.

Here are some of the most common types of rice found on supermarket shelves:

Basmati. This long-grain brown or white rice grown in the Far East has a nutlike flavor and aroma that can be attributed to its aging process. Nutritionally, it is similar to other rice. Texmati rice, a cross between basmati

Celebrate a bountiful harvest with Fettuccine Primavera (page 114). A generous one-cup serving is low in fat and calories and high in healthful fiber.

and American long-grain rice, has a flavor similar to that of basmati. Wehani rice is a flavorful whole-grain basmati hybrid that tastes similar to cracked wheat when cooked. Wild pecan rice is a basmati hybrid that has a pecanlike flavor.

Brown. A long-grain variety that retains its bran during processing, brown rice is actually tan-colored and has a nutlike flavor and chewy texture. Nutritionally, brown rice is similar to enriched white rice, but it contains up to three times more fiber per serving. Brown rice requires longer cooking than white rice — as long as 45 minutes versus about 20 minutes for white.

Converted. Also known as parboiled rice, converted rice is a long-grain variety that is soaked, steamed, and dried before the hull is removed. When cooked, the grains are fluffy and separate. Compared with regular white rice, converted rice retains slightly more nutrients and may require increased cooking time and more liquid.

Instant. Available in white and brown varieties, instant rice is a long-grain variety that has been fully or partially cooked before being dehydrated and packaged. The appearance, texture, and taste of instant rice are a little different from that of regular white or brown rice. The cooked grains are split and slightly soft in texture, and some of their flavor is lost due to the large amount of processing that takes place before packaging. Instant rice actually takes about 10 minutes to cook.

Wild. Technically not a rice at all, wild rice is actually the seed of a marsh grass native to the northern Great Lakes area of the United States. It is a long, slender, dark brown or black grain that is popular for its nutty flavor and chewy texture. Wild rice takes about one hour to cook.

Cooking Grains

Each type of grain requires a different cooking time, calls for a different amount of water, and yields a different amount of cooked product. Check package directions for the specific product you are using or follow recipe directions for preparation.

When cooking rice, regardless of the type, cover it tightly and cook it in the amount of water called for until it is tender and all the liquid has been absorbed. Use a saucepan that is large enough to hold three or four times the amount of rice being cooked. To ensure success, do not lift the lid until you are sure the rice is almost done. Once the liquid has been absorbed, remove the saucepan from the heat. Let stand, covered, five minutes; then fluff the rice with a fork just before serving.

BULGUR-VEGETABLE PILAF

2 cups canned no-salt-added
  chicken broth, undiluted
1 cup bulgur (cracked wheat),
  uncooked
¾ cup chopped onion
½ cup sliced green onions
½ cup grated carrot
½ teaspoon salt
¼ teaspoon garlic powder
1 tablespoon chopped fresh parsley

Bring broth to a boil in a medium saucepan; add bulgur. Cover, reduce heat, and simmer 15 minutes. Stir in chopped onion and next 4 ingredients; cover and cook 10 minutes or until bulgur is tender and liquid is absorbed. Stir in parsley. Yield: 7 servings (89 calories [9% from fat] per ½-cup serving).

FAT 0.9g (SAT 0.2g, MONO 0.3g, POLY 0.2g)
PROTEIN 3.4g CARBOHYDRATE 17.8g
FIBER 4.4g CHOLESTEROL 0mg SODIUM 213mg

LEMON COUSCOUS

2¼ cups water
⅓ cup thinly sliced green onions
¼ teaspoon salt
1⅓ cups couscous, uncooked
2¼ teaspoons grated lemon rind

Combine first 3 ingredients in a medium saucepan; stir well. Bring to a boil; remove from heat. Stir in couscous and lemon rind; cover and let stand 5 minutes or until couscous is tender and liquid is absorbed.

Fluff couscous with a fork, and transfer to a serving bowl. Yield: 8 servings (103 calories [0% from fat] per ½-cup serving).

FAT 0.0g (SAT 0.0g, MONO 0.0g, POLY 0.0g)
PROTEIN 3.6g CARBOHYDRATE 21.7g
FIBER 0.2g CHOLESTEROL 0mg SODIUM 74mg

GARLIC CHEESE GRITS

Vegetable cooking spray
1½ tablespoons chopped onion
1 clove garlic, minced
1¾ cups skim milk
1½ cups water
¾ cup quick-cooking grits,
  uncooked
1 egg, lightly beaten
1 egg white, lightly beaten
1 cup (4 ounces) shredded reduced-
  fat sharp Cheddar cheese
¼ teaspoon salt
⅛ teaspoon hot sauce
2¼ teaspoons low-sodium
  Worcestershire sauce

Coat a large saucepan with cooking spray; place over medium-high heat until hot. Add onion and garlic; sauté until tender. Stir in milk and water; bring to a boil. Stir in grits. Cover, reduce heat, and simmer 5 minutes or until thickened, stirring occasionally. Remove from heat.

Combine egg and remaining ingredients; stir well. Gradually stir about one-fourth of grits mixture into egg mixture; add to remaining grits mixture, stirring until cheese melts.

Pour grits mixture into a 1½-quart casserole coated with cooking spray. Bake at 350° for 30 to 35 minutes or until set. Yield: 6 servings (168 calories [26% from fat] per serving).

FAT 4.8g (SAT 2.5g, MONO 0.4g, POLY 0.2g)
PROTEIN 11.4g CARBOHYDRATE 19.7g
FIBER 1.0g CHOLESTEROL 50mg SODIUM 303mg

TEX-MEX HOMINY

Vegetable cooking spray
¼ cup chopped green onions
1 clove garlic, minced
2 (15½-ounce) cans golden hominy, drained
1 (10-ounce) can diced tomatoes and green chiles, undrained
1 teaspoon chili powder
½ teaspoon ground cumin
¼ teaspoon salt
¼ teaspoon pepper
½ cup (2 ounces) shredded reduced-fat Monterey Jack cheese

Coat a large nonstick skillet with cooking spray; place over medium-heat until hot. Add green onions and garlic; sauté until tender. Stir in hominy and next 5 ingredients; cook 5 minutes, stirring occasionally.

Pour mixture into a 1½-quart baking dish coated with cooking spray. Cover and bake at 350° for 20 minutes or until heated. Uncover and sprinkle with cheese. Bake an additional 5 minutes or until cheese melts. Yield: 6 servings (108 calories [20% from fat] per serving).

FAT 2.4g (SAT 1.1g, MONO 0.2g, POLY 0.3g)
PROTEIN 4.1g CARBOHYDRATE 16.0g
FIBER 0.3g CHOLESTEROL 6mg SODIUM 572mg

CONFETTI RICE

Vegetable cooking spray
2 teaspoons reduced-calorie margarine
1 cup long-grain rice, uncooked
½ cup sliced green onions
1½ cups canned low-sodium chicken broth, undiluted
½ cup dry sherry
1 (2½-ounce) jar sliced mushrooms, undrained
1 (2-ounce) jar diced pimiento, undrained
½ teaspoon salt
½ teaspoon freshly ground pepper
⅛ teaspoon garlic powder

Coat a large saucepan with cooking spray; add margarine. Place over medium-high heat until margarine melts. Add rice and green onions; sauté until rice is lightly browned. Stir in broth and remaining ingredients. Bring to a boil; cover, reduce heat, and simmer 20 to 25 minutes or until rice is tender and liquid is absorbed. Yield: 8 servings (111 calories [10% from fat] per ½-cup serving).

FAT 1.2g (SAT 0.2g, MONO 0.4g, POLY 0.4g)
PROTEIN 2.6g CARBOHYDRATE 21.9g
FIBER 0.5g CHOLESTEROL 0mg SODIUM 210mg

CREOLE RICE

Vegetable cooking spray
1 teaspoon reduced-calorie margarine
1 cup long-grain rice, uncooked
½ cup chopped onion
½ cup chopped green pepper
1 (14½-ounce) can no-salt-added stewed tomatoes
1 (13¾-ounce) can no-salt-added chicken broth, undiluted
1 teaspoon dried parsley flakes
½ teaspoon garlic powder
½ teaspoon dried whole oregano
¼ teaspoon salt

Coat a large nonstick skillet with cooking spray; add margarine. Place over medium-high heat until margarine melts. Add rice; sauté 2 to 3 minutes or until lightly browned, stirring frequently. Add onion and green pepper; sauté 3 to 4 minutes or until vegetables are tender. Remove from heat, and set aside.

Drain tomatoes, reserving liquid; set tomatoes aside. Add enough water to tomato liquid to equal ¾ cup. Combine tomato liquid and chicken broth in a medium saucepan; bring to a boil. Stir in rice mixture, tomato, parsley flakes, and remaining ingredients. Bring to a boil; cover, reduce heat, and simmer 20 to 25 minutes or until rice is tender and liquid is absorbed. Yield: 9 servings (107 calories [5% from fat] per ½-cup serving).

FAT 0.6g (SAT 0.1g, MONO 0.2g, POLY 0.2g)
PROTEIN 2.4g CARBOHYDRATE 22.5g
FIBER 0.9g CHOLESTEROL 0mg SODIUM 80mg

GREEN CHILE RICE

Vegetable cooking spray
½ cup chopped onion
2 cups cooked long-grain rice
　(cooked without salt or fat)
1 (8-ounce) carton nonfat sour
　cream alternative
1 (4-ounce) can chopped green
　chiles, drained
½ cup nonfat cottage cheese
½ teaspoon salt
¼ teaspoon ground bay leaves
¼ teaspoon pepper
¾ cup (3 ounces) shredded
　reduced-fat sharp Cheddar cheese

Coat a nonstick skillet with cooking spray; place over medium-high heat until hot. Add onion; sauté until tender. Stir in rice and next 6 ingredients. Stir in half of Cheddar cheese.

Spoon rice mixture into a 1-quart casserole coated with cooking spray. Bake at 375° for 20 minutes. Sprinkle with remaining half of cheese. Bake an additional 5 minutes or until cheese melts. Yield: 6 servings (165 calories [16% from fat] per serving).

FAT 2.9g (SAT 1.6g, MONO 0.8g, POLY 0.1g)
PROTEIN 11.2g   CARBOHYDRATE 22.0g
FIBER 0.8g   CHOLESTEROL 10mg   SODIUM 419mg

Adding dried apricots and prunes is a delicious way to lightly sweeten rice and enhance the grain's wholesome reputation. Fruited Rice goes well with poultry and pork.

FRUITED RICE

Vegetable cooking spray
1 teaspoon reduced-calorie
　margarine
½ cup chopped onion
2 cups canned low-sodium
　chicken broth, undiluted
1 cup long-grain rice, uncooked
¼ cup diced dried apricots
¼ cup diced dried pitted
　prunes
¼ teaspoon ground thyme

Coat a large saucepan with vegetable cooking spray; add margarine. Place over medium-high heat until margarine melts. Add onion; sauté 3 to 4 minutes or until tender. Add chicken broth; bring to a boil. Stir in rice and remaining ingredients; cover, reduce heat, and simmer 20 to 25 minutes or until rice is tender and liquid is absorbed. Yield: 6 servings (167 calories [8% from fat] per ½-cup serving).

FAT 1.5g (SAT 0.3g, MONO 0.5g, POLY 0.3g)
PROTEIN 3.5g   CARBOHYDRATE 35.1g
FIBER 0.8g   CHOLESTEROL 0mg   SODIUM 42mg

Fluff cooked rice gently with a fork just before serving to separate the grains and combine any added ingredients.

ORIENTAL RICE

Vegetable cooking spray
¾ cup finely chopped onion
3½ cups canned low-sodium
  chicken broth, undiluted
1½ tablespoons dry sherry
1½ tablespoons low-sodium soy
  sauce
1½ teaspoons dark sesame oil
¾ teaspoon hot sauce
1¾ cups converted rice, uncooked
¾ cup sliced green onions

Coat a large saucepan with cooking spray; place over medium-high heat until hot. Add onion; sauté until tender. Stir in broth and next 4 ingredients; bring to a boil. Remove from heat, and stir in rice. Cover, reduce heat, and simmer 20 to 25 minutes or until rice is tender and liquid is absorbed. Remove from heat, and stir in green onions. Yield: 12 servings (118 calories [10% from fat] per ½-cup serving).

FAT 1.3g (SAT 0.3g, MONO 0.5g, POLY 0.4g)
PROTEIN 2.7g CARBOHYDRATE 23.1g
FIBER 0.5g CHOLESTEROL 0mg SODIUM 76mg

SAFFRON RICE

Vegetable cooking spray
¼ cup chopped onion
1 clove garlic, minced
⅔ cup long-grain rice, uncooked
1⅓ cups canned no-salt-added
  chicken broth, undiluted
¼ teaspoon salt
⅛ teaspoon ground saffron

Coat a saucepan with cooking spray; place over medium-high heat until hot. Add onion and garlic; sauté until tender. Add rice; cook 1 minute, stirring constantly. Stir in chicken broth, salt, and saffron. Bring to a boil; cover, reduce heat, and simmer 20 to 25 minutes or until rice is tender and liquid is absorbed. Yield: 4 servings (129 calories [3% from fat] per ½-cup serving).

FAT 0.4g (SAT 0.1g, MONO 0.1g, POLY 0.1g)
PROTEIN 2.6g CARBOHYDRATE 27.0g
FIBER 0.5g CHOLESTEROL 0mg SODIUM 150mg

SPICY MEXICAN RICE

Vegetable cooking spray
⅔ cup long-grain rice, uncooked
⅓ cup chopped onion
⅓ cup chopped green pepper
1 cup chopped tomato
½ teaspoon chili powder
¼ teaspoon salt
¼ teaspoon garlic powder
¼ teaspoon ground red pepper
1⅓ cups canned no-salt-added beef
  broth, undiluted

Coat a large nonstick skillet with vegetable cooking spray; place over medium-high heat until hot. Add rice, onion, and green pepper; sauté until rice is lightly browned and vegetables are crisp-tender. Stir in tomato and remaining ingredients. Bring to a boil; cover, reduce heat, and simmer 20 to 25 minutes or until rice is tender and liquid is absorbed. Yield: 6 servings (94 calories [4% from fat] per ½-cup serving).

FAT 0.4g (SAT 0.1g, MONO 0.1g, POLY 0.1g)
PROTEIN 2.1g CARBOHYDRATE 19.8g
FIBER 1.0g CHOLESTEROL 0mg SODIUM 106mg

JALAPEÑO RICE DRESSING

1⅓ cups water
⅔ cup long-grain rice, uncooked
1 cup cornmeal
½ teaspoon salt
½ teaspoon baking soda
1 cup skim milk
1 (8¾-ounce) can no-salt-added
  cream-style corn
½ cup chopped onion
½ cup frozen egg substitute,
  thawed
1 tablespoon vegetable oil
3 jalapeño peppers, seeded and
  minced
Vegetable cooking spray
¾ cup (3 ounces) shredded
  reduced-fat Monterey Jack cheese

Bring water to a boil in a saucepan; stir in rice. Cover, reduce heat, and simmer 20 to 25 minutes or until rice is tender and liquid is absorbed.

Combine cornmeal, salt, and baking soda in a large bowl; stir well. Stir in rice, milk, and next 5 ingredients. Pour mixture into an 11- x 7- x 2-inch baking dish coated with vegetable cooking spray. Bake, uncovered, at 350° for 40 to 45 minutes or until golden. Sprinkle evenly with cheese; bake an additional 5 minutes or until cheese melts. Yield: 12 servings (136 calories [20% from fat] per serving).

FAT 3.1g (SAT 1.1g, MONO 0.5g, POLY 0.8g)
PROTEIN 5.8g CARBOHYDRATE 21.8g
FIBER 1.6g CHOLESTEROL 5mg SODIUM 208mg

Wild Rice with Mushrooms is a hearty side dish that will earn the status of a special request recipe. Its nutlike flavor complements most meats and fish.

BROWN RICE PILAF

½ cup diced carrot
½ cup diced sweet red pepper
1 cup brown rice, uncooked
2 large cloves garlic, minced
½ teaspoon salt
½ teaspoon dried whole oregano
½ teaspoon dried whole thyme
3 cups water

Arrange carrot and red pepper in a vegetable steamer over boiling water. Cover and steam 2 to 3 minutes or until vegetables are crisp-tender. Drain well, and set aside.

Combine rice and remaining ingredients in a large saucepan. Bring to a boil; cover, reduce heat, and simmer 45 minutes.

Add vegetable mixture to rice mixture; toss gently. Cover and cook an additional 5 minutes or until rice is tender and liquid is absorbed. Yield: 8 servings (93 calories [7% from fat] per ½-cup serving).

FAT 0.7g (SAT 0.2g, MONO 0.3g, POLY 0.3g)
PROTEIN 2.1g   CARBOHYDRATE 19.6g
FIBER 1.3g   CHOLESTEROL 0mg   SODIUM 152mg

Flavorful Rice Without All the Fat

Increase the flavor of rice without adding a lot of fat or calories by cooking it in chicken broth, beef broth, or consommé. Orange juice or apple juice can add the perfect flavor to rice that will accompany pork or poultry.

WILD RICE WITH MUSHROOMS

½ cup wild rice, uncooked
1½ cups canned no-salt-added chicken broth, undiluted
Vegetable cooking spray
2 teaspoons olive oil
2 large shallots, minced
1½ cups thinly sliced fresh mushrooms
1 cup coarsely chopped sweet red pepper
⅓ cup dry sherry
½ teaspoon salt
¼ teaspoon pepper
¼ cup minced fresh parsley

Rinse rice in 3 changes of hot water; drain well. Bring chicken broth to a boil in a medium saucepan. Add rice; cover, reduce heat, and simmer 1 hour or until rice is tender and liquid is absorbed. Set aside.

Coat a medium nonstick skillet with cooking spray; add oil. Place over medium-high heat until hot. Add shallot, mushrooms, and sweet red pepper; sauté until tender. Stir in sherry, salt, and pepper. Bring mixture to a boil; reduce heat, and simmer, uncovered, 2 minutes. Remove from heat, and stir in rice and parsley. Yield: 6 servings (89 calories [25% from fat] per ½-cup serving).

FAT 2.5g (SAT 0.4g, MONO 1.4g, POLY 0.4g)
PROTEIN 3.3g   CARBOHYDRATE 14.1g
FIBER 1.4g   CHOLESTEROL 0mg   SODIUM 234mg

Colorful Vegetable Risotto

4 cups canned low-sodium chicken
  broth, undiluted
1 tablespoon lemon juice
Vegetable cooking spray
1 cup Arborio rice, uncooked
½ cup diced carrot
½ cup sliced fresh mushrooms
½ cup diced sweet red pepper
½ small zucchini, cut into julienne
  strips
2 tablespoons minced shallots
2 tablespoons grated Parmesan
  cheese
¼ teaspoon salt
¼ teaspoon pepper

Combine chicken broth and lemon juice in a medium saucepan. Bring to a boil; cover, reduce heat to low, and keep warm.

Coat a large nonstick skillet with vegetable cooking spray; place skillet over medium-high heat until hot. Add uncooked rice, carrot, mushrooms, sweet red pepper, zucchini, and shallots. Sauté mixture 2 to 3 minutes or until rice is translucent and vegetables are crisp-tender.

Add 1 cup warm broth mixture to rice mixture. Bring to a boil; reduce heat, and simmer, stirring constantly, 5 minutes or until liquid is absorbed. Repeat procedure 6 times, adding ½ cup warm broth mixture at a time (the entire process should take about 30 minutes). Cook, stirring constantly, until rice is tender and liquid is absorbed.

Remove rice mixture from heat; add cheese, salt, and pepper, stirring gently to blend. Yield: 8 servings (123 calories [11% from fat] per ½-cup serving).

FAT 1.5g (SAT 0.5g, MONO 0.5g, POLY 0.3g)
PROTEIN 3.8g CARBOHYDRATE 23.6g
FIBER 0.9g CHOLESTEROL 1mg SODIUM 140mg

LEGUMES

Legumes are plants that produce pods containing edible seeds. The best known are black beans, black-eyed peas, chick-peas (garbanzo beans), kidney beans, lentils, lima beans, peas (split, whole, yellow, and green), pinto beans, and white beans (navy and Great Northern).

Legumes are packed with complex carbohydrates, fiber, vitamins, minerals, and protein — more protein than any other edible plant food. At the same time, legumes have no cholesterol, are very low in fat and sodium, and are inexpensive to prepare.

Sorting and Soaking Legumes

Before cooking, always rinse and sort legumes to remove any debris that may have been missed in the initial cleaning.

All dried legumes, except split peas, lentils, and black-eyed peas, must be soaked before cooking. For the longer soaking method, cover legumes with cold water to two inches above the legumes, removing any that float to the top (these legumes are premature). Soak the legumes at room temperature for six to eight hours or overnight.

For a quicker soaking method, cover the legumes with cold water to two inches above the legumes, removing any that float to the top. Bring to a rolling boil over medium-high heat; boil two minutes. Remove from heat; cover, and let stand one hour. Drain and cook as directed.

Cooking Legumes

The cooking time varies with the age of the legumes. The older they are, the longer they take to cook. Rapid boiling and frequent stirring will cause legume skins to break, so don't try to rush the cooking process. To test for doneness, press a cooked legume between your fingers; it should be slightly firm, not mushy, and the skin should be tender.

Acidic ingredients such as tomato, vinegar, and molasses tend to harden the legumes' skin and lengthen the cooking time. This hardening also occurs when salt is added to the cooking water. Add these ingredients only after the legumes have cooked.

Cuban Black Beans and Rice

Olive oil-flavored vegetable
  cooking spray
1 cup chopped onion
½ cup chopped green pepper
½ teaspoon ground cumin
⅛ teaspoon ground coriander
⅛ teaspoon ground red pepper
1 (15-ounce) can black beans,
  rinsed and drained
1 cup cooked long-grain rice
  (cooked without salt or fat)
¾ cup chopped tomato
1 tablespoon red wine vinegar

Coat a nonstick skillet with cooking spray; place over medium heat until hot. Add onion and green pepper; sauté until crisp-tender. Add cumin, coriander, and red pepper; sauté 3 minutes. Stir in beans and remaining ingredients, and cook until heated. Yield: 6 servings (107 calories [5% from fat] per ½-cup serving).

FAT 0.6g (SAT 0.1g, MONO 0.1g, POLY 0.2g)
PROTEIN 4.8g CARBOHYDRATE 21.3g
FIBER 2.8g CHOLESTEROL 0mg SODIUM 112mg

SOUTHWESTERN BLACK BEANS

1½ cups dried black beans
2½ cups water
1 cup chopped onion
3 cloves garlic, minced
1 jalapeño pepper, seeded and
    minced
1 bay leaf
½ teaspoon salt
¼ teaspoon pepper
¼ cup (1 ounce) shredded reduced-
    fat Monterey Jack cheese

Sort and wash beans; place beans in a saucepan. Cover with water to a depth of 2 inches above beans; let soak overnight. Drain and rinse beans.

Combine beans, 2½ cups water, and next 4 ingredients in pan. Bring to a boil; cover, reduce heat, and simmer 1 hour or until beans are tender. Remove and discard bay leaf.

Drain and mash beans; stir in salt and pepper. Transfer bean mixture to a serving bowl; sprinkle evenly with cheese. Cover and let stand until cheese melts. Serve immediately. Yield: 6 servings (193 calories [7% from fat] per ½-cup serving).

FAT 1.6g (SAT 0.7g, MONO 0.1g, POLY 0.4g)
PROTEIN 12.3g   CARBOHYDRATE 33.8g
FIBER 7.0g   CHOLESTEROL 3mg   SODIUM 229mg

CALICO LIMA BEANS

Vegetable cooking spray
1 teaspoon reduced-calorie
    margarine
⅔ cup chopped onion
½ cup chopped celery
½ cup chopped green pepper
1 (16-ounce) package frozen lima
    beans
1 cup seeded, diced tomato
1 cup spicy-hot vegetable juice
    cocktail

Coat a large nonstick skillet with cooking spray; add margarine. Place

over medium heat until margarine melts. Add onion, celery, and pepper; sauté 3 to 4 minutes or until tender. Stir in lima beans, tomato, and vegetable juice cocktail. Bring mixture to a boil; cover, reduce heat, and simmer 12 to 15 minutes or until beans are tender, stirring occasionally. Yield: 9 servings (81 calories [6% from fat] per ½-cup serving).

FAT 0.6g (SAT 0.1g, MONO 0.1g, POLY 0.2g)
PROTEIN 4.3g   CARBOHYDRATE 15.1g
FIBER 1.6g   CHOLESTEROL 0mg   SODIUM 185mg

SOUTHERN-STYLE BLACK-EYED PEAS

4 cups shelled fresh black-eyed
    peas
2 cups water
¾ cup minced onion
½ cup chopped lean cooked ham
½ teaspoon salt
¼ teaspoon pepper

Combine all ingredients in a large saucepan, stirring well. Bring mixture

to a boil over medium-high heat; cover, reduce heat, and simmer 30 to 35 minutes or until peas are tender, stirring occasionally. Yield: 10 servings (88 calories [9% from fat] per ½-cup serving).

FAT 0.9g (SAT 0.3g, MONO 0.2g, POLY 0.2g)
PROTEIN 6.7g   CARBOHYDRATE 13.7g
FIBER 1.3g   CHOLESTEROL 4mg   SODIUM 231mg

HERBED LENTILS WITH PIMIENTO

4 cups water
1 small onion, chopped
1 stalk celery, halved
½ teaspoon dried whole thyme
1 bay leaf
½ teaspoon whole black
    peppercorns
1 cup dried lentils
3 tablespoons water
3 tablespoons red wine vinegar
¼ teaspoon chicken-flavored
    bouillon granules
1½ teaspoons Dijon mustard
½ teaspoon salt
1 (4-ounce) jar diced pimiento,
    drained
2 tablespoons sliced green onions
1 tablespoon chopped fresh parsley

Combine first 4 ingredients in a large saucepan. Place bay leaf and peppercorns on a small piece of cheesecloth; tie ends of cheesecloth securely. Add cheesecloth bag to mixture in pan. Bring to a boil; cover, reduce heat, and simmer 20 minutes. Add lentils. Cover and cook 25 to 30 minutes or until lentils are tender. Remove and discard celery and cheesecloth bag.

Combine water, vinegar, bouillon granules, mustard, and salt in a small bowl; stir well. Add vinegar mixture, pimiento, green onions, and parsley to lentil mixture; toss gently to combine. Yield: 6 servings (132 calories [3% from fat] per ½-cup serving).

FAT 0.5g (SAT 0.1g, MONO 0.1g, POLY 0.2g)
PROTEIN 10.3g   CARBOHYDRATE 22.7g
FIBER 4.4g   CHOLESTEROL 0mg   SODIUM 274mg

OLD-FASHIONED BAKED BEANS

1 (16-ounce) package dried
    navy beans
1½ quarts water
2 cups chopped onion
1 cup reduced-calorie catsup
½ cup chopped lean cooked
    ham
½ cup molasses
1 tablespoon prepared mustard
½ teaspoon salt
½ teaspoon pepper
Vegetable cooking spray

Sort and wash beans; place beans in a large Dutch oven. Cover with water to a depth of 2 inches above beans; let soak overnight. Drain and rinse beans.

Combine beans, 1½ quarts water, and chopped onion in pan. Bring to a boil; cover, reduce heat, and simmer 2 hours. Drain bean mixture, reserving 2 cups cooking liquid.

Combine bean mixture, reserved cooking liquid, catsup, and next 5 ingredients in a large bowl; stir well. Pour mixture into a 3-quart casserole coated with cooking spray. Bake, uncovered, at 350° for 1 hour and 30 minutes or until beans are tender. Yield: 15 servings (150 calories [4% from fat] per ½-cup serving).

FAT 0.7g (SAT 0.2g, MONO 0.1g, POLY 0.2g)
PROTEIN 8.0g CARBOHYDRATE 28.2g
FIBER 3.4g CHOLESTEROL 2mg SODIUM 171mg

Before cooking, carefully sort through the dried beans to remove and discard any rocks or darkened or blemished beans that may have been overlooked during packaging.

Old-Fashioned Baked Beans gets its traditional flavor from ham — in this case, lean cooked ham that helps keep the fat content low.

The enticing aroma of Old-Fashioned Baked Beans will draw family members to the kitchen long before the dish is ready.

To test the baked beans for doneness, you can spear a couple with a fork or you can press 1 or 2 beans between your fingers to feel how tender they are.

Pastas

For years, spaghetti with meat sauce and macaroni and cheese were the most common pasta dishes. Today, such pastas as capellini, fettuccine, linguine, and tortellini, just to name a few, have become household words.

When it comes to low-fat eating, the amount of fat in pasta is not as much of a concern as the fat in the rich sauce that usually accompanies it. The recipes featured in this section offer a variety of low-fat pasta dishes.

Pastas are available many shapes, sizes, flavors, and colors. Whether you choose dried, fresh, or frozen pasta, the nutritional value is about the same and all contain very little fat. Even egg noodles contain only a modest amount of fat and cholesterol.

Dried pastas are a favorite because they are inexpensive and have a long shelf life. The best dried pastas are made from semolina, a high-protein flour milled from durum wheat.

Fresh pasta is often made with eggs and all-purpose flour, and it cooks quickly. Look for fresh pasta in the refrigerator section at the supermarket or in specialty stores.

Cook pasta in plenty of water — about six quarts to a pound of dried pasta. It is not necessary to add the salt and oil that are called for on some packages. Bring the water to a rolling boil, and add the pasta a little at a time so the water does not stop boiling. For long pasta such as spaghetti, hold one end and gently push the other end into the water as it softens.

Pasta is best cooked "al dente," or "to the tooth," so that it is soft and pliable but firm enough to have a slight resistance when chewed. Start testing dried pasta for doneness after four or five minutes of cooking; test fresh pasta after about one minute.

Macaroni and Cheese

1 (8-ounce) package elbow
   macaroni, uncooked
Vegetable cooking spray
3 tablespoons margarine
¼ cup finely chopped onion
¼ cup all-purpose flour
2 cups evaporated skimmed milk,
   divided
1½ cups (6 ounces) shredded
   reduced-fat sharp Cheddar cheese
½ teaspoon salt
½ teaspoon dry mustard
¼ teaspoon pepper
¼ cup frozen egg substitute,
   thawed
Paprika

Cook macaroni according to package directions, omitting salt and fat; drain well, and set aside.

Coat a medium saucepan with vegetable cooking spray; add margarine. Place over medium-high heat until margarine melts. Add onion; sauté until tender. Combine flour and ½ cup milk; stir until smooth. Add flour mixture to onion, stirring well. Add remaining 1½ cups milk to flour mixture. Cook over medium heat, stirring constantly, until mixture is thickened and bubbly. Remove from heat; add cheese and next 3 ingredients, stirring until cheese melts. Gradually stir about one-fourth of hot mixture into egg substitute; add to remaining hot mixture, stirring constantly.

Combine macaroni and cheese sauce; stir well. Pour mixture into a 2-quart casserole coated with cooking spray. Sprinkle with paprika. Bake at 350° for 30 to 35 minutes or until bubbly. Yield: 10 servings (223 calories [29% from fat] per serving).

FAT 7.3g (SAT 2.7g, MONO 2.5g, POLY 1.4g)
PROTEIN 12.8g CARBOHYDRATE 26.3g
FIBER 0.7g CHOLESTEROL 13mg SODIUM 350mg

Almond Orzo

2 quarts water
⅔ cup orzo, uncooked
3 tablespoons grated Parmesan
   cheese
2 tablespoons blanched slivered
   almonds, toasted
2 tablespoons skim milk
¼ teaspoon salt
⅛ teaspoon paprika

Bring water to a boil in a saucepan. Add orzo; allow water to return to a boil. Cook, uncovered, 10 to 12 minutes or just until orzo is tender; drain well.

Combine cooked orzo, Parmesan cheese, and remaining ingredients in a medium bowl; toss well. Yield: 4 servings (156 calories [18% from fat] per ½-cup serving).

FAT 3.2g (SAT 0.9g, MONO 1.4g, POLY 0.6g)
PROTEIN 6.5g CARBOHYDRATE 25.0g
FIBER 1.1g CHOLESTEROL 3mg SODIUM 223mg

Greek-Style Capellini lends an ethnic flair to healthy eating.

CARAWAY FETTUCCINE

⅓ cup evaporated skimmed milk
⅓ cup Chablis or other dry white
   wine
1½ tablespoons reduced-calorie
   margarine
3 cups cooked fettuccine (cooked
   without salt or fat)
3 tablespoons minced fresh parsley
2 teaspoons caraway seeds
¼ teaspoon salt
⅛ teaspoon garlic powder

Combine milk, wine, and margarine in a saucepan; place over medium heat. Cook, stirring constantly,
until margarine melts. Add fettuccine
and remaining ingredients. Cook,
tossing gently, until thoroughly
heated. Yield: 4 servings (235 calories
[15% from fat] per ¾-cup serving).

FAT 3.9g (SAT 0.5g, MONO 1.2g, POLY 1.6g)
PROTEIN 8.4g   CARBOHYDRATE 41.6g
FIBER 2.4g   CHOLESTEROL 1mg   SODIUM 216mg

GREEK-STYLE CAPELLINI

6 ounces capellini, uncooked
1 pound fresh broccoli
Vegetable cooking spray
1 teaspoon olive oil
1 clove garlic, minced
½ cup canned low-sodium chicken
   broth, undiluted
1 teaspoon Greek seasoning
2 cups peeled, seeded, and chopped
   tomato
2 tablespoons sliced ripe olives
¼ teaspoon freshly ground pepper
½ cup (2 ounces) crumbled feta
   cheese

Prepare capellini according to
package directions, omitting salt and
fat. Drain well, and set aside.

Trim off large leaves of broccoli;
remove tough ends of lower stalks.
Wash broccoli thoroughly, and cut
into small flowerets; cut stems
diagonally into ½-inch pieces.

Coat a large nonstick skillet with
cooking spray; add oil. Place over medium-high heat until hot. Add garlic;
sauté 1 minute. Add broccoli; sauté
until crisp-tender. Stir in broth and
Greek seasoning. Bring to a boil; stir
in tomato and capellini. Reduce heat,
and simmer until thoroughly heated.
Add olives and pepper; toss gently.
Transfer to a serving bowl, and sprinkle with cheese. Serve immediately.
Yield: 7 servings (149 calories [22%
from fat] per 1-cup serving).

FAT 3.6g (SAT 1.5g, MONO 1.3g, POLY 0.5g)
PROTEIN 6.3g   CARBOHYDRATE 23.9g
FIBER 2.6g   CHOLESTEROL 7mg   SODIUM 316mg

Try a Different Pasta

Uncooked pastas of similar sizes
and shapes can be interchanged in
recipes when measured by weight,
not volume. However, cooked pasta
must be substituted cup for cup.
Allow 1 ounce of dry pasta or
½ to 1 cup cooked pasta per serving.

Linguine, spaghetti, or vermicelli:
4 ounces dry = 2 to 3 cups cooked
8 ounces dry = 4 to 5 cups cooked
16 ounces dry = 8 to 9 cups cooked

Macaroni, penne, rotini, or shells:
4 ounces dry = 2½ cups cooked
8 ounces dry = 4½ cups cooked

Fine or medium egg noodles:
4 ounces dry = 2 to 3 cups cooked
8 ounces dry = 4 to 5 cups cooked

Fettuccine Primavera

½ pound fresh asparagus spears
Vegetable cooking spray
2 tablespoons reduced-calorie margarine
2 cups sliced fresh mushrooms
1 cup small broccoli flowerets
1 cup thinly sliced carrot
½ cup sliced green onions
½ cup medium-size sweet red pepper, cut into julienne strips
2 cloves garlic, minced
3 tablespoons chopped fresh basil
½ cup Chablis or other dry white wine
¼ teaspoon salt
¼ teaspoon pepper
3½ cups cooked fettuccine (cooked without salt or fat)
3 tablespoons freshly grated Parmesan cheese

Snap off tough ends of asparagus. Remove scales from spears with a knife or vegetable peeler, if desired. Cut asparagus diagonally into ¾-inch pieces.

Coat a large nonstick skillet with cooking spray; add margarine. Place over medium-high heat until margarine melts. Add asparagus, mushrooms, and next 6 ingredients; sauté until vegetables are crisp-tender. Add wine, salt, and pepper; cook 2 minutes, stirring constantly. Add fettuccine and cheese; toss well. Serve immediately. Yield: 7 servings (169 calories [12% from fat] per 1-cup serving).

FAT 2.3g (SAT 0.5g, MONO 0.6g, POLY 0.8g)
PROTEIN 6.6g CARBOHYDRATE 31.4g
FIBER 3.2g CHOLESTEROL 1mg SODIUM 139mg

Ratatouille and Pasta Toss

Vegetable cooking spray
1¼ cups chopped onion
1 clove garlic, minced
1 (1-pound) eggplant, cubed
1 (28-ounce) can no-salt-added whole tomatoes, undrained and chopped
½ teaspoon dried whole basil
½ teaspoon dried whole thyme
¼ teaspoon salt
¼ teaspoon dried fennel seeds, crushed
1 bay leaf
3 cups cooked fusilli (cooked without salt or fat)
½ cup grated Parmesan cheese
½ cup chopped fresh parsley

Coat a large Dutch oven with cooking spray; place over medium heat until hot. Add onion and garlic; sauté 3 to 4 minutes or until tender. Add eggplant; cook 3 minutes, stirring occasionally. Stir in tomato and next 5 ingredients. Bring to a boil; cover, reduce heat, and simmer 20 minutes, stirring occasionally.

Remove and discard bay leaf. Add fusilli, cheese, and parsley; toss well. Yield: 9 servings (128 calories [13% from fat] per 1-cup serving).

FAT 1.8g (SAT 0.9g, MONO 0.5g, POLY 0.2g)
PROTEIN 5.8g CARBOHYDRATE 23.1g
FIBER 2.8g CHOLESTEROL 4mg SODIUM 164mg

Linguine in Sour Cream-Wine Sauce

6 ounces linguine, uncooked
¼ cup nonfat sour cream alternative
3 tablespoons Chablis or other dry white wine
1½ tablespoons grated Parmesan cheese
⅛ teaspoon salt
⅛ teaspoon pepper
Vegetable cooking spray
1⅓ cups sliced fresh mushrooms
½ cup chopped green onions
1 tablespoon chopped fresh parsley

Cook linguine according to package directions, omitting salt and fat. Drain well. Combine sour cream alternative and next 4 ingredients in a medium bowl; stir well. Add linguine; toss well, and set aside.

Coat a large nonstick skillet with vegetable cooking spray; place over medium heat until hot. Add mushrooms and green onions; sauté until tender.

Add linguine mixture; cook, tossing gently, until mixture is thoroughly heated. Transfer linguine mixture to a serving bowl; sprinkle with parsley, and serve immediately. Yield: 4 servings (186 calories [7% from fat] per ¾-cup serving).

FAT 1.5g (SAT 0.5g, MONO 0.3g, POLY 0.3g)
PROTEIN 7.8g CARBOHYDRATE 34.6g
FIBER 1.5g CHOLESTEROL 1mg SODIUM 125mg

Gently push long pasta such as spaghetti into boiling water as the pasta softens. By following this method, you don't have to break the pasta to fit it into the pan.

Pasta and Red Peppers

4½ ounces linguine, uncooked
Vegetable cooking spray
1½ teaspoons reduced-calorie
   margarine
1 medium-size sweet red pepper,
   cut into strips
¼ cup sliced green onions
1 large clove garlic, minced
⅓ cup commercial oil-free Italian
   dressing

Cook linguine according to package directions, omitting salt and fat. Drain well, and set aside.

Coat a medium nonstick skillet with cooking spray; add margarine. Place over medium-high heat until margarine melts. Add pepper, green onions, and garlic; sauté until tender. Stir in Italian dressing; cook until thoroughly heated, stirring occasionally. Add pasta; cook, tossing gently, just until mixture is thoroughly heated. Yield: 2 servings (293 calories [10% from fat] per 1-cup serving).

FAT 3.4g (SAT 0.9g, MONO 2.2g, POLY 2.9g)
PROTEIN 9.1g CARBOHYDRATE 56.2g
FIBER 2.6g CHOLESTEROL 0mg SODIUM 467mg

Basic Pasta

2 eggs
1 teaspoon olive oil
½ teaspoon salt
1¼ cups plus 1 tablespoon
   all-purpose flour, divided

Position mixing blade in food processor bowl; add eggs, olive oil, and salt. Process 30 seconds or until blended. Add 1¼ cups flour; process 30 seconds to 1 minute or until mixture forms a ball.

Sprinkle remaining 1 tablespoon flour evenly over work surface. Turn dough out onto floured surface. Knead dough until smooth and elastic (about 10 to 15 minutes). Wrap dough in plastic wrap, and let rest 10 minutes. Use Basic Pasta dough to create one of the variations below.

Cannelloni: Divide Basic Pasta dough into 2 equal portions. Working with 1 portion at a time, pass dough through smooth rollers of pasta machine on widest setting. Continue moving the width gauge to narrower settings; pass dough through rollers once at each setting.

Roll dough to desired thinness (about ⅛ inch). Cut each dough sheet into 7 (5¾- x 5-inch) rectangles. Hang pasta on a wooden drying rack (dry no longer than 30 minutes). Cook pasta in 3 quarts boiling water 2 minutes. Drain. Yield: 14 shells (55 calories [20% from fat] each).

FAT 1.2g (SAT 0.3g, MONO 0.5g, POLY 0.2g)
PROTEIN 2.1g CARBOHYDRATE 8.6g
FIBER 0.3g CHOLESTEROL 32mg SODIUM 93mg

Fettuccine: Divide Basic Pasta dough into 4 equal portions. Working with 1 portion at a time, pass dough through smooth rollers of pasta machine on widest setting. Continue moving the width gauge to narrower settings; pass dough through rollers once at each setting.

Roll dough to desired thinness (about 1⁄16 inch). Pass each dough sheet through fettuccine cutting rollers of machine. Hang pasta on a wooden drying rack (dry no longer than 30 minutes). Cook pasta in 3 quarts boiling water 2 minutes. Drain; serve immediately. Yield: 6 servings (127 calories [19% from fat] per ½-cup serving).

FAT 2.7g (SAT 0.7g, MONO 1.2g, POLY 0.4g)
PROTEIN 4.9g CARBOHYDRATE 20.1g
FIBER 0.7g CHOLESTEROL 74mg SODIUM 218mg

Lasagna: Divide Basic Pasta dough into 4 equal portions. Working with 1 portion at a time, pass dough through smooth rollers of pasta machine on widest setting. Continue moving the width gauge to narrower settings; pass dough through rollers once at each setting.

Roll dough to desired thinness (about 1⁄16 inch). Cut each dough sheet into 4 (11- x 2-inch) strips. Hang pasta on a wooden drying rack (dry no longer than 30 minutes). Cook pasta in 3 quarts boiling water 2 minutes. Drain. Yield: 16 noodles (48 calories [19% from fat] each).

FAT 1.0g (SAT 0.3g, MONO 0.5g, POLY 0.2g)
PROTEIN 1.8g CARBOHYDRATE 7.5g
FIBER 0.3g CHOLESTEROL 28mg SODIUM 82mg

MEATLESS MAIN DISHES

Today's meatless meals have come a long way from the tofu and sprouts of a couple of decades ago. Whether you are a strict vegetarian or you simply want to cut down on fat by choosing a meatless meal once or twice a week, the recipes in this chapter prove that a meal without meat can be satisfying and delicious.

Many Americans are incorporating low-fat eating into their diets, and meatless main dishes are gaining popularity. Hearty grains, legumes, pastas, reduced-fat cheeses, and fresh vegetables are the primary ingredients in these recipes that are low in fat and high in protein and fiber. These meatless main dishes are also rich sources of vitamins and minerals.

Protein is made of up of 22 amino acids. Eight of these cannot be manufactured by the body and must be obtained from food sources, whether animal or vegetable. Animal products such as meat and eggs contain all eight of these essential amino acids, making them complete proteins. Plant foods are missing one or more essential amino acids.

Strict vegetarians count on plant sources to provide all amino acids. This makes it necessary to eat plant foods that have complementary proteins — those that work together to supply all the essential amino acids. Examples of complementary combinations include red beans and rice, corn and lima beans, lentils and spaghetti, and tofu and couscous.

If you are not a strict vegetarian or are just trying to cut back on your consumption of meat, combine a plant food with eggs or low-fat dairy products, both of which are complete proteins. (But keep in mind that egg yolks are high in cholesterol and should be limited to four per week for healthy eating. Fortunately, most of the protein is found in the egg white.) An example of this combination is a vegetable lasagna. The incomplete protein of lasagna noodles is paired with the complete protein of part-skim ricotta and part-skim mozzarella cheeses, and grated Parmesan cheese.

Be aware that butter or margarine, sour cream, and whole milk cheeses can turn meatless main dishes into high-fat disasters. Keep fat to a minimum with products such as skim milk, evaporated skimmed milk, low-fat or nonfat yogurt, reduced-calorie margarine, and reduced-fat cheeses that contain no more than five grams of fat per ounce.

Many low-fat dairy products, especially cheeses, are high in sodium, so some of these meatless main dishes are not considered to be low-sodium entrées. If you are trying to reduce your sodium intake, note the sodium value in the nutrient grid following each recipe. The sodium content can

Vegetable Lasagna (page 124) shows that meatless meals can skimp on fat and calories yet be filled with flavor. One generous serving has a slim 233 calories.

be reduced by omitting any salt that is called for in the ingredient list.

The recipes in this chapter have been analyzed for nutritional content to ensure that they meet dietary requirements for protein. Each serving of these meatless dishes contains at least 10 grams of protein, which is sufficient for a main dish.

BAKED BARLEY AND BEANS

1 cup pearl barley, uncooked
2½ cups canned low-sodium chicken broth, undiluted
Vegetable cooking spray
2 cups sliced fresh mushrooms
1 cup chopped onion
½ cup diced green pepper
1 (15-ounce) can black beans, rinsed and drained
½ teaspoon salt
¼ teaspoon pepper
3 tablespoons sunflower kernels

Spread barley on a baking sheet; bake at 350° for 8 minutes or until lightly browned. Combine barley and chicken broth in a medium saucepan; bring to a boil. Cover, reduce heat, and simmer 20 minutes or until barley is tender and liquid is absorbed.

Coat a nonstick skillet with cooking spray; place over medium-high heat until hot. Add mushrooms, onion, and green pepper; sauté until tender. Stir in barley, beans, salt, and pepper; spoon mixture into a 1½-quart baking dish coated with cooking spray. Cover and bake at 350° for 30 minutes or until thoroughly heated. Sprinkle with sunflower kernels; bake, uncovered, an additional 5 minutes. Yield: 5 servings (269 calories [16% from fat] per serving).

FAT 4.8g (SAT 0.8g, MONO 1.1g, POLY 2.6g)
PROTEIN 11.3g CARBOHYDRATE 48.1g
FIBER 9.6g CHOLESTEROL 0mg SODIUM 399mg

BLACK BEAN ENCHILADAS

2 (15-ounce) cans black beans, rinsed and drained
Vegetable cooking spray
1¼ cups finely chopped onion
2 cloves garlic, minced
1 tablespoon lime juice
½ teaspoon dried whole oregano
¼ teaspoon salt
½ cup nonfat sour cream alternative
1 tablespoon plus 1 teaspoon minced fresh cilantro
8 (6-inch) corn tortillas
Enchilada Sauce (page 185)
1 cup (4 ounces) shredded reduced-fat Monterey Jack cheese

Mash half of beans; set mashed and unmashed beans aside.

Coat a nonstick skillet with cooking spray; place over medium-high heat until hot. Add onion and garlic; sauté until tender. Stir in mashed and unmashed beans, lime juice, oregano, and salt; set aside.

Combine sour cream and cilantro; stir well, and set aside.

Wrap tortillas in aluminum foil; bake at 325° for 12 minutes or until thoroughly heated. Spread 1 tablespoon sour cream mixture over surface of each tortilla. Spoon bean mixture evenly down center of each tortilla. Loosely roll up tortillas.

Spread ¾ cup Enchilada Sauce in an 11- x 7- x 2-inch baking dish coated with cooking spray. Arrange tortillas, seam side down, over sauce. Top tortillas with remaining Enchilada Sauce. Cover and bake at 350° for 15 minutes. Sprinkle evenly with cheese. Bake, uncovered, an additional 5 minutes or until cheese melts. Yield: 8 servings (238 calories [23% from fat] per serving).

FAT 6.1g (SAT 2.1g, MONO 0.9g, POLY 1.6g)
PROTEIN 13.5g CARBOHYDRATE 34.3g
FIBER 5.4g CHOLESTEROL 9mg SODIUM 507mg

SPAGHETTI WITH GARBANZO SAUCE

Vegetable cooking spray
2 teaspoons vegetable oil
1 medium onion, coarsely chopped
1 medium-size green pepper, chopped
2 cloves garlic, minced
1 tablespoon chopped fresh parsley
1 (15-ounce) can garbanzo beans, drained
2 (8-ounce) cans no-salt-added tomato sauce
½ teaspoon dried whole oregano
¼ teaspoon dried whole basil
¼ teaspoon pepper
2 cups cooked spaghetti (cooked without salt or fat)
½ cup (2 ounces) finely shredded reduced-fat sharp Cheddar cheese
1½ tablespoons grated Parmesan cheese

Coat a large nonstick skillet with vegetable cooking spray; add oil. Place over medium-high heat until hot. Add onion, green pepper, garlic, and parsley; sauté 3 to 4 minutes or until vegetables are tender. Add beans and next 4 ingredients; stir well. Bring mixture to a boil over medium heat, stirring occasionally. Cover, reduce heat, and simmer 30 minutes, stirring occasionally.

To serve, top spaghetti with bean mixture. Sprinkle evenly with Cheddar cheese and Parmesan cheese. Yield: 4 servings (438 calories [17% from fat] per serving).

FAT 8.4g (SAT 2.7g, MONO 1.3g, POLY 2.4g)
PROTEIN 19.2g CARBOHYDRATE 72.4g
FIBER 7.6g CHOLESTEROL 11mg SODIUM 294mg

Whether you're planning a Mexican fiesta or a quick meal for hearty appetites, put Bean and Corn Burritos on the menu.

PINTO-TORTILLA MELTS

1 (15-ounce) can pinto beans,
  drained and mashed
½ teaspoon chili powder
¼ teaspoon ground cumin
⅛ teaspoon ground red pepper
6 (6-inch) corn tortillas
¼ cup minced fresh cilantro
2 (4-ounce) cans chopped green
  chiles, undrained
¾ cup (3 ounces) shredded
  reduced-fat sharp Cheddar cheese
Green Chile Sauce

Combine first 4 ingredients; stir well. Spread 2½ tablespoons bean mixture over surface of each tortilla. Top each evenly with cilantro, green chiles, and cheese.

Place tortillas on baking sheet. Bake at 450° for 3 to 5 minutes or until cheese melts. Serve with Green Chile Sauce. Yield: 6 servings (179 calories [20% from fat] per serving).

Green Chile Sauce

1½ cups chopped tomato
⅓ cup chopped onion
1 (4-ounce) can chopped green
  chiles, undrained
1 clove garlic, minced
½ teaspoon chicken-flavored
  bouillon granules

Combine all ingredients in a saucepan. Bring to a boil over medium heat; reduce heat, and simmer, uncovered, 25 minutes, stirring occasionally. Transfer mixture to a bowl; cover and chill. Yield: 1¼ cups.

FAT 4.0g (SAT 1.8g, MONO 1.0g, POLY 0.6g)
PROTEIN 10.4g   CARBOHYDRATE 27.4g
FIBER 4.5g   CHOLESTEROL 9mg   SODIUM 375mg

BEAN AND CORN BURRITOS

Vegetable cooking spray
½ cup chopped onion
¼ cup diced green pepper
1 teaspoon minced pickled jalapeño
  pepper
1 clove garlic, minced
1 teaspoon ground cumin
⅛ teaspoon ground white pepper
1 (16-ounce) can light red kidney
  beans, drained and mashed
½ cup frozen whole kernel corn,
  thawed and drained
4 (8-inch) flour tortillas
¾ cup (3 ounces) shredded
  reduced-fat sharp Cheddar cheese
1 cup commercial medium salsa
¼ cup nonfat sour cream
  alternative
Jalapeño pepper slices (optional)
Fresh cilantro sprigs (optional)

Coat a small nonstick skillet with cooking spray; place over medium heat until hot. Add onion, green pepper, jalapeño pepper, and garlic; sauté until tender. Stir in cumin and white pepper. Cook 1 minute, stirring constantly. Remove from heat; stir in mashed beans and corn.

Spread ½ cup bean mixture evenly over surface of each tortilla. Sprinkle 3 tablespoons cheese down center of each tortilla. Roll up tortillas, and place seam side down on a medium baking sheet. Bake at 425° for 7 to 8 minutes or until thoroughly heated.

For each serving, top each burrito with ¼ cup salsa and 1 tablespoon sour cream. If desired, garnish with jalapeño pepper slices and fresh cilantro sprigs. Yield: 4 servings (355 calories [20% from fat] per serving).

FAT 7.8g (SAT 3.2g, MONO 2.6g, POLY 1.2g)
PROTEIN 18.5g   CARBOHYDRATE 57.1g
FIBER 5.4g   CHOLESTEROL 14mg   SODIUM 316mg

SPICY RED BEANS AND VEGETABLE RICE

¾ pound dried kidney beans
Vegetable cooking spray
1½ tablespoons vegetable oil
1¼ cups chopped onion
2 cloves garlic, minced
2½ cups water
1 tablespoon beef-flavored bouillon
   granules
1 tablespoon honey
½ teaspoon dried whole oregano
½ teaspoon hot sauce
2 bay leaves
Vegetable Rice

Sort and wash beans; place in a Dutch oven. Cover with water to a depth of 2 inches above beans; let soak 8 hours. Drain and rinse beans. Set beans aside.

Coat pan with cooking spray; add oil. Place over medium-high heat until hot. Add onion and garlic; sauté 3 to 4 minutes or until tender. Add beans, water, and next 5 ingredients; bring to a boil. Cover, reduce heat, and simmer 2 hours or until beans are tender. Remove and discard bay leaves. Place ½ cup Vegetable Rice in each of 8 individual serving bowls; top each evenly with bean mixture. Yield: 8 servings (327 calories [11% from fat] per serving).

Vegetable Rice
Vegetable cooking spray
1 cup chopped onion
1 cup finely chopped carrot
1 cup finely chopped celery
¾ cup finely chopped sweet red
   pepper
½ cup finely chopped green pepper
2 cloves garlic, minced
2⅓ cups water
1 teaspoon Cajun seasoning
1⅓ cups long-grain rice, uncooked
2 tablespoons chopped fresh
   parsley

Coat a large nonstick skillet with vegetable cooking spray; place over medium-high heat until hot. Add onion and next 5 ingredients; sauté 3 to 4 minutes or until tender. Remove vegetable mixture from heat; set aside, and keep warm.

Combine water and Cajun seasoning in a medium saucepan, stirring well; bring to a boil. Stir in rice. Cover, reduce heat, and simmer 20 to 25 minutes or until rice is tender and liquid is absorbed.

Combine vegetable mixture and cooked rice in a large bowl; add chopped parsley, and toss gently to combine. Yield: 4 cups.

FAT 3.9g (SAT 0.8g, MONO 1.0g, POLY 1.8g)
PROTEIN 13.4g CARBOHYDRATE 60.3g
FIBER 6.8g CHOLESTEROL 0mg SODIUM 536mg

CURRIED SPLIT PEAS WITH RICE

1⅔ cups dried yellow split peas
5 cups water
Vegetable cooking spray
1½ tablespoons reduced-calorie
   margarine
3 cups chopped onion
1 tablespoon grated unsweetened
   coconut
1 teaspoon crushed red pepper
   flakes
2 teaspoons peeled, grated
   gingerroot
½ teaspoon ground bay leaves
2 tablespoons all-purpose flour
1 tablespoon curry powder
1 cup skim milk
½ cup canned no-salt-added
   chicken broth, undiluted
1 teaspoon lemon juice
½ teaspoon salt
4½ cups cooked long-grain rice
   (cooked without salt or fat)
¼ cup sliced green onions
¼ cup raisins

Combine peas and water in a Dutch oven. Bring to a boil; cover, reduce heat, and simmer 40 to 45 minutes or until peas are tender. Drain well, and set aside.

Coat a large nonstick skillet with vegetable cooking spray; add margarine. Place over medium heat until margarine melts. Add onion and next 4 ingredients; sauté 3 to 4 minutes or until onion is tender. Add flour and curry powder, stirring well. Cook 1 minute, stirring constantly. Gradually add milk and chicken broth to flour mixture. Cook over medium heat, stirring constantly, until mixture is thickened and bubbly.

Remove from heat; stir in peas, lemon juice, and salt. Cook until mixture is thoroughly heated, stirring occasionally. For each serving, top ¾ cup rice with 1 cup pea mixture. Top each serving with 2 teaspoons green onions and 2 teaspoons raisins. Yield: 6 servings (448 calories [8% from fat] per serving).

FAT 4.0g (SAT 1.2g, MONO 1.0g, POLY 1.2g)
PROTEIN 19.5g CARBOHYDRATE 85.1g
FIBER 5.9g CHOLESTEROL 1mg SODIUM 269mg

Creole Black-Eyed Peas and Polenta is a flavorful blend of traditional Southern and Italian favorites. And with over 14 grams of protein per serving, it makes a hearty meatless main dish.

CREOLE BLACK-EYED PEAS AND POLENTA

3 cups water
¾ teaspoon salt
¾ cup instant polenta
¼ cup freshly grated Parmesan
　cheese
Vegetable cooking spray
3½ cups frozen black-eyed peas
2 cups water
1¼ cups chopped onion
1¼ cups chopped green pepper
2 cloves garlic, minced
2 (14½-ounce) cans no-salt-added
　stewed tomatoes, undrained and
　chopped
1 tablespoon low-sodium
　Worcestershire sauce
½ teaspoon salt
¼ teaspoon ground red pepper
¼ teaspoon black pepper
¼ teaspoon hot sauce
Fresh parsley sprigs (optional)

Combine 3 cups water and salt in a medium saucepan; bring to a boil. Add polenta in a slow, steady stream, stirring constantly. Reduce heat to medium, and cook 20 minutes, stirring constantly, until mixture pulls away from sides of pan. Add Parmesan cheese, stirring until cheese melts.

Spoon polenta mixture into a 9- x 5- x 3-inch loafpan coated with vegetable cooking spray. Set aside, and let cool completely.

Combine peas and 2 cups water in a large saucepan. Bring to a boil; cover, reduce heat, and simmer 20 minutes. Drain and set aside.

Coat a large nonstick skillet with vegetable cooking spray; place over medium heat until hot. Add onion, green pepper, and garlic; sauté until tender. Stir in peas, tomato, and next 5 ingredients; bring mixture to a boil. Reduce heat; simmer, uncovered, 10 minutes or until peas are tender, stirring occasionally.

Turn polenta out onto a cutting board; cut crosswise into 18 (½-inch) slices. Arrange 3 slices in a fan pattern on each of 6 individual serving plates; top each serving with 1 cup pea mixture. Garnish each serving with fresh parsley sprigs, if desired. Yield: 6 servings (274 calories [8% from fat] per serving).

FAT 2.5g (SAT 1.1g, MONO 0.6g, POLY 0.4g)
PROTEIN 14.2g CARBOHYDRATE 50.3g
FIBER 5.5g CHOLESTEROL 3mg SODIUM 601mg

Polenta is a cornmeal-based mixture that originated in northern Italy. The cooked mixture is done when it pulls away from the sides of the pan and forms a ball.

Press the cooked polenta mixture into a 9- x 5- x 3-inch loafpan that has been coated with cooking spray. A flexible rubber spatula makes this an easy task.

Turn out the loaf-shaped polenta onto a cutting board and cut into ½-inch slices. Each serving consists of 3 slices of polenta topped with 1 cup of the pea mixture.

LENTIL SPAGHETTI

Vegetable cooking spray
1 tablespoon reduced-calorie
  margarine
1 cup diced onion
1 cup diced celery
1 cup diced carrot
1 cup chopped zucchini
1 cup sliced fresh mushrooms
2 cloves garlic, minced
2 (14½-ounce) cans no-salt-added
  whole tomatoes, undrained and
  chopped
1½ cups water
1½ cups canned no-salt-added
  chicken broth, undiluted
1½ cups dried lentils
1¼ teaspoons dried Italian
  seasoning
1 bay leaf
½ teaspoon salt
¼ teaspoon pepper
8 cups cooked spaghetti (cooked
  without salt or fat)
¼ cup freshly grated Parmesan
  cheese

Coat a Dutch oven with vegetable cooking spray; add margarine. Place over medium-high heat until margarine melts. Add onion and next 5 ingredients; sauté 3 or 4 minutes or until crisp-tender.

Stir in tomato and next 5 ingredients. Bring to a boil; cover, reduce heat, and simmer 30 minutes, stirring occasionally. Uncover and cook an additional 10 minutes, stirring occasionally. Stir in salt and pepper. Remove and discard bay leaf.

For each serving, top 1 cup spaghetti with 1 cup lentil mixture. Sprinkle evenly with cheese. Yield: 8 servings (402 calories [10% from fat] per serving).

FAT 4.6g (SAT 1.6g, MONO 1.2g, POLY 1.1g)
PROTEIN 21.3g CARBOHYDRATE 69.9g
FIBER 8.4g CHOLESTEROL 5mg SODIUM 338mg

LENTIL AND MUSHROOM STROGANOFF

1¼ cups dried lentils
3½ cups water
Vegetable cooking spray
2½ cups sliced fresh mushrooms
1 cup chopped onion
2 cloves garlic, minced
2 tablespoons all-purpose flour
2 teaspoons dry mustard
1 (10¾-ounce) can 99% fat-free
  cream of mushroom soup
½ cup nonfat sour cream
  alternative
½ teaspoon freshly ground pepper
5 cups cooked fettuccine (cooked
  without salt or fat)
2 tablespoons chopped fresh parsley

Combine dried lentils and water in a Dutch oven. Bring to a boil; cover, reduce heat, and simmer 30 to 35 minutes or until lentils are tender. Drain well. Set aside, and keep warm.

Coat a nonstick skillet with cooking spray; place over medium heat until hot. Add mushrooms, onion, and garlic; sauté until tender. Combine flour and mustard; add to mushroom mixture. Cook 1 minute, stirring constantly. Stir in lentils, soup, sour cream, and pepper. Cook over low heat, stirring occasionally, until thoroughly heated (do not boil).

For each serving, top 1 cup fettuccine with 1 cup lentil mixture. Sprinkle with parsley. Yield: 5 servings (450 calories [6% from fat] per serving).

FAT 3.1g (SAT 0.2g, MONO 0.2g, POLY 0.7g)
PROTEIN 24.2g CARBOHYDRATE 81.5g
FIBER 9.0g CHOLESTEROL 3mg SODIUM 278mg

LENTIL PASTICCIO

1 cup elbow macaroni, uncooked
¾ cup dried lentils
¾ cup chopped onion
1 medium carrot, finely chopped
1 clove garlic, minced
1¾ cups water
1 (8-ounce) can no-salt-added
  tomato sauce
2 tablespoons chopped fresh parsley
¼ teaspoon ground cinnamon
1 tablespoon margarine
1½ tablespoons all-purpose flour
1 cup skim milk
¼ cup grated Parmesan cheese
¼ teaspoon salt
¼ cup frozen egg substitute, thawed
Vegetable cooking spray

Cook macaroni according to package directions, omitting salt and fat; drain well, and set aside.

Combine lentils and next 4 ingredients in a saucepan. Bring to a boil; cover, reduce heat, and simmer 35 minutes. (Do not overcook lentils.) Stir in tomato sauce, parsley, and cinnamon. Set aside.

Melt margarine in a saucepan over medium heat; add flour, stirring until smooth. Cook 1 minute, stirring constantly. Gradually add milk; cook, stirring constantly, until mixture is thickened and bubbly. Add Parmesan cheese and salt, stirring until cheese melts. Let cool; stir in egg substitute.

Layer half each of macaroni and lentil mixture in a 10- x 6- x 2-inch baking dish coated with cooking spray. Repeat layers; pour cheese mixture over top. Bake, uncovered, at 350° for 45 minutes or until lightly browned. Let stand 10 minutes. Yield: 6 servings (240 calories [14% from fat] per serving).

FAT 3.7g (SAT 1.2g, MONO 1.2g, POLY 0.9g)
PROTEIN 14.1g CARBOHYDRATE 38.3g
FIBER 4.5g CHOLESTEROL 3mg SODIUM 235mg

Vegetable-Cheese Cannelloni

8 cannelloni shells, uncooked
1 (14½-ounce) can no-salt-added whole tomatoes, undrained
1 (8-ounce) can no-salt-added tomato sauce
2 tablespoons no-salt-added tomato paste
¼ cup finely chopped green pepper
¼ cup finely chopped shallots
1 clove garlic, crushed
½ teaspoon dried whole basil
Vegetable cooking spray
1 cup shredded carrot
1 cup shredded zucchini
½ cup diced fresh mushrooms
2 tablespoons chopped fresh parsley
2 cups 1% low-fat cottage cheese
¼ cup frozen egg substitute, thawed
2 tablespoons grated Parmesan cheese
½ teaspoon dried whole basil
⅛ teaspoon ground nutmeg
⅛ teaspoon ground white pepper

Cook cannelloni shells according to package directions, omitting salt and fat; drain and set aside.

Place tomatoes in container of an electric blender or food processor; top with cover, and process until smooth. Transfer tomato puree to a saucepan; stir in tomato sauce and next 5 ingredients. Bring to a boil; reduce heat, and simmer, uncovered, 20 minutes, stirring occasionally. Spread ½ cup tomato mixture in an 11- x 7- x 2-inch baking dish coated with cooking spray; set aside. Reserve remaining tomato mixture.

Coat a large nonstick skillet with cooking spray; place over medium-high heat until hot. Add carrot, zucchini, mushrooms, and parsley; sauté until crisp-tender. Drain vegetable mixture well on paper towels.

Combine cottage cheese and remaining ingredients in container of electric blender or food processor. Top with cover, and process until mixture is smooth. Combine vegetable mixture and cheese mixture in a large bowl; stir well.

Spoon vegetable-cheese mixture evenly into cannelloni shells, and place in baking dish. Spoon remaining tomato mixture evenly over shells. Cover and bake at 375° for 20 minutes or until thoroughly heated. Yield: 4 servings (250 calories [16% from fat] per serving).

FAT 4.5g (SAT 1.6g, MONO 1.1g, POLY 0.7g)
PROTEIN 24.7g CARBOHYDRATE 28.1g
FIBER 1.7g CHOLESTEROL 21mg SODIUM 728mg

Spinach-Stuffed Manicotti

1 (8-ounce) box manicotti shells, uncooked
Vegetable cooking spray
¾ cup diced onion
¾ cup diced green pepper
2 (14½-ounce) cans no-salt-added whole tomatoes, undrained and chopped
1 (8-ounce) can no-salt-added tomato sauce
1 (6-ounce) can no-salt-added tomato paste
1 tablespoon brown sugar
1 teaspoon dried whole oregano
½ teaspoon salt
¼ teaspoon pepper
2 (10-ounce) packages frozen chopped spinach, thawed and drained
1 (15-ounce) carton part-skim ricotta cheese
1 cup (4 ounces) shredded part-skim mozzarella cheese
3 tablespoons grated Parmesan cheese
2 teaspoons dried Italian seasoning
¼ teaspoon nutmeg
¼ teaspoon pepper

Cook manicotti shells according to package directions, omitting salt and fat. Drain well, and set aside.

Coat a large saucepan with cooking spray; place over medium-high until hot. Add onion and green pepper; sauté until tender. Stir in tomato and next 6 ingredients. Bring to a boil; cover, reduce heat and simmer 20 minutes, stirring occasionally.

Drain spinach; press between paper towels until barely moist. Combine spinach, ricotta cheese, and remaining ingredients in a medium bowl; stir well. Spoon cheese mixture evenly into manicotti shells.

Spoon half of tomato mixture into a 13- x 9- x 2-inch baking dish coated with cooking spray. Place shells in dish; top with remaining tomato mixture. Cover and bake at 350° for 40 to 45 minutes or until thoroughly heated. Yield: 7 servings (242 calories [29% from fat] per serving).

FAT 7.6g (SAT 3.7g, MONO 2.0g, POLY 0.7g)
PROTEIN 20.3g CARBOHYDRATE 28.6g
FIBER 5.3g CHOLESTEROL 31mg SODIUM 542mg

Carefully spoon the filling for Spinach-Stuffed Manicotti into the cooked pasta shells. Cooked shells are fragile and should be handled with care.

Vegetable Lasagna

6 lasagna noodles, uncooked
Vegetable cooking spray
1½ cups chopped onion
1 cup chopped green pepper
3 cloves garlic, minced
2½ cups coarsely chopped zucchini
2 cups peeled, chopped tomato
2 cups sliced fresh mushrooms
¾ cup shredded carrot
¾ cup chopped celery
2 (8-ounce) cans no-salt-added
   tomato sauce
1 (6-ounce) can no-salt-added
   tomato paste
2 tablespoons red wine vinegar
1 tablespoon dried Italian seasoning
½ teaspoon salt
½ teaspoon pepper
¼ teaspoon fennel seeds
2 cups part-skim ricotta cheese
1¼ cups (5 ounces) shredded part-
   skim mozzarella cheese, divided
2 tablespoons grated Parmesan
   cheese

Cook noodles according to package directions, omitting salt and fat. Drain well, and set aside.

Coat a large Dutch oven with cooking spray; place over medium-high heat until hot. Add onion, green pepper, and garlic; sauté until tender. Stir in zucchini and next 11 ingredients. Cover, reduce heat, and simmer 30 minutes, stirring occasionally. Remove from heat, and set aside.

Combine ricotta cheese and ¾ cup mozzarella cheese; stir well. Spoon 2 cups vegetable mixture into a 13- x 9- x 2-inch baking dish coated with cooking spray. Arrange 3 noodles lengthwise in a single layer over vegetable mixture; top with half of cheese mixture. Repeat layers; top with remaining vegetable mixture.

Cover and bake at 350° for 25 minutes. Uncover and sprinkle with remaining ½ cup mozzarella cheese and Parmesan cheese. Bake, uncovered, an additional 8 to 10 minutes or until cheese melts. Let stand 10 minutes before serving. Yield: 10 servings (233 calories [28% from fat] per serving).

FAT 7.2g (SAT 4.2g, MONO 1.9g, POLY 0.5g)
PROTEIN 14.2g CARBOHYDRATE 29.2g
FIBER 2.8g CHOLESTEROL 24mg SODIUM 296mg

Italian Rotini Casserole

Vegetable cooking spray
1½ cups diced zucchini
½ cup chopped fresh mushrooms
¼ cup chopped onion
1½ tablespoons reduced-calorie
   margarine
1 tablespoon all-purpose flour
1¼ cups no-salt-added tomato
   juice
½ teaspoon dried whole basil
½ teaspoon dried whole oregano
¼ teaspoon salt
3 cups cooked tricolor rotini
   (cooked without salt or fat)
1 (16-ounce) can light red kidney
   beans, drained
1½ cups (6 ounces) shredded part-
   skim mozzarella cheese
1½ tablespoons grated Parmesan
   cheese

Coat a small nonstick skillet with vegetable cooking spray; place over medium-high heat until hot. Add zucchini, mushrooms, and onion; sauté until tender. Remove from heat, and set aside.

Melt margarine in a small, heavy saucepan over medium heat; add flour, stirring until smooth. Cook 1 minute, stirring constantly. Gradually add tomato juice; cook, stirring constantly, until mixture is thickened and bubbly. Remove from heat, and stir in basil, oregano, and salt.

Combine sauce mixture, vegetable mixture, pasta, beans, and mozzarella cheese in a large bowl; stir well. Pour mixture into a 2-quart casserole coated with vegetable cooking spray. Sprinkle evenly with Parmesan cheese. Cover and bake at 350° for 20 minutes; uncover and bake an additional 10 minutes or until thoroughly heated. Yield: 6 servings (294 calories [24% from fat] per serving).

FAT 7.7g (SAT 3.5g, MONO 2.2g, POLY 1.4g)
PROTEIN 16.8g CARBOHYDRATE 40.3g
FIBER 3.5g CHOLESTEROL 17mg SODIUM 287mg

Whole Wheat Spaghetti With Ratatouille Sauce

Vegetable cooking spray
1 cup chopped onion
½ cup chopped green pepper
1 large clove garlic, minced
3 cups peeled, cubed eggplant
   (about 1 small)
¾ cup sliced fresh mushrooms
¾ cup julienne-cut yellow squash
¾ cup julienne-cut zucchini
1½ cups peeled, seeded, and
   chopped tomato
1 (8-ounce) can no-salt-added
   tomato sauce
2 tablespoons minced fresh parsley
2 tablespoons Burgundy or other
   dry red wine
1¼ teaspoons dried whole basil
1¼ teaspoons dried whole oregano
¾ teaspoon salt
½ teaspoon pepper
4 cups cooked whole wheat
   spaghetti (cooked without salt
   or fat)
¼ cup freshly grated Parmesan
   cheese

Coat a Dutch oven with cooking spray; place over medium-high heat until hot. Add onion, green pepper, and garlic; sauté until tender. Add eggplant, mushrooms, yellow squash, and zucchini; cook 5 minutes or until vegetables are crisp-tender, stirring occasionally. Add tomato and next 7 ingredients; cook over medium heat, stirring occasionally, until mixture is thoroughly heated.

For each serving, top 1 cup spaghetti with 1 cup vegetable mixture. Sprinkle evenly with Parmesan cheese. Yield: 4 servings (293 calories [11% from fat] per serving).

FAT 3.5g (SAT 1.4g, MONO 0.7g, POLY 0.6g)
PROTEIN 13.6g CARBOHYDRATE 57.7g
FIBER 4.9g CHOLESTEROL 5mg SODIUM 585mg

VEGETABLE ENCHILADA CASSEROLE

Vegetable cooking spray
¾ cup chopped green pepper
½ cup chopped green onions
2 cloves garlic, minced
1 small eggplant, peeled and chopped
1 medium zucchini, sliced
½ pound fresh mushrooms, sliced
1 (8-ounce) can no-salt-added tomato sauce
1 (8-ounce) can chopped green chiles, drained
1 cup chopped tomato
1 teaspoon sugar
½ teaspoon chili powder
⅛ teaspoon ground cumin
6 (8-inch) flour tortillas
½ cup (2 ounces) shredded reduced-fat mild Cheddar cheese
½ cup (2 ounces) shredded reduced-fat Monterey Jack cheese
¼ cup sliced ripe olives

Coat a large nonstick skillet with cooking spray; place over medium-high heat until hot. Add green pepper, green onions, and garlic; sauté until crisp-tender. Add eggplant, zucchini, and mushrooms; sauté 4 to 5 minutes or until vegetables are tender, stirring occasionally. Stir in tomato sauce and next 5 ingredients; cover and simmer 30 minutes, stirring occasionally.

Coat a 13- x 9- x 2-inch baking dish with cooking spray. Arrange half of tortillas in bottom of baking dish; top with vegetable mixture. Arrange remaining half of tortillas over vegetable mixture.

Cover and bake at 350° for 25 to 30 minutes or until thoroughly heated. Sprinkle with shredded cheeses and olives; bake, uncovered, an additional 5 minutes or until cheese melts. Yield: 6 servings (278 calories [25% from fat] per serving).

FAT 7.9g (SAT 3.1g, MONO 1.8g, POLY 1.3g)
PROTEIN 11.8g CARBOHYDRATE 44.9g
FIBER 4.0g CHOLESTEROL 12mg SODIUM 210mg

MUSHROOM-SPINACH CALZONES

1 package dry yeast
1 cup warm water (105° to 115°), divided
1 tablespoon honey
½ teaspoon salt
1¾ cups whole wheat flour
1 cup unbleached flour
3 tablespoons whole wheat flour, divided
Vegetable cooking spray
1½ cups sliced fresh mushrooms
1½ cups tightly packed chopped fresh spinach
¾ cup chopped onion
¾ cup diced sweet red pepper
½ cup shredded carrot
¼ cup commercial oil-free Italian dressing
1½ cups (6 ounces) shredded part-skim mozzarella cheese
¼ teaspoon freshly ground pepper
1 egg white
1 tablespoon water

Dissolve yeast in ¼ cup warm water in a large bowl; let stand 5 minutes. Combine remaining ¾ cup warm water, honey, and salt; add to yeast mixture, stirring gently. Gradually stir in 1¾ cups whole wheat flour and enough of unbleached flour to make a soft dough.

Sprinkle 1 tablespoon whole wheat flour evenly over work surface. Turn dough out onto surface, and knead until smooth and elastic (about 8 to 10 minutes). Place dough in a large bowl coated with cooking spray, turning to coat top. Cover and let rise in a warm place (85°), free from drafts, 45 minutes or until doubled in bulk.

Coat a large nonstick skillet with cooking spray; place over medium-high heat until hot. Add mushrooms and next 4 ingredients; sauté until vegetables are crisp-tender. Remove from heat; stir in dressing. Set aside.

Punch dough down, and divide into 6 equal portions. Shape each portion into a ball; cover and let rest 5 minutes. Sprinkle 1 teaspoon whole wheat flour evenly over work surface. Turn 1 portion of dough out onto floured surface, and roll to a 7½-inch circle. Repeat procedure with remaining 1 tablespoon plus 2 teaspoons whole wheat flour and remaining portions of dough.

Spoon vegetable mixture evenly over half of each circle. Sprinkle cheese and ground pepper evenly over each. Brush edges of circles with water. Fold circles in half; crimp edges to seal. Combine egg white and 1 tablespoon water; brush calzones with egg white mixture. Place calzones on a large ungreased baking sheet. Bake at 425° for 10 minutes or until golden. Yield: 6 servings (318 calories [17% from fat] per serving).

FAT 5.9g (SAT 3.1g, MONO 1.5g, POLY 0.6g)
PROTEIN 16.4g CARBOHYDRATE 52.8g
FIBER 7.3g CHOLESTEROL 16mg SODIUM 461mg

Italian Stuffed Eggplant

2 medium eggplants
Vegetable cooking spray
1¼ cups chopped onion
1¼ cups diced zucchini
1 cup sliced fresh mushrooms
¾ cup chopped green pepper
1 clove garlic, minced
¾ cup chopped tomato
1 (8-ounce) can no-salt-added
    tomato sauce
1 cup cooked brown rice (cooked
    without salt or fat)
¼ cup grated Parmesan cheese
1 tablespoon unsalted sunflower
    kernels, toasted
1 teaspoon dried Italian seasoning
1 cup (4 ounces) shredded part-
    skim mozzarella cheese

Wash eggplants; cut each in half lengthwise. Carefully remove pulp, leaving a ¼-inch-thick shell. Chop pulp, reserving 2 cups. (Reserve remaining pulp for other uses.) Set eggplant shells aside.

Coat a nonstick skillet with cooking spray; place over medium heat until hot. Add onion and next 4 ingredients; sauté until tender. Stir in 2 cups reserved eggplant, tomato, and tomato sauce. Cook, uncovered, 15 minutes, stirring occasionally. Remove from heat; stir in rice, Parmesan cheese, sunflower kernels, and Italian seasoning.

Place eggplant shells in a shallow baking dish coated with cooking spray. Spoon vegetable mixture evenly into shells. Bake, uncovered, at 350° for 10 minutes or until thoroughly heated. Sprinkle with cheese; bake an additional 5 minutes or until cheese melts. Yield 4 servings (295 calories [28% from fat] per serving).

FAT 9.2g (SAT 4.2g, MONO 2.3g, POLY 1.8g)
PROTEIN 16.1g CARBOHYDRATE 41.4g
FIBER 7.6g CHOLESTEROL 20mg SODIUM 258mg

Baked Potatoes with Broccoli and Cheese

6 (8-ounce) baking potatoes
½ cup plain nonfat yogurt
3 tablespoons minced onion
¼ teaspoon salt
⅛ teaspoon ground white pepper
5 cups chopped fresh broccoli
2 teaspoons reduced-calorie
    margarine
2 tablespoons cornstarch
1 tablespoon plus 1 teaspoon water
⅔ cup canned low-sodium chicken
    broth, undiluted
⅔ cup skim milk
¾ cup (3 ounces) shredded
    reduced-fat mild Cheddar cheese

Scrub potatoes; bake at 400° for 1 hour or until soft. Let cool to touch. Cut a lengthwise strip (1 inch wide) from top of each potato; carefully scoop out pulp, leaving shells intact.

Combine potato pulp, yogurt, and next 3 ingredients in a large bowl. Beat at medium speed of an electric mixer until light and fluffy; spoon mixture evenly into shells. Bake at 400° for 25 to 30 minutes or until thoroughly heated.

Arrange broccoli in a vegetable steamer over boiling water. Cover and steam 8 minutes. Set aside.

Melt margarine in a heavy saucepan over medium heat. Combine cornstarch and water, stirring well; add to margarine, stirring until smooth. Cook 1 minute, stirring constantly. Gradually add chicken broth and milk; cook, stirring constantly, until thickened. Add cheese and broccoli, stirring until cheese melts. Spoon mixture evenly over potatoes. Yield: 6 servings (352 calories [10% from fat] per serving).

FAT 4.1g (SAT 1.8g, MONO 0.3g, POLY 0.6g)
PROTEIN 13.5g CARBOHYDRATE 67.2g
FIBER 6.5g CHOLESTEROL 10mg SODIUM 282mg

Hearty Vegetable Pizza with Oatmeal Crust

1 cup regular oats, uncooked
1 package dry yeast
½ cup plus 2 tablespoons warm
    water (105° to 115°)
1 teaspoon sugar
½ teaspoon salt
1½ tablespoons vegetable oil
½ cup whole wheat flour
¼ cup all-purpose flour
2 tablespoons all-purpose flour,
    divided
Vegetable cooking spray
1 (10-ounce) package frozen
    chopped spinach
2 cups thinly sliced leeks
1 small sweet red pepper, cut into
    strips
1 clove garlic, minced
⅔ cup no-salt-added tomato sauce
½ teaspoon dried Italian seasoning
½ cup sliced fresh mushrooms
6 cherry tomatoes, quartered
1 cup (4 ounces) shredded part-
    skim mozzarella cheese

Place oats in container of an electric blender or food processor; top with cover, and process until oats resemble flour.

Dissolve yeast in warm water in a large mixing bowl; let stand 5 minutes. Add ground oats, sugar, salt, and oil; beat at medium speed of an electric mixer until well blended. Add whole wheat flour; beat at medium speed of an electric mixer 1 minute. Gradually stir in ¼ cup all-purpose flour to make a soft dough.

Sprinkle 1 tablespoon all-purpose flour evenly over work surface; turn dough out onto floured surface, and knead until smooth and elastic (about 5 minutes). Place dough in a large bowl coated with cooking spray, turning to coat top. Cover and let rise in a warm place (85°), free from drafts, 1 hour or until doubled in bulk.

Cook spinach according to package directions, omitting salt; drain. Press spinach between paper towels until barely moist; set aside.

Coat a large nonstick skillet with cooking spray; place over medium-high heat until hot. Add leeks, pepper, and garlic; sauté until tender. Stir in spinach; set aside.

Punch down dough. Sprinkle remaining 1 tablespoon all-purpose flour evenly over work surface. Turn dough out onto floured surface; roll to a 14-inch circle. Place circle on a 12-inch pizza pan coated with cooking spray. Turn excess dough under to form a rim. Prick bottom of crust with a fork. Bake at 400° for 5 minutes. Combine tomato sauce and Italian seasoning; spread over crust. Top with spinach mixture, mushrooms, and tomato. Bake at 400° for 12 to 15 minutes or until crust is lightly browned. Sprinkle with cheese. Bake an additional 5 minutes or until cheese melts. To serve, cut pizza into 8 wedges. Yield: 4 servings (383 calories [29% from fat] per serving).

FAT 12.3g (SAT 4.2g, MONO 3.3g, POLY 3.6g)
PROTEIN 18.1g CARBOHYDRATE 53.5g
FIBER 9.5g CHOLESTEROL 16mg SODIUM 504mg

What Is Tofu?

Tofu, or soybean curd, is made by a process similar to that used to produce cottage cheese. An iron-rich liquid is extracted from ground, cooked soybeans; then a coagulant is added to the liquid. The coagulant causes a curd to form. This curd is then pressed to make tofu. Firm tofu can be cut up and added to stir-fries, salads, and casseroles. Soft tofu is perfect for use in dips and spreads.

QUICK MOROCCAN COUSCOUS

Vegetable cooking spray
⅓ cup chopped green onions
2 cups canned low-sodium chicken broth, undiluted
1 (15-ounce) can garbanzo beans, drained
½ cup raisins
½ teaspoon salt
½ teaspoon ground cumin
¼ teaspoon ground ginger
¼ teaspoon ground turmeric
¼ teaspoon crushed red pepper
1 cup couscous, uncooked
6 ounces firm tofu, cubed
3 tablespoons slivered almonds, toasted
2 tablespoons minced fresh parsley

Coat a medium saucepan with vegetable cooking spray; place over medium-high heat until hot. Add green onions; sauté 2 to 3 minutes or until crisp-tender. Add broth and next 7 ingredients; bring to a boil. Remove from heat. Add couscous and tofu; cover and let stand 5 minutes or until couscous is tender and liquid is absorbed. Add almonds and parsley; toss gently to combine. Yield: 6 servings (270 calories [17% from fat] per 1-cup serving).

FAT 5.0g (SAT 0.7g, MONO 2.0g, POLY 1.8g)
PROTEIN 11.7g CARBOHYDRATE 46.8g
FIBER 3.2g CHOLESTEROL 0mg SODIUM 231mg

TOFU-ZUCCHINI STROGANOFF

1 (10½-ounce) package firm tofu
Vegetable cooking spray
1 teaspoon vegetable oil
1 medium zucchini, cut into julienne strips
1 medium-size sweet red pepper, cut into julienne strips
½ pound fresh mushrooms, sliced
2 cloves garlic, minced
⅔ cup skim milk
1 tablespoon all-purpose flour
1 teaspoon beef-flavored bouillon granules
½ teaspoon dried whole dillweed
1 tablespoon Neufchâtel cheese, softened
4 cups cooked medium egg noodles (cooked without salt or fat)

Wrap tofu in several layers of cheesecloth or paper towels; press lightly to remove excess moisture. Remove cheesecloth; cut tofu into ½-inch cubes.

Coat a large nonstick skillet with vegetable cooking spray; add oil. Place over medium-high heat until hot. Add tofu; sauté 3 to 4 minutes or until lightly browned. Drain tofu; pat dry with paper towels. Wipe skillet with a paper towel.

Coat skillet with vegetable cooking spray; place over medium-high heat until hot. Add zucchini and next 3 ingredients; sauté until tender. Remove vegetable mixture from skillet, and set aside. Wipe skillet dry with a paper towel.

Combine milk, flour, bouillon granules, and dillweed in a small bowl, stirring well. Add flour mixture to skillet; bring to a boil over medium heat, stirring constantly. Add cheese; cook, stirring constantly, until cheese melts. Add tofu and vegetable mixture. Cook over low heat, stirring constantly, until thoroughly heated. To serve, spoon tofu mixture evenly over noodles. Yield: 4 servings (339 calories [22% from fat] per serving).

FAT 8.4g (SAT 1.9g, MONO 2.0g, POLY 3.3g)
PROTEIN 17.0g CARBOHYDRATE 50.7g
FIBER 5.9g CHOLESTEROL 56mg SODIUM 293mg

MEATS

Can a juicy steak or pork chop be part of a low-fat eating plan? The answer is a resounding YES! Today, beef, veal, lamb, and pork are leaner than ever before. And with wise shopping and low-fat cooking methods, red meats can easily fit into a lifestyle of healthy eating.

A lean revolution has hit the meat counter, making many cuts of meat good choices for low-fat eating. Lean meats contribute high-quality protein to the diet and are good sources of iron, zinc, vitamin B_{12}, niacin, and riboflavin.

However, even lean meats contain saturated fat that can raise blood cholesterol levels. For this reason, the AHA recommends that a low-fat diet include no more than six ounces of cooked lean meat daily.

The recipes in this section have been developed to contain little, if any, added fat in order to keep the percent of calories from fat at 30 percent or less. But some cuts of meat, such as a beef flank steak, naturally derive more than 30 percent of calories from fat, even though the cut is still considered lean. If this is the case, the meat dish should be accompanied by dishes that are very low in fat such as a side dish of rice or pasta that has been cooked without fat and a green salad with nonfat dressing.

Selecting Lean Meats

Some cuts of meat are higher in fat than others. The key to choosing lean cuts is to select those that have more muscle than fat. Also, look for cuts with the least amount of marbling, or flecks of fat. The nutritional content of the leanest cuts of beef and other meats is shown in the chart on page 147.

Cooking Lean Meats

Low-fat cooking techniques for meats include roasting, broiling, grilling, braising, and stir-frying. (See page 14 for descriptions of these cooking methods.) The most important thing to remember about cooking lean meats is that they cook faster than high-fat meats. Using a meat thermometer is the best way to determine doneness in lean cuts.

To get an accurate reading from a meat thermometer, insert it into the thickest part of the meat, being careful not to let the thermometer rest in a fatty area or touch a bone. When the meat reaches the desired degree of doneness, push the thermometer farther into the meat; if the temperature drops, continue cooking. If the temperature stays the same, remove the meat from the heat source, and let stand 10 minutes before serving.

Colorful Stuffed Pork Roast (page 142) is a hearty example of healthy eating. Perfect for a casual dinner party, this roast is filled with rice, mushrooms, and dried apricots.

129

Although Americans have reduced the amount of beef they consume, it continues to be a favorite food. And with the increasing popularity of low-fat cooking, lean cuts of beef are being placed on healthy menus.

The USDA assigns grades to indicate the lean-to-fat ratio in a cut of beef. Use these grades as a guideline to help you select the leanest cuts of beef for your recipes:

Prime. Usually found only in finer restaurants and select meat stores, Prime is the highest grade of beef and the most expensive. Prime cuts of beef contain the most marbling.

Choice. Choice is the grade of beef most often found in the supermarket. It is similar to Prime but has less marbling, so it is leaner.

Select. Select, which previously was called "Good," is the leanest beef because it contains the least amount of marbling.

BEEF TENDERLOIN AU POIVRE

1 (3-pound) beef tenderloin
3 tablespoons reduced-calorie margarine, divided
½ teaspoon whole white peppercorns, coarsely crushed
½ teaspoon whole green peppercorns, coarsely crushed
½ teaspoon whole black peppercorns, coarsely crushed
Vegetable cooking spray
12 small round red potatoes (about 3 pounds)
3 tablespoons water
2 tablespoons minced fresh chives
1 teaspoon coarsely ground pepper
½ teaspoon salt
3 tablespoons brandy

Trim excess fat from tenderloin. Combine 1½ teaspoons margarine and next 3 ingredients in a small bowl, stirring well; rub peppercorn mixture evenly over entire surface of tenderloin.

Place tenderloin on a rack in a roasting pan coated with vegetable cooking spray. Insert meat thermometer into thickest part of tenderloin, if desired.

Cut potatoes crosswise into ¼-inch slices, cutting to but not through bottom of potatoes. Arrange potatoes, cut side up, around tenderloin. Combine remaining 2½ tablespoons margarine, water, chives, pepper, and salt in a small bowl, stirring well; brush potatoes evenly with half of margarine mixture.

Bake at 400° for 20 minutes. Reduce heat to 375°, and bake an additional 35 to 40 minutes or until meat thermometer registers 140° (rare) or 160° (medium). Remove tenderloin from oven; transfer to a large serving platter. Set aside, and keep warm.

Brush potatoes evenly with remaining half of margarine mixture; bake an additional 15 to 17 minutes or until potatoes are tender and slices have fanned out slightly.

Slice tenderloin diagonally across grain into ¼-inch slices; arrange potatoes around tenderloin.

Pour brandy into a small, long-handled saucepan; heat over low heat just until warm (do not boil). Remove saucepan from heat. Ignite brandy with a long match, and pour evenly over tenderloin. Yield: 12 servings (270 calories [29% from fat] per serving).

FAT 8.8g (SAT 3.2g, MONO 3.3g, POLY 0.8g)
PROTEIN 25.9g CARBOHYDRATE 19.1g
FIBER 2.2g CHOLESTEROL 69mg SODIUM 172mg

MUSHROOM-STUFFED BEEF TENDERLOIN

Vegetable cooking spray
¾ pound fresh mushrooms, sliced
¾ pound chopped fresh spinach
1½ cups chopped green onions
¼ cup chopped fresh parsley
½ teaspoon salt
1 (4-pound) beef tenderloin
1 teaspoon salt-free herb-and-spice blend
½ cup low-sodium soy sauce
⅓ cup dry sherry
2 tablespoons brown sugar
2 tablespoons honey
2 cloves garlic, minced

Coat a large nonstick skillet with cooking spray; place over medium-high heat until hot. Add mushrooms, spinach, and green onions; sauté 3 to 4 minutes or until mushrooms and green onions are tender. Remove skillet from heat; stir in parsley and salt. Set aside.

Trim excess fat from tenderloin. Slice tenderloin lengthwise to but not through the center, leaving one long side connected. Sprinkle herb-and-spice blend into opening of tenderloin. Spoon mushroom mixture into opening.

Fold top side of tenderloin over mushroom mixture, and tie securely with heavy string at 2-inch intervals. Place tenderloin in a large, shallow baking dish. Combine soy sauce and remaining ingredients in a small bowl; pour over tenderloin. Cover and marinate in refrigerator 8 hours, turning occasionally.

Remove tenderloin from marinade, reserving marinade. Place tenderloin, seam side down, on a rack in a roasting pan coated with cooking spray. Insert meat thermometer into thickest part of tenderloin, if desired. Bake at 425° for 45 minutes to 1 hour or until thermometer registers 140° (rare) or 160° (medium), basting occasionally with marinade.

Let tenderloin stand 10 minutes. Remove string; slice tenderloin diagonally across grain into ¼-inch slices. Yield: 16 servings (178 calories [34% from fat] per serving).

FAT 6.8g (SAT 2.6g, MONO 2.6g, POLY 0.4g)
PROTEIN 21.3g CARBOHYDRATE 6.7g
FIBER 1.4g CHOLESTEROL 60mg SODIUM 333mg

BEEF TENDERLOIN WITH SHERRIED MUSHROOMS

Vegetable cooking spray
½ pound fresh mushrooms, sliced
1 large clove garlic, minced
½ cup dry sherry
6 (4-ounce) beef tenderloin steaks
1 teaspoon salt-free lemon-pepper seasoning

Coat a large nonstick skillet with vegetable cooking spray; place over medium-high heat until hot. Add mushrooms and garlic; sauté 3 to 4 minutes or until mushrooms are tender. Add sherry; cook until liquid evaporates, stirring frequently. Set mixture aside, and keep warm.

Sprinkle both sides of each steak evenly with lemon-pepper seasoning. Coat grill rack with cooking spray; place on grill over medium-hot coals. Place steaks on rack; cook 5 minutes on each side or until desired degree of doneness. Arrange steaks on a serving platter; top evenly with mushroom mixture. Yield: 6 servings (214 calories [40% from fat] per serving).

FAT 9.4g (SAT 3.6g, MONO 3.6g, POLY 0.5g)
PROTEIN 28.3g CARBOHYDRATE 2.9g
FIBER 0.6g CHOLESTEROL 81mg SODIUM 65mg

MANDARIN STEAK

1 (1½-pound) lean boneless beef sirloin steak
1 cup unsweetened orange juice
3 tablespoons lemon juice
1 teaspoon hot sauce
6 green onions, cut into 2-inch pieces
Vegetable cooking spray
1 tablespoon cornstarch
½ teaspoon salt
1 (11-ounce) can mandarin oranges in heavy syrup, drained
4½ cups cooked long-grain rice (cooked without salt or fat)

Trim fat from steak. Place steak in a zip-top heavy-duty plastic bag. Combine orange juice and next 3 ingredients; stir well. Pour over steak; seal bag, and shake until steak is well coated. Marinate in refrigerator 2 to 4 hours, turning bag occasionally.

Remove steak from marinade. Strain marinade, reserving green onions; set green onions and marinade aside. Place steak on rack of a broiler pan coated with cooking spray; broil 5½ inches from heat 12 minutes. Turn steak, and top with green onions; broil an additional 10 minutes or to desired degree of doneness. Cut steak diagonally across grain into thin slices. Set meat and green onions aside; keep warm.

Combine marinade, cornstarch, and salt in a small saucepan. Bring to a boil over medium heat; boil 1 minute, stirring constantly. Combine steak, green onions, marinade mixture, and mandarin oranges in a large bowl; toss gently. Spoon rice onto a large serving platter; top with steak mixture. Yield: 6 servings (402 calories [19% from fat] per serving).

FAT 8.3g (SAT 3.3g, MONO 3.6g, POLY 0.4g)
PROTEIN 31.5g CARBOHYDRATE 47.9g
FIBER 1.1g CHOLESTEROL 82mg SODIUM 266mg

BEEF BURGUNDY

1 (1½-pound) lean boneless beef sirloin steak
Vegetable cooking spray
1 large onion, sliced and separated into rings
½ teaspoon salt
½ teaspoon dried whole oregano
½ teaspoon pepper
¼ teaspoon garlic powder
¼ teaspoon dried whole thyme
2 bay leaves
1 (13¾-ounce) can no-salt-added beef broth, undiluted
1¼ cups Burgundy or other dry red wine
1½ cups sliced fresh mushrooms
3 tablespoons cornstarch
½ cup water
¼ teaspoon browning-and-seasoning sauce
6 cups cooked medium egg noodles (cooked without salt or fat)

Partially freeze steak; trim fat from steak. Slice steak diagonally across grain into ¼-inch strips. Coat a Dutch oven with cooking spray; place over medium heat until hot. Add steak, and cook until browned. Stir in onion and next 8 ingredients. Bring to a boil; cover, reduce heat, and simmer 20 minutes, stirring occasionally. Add sliced mushrooms; cover and simmer 5 minutes.

Combine cornstarch, water, and browning-and-seasoning sauce; stir well. Add to steak mixture, stirring constantly. Bring mixture to a boil; boil 1 minute or until thickened, stirring constantly. Remove and discard bay leaves. To serve, spoon steak mixture over cooked noodles. Yield: 6 servings (409 calories [18% from fat] per serving).

FAT 8.3g (SAT 2.6g, MONO 3.1g, POLY 1.0g)
PROTEIN 32.7g CARBOHYDRATE 48.3g
FIBER 4.4g CHOLESTEROL 122mg SODIUM 281mg

Add visual appeal to your next barbecue with Spirited Beef Kabobs. Marinate the steak for several hours before grilling to make it tender and flavorful.

SAVORY POT ROAST

1 (3-pound) beef eye-of-round roast
2 cloves garlic, thinly sliced
¼ cup all-purpose flour
½ teaspoon salt
½ teaspoon coarsely ground pepper
Vegetable cooking spray
1 medium onion, sliced
1 bay leaf
1 cup Burgundy or other dry
   red wine
1 (8-ounce) can no-salt-added
   tomato sauce
1 tablespoon brown sugar
1 teaspoon dried whole oregano
1 teaspoon prepared horseradish
1 teaspoon prepared mustard
Fresh oregano sprigs (optional)

SPIRITED BEEF KABOBS

1 (1½-pound) lean boneless beef
   sirloin steak
¼ cup low-sodium soy sauce
¼ cup whiskey
¼ cup Dijon mustard
2 teaspoons lemon juice
½ teaspoon pepper
¼ teaspoon salt
2 cloves garlic, crushed
12 boiling onions or 3 small
   onions, quartered
12 large fresh mushrooms
1 large sweet red pepper, cut into
   12 (1-inch) pieces
2 medium zucchini, cut into
   12 (1-inch) pieces
Vegetable cooking spray

Trim fat from steak; cut steak into 1-inch pieces. Place steak in a zip-top heavy-duty plastic bag. Combine soy sauce and next 6 ingredients in a small bowl; stir well. Pour over steak;

seal bag, and shake until steak is well coated. Marinate in refrigerator 8 hours, turning bag occasionally.

Cook onions in boiling water to cover 3 minutes; drain well, and set onions aside.

Remove steak from marinade, reserving marinade. Thread steak, onions, mushrooms, sweet red pepper, and zucchini alternately on 12 (12-inch) skewers.

Coat grill rack with vegetable cooking spray; place on grill over medium-hot coals. Place kabobs on rack, and cook 12 to 14 minutes or to desired degree of doneness, turning and basting frequently with marinade. Yield: 6 servings (282 calories [30% from fat] per serving).

FAT 8.7g (SAT 3.2g, MONO 3.8g, POLY 0.7g)
PROTEIN 29.1g   CARBOHYDRATE 17.2g
FIBER 3.4g   CHOLESTEROL 76mg   SODIUM 718mg

Trim fat from roast. Cut 1-inch slits in roast, and insert a garlic slice into each slit. Combine flour, salt, and pepper; stir well. Dredge roast in flour mixture.

Coat a Dutch oven with cooking spray; place over medium-high heat until hot. Add roast; cook until browned on all sides. Add onion and bay leaf to pan. Combine wine and next 5 ingredients, stirring well; pour over roast. Bring to a boil; cover, reduce heat, and simmer 1 to 1½ hours or until roast is tender. Remove and discard bay leaf.

Transfer roast and onion to a serving platter, using a slotted spoon. Spoon remaining sauce over roast. Garnish with fresh oregano sprigs, if desired. Yield: 12 servings (175 calories [26% from fat] per serving).

FAT 5.0g (SAT 1.8g, MONO 2.1g, POLY 0.3g)
PROTEIN 25.4g   CARBOHYDRATE 5.8g
FIBER 0.4g   CHOLESTEROL 61mg   SODIUM 169mg

Steak Sukiyaki

1 pound lean boneless round steak
½ cup water
¼ cup low-sodium soy sauce
1 tablespoon cornstarch
2 tablespoons dry sherry
1 teaspoon peeled, minced
    gingerroot
½ teaspoon salt
¼ teaspoon crushed red pepper
Vegetable cooking spray
2 teaspoons vegetable oil
1 cup thinly sliced onion
¾ cup diagonally sliced celery
⅓ cup bamboo shoots
⅓ cup sliced water chestnuts
⅓ cup sliced green onions
1 cup fresh bean sprouts
1 cup sweet red pepper strips
½ cup sliced fresh mushrooms
3 cups cooked long-grain rice
    (cooked without salt or fat)

Partially freeze steak; trim fat from steak. Slice steak diagonally across grain into ¼-inch strips. Combine water and next 6 ingredients; set aside.

Coat a wok or large nonstick skillet with cooking spray; add oil. Place over medium-high heat (375°) until hot. Add steak, and stir-fry 3 minutes. Remove steak from wok; drain. Wipe drippings from wok.

Coat wok with cooking spray; place over medium-high heat until hot. Add onion and celery; stir-fry 3 minutes. Add bamboo shoots and water chestnuts; stir-fry 3 minutes. Add green onions, bean sprouts, pepper strips, and mushrooms; stir-fry 1 to 2 minutes. Add soy sauce mixture and steak; cook until thickened and thoroughly heated. Serve over rice. Yield: 6 servings (282 calories [21% from fat] per serving).

FAT 6.6g (SAT 2.0g, MONO 2.5g, POLY 1.1g)
PROTEIN 20.4g CARBOHYDRATE 33.2g
FIBER 2.1g CHOLESTEROL 48mg SODIUM 510mg

Beef Fajitas

3 pounds lean boneless round steak
3 (5½-ounce) cans no-salt-added
    vegetable juice cocktail
⅔ cup lime juice
½ cup chopped fresh cilantro
¼ teaspoon black pepper
¼ teaspoon ground red pepper
2 large cloves garlic, minced
12 (6-inch) flour tortillas
Vegetable cooking spray
1 cup sweet red pepper strips
1 cup green pepper strips
1½ cups sliced onion
¾ cup commercial salsa
¾ cup nonfat sour cream
    alternative

Partially freeze steak; trim fat from steak. Slice steak diagonally across grain into ¼-inch strips. Place steak in a zip-top heavy-duty plastic bag. Combine vegetable juice cocktail and next 5 ingredients; pour over steak. Seal bag; shake until steak is well coated. Marinate in refrigerator 4 to 6 hours, turning bag occasionally.

Wrap tortillas in aluminum foil. Bake at 325° for 15 minutes. Set aside, and keep warm.

Remove steak from marinade, reserving marinade. Coat a nonstick skillet with cooking spray; place over medium-high heat until hot. Add steak; cook until browned, stirring frequently. Add marinade, pepper strips, and onion; reduce heat, and simmer until vegetables are crisp-tender. Remove mixture from skillet, using a slotted spoon, and divide evenly among tortillas; roll up tortillas. Top each with 1 tablespoon salsa and 1 tablespoon sour cream. Yield: 12 servings (264 calories [21% from fat] per serving).

FAT 6.2g (SAT 1.8g, MONO 2.4g, POLY 0.9g)
PROTEIN 22.7g CARBOHYDRATE 31.0g
FIBER 2.2g CHOLESTEROL 48mg SODIUM 57mg

Beef and Broccoli Stir-Fry

1½ pounds lean boneless round
    steak
⅓ cup rice wine or dry white wine
3 tablespoons low-sodium soy
    sauce, divided
1 tablespoon cornstarch
3 tablespoons water
3 tablespoons honey
¼ teaspoon crushed red pepper
Vegetable cooking spray
2 teaspoons vegetable oil, divided
4 cups fresh broccoli flowerets

Partially freeze steak; trim fat from steak. Slice steak diagonally across grain into ¼-inch strips. Place in a zip-top heavy-duty plastic bag. Combine wine, 2 tablespoons soy sauce, and cornstarch; pour over steak. Seal bag; shake until steak is coated. Marinate in refrigerator 2 hours.

Combine water, honey, remaining 1 tablespoon soy sauce, and red pepper; stir well, and set aside.

Coat a wok or large nonstick skillet with cooking spray; add 1 teaspoon oil. Place over medium-high heat (375°) until hot. Add broccoli, and stir-fry 4 minutes. Remove broccoli from wok. Set aside; keep warm.

Remove steak from marinade, reserving marinade. Add remaining 1 teaspoon oil to wok; place wok over medium-high heat until hot. Add steak, and stir-fry 4 minutes or until done. Remove steak from wok; drain. Wipe drippings from wok.

Add steak, honey mixture, and marinade to wok; cook until thoroughly heated. Arrange broccoli on individual plates; top evenly with steak mixture. Yield: 6 servings (230 calories [27% from fat] per serving).

FAT 7.0g (SAT 2.1g, MONO 2.5g, POLY 1.1g)
PROTEIN 28.3g CARBOHYDRATE 12.4g
FIBER 1.4g CHOLESTEROL 71mg SODIUM 260mg

STIR-FRIED BEEF AND VEGETABLES

1½ pounds lean boneless top
    round steak
¼ cup water
3 tablespoons low-sodium
    Worcestershire sauce
3 cloves garlic, minced
½ teaspoon seasoned salt
½ teaspoon pepper
Vegetable cooking spray
4½ cups fresh broccoli flowerets
3 cups sliced fresh mushrooms
1 small sweet red pepper, cut into
    strips
18 pearl onions, peeled
1 (10-ounce) package frozen
    French-style green beans,
    thawed
2 tablespoons cornstarch
1½ tablespoons water
8 cups cooked long-grain rice
    (cooked without salt or fat)

Partially freeze steak; trim fat from
steak. Slice steak diagonally across
grain into ¼-inch strips. Place steak
in a zip-top heavy-duty plastic bag.

Combine ¼ cup water and next 4 ingredients in a small bowl; stir well.
Pour over steak; seal bag, and shake
until steak is well coated. Marinate in
refrigerator 2 to 4 hours, turning bag
occasionally.

Remove steak from marinade, reserving marinade. Coat a wok or large
nonstick skillet with cooking spray.
Place over medium-high heat (375°)
until hot. Add steak, and stir-fry 3
minutes. Add broccoli and next 3 ingredients; stir-fry 5 minutes or until
vegetables are crisp-tender. Add green
beans, and stir-fry 1 minute.

Combine cornstarch, marinade,
and 1½ tablespoons water; add to
steak mixture. Cook, stirring constantly, until mixture is thickened and
thoroughly heated. Serve steak mixture over rice. Yield: 8 servings (386
calories [10% from fat] per serving).

FAT 4.1g (SAT 1.3g, MONO 1.4g, POLY 0.4g)
PROTEIN 26.3g   CARBOHYDRATE 60.2g
FIBER 4.2g   CHOLESTEROL 48mg   SODIUM 109mg

Cut the steak for Stir-Fried Beef and Vegetables diagonally across the grain into thin strips. Partially freezing the steak before slicing makes this job easier.

Stir-frying is a cooking method in which small pieces of food are quickly cooked in a large skillet or wok over high heat while being stirred constantly.

Add a solution of cornstarch and water near the end of the cooking time to thicken the beef mixture. Cook, stirring constantly, just until the mixture is thoroughly heated.

Stir-Fried Beef and Vegetables is low-fat cooking at its best. Brightly colored vegetables add vitamins, minerals, and fiber to this nutritious meal.

GARLIC FLANK STEAK

1 (1½-pound) lean flank steak
¼ cup lime juice
¼ cup tequila
¼ cup minced fresh cilantro
4 cloves garlic, crushed
2 teaspoons coarsely ground pepper
Vegetable cooking spray

Trim fat from steak. Score steak on both sides. Place steak in a zip-top heavy-duty plastic bag. Combine lime juice and next 4 ingredients in a small bowl; stir well. Pour over steak; seal bag, and shake until steak is well coated. Marinate in refrigerator 8 hours, turning bag occasionally.

Remove steak from marinade; discard marinade. Coat grill rack with vegetable cooking spray; place on grill over medium-hot coals. Place steak on rack; cook 6 minutes on each side or to desired degree of doneness. Slice steak diagonally across grain into ¼-inch slices. Yield: 6 servings (231 calories [54% from fat] per serving).

FAT 13.9g (SAT 5.9g, MONO 5.8g, POLY 0.4g)
PROTEIN 23.5g CARBOHYDRATE 0.8g
FIBER 0.2g CHOLESTEROL 64mg SODIUM 77mg

MARINATED LONDON BROIL

1 (1-pound) flank steak
1 tablespoon prepared mustard
2 tablespoons Burgundy or other
   dry red wine
2 tablespoons lemon juice
2 tablespoons low-sodium soy sauce
2 tablespoons low-sodium
   Worcestershire sauce
Vegetable cooking spray

Trim fat from steak. Score steak on both sides; brush both sides of steak with mustard. Place steak in a zip-top heavy-duty plastic bag. Combine wine and next 3 ingredients in a small bowl; stir well. Pour over steak; seal bag, and shake until steak is well coated. Marinate in refrigerator 8 hours, turning bag occasionally.

Remove steak from marinade, reserving marinade. Place steak on rack of a broiler pan coated with cooking spray. Broil 5½ inches from heat 6 to 7 minutes on each side or until desired degree of doneness, basting occasionally with marinade. Slice steak diagonally across grain into ¼-inch slices. Yield: 4 servings (227 calories [52% from fat] per serving).

FAT 13.1g (SAT 5.4g, MONO 5.5g, POLY 0.4g)
PROTEIN 21.8g CARBOHYDRATE 2.5g
FIBER 0.0g CHOLESTEROL 60mg SODIUM 344mg

Scoring is a process in which shallow cuts are made diagonally across a food, such as a flank steak, at 1-inch intervals to allow the food to absorb the marinade.

PARSLIED MEAT LOAF

2 pounds ground round
1¼ cups regular oats, uncooked
1 cup chopped fresh parsley
¾ cup chopped onion
¼ cup frozen egg substitute, thawed
2 tablespoons chopped green
   pepper
1 large clove garlic, minced
½ teaspoon salt
½ teaspoon dried whole thyme
½ teaspoon black pepper
¼ teaspoon ground allspice
⅛ teaspoon ground nutmeg
⅛ teaspoon ground red pepper
Vegetable cooking spray
¼ cup catsup

Combine first 13 ingredients in a large bowl; stir well. Shape mixture into a 9- x 5-inch loaf; place loaf on a rack in a roasting pan coated with cooking spray. Bake at 350° for 1 hour and 15 minutes. Spread catsup evenly over meat loaf; bake an additional 5 minutes. Remove from oven; let stand 5 minutes before serving. Yield: 10 servings (188 calories [30% from fat] per serving).

FAT 6.2g (SAT 2.1g, MONO 2.6g, POLY 0.5g)
PROTEIN 22.0g CARBOHYDRATE 10.1g
FIBER 1.6g CHOLESTEROL 56mg SODIUM 244mg

The Search for Low-Fat Ground Beef

Some butchers label ground beef as regular, lean, or extra-lean, while others label it hamburger, ground beef, ground chuck, ground sirloin, or ground round. Still others indicate the amount of fat in their products by stating the percentage of lean in the meat, for example, 85 percent lean ground beef. With the current emphasis on fat reduction in meats, ground beef with lean contents as high as 95 percent may be available.

Generally, ground round and ground sirloin are the leanest choices, followed by ground chuck and ground beef. Choose a ground beef with the highest percentage of lean to fat, such as ground round. Or select a lean top round steak and ask the butcher to trim away all visible fat and grind the steak for you.

Veal is the meat from calves no older than three months. The calves weigh 350 pounds or less and have been fed a diet consisting primarily of milk. Although veal is limited in supply and therefore relatively expensive in cost per pound, there is minimal waste in most retail cuts.

Along with being the most delicately flavored of all meats, veal has little or no marbling, which makes it low in fat. But most cuts of veal are higher in cholesterol than most lean cuts of beef.

Veal ranges in color from ivory with a blush of pink to pale pink, depending on the age and diet of the animal. The meat should be fine-grained and velvety in texture.

Because veal comes from such young animals, most cuts are considered lean, with the leg, shoulder, loin, and sirloin being the leanest. See page 147 for a comparison of the fat, saturated fat, and cholesterol contents of veal and other cuts of meat.

VEAL ROAST WITH MUSHROOM SAUCE

1 (3-pound) boneless veal roast
½ cup brandy
¼ cup sherry wine vinegar
¼ cup minced shallot
1 clove garlic, minced
1 tablespoon minced fresh parsley
1 teaspoon dried whole thyme
½ teaspoon freshly ground pepper
¼ teaspoon salt
Vegetable cooking spray
2 cups water
Mushroom Sauce

Trim excess fat from roast. Place roast in a large zip-top heavy-duty plastic bag. Combine brandy and next 7 ingredients in a small bowl; stir well. Pour brandy mixture over roast; seal bag, and shake until roast is well coated. Marinate roast in refrigerator 8 hours, turning bag occasionally.

Remove roast from marinade, reserving marinade. Place roast on a rack in a roasting pan coated with cooking spray. Insert meat thermometer into thickest part of roast, if desired. Pour water into roasting pan. Cover and bake at 325° for 1 hour and 25 minutes. Uncover and bake 1 hour or until meat thermometer registers 160° (medium), basting frequently with marinade.

Let roast stand 10 minutes; slice roast diagonally across grain into ¼-inch slices. Serve roast with Mushroom Sauce. Yield: 12 servings (200 calories [25% from fat] per serving).

Mushroom Sauce
Vegetable cooking spray
4 cups sliced fresh shiitake mushrooms
2 cups hot water
¼ cup all-purpose flour
2 teaspoons beef-flavored bouillon granules

Coat a large nonstick skillet with cooking spray; place over medium-high heat until hot. Add mushrooms; sauté until tender. Add hot water, flour, and bouillon granules, stirring until smooth. Bring to a boil; reduce heat, and simmer until thickened, stirring constantly. Yield: 2½ cups.

FAT 5.5g (SAT 1.5g, MONO 1.8g, POLY 0.5g)
PROTEIN 25.7g CARBOHYDRATE 3.9g
FIBER 0.4g CHOLESTEROL 92mg SODIUM 307mg

Bourbon-Roasted Veal with Onion Relish

1 (3-pound) boneless veal roast
1 large clove garlic, halved
⅔ cup bourbon
¼ cup water
½ teaspoon hot sauce
¾ teaspoon pepper, divided
½ teaspoon salt
Vegetable cooking spray
Flowering kale leaves (optional)
Onion Relish

Trim excess fat from roast; rub surface of roast with garlic. Place roast in a large zip-top heavy-duty plastic bag. Combine bourbon, water, hot sauce, and ½ teaspoon pepper in a small bowl; stir well. Pour bourbon mixture over roast; seal bag, and shake until roast is well coated. Marinate roast in refrigerator 8 hours, turning bag occasionally.

Remove roast from marinade; discard marinade. Sprinkle roast evenly with remaining ¼ teaspoon pepper and salt. Place roast on a rack in a roasting pan coated with vegetable cooking spray. Insert meat thermometer into thickest part of roast, if desired. Cover and bake at 325° for 1 hour and 25 minutes. Uncover and bake 1 hour or until meat thermometer registers 160° (medium).

Let stand 10 minutes; slice roast diagonally across grain into ¼-inch slices. Arrange slices on a serving platter; garnish with flowering kale leaves, if desired. Serve with Onion Relish. Yield: 12 servings (180 calories [27% from fat] per serving).

Onion Relish
Vegetable cooking spray
3 medium onions, quartered and thinly sliced
1½ tablespoons brown sugar
1 tablespoon chopped fresh thyme
3 tablespoons white wine vinegar
½ teaspoon pepper

Coat a large saucepan with cooking spray; place over medium heat until hot. Add sliced onion; cover, reduce heat, and simmer 2 hours, stirring occasionally.

Add brown sugar, thyme, vinegar, and pepper; stir well. Cook, uncovered, stirring frequently, 5 to 6 minutes or until mixture is slightly thickened. Serve relish at room temperature. Yield: 1¼ cups.

FAT 5.3g (SAT 1.5g, MONO 1.8g, POLY 0.5g)
PROTEIN 25.5g   CARBOHYDRATE 5.6g
FIBER 0.9g   CHOLESTEROL 92mg   SODIUM 268mg

Savory Italian-Style Veal Chops

4 (6-ounce) lean veal loin chops (¾ inch thick)
¾ teaspoon dried Italian seasoning
⅛ teaspoon pepper
Vegetable cooking spray
¼ cup water
¼ cup Chablis or other dry white wine
½ teaspoon chicken-flavored bouillon granules
1 clove garlic, crushed
1 small onion, thinly sliced
2 cups sliced fresh mushrooms
½ teaspoon dried whole rosemary, crushed
1 tablespoon chopped fresh parsley

Trim fat from chops; sprinkle chops evenly with Italian seasoning and pepper. Coat a large nonstick skillet with cooking spray; place over medium-high heat until hot. Add chops; cook 3 to 4 minutes on each side or until browned. Remove chops from skillet, and set aside.

Add water and next 3 ingredients to skillet. Bring to a boil; reduce heat, and simmer 2 minutes. Place onion in an 11- x 7- x 2-inch baking dish coated with cooking spray; top with chops. Pour wine mixture over chops, and top with mushroom and rosemary. Cover and bake at 350° for 30 to 35 minutes or until chops are tender. Sprinkle chops evenly with parsley. Yield: 4 servings (160 calories [25% from fat] per serving).

FAT 4.4g (SAT 1.2g, MONO 1.2g, POLY 0.5g)
PROTEIN 24.2g   CARBOHYDRATE 5.4g
FIBER 1.3g   CHOLESTEROL 91mg   SODIUM 211mg

Delicate shiitake mushrooms give Veal Roast with Mushroom Sauce its unique flavor. Serve steamed baby vegetables as an impressive side dish.

Rosemary Grilled Veal Chops

6 (6-ounce) lean veal loin chops
  (¾ inch thick)
½ cup Chablis or other dry white
  wine
2 tablespoons lemon juice
4 cloves garlic, minced
2 teaspoons dried whole rosemary,
  crushed
¼ teaspoon pepper
⅛ teaspoon salt
Vegetable cooking spray

Trim fat from chops. Place chops in a zip-top heavy-duty plastic bag. Combine wine and next 5 ingredients; stir well. Pour over chops; seal bag, and shake until chops are well coated. Marinate in refrigerator 2 to 4 hours, turning bag occasionally.

Remove chops from marinade, reserving marinade. Coat grill rack with vegetable cooking spray; place on grill over medium-hot coals. Place chops on rack, and cook 15 to 20 minutes or to desired degree of doneness, turning and basting frequently with marinade. Yield: 6 servings (159 calories [30% from fat] per serving).

FAT 5.3g (SAT 1.4g, MONO 1.8g, POLY 0.5g)
PROTEIN 25.1g CARBOHYDRATE 1.3g
FIBER 0.1g CHOLESTEROL 92mg SODIUM 118mg

Veal Scaloppine

1 pound veal cutlets (¼ inch thick)
Freshly ground pepper
Vegetable cooking spray
2 teaspoons olive oil, divided
½ pound fresh mushrooms, sliced
½ small green pepper, cut into thin
  strips
½ medium-size sweet red pepper,
  cut into thin strips
½ cup Chablis or other dry white
  wine
¼ cup canned no-salt-added
  chicken broth, undiluted
1 tablespoon lemon juice
½ teaspoon salt
1 tablespoon cornstarch
2 tablespoons water
2 tablespoons chopped fresh parsley
2 cups cooked vermicelli (cooked
  without salt or fat)

Trim fat from cutlets. Place cutlets between 2 sheets of heavy-duty plastic wrap; flatten to ⅛-inch thickness, using a meat mallet or rolling pin. Sprinkle cutlets with ground pepper.

Coat a large nonstick skillet with cooking spray; add 1 teaspoon oil. Place over medium heat until hot. Add half of veal; cook 3 minutes on each side or until browned. Remove veal from skillet; drain and pat dry with paper towels. Set aside, and keep warm. Wipe drippings from skillet with a paper towel. Repeat procedure with remaining 1 teaspoon oil and half of veal.

Coat skillet with cooking spray; place over medium heat until hot. Add mushrooms and pepper strips; sauté until crisp-tender. Stir in wine and next 3 ingredients; bring to a boil. Reduce heat; simmer 1 minute.

Combine cornstarch and water, stirring well; add to mushroom mixture. Cook, stirring constantly, until thickened. Remove from heat, and stir in parsley. Place vermicelli on a large serving platter. Arrange veal over vermicelli, and top evenly with sauce. Yield: 4 servings (375 calories [22% from fat] per serving).

FAT 9.3g (SAT 2.0g, MONO 3.8g, POLY 1.2g)
PROTEIN 34.0g CARBOHYDRATE 37.5g
FIBER 3.2g CHOLESTEROL 100mg SODIUM 385mg

Veal Margarita Flambé

1 pound veal cutlets (¼ inch thick)
Vegetable cooking spray
1 tablespoon reduced-calorie
  margarine, divided
2 teaspoons all-purpose flour
½ cup canned no-salt-added
  chicken broth, undiluted
½ teaspoon salt
Dash of pepper
2 tablespoons Cointreau or other
  orange-flavored liqueur
1½ tablespoons fresh lime juice
1 tablespoon tequila
½ teaspoon grated lime rind

Trim fat from cutlets. Coat a large nonstick skillet with vegetable cooking spray; add 1 teaspoon margarine. Place over medium-high heat until margarine melts. Add half of veal, and cook 3 minutes on each side or until veal is browned. Remove veal from skillet; drain and pat dry with paper towels.

Transfer veal to a serving platter; set aside, and keep warm. Wipe drippings from skillet with a paper towel. Repeat procedure with 1 teaspoon margarine and remaining half of veal.

Combine flour and chicken broth, stirring until smooth. Combine flour mixture, remaining 1 teaspoon margarine, salt, and pepper in skillet, stirring well. Cook over medium heat, stirring constantly, until mixture is thickened and bubbly. Stir in Cointreau and lime juice.

Pour tequila into side of skillet. Ignite tequila with a long match; let flames die down. Pour sauce over veal, and sprinkle evenly with lime rind. Yield: 4 servings (212 calories [33% from fat] per serving).

FAT 7.7g (SAT 1.9g, MONO 2.7g, POLY 1.3g)
PROTEIN 27.5g CARBOHYDRATE 4.5g
FIBER 0.0g CHOLESTEROL 100mg SODIUM 413mg

VEAL PICCATA

1 pound veal cutlets (¼ inch thick)
¼ cup all-purpose flour
Vegetable cooking spray
1 teaspoon olive oil
½ cup dry sherry
¼ cup lemon juice
2 tablespoons capers
Lemon slices (optional)
Chopped fresh parsley (optional)

Trim fat from cutlets. Dredge cutlets in flour. Coat a large nonstick skillet with cooking spray; add oil. Place over medium-high heat until hot. Add veal, and cook 3 minutes on each side or until browned. Remove veal from skillet; drain and pat dry with paper towels. Transfer veal to a serving platter. Set aside; keep warm.

Add sherry, lemon juice, and capers to skillet; stir well, scraping bottom of pan to loosen brown bits. Cook over medium-high heat, stirring occasionally, until mixture is reduced by half. Pour sauce over veal. If desired, garnish with lemon slices and fresh parsley. Yield: 4 servings (178 calories [24% from fat] per serving).

FAT 4.6g (SAT 1.1g, MONO 1.9g, POLY 0.5g)
PROTEIN 24.0g   CARBOHYDRATE 8.7g
FIBER 0.2g   CHOLESTEROL 94mg   SODIUM 435mg

VEAL CUTLETS IN GREEN PEPPERCORN SAUCE

1 pound veal cutlets (¼ inch thick)
Vegetable cooking spray
1½ cups canned no-salt-added beef broth, undiluted
½ cup Burgundy or other dry red wine
2 large cloves garlic, crushed
2 bay leaves
1½ tablespoons green peppercorns, drained and divided
½ teaspoon salt
1 tablespoon plus 1 teaspoon cornstarch
2 tablespoons water

Trim fat from cutlets. Coat a large nonstick skillet with cooking spray; place over medium-high heat until hot. Add veal; cook 3 minutes on each side or until browned. Remove veal from skillet; drain and pat dry with paper towels. Wipe drippings from skillet with a paper towel.

Combine broth and next 5 ingredients in skillet; stir well. Add veal to skillet. Bring to a boil; cover, reduce heat, and simmer 20 minutes or until veal is tender. Remove veal from skillet, and set aside. Remove and discard bay leaves.

Combine cornstarch and water, stirring well; add to broth mixture. Cook, stirring constantly, until thickened. Return veal to skillet, and cook just until thoroughly heated. Yield: 4 servings (194 calories [27% from fat] per serving).

FAT 5.8g (SAT 1.6g, MONO 2.0g, POLY 0.5g)
PROTEIN 27.7g   CARBOHYDRATE 4.2g
FIBER 0.3g   CHOLESTEROL 100mg   SODIUM 375mg

Fresh parsley, lemon juice, and capers are the classic ingredients in Veal Piccata. A garnish of lemon slices hints at the flavor and adds contrasting color to this entrée.

Lamb

Lamb is a delicately flavored meat that is generally very tender. The meat comes from lamb that is about six to eight months old, so it has very little marbling, making it low in fat. At one year of age, lamb becomes mutton, which is more popular in Europe than it is in the United States.

Lean fresh lamb should have a pink to light red color and a thin layer of firm, white fat surrounding it. Any excess fat should be trimmed before cooking. The texture of the meat should be firm and fine-grained. The older the lamb, the darker the meat becomes.

A thin, parchment-like membrane called fell may be found on the outside of larger cuts of lamb. It is generally removed from chops before marketing, but it is left on larger cuts such as the leg to keep the meat juicy and help retain the shape of the meat during cooking.

Lean cuts of lamb are excellent for low-fat eating. The leanest cuts are the leg, sirloin, and loin, as shown in the chart of nutritional comparisons for meats on page 147.

Roasted Rack of Lamb With Bordelaise Sauce

1 (2-pound) rack of lamb (8 chops)
¼ cup soft whole wheat
  breadcrumbs
½ teaspoon minced garlic
½ teaspoon dried parsley flakes
½ teaspoon dried whole rosemary,
  crushed
¼ teaspoon freshly ground pepper
Vegetable cooking spray
Bordelaise Sauce

Trim fat from rack, leaving only small eye of rib. Strip rib tips of all meat and fat. Combine breadcrumbs and next 4 ingredients in a small bowl; stir well. Pat mixture evenly over meat portion of rack. Place rack of lamb, bone side down, on rack of a broiler pan coated with vegetable cooking spray. Insert meat thermometer into rack, making sure it does not touch bone.

Bake at 450° for 25 to 30 minutes or until meat thermometer registers 150° (medium rare) or 160° (medium). Let rack of lamb stand 10 minutes before serving. Cut into 8 chops, and serve with Bordelaise Sauce. Yield: 4 servings (255 calories [44% from fat] per serving).

Bordelaise Sauce
Vegetable cooking spray
1 shallot, minced
2 tablespoons all-purpose flour
⅔ cup canned no-salt-added beef
  broth, undiluted and divided
⅓ cup Burgundy or other dry red
  wine
¾ teaspoon dried parsley flakes
¼ teaspoon dried whole thyme
¼ teaspoon salt
⅛ teaspoon pepper

Coat a small saucepan with vegetable cooking spray; place over medium heat until hot. Add shallot; sauté until tender.

Combine flour and ¼ cup broth, stirring until smooth. Add flour mixture to saucepan; stir in remaining broth, wine, parsley, and thyme. Cook, stirring constantly, until mixture is thickened. Remove saucepan from heat, and stir in salt and pepper. Yield: 1 cup.

FAT 12.5g (SAT 4.4g, MONO 4.9g, POLY 1.3g)
PROTEIN 26.7g CARBOHYDRATE 6.9g
FIBER 0.4g CHOLESTEROL 84mg SODIUM 248mg

Spicy Lamb with Couscous

1 pound lean boneless lamb
Vegetable cooking spray
1½ cups no-salt-added tomato
  juice
1 cup chopped green pepper
1 cup chopped sweet red pepper
2 tablespoons chopped onion
3 cloves garlic, minced
1 tablespoon lemon juice
½ teaspoon ground coriander
½ teaspoon ground cumin
¼ teaspoon salt
¼ teaspoon ground ginger
¼ teaspoon paprika
1½ cups canned no-salt-added
  chicken broth, undiluted
¾ cup couscous, uncooked

Trim fat from lamb; cut lamb into 1-inch pieces. Coat a large saucepan with vegetable cooking spray; place over medium-high heat until hot. Add lamb; cook until browned on all sides. Drain and pat dry with paper towels. Wipe drippings from pan with a paper towel.

Return lamb to pan; add tomato juice and next 10 ingredients. Bring mixture to a boil; cover, reduce heat, and simmer 45 minutes or until lamb is tender.

Bring chicken broth to a boil in a medium saucepan. Remove from heat. Add couscous; cover and let stand 5 minutes or until couscous is tender and liquid is absorbed. Fluff couscous with a fork, and transfer to a serving platter; top with lamb mixture. Yield: 4 servings (251 calories [28% from fat] per serving).

FAT 7.9g (SAT 2.6g, MONO 2.9g, POLY 0.6g)
PROTEIN 27.7g CARBOHYDRATE 16.7g
FIBER 1.7g CHOLESTEROL 76mg SODIUM 271mg

Sweet-and-Savory Lamb Chops takes less than 30 minutes to prepare. A serving of Minted English Peas (page 201) and a dinner roll round out this family meal.

GRILLED PESTO LAMB CHOPS

⅓ cup tightly packed fresh basil leaves
1½ teaspoons grated Parmesan cheese
1½ teaspoons pine nuts
1 clove garlic, halved
2 tablespoons plain nonfat yogurt
4 (4-ounce) lean lamb rib chops
Vegetable cooking spray
Fresh basil sprigs (optional)

Position knife blade in food processor bowl; add first 4 ingredients. Process until smooth. Transfer mixture to a small bowl; stir in yogurt. Cover and chill 30 minutes.

Trim fat from chops. Coat grill rack with vegetable cooking spray; place on grill over medium-hot coals. Place chops on rack, and cook 5 minutes. Turn chops; spread basil mixture evenly over chops. Cook 5 minutes or to desired degree of doneness. Garnish with fresh basil sprigs, if desired. Yield: 2 servings (214 calories [41% from fat] per serving).

FAT 9.8g (SAT 3.4g, MONO 4.0g, POLY 0.8g)
PROTEIN 27.8g CARBOHYDRATE 2.1g
FIBER 0.1g CHOLESTEROL 84mg SODIUM 108mg

SWEET-AND-SAVORY LAMB CHOPS

8 (3-ounce) lean lamb loin chops (1 inch thick)
2 cloves garlic, halved
1 tablespoon minced fresh rosemary
¼ teaspoon freshly ground pepper
Vegetable cooking spray
¼ cup honey
2 tablespoons stone ground mustard
Fresh rosemary sprigs (optional)
Lemon slices (optional)

Trim fat from chops. Rub both sides of chops with cut side of garlic. Press rosemary and pepper evenly onto both sides of chops. Place chops on rack of a broiler pan coated with cooking spray. Combine honey and mustard in a small bowl; stir well, and set aside.

Broil chops 5½ inches from heat 6 minutes. Turn chops, and spread with honey mixture; broil an additional 8 minutes or to desired degree of doneness. If desired, garnish with fresh rosemary sprigs and lemon slices. Yield: 4 servings (259 calories [31% from fat] per serving).

FAT 8.9g (SAT 3.0g, MONO 3.6g, POLY 0.6g)
PROTEIN 26.1g CARBOHYDRATE 18.7g
FIBER 0.2g CHOLESTEROL 81mg SODIUM 214mg

You'll have a hard time finding a "fat pig" at the market today. Pork producers have put their hogs on a diet, and today's pork is significantly lower in fat than ever before.

Even though the cuts of pork you buy in the supermarket are virtually free of trichinae (the parasites that cause the disease trichinosis), it is still recommended that precautions be taken during handling and preparation. Wash anything that comes in contact with raw pork, and cook pork to an internal temperature of 160° (medium). At this temperature, pork will be safe to eat while remaining tender, juicy, and slightly pink in the middle.

Fresh pork should be grayish pink or rose-colored, while cured pork should be deep pink in color. The leanest cuts of pork include the tenderloin and the leg (fresh ham). See page 147 for the calorie, fat, and cholesterol content of several pork cuts.

GARLIC-ROSEMARY PORK ROAST

1 (3½-pound) lean boneless double pork loin roast, tied
4 cloves garlic, crushed
2 tablespoons chopped fresh rosemary
2 tablespoons chopped fresh chives
2 tablespoons chopped fresh parsley
Vegetable cooking spray

Untie roast, and trim fat. Retie roast. Rub garlic over surface of roast. Combine rosemary, chives, and parsley; sprinkle evenly over roast. Cover and chill 2 to 4 hours.

Place roast on rack of a broiler pan coated with vegetable cooking spray.

Insert meat thermometer into thickest part of roast, if desired. Place roast in a 450° oven. Reduce heat to 325°, and bake 2 hours or until meat thermometer registers 160°.

Let roast stand 10 minutes. Remove string from roast, and slice diagonally across grain into thin slices. Yield: 14 servings (202 calories [51% from fat] per serving).

FAT 11.5g (SAT 4.0g, MONO 5.2g, POLY 1.4g)
PROTEIN 22.3g CARBOHYDRATE 0.5g
FIBER 0.1g CHOLESTEROL 75mg SODIUM 58mg

COLORFUL STUFFED PORK ROAST

2 (6-ounce) packages long-grain and wild rice mix
¾ cup boiling water
¾ cup dried apricots
Vegetable cooking spray
¾ cup chopped fresh mushrooms
½ cup chopped green onions
½ cup chopped sweet red pepper
2 cloves garlic, minced
¼ cup plus 2 tablespoons chopped water chestnuts
2 tablespoons chopped fresh parsley
½ teaspoon freshly ground pepper
1 (4-pound) lean boneless double pork loin roast, tied
½ cup apricot jam, melted and divided

Prepare rice mix according to package directions, omitting salt and fat. Set aside.

Pour boiling water over apricots; let stand 20 minutes. Drain well. Finely chop apricots, and set aside.

Coat a large nonstick skillet with cooking spray; place over medium-high heat until hot. Add mushrooms, green onions, sweet red pepper, and garlic; sauté 4 to 5 minutes or until vegetables are tender. Stir in rice, apricots, water chestnuts, parsley, and ground pepper.

Untie roast, and trim fat. Spread 1¼ cups rice mixture over inside of roast. Retie roast. Set remaining rice mixture aside; keep warm. Place roast on a rack in a roasting pan coated with cooking spray; brush roast with half of jam. Insert meat thermometer into thickest part of roast, if desired. Bake at 350° for 1 hour and 40 minutes or until meat thermometer registers 160°, basting frequently with remaining half of jam.

Let roast stand 10 minutes. Spread remaining rice mixture on a large serving platter; place roast on top of rice mixture. Remove string from roast; slice diagonally across grain into 16 slices. Yield: 16 servings (309 calories [31% from fat] per serving).

FAT 10.7g (SAT 3.7g, MONO 4.8g, POLY 1.4g)
PROTEIN 22.8g CARBOHYDRATE 30.2g
FIBER 1.8g CHOLESTEROL 67mg SODIUM 418mg

Untie a double pork loin roast, and trim any fat on the outside of the roast. Then open up the roast, and trim any fat on the inside. Retie the roast before baking.

SPICY-HOT SMOKED PORK

Hickory chips
1 (3-pound) lean boneless double
    pork loin roast, tied
1 cup cider vinegar
1 tablespoon hot sauce
1 teaspoon low-sodium
    Worcestershire sauce
½ teaspoon salt
½ teaspoon cracked black pepper
½ teaspoon ground red pepper
Vegetable cooking spray

Soak hickory chips in water for at least 30 minutes.

Untie roast, and trim fat. Retie roast. Place roast in a zip-top heavy-duty plastic bag. Combine vinegar and next 5 ingredients; pour over roast. Seal bag; shake until roast is well coated. Marinate in refrigerator 8 hours, turning bag occasionally.

Prepare charcoal fire in meat smoker; let burn 20 minutes. Place hickory chips on coals. Place water pan in smoker; add hot water to pan until water reaches fill line on pan.

Remove roast from marinade; discard marinade. Coat grill rack with cooking spray; place rack in smoker. Place roast on rack. Insert meat thermometer into thickest part of roast, if desired. Cover with smoker lid; cook 5 hours or until thermometer registers 160°. Refill water pan and add additional charcoal as needed.

Let roast stand 10 minutes. Remove string; slice diagonally across grain into thin slices. Yield: 12 servings (200 calories [52% from fat] per serving).

FAT 11.5g (SAT 4.0g, MONO 5.2g, POLY 1.4g)
PROTEIN 22.1g CARBOHYDRATE 0.2g
FIBER 0.0g CHOLESTEROL 74mg SODIUM 159mg

Savor the Oriental flavor of Pineapple-Ginger Pork Tenderloins. One serving has 232 calories and less than five grams of fat.

PINEAPPLE-GINGER PORK TENDERLOINS

2 (¾-pound) pork tenderloins
½ cup unsweetened pineapple juice
2 tablespoons peeled, minced
    gingerroot
2 tablespoons low-sodium soy sauce
2 cloves garlic, minced
½ teaspoon dry mustard
Vegetable cooking spray
12 slices fresh pineapple (½ inch
    thick)
Fresh parsley sprigs (optional)

Trim fat from tenderloins. Place tenderloins in a zip-top heavy-duty plastic bag. Combine pineapple juice and next 4 ingredients; stir well. Pour over tenderloins; seal bag, and shake until tenderloins are well coated. Marinate in refrigerator 8 hours, turning bag occasionally.

Remove pork tenderloins from marinade, reserving marinade. Insert a meat thermometer into thickest part of tenderloin, if desired. Coat grill rack with vegetable cooking spray; place on grill over medium coals. Place tenderloins on rack, and cook 35 to 45 minutes or until thermometer reaches 160°, turning and basting occasionally with marinade.

Transfer tenderloins to a serving platter; let stand 10 minutes. Place pineapple slices on grill rack; cook 5 to 7 minutes on each side or until browned. Slice tenderloin diagonally across grain into thin slices. Arrange pineapple on platter with tenderloin. Garnish with fresh parsley sprigs, if desired. Yield: 6 servings (232 calories [19% from fat] per serving).

FAT 4.9g (SAT 1.4g, MONO 1.9g, POLY 0.7g)
PROTEIN 24.6g CARBOHYDRATE 22.9g
FIBER 2.5g CHOLESTEROL 77mg SODIUM 166mg

JALISCO-STYLE PORK TENDERLOINS

2 (¾-pound) pork tenderloins
Vegetable cooking spray
2 teaspoons grated orange rind
1 cup fresh orange juice
1 medium onion, sliced
1 tablespoon commercial steak
  sauce
¼ teaspoon garlic powder
⅛ teaspoon crushed red pepper
⅛ teaspoon ground cinnamon
⅛ teaspoon ground cloves

Trim fat from tenderloins. Coat a Dutch oven with cooking spray; place over medium-high heat until hot. Add tenderloins; cook 10 minutes or until browned, turning occasionally.

Combine orange rind and remaining ingredients in a small bowl; stir well. Pour orange juice mixture over tenderloins. Insert a meat thermometer into thickest part of tenderloin, if desired. Bring mixture in pan to a boil; cover, reduce heat, and simmer 1 hour and 10 minutes or until meat thermometer registers 160°, basting occasionally with juices.

Transfer tenderloins to a serving platter using a slotted spoon. Let stand 10 minutes; slice diagonally across grain into thin slices. Serve tenderloins with onion mixture. Yield: 6 servings (159 calories [17% from fat] per serving).

FAT 3.0g (SAT 1.0g, MONO 1.3g, POLY 0.3g)
PROTEIN 24.4g CARBOHYDRATE 7.6g
FIBER 0.6g CHOLESTEROL 74mg SODIUM 103mg

ORIENTAL PORK TENDERLOINS

2 (¾-pound) pork tenderloins
½ cup reduced-calorie catsup
2 tablespoons brown sugar
2 tablespoons low-sodium soy
  sauce
½ teaspoon ground ginger
1 clove garlic, minced
Vegetable cooking spray
Fresh parsley sprigs (optional)

Trim fat from tenderloins. Place tenderloins in a zip-top heavy-duty plastic bag. Combine catsup and next 4 ingredients in a small bowl; stir well. Pour catsup mixture over tenderloins; seal bag, and shake until tenderloins are well coated. Marinate in refrigerator 8 hours, turning bag occasionally.

Remove tenderloins from marinade, reserving marinade. Place tenderloins on a rack in a roasting pan coated with cooking spray. Insert meat thermometer into thickest part of tenderloin, if desired. Bake at 400° for 45 to 50 minutes or until meat thermometer registers 160°, basting frequently with marinade.

Transfer tenderloins to a serving platter. Let stand 10 minutes; slice diagonally across grain into thin slices. Garnish with fresh parsley sprigs, if desired. Yield: 6 servings (163 calories [24% from fat] per serving).

FAT 4.1g (SAT 1.4g, MONO 1.8g, POLY 0.5g)
PROTEIN 24.1g CARBOHYDRATE 5.2g
FIBER 0.0g CHOLESTEROL 77mg SODIUM 222mg

CRANBERRY-GINGER PORK CHOPS

4 (6-ounce) lean center-cut loin
  pork chops
½ cup cranberry juice cocktail
  concentrate, thawed and
  undiluted
3 tablespoons sliced green onions
1 tablespoon peeled, grated
  gingerroot
¼ teaspoon ground red pepper
Vegetable cooking spray

Trim fat from chops. Place chops in a zip-top heavy-duty plastic bag. Combine cranberry juice cocktail and next 3 ingredients; pour over chops. Seal bag; shake until chops are well coated. Marinate in refrigerator 8 hours, turning bag occasionally.

Remove chops from marinade, reserving marinade. Coat grill rack with cooking spray, and place on grill over medium-hot coals. Place chops on rack, and cook 5 to 6 minutes on each side or until desired degree of doneness, basting frequently with marinade. Yield: 4 servings (342 calories [30% from fat] per serving).

FAT 11.4g (SAT 4.1g, MONO 5.3g, POLY 1.5g)
PROTEIN 24.4g CARBOHYDRATE 34.7g
FIBER 0.2g CHOLESTEROL 77mg SODIUM 69mg

Trim any fat around the edge of bone-in or boneless pork chops to keep them as low in fat as possible.

HERBED DIJON PORK CHOPS

2 pounds lean boneless center-cut
   loin pork chops (¾ inch thick)
½ cup fine, dry breadcrumbs
1 tablespoon dried parsley flakes
½ teaspoon dried whole rosemary,
   crushed
¼ teaspoon pepper
½ cup country-style Dijon mustard
Vegetable cooking spray

Trim fat from chops. Combine breadcrumbs and next 3 ingredients. Brush mustard over both sides of chops; dredge in breadcrumb mixture.

Coat a large nonstick skillet with cooking spray; place over medium-high heat until hot. Add chops; cook 4 to 6 minutes on each side or until tender. Yield: 8 servings (221 calories [40% from fat] per serving).

FAT 9.9g (SAT 3.1g, MONO 4.8g, POLY 1.2g)
PROTEIN 24.3g CARBOHYDRATE 5.7g
FIBER 0.3g CHOLESTEROL 68mg SODIUM 564mg

RANCHER PORK CHOPS

1½ pounds lean boneless center-cut
   loin pork chops (¾ inch thick)
Vegetable cooking spray
1 cup chopped onion
1 (14½-ounce) can no-salt-added
   whole tomatoes, drained and
   chopped
1 (4-ounce) can chopped green
   chiles, drained
2 cloves garlic, minced
¼ teaspoon salt

Trim fat from chops; set aside. Coat a large nonstick skillet with cooking spray; place over medium-high heat until hot. Add onion; sauté until tender. Add tomato and remaining ingredients; stir well. Add chops to skillet, spooning vegetable mixture over chops. Cover, reduce heat, and simmer 25 minutes or until chops are tender. Yield: 6 servings (161 calories [35% from fat] per serving).

FAT 6.3g (SAT 2.2g, MONO 2.8g, POLY 0.7g)
PROTEIN 19.8g CARBOHYDRATE 5.3g
FIBER 1.0g CHOLESTEROL 54mg SODIUM 180mg

BOUDIN BLANC

2 medium onions, quartered
⅓ cup minced fresh parsley
Vegetable cooking spray
½ pound skinned, boned chicken
   breast halves
½ pound lean ground pork
1 cup soft breadcrumbs
½ cup frozen egg substitute, thawed
¼ cup instant nonfat dry milk
   powder
1 teaspoon ground white pepper
½ teaspoon salt
¼ teaspoon ground ginger
¼ teaspoon ground cinnamon
¼ teaspoon ground nutmeg
¼ teaspoon ground allspice
5 to 6 feet pork sausage casing
4 cups water

Position knife blade in food processor bowl. Add onion and parsley. Process until onion is coarsely chopped. Coat a nonstick skillet with cooking spray; place over medium heat until hot. Add onion mixture; sauté until onion is tender. Remove from heat.

Add chicken to processor bowl; process until finely chopped. Add onion mixture, ground pork, and next 9 ingredients. Process 1 to 2 minutes or until mixture is smooth.

Rinse pork casing thoroughly in warm water; drain well. Tie one end of casing securely with cotton string. Insert a large, wide-mouth tip into large pastry bag. Fill bag with sausage mixture. Slip open end of casing over tip of bag. Pipe sausage mixture into casing, using hand to force mixture evenly into casing. Tie open end of casing with string.

Combine water and sausage in a large Dutch oven. Bring to a boil; cover, reduce heat, and simmer 20 to 30 minutes or until sausage is done. Remove sausage from water. Chill until ready to serve.

To serve, cut sausage into ¼-inch slices. Coat a nonstick skillet with cooking spray; place over medium-high heat until hot. Add sausage slices; cook until sausage is browned on both sides. Yield: 8 servings (140 calories [19% from fat] per serving).

FAT 3.0g (SAT 1.0g, MONO 1.2g, POLY 0.4g)
PROTEIN 16.6g CARBOHYDRATE 10.8g
FIBER 1.1g CHOLESTEROL 34mg SODIUM 273mg

APRICOT-GLAZED HAM

1 (2-pound) lean cooked, boneless
   ham, cut into 8 slices
Vegetable cooking spray
⅓ cup reduced-calorie apricot
   spread
2 tablespoons unsweetened orange
   juice
2 tablespoons spicy hot mustard
1 teaspoon low-sodium soy sauce
½ teaspoon peeled, grated
   gingerroot

Arrange ham slices in a 13- x 9- x 2-inch baking dish coated with cooking spray. Combine apricot spread and remaining ingredients; spoon mixture evenly over ham slices.

Cover and bake at 325° for 15 minutes or until thoroughly heated. Yield: 8 servings (158 calories [27% from fat] per serving).

FAT 4.7g (SAT 1.4g, MONO 2.1g, POLY 0.4g)
PROTEIN 19.0g CARBOHYDRATE 10.5g
FIBER 0.2g CHOLESTEROL 48mg SODIUM 1,198mg

Wild Game

Buffalo and venison are showing up on restaurant menus and in some supermarkets, particularly in the western United States.

Because wild game doesn't get fat, it is lower in fat than most meats, but the cholesterol content is similar to that of other red meats. Trim any visible fat from wild game before cooking, even though there isn't much of it. The strong, gamey flavor is exaggerated in the fat, so you want to remove as much as possible.

Cook tender cuts of game, such as roasts and steaks, at low temperatures until they reach 140° (rare) or 160° (medium). Marinating a tougher cut of game in an acid-based marinade will tenderize the meat, help prevent it from drying out, and enhance its flavor. As with other lean meats, overcooking toughens and drys out game.

All cuts of game, especially the tougher ones, can be braised or stewed. Both methods keep the meat moist and help make it tender.

SOUTHWESTERN BUFFALO STEAKS

1 (1-pound) top sirloin buffalo steak (½ inch thick)
1¼ teaspoons ground cumin
¼ teaspoon salt
¼ teaspoon pepper
Vegetable cooking spray
1 cup Spicy Jalapeño-Fruit Sauce (page 185)

Trim fat from steak; cut steak into 4 equal pieces. Place steak between 2 sheets of heavy-duty plastic wrap, and flatten to ⅜-inch thickness, using a meat mallet or rolling pin. Combine cumin, salt, and pepper; rub mixture onto both sides of steaks.

Coat a medium nonstick skillet with cooking spray; place over medium heat until hot. Add steaks; cook 4 minutes on each side or until desired degree of doneness. Serve each steak with ¼ cup Spicy Jalapeño-Fruit Sauce. Yield: 4 servings (170 calories [12% from fat] per serving).

FAT 2.2g (SAT 0.6g, MONO 0.6g, POLY 0.5g)
PROTEIN 24.2g CARBOHYDRATE 14.3g
FIBER 3.1g CHOLESTEROL 50mg SODIUM 417mg

BURGUNDY BUFFALO BURGER STEAKS

Vegetable cooking spray
1 cup finely chopped onion
2 cloves garlic, minced
1½ pounds ground buffalo
¼ cup Burgundy or other dry red wine
1 teaspoon dry mustard
½ teaspoon salt
¼ teaspoon pepper
¼ teaspoon dried whole thyme

Coat a large nonstick skillet with cooking spray; place over medium-high heat until hot. Add onion and garlic; sauté until tender. Remove from heat; set aside, and let cool.

Combine onion mixture, buffalo, and remaining ingredients in a large bowl. Shape mixture into 6 patties. Coat skillet with cooking spray; place over medium-high heat until hot. Add patties, and cook 4 to 5 minutes on each side or to desired degree of doneness. Drain on paper towels. Yield: 6 servings (126 calories [13% from fat] per serving).

FAT 1.8g (SAT 0.5g, MONO 0.5g, POLY 0.3g)
PROTEIN 23.3g CARBOHYDRATE 2.6g
FIBER 0.5g CHOLESTEROL 52mg SODIUM 245mg

MARINATED VENISON STEAKS

6 (4-ounce) lean, boneless venison loin steaks (½ inch thick)
¼ cup Burgundy or other dry red wine
1½ tablespoons low-sodium soy sauce
1 clove garlic, minced
¾ teaspoon dried whole thyme
¼ teaspoon salt
¼ teaspoon pepper
¼ teaspoon hot sauce
1 bay leaf
Vegetable cooking spray

Trim fat from steaks; place steaks in a zip-top heavy-duty plastic bag. Combine wine and next 7 ingredients; stir well. Pour over steaks; seal bag, and shake until steaks are well coated. Marinate in refrigerator 8 hours, turning bag occasionally.

Remove steaks from marinade, reserving marinade. Remove and discard bay leaf. Coat grill rack with vegetable cooking spray; place on grill over medium-hot coals. Place steaks on rack, and cook 3 minutes on each side or to desired degree of doneness, basting occasionally with marinade. Yield: 6 servings (133 calories [19% from fat] per serving).

FAT 2.8g (SAT 1.0g, MONO 0.7g, POLY 0.5g)
PROTEIN 24.8g CARBOHYDRATE 0.4g
FIBER 0.1g CHOLESTEROL 92mg SODIUM 209mg

VENISON POT ROAST WITH VEGETABLES

3 pounds venison roast
3 tablespoons all-purpose flour
½ teaspoon salt
½ teaspoon pepper
Vegetable cooking spray
1 tablespoon vegetable oil
1 medium onion, sliced
1 cup apple cider
1 cup canned no-salt-added
    beef broth, undiluted
1 teaspoon dried whole
    thyme
1 bay leaf
8 small red potatoes, peeled
    (about 1¼ pounds)
6 carrots, scraped and quartered
4 stalks celery, cut into 2-inch
    pieces

Trim excess fat from roast. Combine flour, salt, and pepper in a shallow dish; stir well. Dredge roast in flour mixture.

Coat a large Dutch oven with vegetable cooking spray; add oil. Place over medium-high heat until hot. Add roast; cook 5 minutes or until browned on all sides. Add onion, cider, broth, thyme, and bay leaf to pan. Bring mixture to a boil; cover, reduce heat, and simmer 1 hour and 45 minutes.

Add potato, carrot, and celery to pan; cover and simmer an additional 45 to 50 minutes or until roast and vegetables are tender. Transfer roast to a large serving platter; spoon vegetables around roast, using a slotted spoon. Remove and discard bay leaf. Spoon remaining mixture in pan evenly over roast and vegetables. Yield: 8 servings (269 calories [17% from fat] per serving).

FAT 5.3g (SAT 1.6g, MONO 1.4g, POLY 1.5g)
PROTEIN 32.7g CARBOHYDRATE 21.5g
FIBER 2.9g CHOLESTEROL 113mg SODIUM 247mg

COMPARISON OF NUTRITIONAL CONTENT OF MEATS

Cut (3 ounces cooked)	Calories	Fat (grams)	Saturated Fat (grams)	Cholesterol (milligrams)
Beef				
Eye-of-round	156	5.5	2.1	59
Round tip	162	6.4	2.3	69
Top round	162	5.3	1.8	71
Round	165	6.8	2.5	70
Ground round	165	6.8	2.5	70
Tenderloin	173	7.9	3.1	71
Top loin	173	7.6	3.0	65
Sirloin	177	7.4	3.0	76
Ground sirloin	177	7.4	3.0	76
Flank	207	12.7	5.4	60
Ground beef, extra-lean	218	13.9	5.5	71
Ground chuck	228	15.6	6.1	66
Ground beef	244	17.8	7.0	74
Veal				
Leg	128	2.9	1.0	88
Sirloin	143	5.3	2.1	88
Shoulder	145	5.6	2.1	97
Loin	149	5.9	2.2	90
Rib	151	6.3	1.8	98
Cutlets	185	10.5	4.5	88
Lamb				
Leg (shank half)	153	5.7	2.0	74
Leg (whole)	162	6.6	2.4	76
Shoulder	173	9.2	3.5	74
Sirloin	173	7.8	2.8	78
Loin	184	8.3	3.0	81
Rib	200	11.0	4.0	77
Pork				
Ham (lean, cured)	123	4.7	1.5	45
Tenderloin	141	4.1	1.4	79
Leg (whole, fresh ham)	188	9.0	3.1	82
Center loin	204	11.1	3.1	77
Loin	204	11.7	4.1	77
Shoulder	208	12.7	4.4	82
Wild Game				
Buffalo	111	1.5	0.5	52
Venison	134	2.7	1.1	95

POULTRY

The popularity of poultry has soared in recent years. The fact that it is a protein-rich food that is low in total fat, saturated fat, and cholesterol has helped make it a big part of the fat-conscious diet. Also, poultry is economical, easy to cook, and extremely versatile.

Poultry, which includes chicken, Cornish hens, turkey, and wild birds, can be a superstar in any healthful diet. To keep poultry as lean as possible, trim away all visible fat and remove the skin, which contains most of the fat.

Selecting Poultry

When choosing poultry, buy the cut that best suits your time and budget requirements. For example, if your recipe calls for a cup amount of chopped, cooked chicken, the most economical option is to purchase and cook a whole chicken. Or you could spend a bit more and buy skinned, boned breast halves to cook and chop. If the recipe calls for skinned, boned chicken breast halves, you could purchase less expensive breast halves that have the skin and bone, and remove the skin and bone yourself. Keep in mind that the less processed a cut of poultry is, the less expensive it will be per pound.

Packaged poultry should have a USDA inspection mark that indicates the poultry is safe and wholesome. Some poultry products may also carry a state inspection mark. The top grade of poultry, Grade A, is the one seen most often in supermarkets.

Storage and Handling

Poultry is very perishable and should be stored in the coldest section of the refrigerator. Uncooked poultry can be stored safely in the refrigerator for two to three days; cooked poultry can be refrigerated up to four days after preparation. Smaller cuts of poultry can be frozen up to three months for optimum flavor and quality, while large, whole birds will retain their quality up to six months. For best results, remove the poultry from its packaging, rinse, and pat dry. Wrap the meat tightly in heavy-duty plastic wrap or freezer paper before freezing.

The safest way to thaw poultry is in the refrigerator. But to safely thaw more quickly, place the wrapped package in a large bowl of cold water, and allow it to sit at room temperature 30 minutes. Change the water, and repeat this process until the poultry is thawed. Never leave a package of poultry sitting out on the counter to thaw because bacteria thrive at warm temperatures. Thawing in the microwave oven is also a quick way to thaw and should be done according to oven directions. Cook thawed poultry immediately, or refrigerate it until cooking time. Poultry that has been thawed should not be refrozen.

Despite the impressive appearance of this poultry entrée, Apricot Chicken with Bourbon and Pecans (page 152) is simple to prepare.

Chicken

Chicken is considered a nutrient-dense food because it is high in protein, vitamins, and minerals and low in calories, total fat, saturated fat, and cholesterol. Your imagination is the only limit when it comes to the many ways chicken can be prepared. Its delicate flavor, versatility, and low fat content make it an excellent addition to a healthy eating plan.

TEX-MEX ROASTED CHICKEN WITH VEGETABLES

1 (3-pound) broiler-fryer, skinned
Vegetable cooking spray
1 tablespoon white wine vinegar
1 teaspoon ground cumin
1 teaspoon chili powder
½ teaspoon dried whole basil
½ teaspoon dried whole oregano
¼ teaspoon salt
2 cups coarsely chopped yellow squash
2 cups coarsely chopped zucchini
1½ cups unpeeled, seeded, coarsely chopped tomato
1 small sweet red pepper, cut into julienne strips
½ cup chopped shallots

Trim fat from chicken. Remove giblets and neck from chicken; reserve for other uses. Rinse chicken under cold water; pat dry. Place chicken, breast side up, on a rack in a roasting pan coated with cooking spray. Truss chicken. Insert meat thermometer in meaty part of thigh, making sure it does not touch bone.

Combine vinegar and next 5 ingredients; rub chicken with herb mixture. Bake, uncovered, at 375° for 1½ hours or until meat thermometer registers 185°. Transfer chicken to a serving platter, and keep warm.

Coat a large nonstick skillet with cooking spray; place over medium-high heat until hot. Add yellow squash, zucchini, tomato, pepper, and shallots; sauté 3 to 4 minutes or until vegetables are crisp-tender. Arrange vegetable mixture around chicken. Yield: 6 servings (213 calories [31% from fat] per serving).

FAT 7.4g (SAT 1.9g, MONO 2.5g, POLY 1.8g)
PROTEIN 27.7g   CARBOHYDRATE 9.2g
FIBER 2.3g   CHOLESTEROL 79mg   SODIUM 187mg

CHICKEN BRAISED IN WHITE WINE

½ pound small fresh mushrooms
2 cups canned no-salt-added chicken broth, undiluted
1 cup Chablis or other dry white wine
1 (3-pound) broiler-fryer, cut up and skinned
¼ teaspoon salt
¼ teaspoon pepper
Vegetable cooking spray
3 small onions, quartered
2 cloves garlic, minced
3 fresh parsley sprigs
1 fresh thyme sprig
1 bay leaf

Clean mushrooms with damp paper towels; remove stems. Cut mushroom caps in half; set aside. Combine mushroom stems, broth, and wine in a medium saucepan; bring to a boil. Reduce heat, and simmer, uncovered, 40 minutes or until mixture is reduced to 1 cup. Strain broth mixture, reserving liquid; set aside. Discard mushroom stems.

Trim excess fat from chicken. Rinse chicken under cold water; pat dry. Sprinkle chicken with salt and pepper. Coat a large nonstick skillet with vegetable cooking spray; place over medium-high heat until hot. Add chicken; cook until browned on both sides. Remove chicken from skillet; drain on paper towels, and set aside. Wipe drippings from skillet with a paper towel.

Coat skillet with vegetable cooking spray; place over medium-high heat until hot. Add onion and garlic; cook until onion is browned. Add mushroom caps, broth mixture, chicken, parsley, thyme, and bay leaf to skillet. Bring to a boil; cover, reduce heat, and simmer 45 minutes or until chicken is tender. Remove and discard bay leaf. Transfer chicken and vegetables to a serving platter, using a slotted spoon. Discard cooking liquid. Yield: 6 servings (198 calories [32% from fat] per serving).

FAT 7.0g (SAT 1.9g, MONO 2.5g, POLY 1.6g)
PROTEIN 25.6g   CARBOHYDRATE 6.9g
FIBER 1.4g   CHOLESTEROL 73mg   SODIUM 219mg

Food Safety and Poultry

When poultry is handled properly, salmonella (bacteria that can cause food poisoning) can be rendered ineffective. Keep uncooked poultry thoroughly chilled; leaving it at room temperature for any length of time will encourage salmonella growth.

Wash poultry thoroughly before cooking, and always use a clean knife and cutting board during preparation. Wash your hands, the knife, and the cutting board with hot, soapy water immediately after handling poultry to prevent cross-contamination with other foods.

CRISPY OVEN-FRIED CHICKEN

¼ cup plus 2 tablespoons frozen
   egg substitute, thawed
1 tablespoon water
1 cup crispy rice cereal, crushed
⅓ cup toasted wheat germ
1 tablespoon instant minced onion
½ teaspoon salt-free herb seasoning
   blend
¼ teaspoon garlic powder
¼ teaspoon salt
¼ teaspoon pepper
1 (3-pound) broiler-fryer, cut up
   and skinned
¼ cup all-purpose flour
Vegetable cooking spray

Combine egg substitute and water in a shallow dish; stir well. Combine cereal and next 6 ingredients in a shallow dish; stir well.

Place chicken pieces and flour in a large zip-top heavy-duty plastic bag; seal bag, and shake until chicken is well coated.

Dip chicken in egg substitute mixture; dredge in cereal mixture. Place chicken on rack of a broiler pan coated with cooking spray. Bake, uncovered, at 350° for 1 hour or until chicken is tender and golden. Yield: 6 servings (248 calories [19% from fat] per serving).

FAT 5.2g (SAT 1.2g, MONO 1.2g, POLY 1.5g)
PROTEIN 34.3g   CARBOHYDRATE 14.0g
FIBER 1.3g   CHOLESTEROL 99mg   SODIUM 278mg

Most of the fat content of chicken and other types of poultry lies in the skin. Remove the skin before cooking to keep Crispy Oven-Fried Chicken as low in fat as possible.

For less mess, combine the flour and chicken in a large zip-top heavy-duty plastic bag. Seal the bag, and shake it until the chicken is well coated with the flour.

Bake the chicken on the rack of a broiler pan. This allows air to circulate, creating a crisp crust over the entire surface of the chicken rather than just on the top.

If you take Crispy Oven-Fried Chicken on your next picnic, pack enough for second helpings.

Tangy Oven-Barbecued Chicken

½ cup jellied cranberry sauce
¼ cup no-salt-added tomato
 paste
2 tablespoons prepared mustard
1 teaspoon cider vinegar
4 (6-ounce) skinned chicken
 breast halves

Line an 11- x 7- x 2-inch baking dish with aluminum foil; set aside.

Combine first 4 ingredients in container of an electric blender. Top with cover, and process until mixture is smooth. Brush mixture evenly over both sides of chicken; reserve remaining mixture.

Place chicken, bone side up, in prepared dish. Bake, uncovered, at 375° for 25 minutes. Turn chicken, and brush with remaining cranberry mixture. Bake, uncovered, an additional 20 minutes or until chicken is tender. Yield: 4 servings (204 calories [11% from fat] per serving).

FAT 2.4g (SAT 0.4g, MONO 0.6g, POLY 0.4g)
PROTEIN 27.1g   CARBOHYDRATE 17.3g
FIBER 0.8g   CHOLESTEROL 66mg   SODIUM 195mg

Chicken and Asparagus en Papillote

1 pound fresh asparagus spears
4 (4-ounce) skinned, boned
 chicken breast halves
2 small sweet red peppers, cut
 into julienne strips
2 tablespoons low-sodium soy
 sauce
2 teaspoons peeled, grated
 gingerroot
2 teaspoons water
2 teaspoons honey
2 teaspoons dark sesame oil
½ teaspoon sesame seeds, toasted
Vegetable cooking spray

Snap off tough ends of asparagus. Remove scales with a knife or a vegetable peeler, if desired. Cut asparagus into 3-inch pieces. Arrange in a vegetable steamer over boiling water; cover and steam 4 minutes or until crisp-tender. Rinse with cold water; drain well.

Place chicken between 2 sheets of heavy-duty plastic wrap, and flatten to ¼-inch thickness, using a meat mallet or rolling pin. Set aside.

Cut 4 (15-inch) squares of parchment paper; fold each square in half. Trim each into a large heart shape.

Place parchment hearts on 2 large baking sheets, and open out flat.

Divide asparagus and half of pepper strips evenly among parchment hearts. Place vegetables on half of each parchment heart near the crease. Top each with a chicken breast half and remaining pepper strips. Combine soy sauce, gingerroot, water, honey, and oil in a small bowl, stirring well. Drizzle mixture evenly over chicken and vegetables. Sprinkle evenly with sesame seeds.

Fold paper edges over to seal. Starting with rounded edges of hearts, pleat and crimp edges of parchment to make an airtight seal. Spray packets with cooking spray. Bake at 400° for 12 minutes or until bags are puffed and lightly browned.

Place packets on individual serving plates. To serve, cut an opening in the top of each packet, and fold paper back. Serve immediately. Yield: 4 servings (190 calories [21% from fat] per serving).

FAT 4.4g (SAT 0.8g, MONO 1.3g, POLY 1.5g)
PROTEIN 28.7g   CARBOHYDRATE 8.6g
FIBER 2.2g   CHOLESTEROL 66mg   SODIUM 272mg

Apricot Chicken with Bourbon and Pecans

1 (16-ounce) can apricot halves in
 light syrup, undrained
3 tablespoons all-purpose flour
¼ teaspoon salt
⅛ teaspoon ground white pepper
6 (4-ounce) skinned, boned chicken
 breast halves
Vegetable cooking spray
2 teaspoons vegetable oil
1½ teaspoons cornstarch
3 tablespoons bourbon
1 teaspoon lemon juice
3 tablespoons chopped pecans,
 toasted
Fresh parsley sprigs (optional)

Drain apricots, reserving 1 cup syrup; set syrup aside. Place 6 apricot halves, cut side down, on a cutting board. Reserve remaining apricot halves for other uses. Cut slits in apricot halves to ¼ inch from one end, forming a fan. Set aside.

Combine flour, salt, and pepper; dredge chicken in flour mixture. Coat a large nonstick skillet with cooking spray; add oil. Place over medium heat until hot. Add chicken; cook 5 minutes on each side or until browned. Remove chicken from skillet; transfer to a serving platter, and keep warm.

Combine reserved syrup, cornstarch, bourbon, and lemon juice in a saucepan. Bring to a boil; reduce heat, and simmer 2 minutes or until slightly thickened, stirring constantly.

Place a fanned apricot half on each chicken breast; top evenly with sauce. Sprinkle evenly with pecans. Garnish with fresh parsley sprigs, if desired. Yield: 6 servings (227 calories [25% from fat] per serving).

FAT 6.3g (SAT 0.9g, MONO 2.8g, POLY 1.9g)
PROTEIN 27.3g   CARBOHYDRATE 14.6g
FIBER 0.8g   CHOLESTEROL 66mg   SODIUM 174mg

SESAME CHICKEN KABOBS

5 (4-ounce) skinned, boned chicken
   breast halves
½ cup low-sodium soy sauce
½ cup commercial nonfat Catalina
   dressing
¼ cup minced onion
2½ tablespoons lemon juice
1 tablespoon sesame seeds
1 clove garlic, crushed
½ teaspoon ground ginger
1 medium-size green pepper, cut
   into 1-inch pieces
1 medium-size sweet red pepper,
   cut into 1-inch pieces
1 (8-ounce) can pineapple chunks
   in juice, drained
Vegetable cooking spray
6 cups cooked long-grain rice
   (cooked without salt or fat)

Cut chicken into 1-inch cubes;
place in a zip-top heavy-duty plastic
bag. Combine soy sauce and next 6
ingredients in a small bowl; stir well.
Pour over chicken; seal bag, and
shake until chicken is well coated.
Marinate in refrigerator 2 hours,
turning bag occasionally.

Remove chicken from marinade,
reserving marinade. Thread chicken,
pepper pieces, and pineapple alternately on 6 (12-inch) skewers. Coat
grill rack with cooking spray; place
over medium-hot coals. Place kabobs
on rack; cook 15 minutes or until
chicken is done, turning and basting
frequently with marinade. Serve kabobs over rice. Yield: 6 servings (394
calories [9% from fat] per serving).

FAT 3.9g (SAT 0.9g, MONO 1.3g, POLY 1.1g)
PROTEIN 26.8g CARBOHYDRATE 58.8g
FIBER 1.9g CHOLESTEROL 60mg SODIUM 479mg

*Fresh mushrooms, dry sherry, and shallots
give Chicken Breasts with Sherried
Mushrooms its distinguished flavor.*

CHICKEN BREASTS WITH SHERRIED MUSHROOMS

1 (10½-ounce) can low-sodium
   chicken broth, undiluted
2 tablespoons all-purpose flour
¼ teaspoon salt
¼ teaspoon pepper
4 (4-ounce) skinned, boned chicken
   breast halves
Vegetable cooking spray
1 tablespoon reduced-calorie
   margarine, melted
2 cups sliced fresh mushrooms
2 tablespoons minced shallots
¼ cup dry sherry, divided
1½ teaspoons cornstarch
1 tablespoon chopped fresh parsley

Place broth in a small saucepan.
Bring to a boil; cook 5 minutes or until reduced to 1 cup. Set aside.

Combine flour, salt, and pepper;
sprinkle over chicken. Coat a large
nonstick skillet with cooking spray;
place over medium-high heat until
hot. Add chicken; cook 5 minutes on
each side or until browned. Remove
chicken from skillet, and set aside.
Wipe drippings from skillet.

Coat skillet with cooking spray;
add margarine. Place over medium-
high heat until margarine melts. Add
mushrooms and shallots; sauté until
tender. Combine 1 tablespoon sherry
and cornstarch; stir well, and set
aside. Add remaining 3 tablespoons
sherry and broth to skillet. Bring to a
boil; cook until sauce is reduced to ¾
cup. Add cornstarch mixture; cook,
stirring constantly, about 1 minute or
until mixture is thickened.

Return chicken to skillet; cover, reduce heat, and simmer 10 minutes or
until tender. Transfer chicken to a
serving platter; top evenly with
mushroom mixture. Sprinkle with
parsley. Yield: 4 servings (197 calories
[26% from fat] per serving).

FAT 5.6g (SAT 1.3g, MONO 2.1g, POLY 1.6g)
PROTEIN 28.4g CARBOHYDRATE 7.0g
FIBER 0.7g CHOLESTEROL 72mg SODIUM 266mg

CHUTNEY-GLAZED CHICKEN

8 (4-ounce) skinned, boned chicken
  breast halves
Vegetable cooking spray
⅓ cup commercial mango chutney
2 tablespoons Dijon mustard
2 tablespoons dry sherry
2 teaspoons curry powder

Place chicken on rack of a broiler pan coated with cooking spray. Combine chutney and remaining ingredients, stirring well.

Brush chicken with half of chutney mixture. Broil 5½ inches from heat 5 minutes. Turn chicken, and brush evenly with remaining chutney mixture; broil an additional 4 to 5 minutes or until chicken is tender. Yield: 8 servings (164 calories [18% from fat] per serving).

FAT 3.2g (SAT 0.8g, MONO 1.0g, POLY 0.6g)
PROTEIN 24.4g CARBOHYDRATE 7.7g
FIBER 0.2g CHOLESTEROL 66mg SODIUM 192mg

ORIENTAL CHICKEN STIR-FRY

4 (4-ounce) skinned, boned chicken
  breast halves, cut into 1-inch
  cubes
⅓ cup Chablis or other dry white
  wine
⅓ cup teriyaki sauce
2 teaspoons peeled, grated
  gingerroot
1 clove garlic, crushed
1 cup canned no-salt-added chicken
  broth, undiluted
1½ tablespoons low-sodium soy
  sauce
1 tablespoon cornstarch
1½ teaspoons brown sugar
Vegetable cooking spray
1 tablespoon sesame oil, divided
3 cups fresh broccoli flowerets
2 medium-size sweet red peppers,
  cut into julienne strips
½ cup chopped green onions
5 cups cooked long-grain rice
  (cooked without salt or fat)

Place chicken in a zip-top heavy-duty plastic bag. Combine wine, teriyaki sauce, gingerroot, and garlic in a small bowl, stirring well. Pour over chicken; seal bag, and shake until chicken is well coated. Marinate in refrigerator 2 to 4 hours, turning bag occasionally.

Remove chicken from marinade; discard marinade. Combine broth, soy sauce, cornstarch, and brown sugar; stir well, and set aside.

Coat a wok or large nonstick skillet with vegetable cooking spray; add 2 teaspoons oil. Place over medium-high heat (375°) until hot. Add chicken, and stir-fry 4 to 5 minutes or until tender. Remove chicken from wok. Drain and pat dry with paper towels. Wipe drippings from wok with a paper towel.

Add remaining 1 teaspoon oil to wok; place over medium-high heat until hot. Add broccoli, and stir-fry 2 minutes. Add pepper strips and green onions; stir-fry 3 to 4 minutes or until crisp-tender. Remove vegetables from wok, and set aside.

Add broth mixture to wok; cook, stirring constantly, until mixture is thickened. Return chicken and vegetables to wok; cook, stirring constantly, until mixture is thoroughly heated. Serve chicken mixture over rice. Yield: 5 servings (412 calories [14% from fat] per serving).

FAT 6.3g (SAT 1.3g, MONO 2.2g, POLY 1.9g)
PROTEIN 28.7g CARBOHYDRATE 57.5g
FIBER 3.4g CHOLESTEROL 60mg SODIUM 488mg

SWEET-AND-SOUR CHICKEN

1 (20-ounce) can unsweetened
  pineapple chunks, undrained
3 tablespoons white wine vinegar
3 tablespoons low-sodium soy
  sauce
3 tablespoons reduced-calorie
  catsup
1½ tablespoons cornstarch
1½ tablespoons brown sugar
2 teaspoons low-sodium
  Worcestershire sauce
½ teaspoon ground ginger
¼ teaspoon garlic powder
Vegetable cooking spray
3 (4-ounce) skinned, boned chicken
  breast halves, cut into 1-inch
  cubes
½ small sweet red pepper, cut into
  julienne strips
½ small green pepper, cut into
  julienne strips
4 cups cooked long-grain rice
  (cooked without salt or fat)

Drain pineapple chunks, reserving juice. Set pineapple chunks aside. Combine reserved juice, vinegar, and next 7 ingredients in a small bowl; stir well, and set aside.

Coat a large nonstick skillet with cooking spray; place over medium-high heat until hot. Add chicken; cook 5 minutes or until chicken is browned on all sides. Add pineapple and pepper strips; cook 2 to 3 minutes or until pepper is crisp-tender, stirring constantly. Gradually stir pineapple juice mixture into chicken mixture. Cook over medium heat, stirring constantly, until thickened and bubbly. Serve chicken mixture over rice. Yield: 4 servings (443 calories [3% from fat] per serving).

FAT 1.5g (SAT 0.3g, MONO 0.3g, POLY 0.3g)
PROTEIN 23.8g CARBOHYDRATE 78.5g
FIBER 1.4g CHOLESTEROL 49mg SODIUM 364mg

CHICKEN TOSTADAS WITH RED PEPPER SALSA

Vegetable cooking spray
6 (4-ounce) skinned, boned chicken breast halves, cubed
1½ cups chopped onion
2 cloves garlic, minced
Red Pepper Salsa (page 190), divided
¼ cup Chablis or other dry white wine
½ teaspoon chili powder
¼ teaspoon salt
⅛ teaspoon freshly ground pepper
8 (6-inch) corn tortillas
2 cups shredded lettuce
½ cup nonfat sour cream alternative

Coat a large nonstick skillet with cooking spray; place over medium-high heat until hot. Add chicken, onion, and garlic; cook until chicken is browned and onion is tender. Drain chicken mixture, and pat chicken dry with paper towels. Wipe drippings from skillet with a paper towel.

Add chicken mixture, ¾ cup Red Pepper Salsa, wine, chili powder, salt, and pepper to skillet. Bring to a boil; cover, reduce heat, and simmer 10 minutes. Uncover and increase heat to high. Cook an additional 5 minutes or until most of the liquid has evaporated. Set aside; keep warm.

Place tortillas on ungreased baking sheets. Bake at 350° for 15 to 20 minutes or until crisp. Place 1 tortilla on each of 8 individual serving plates. Top each tortilla evenly with lettuce, chicken mixture, remaining 2 cups Red Pepper Salsa, and sour cream. Yield: 8 servings (199 calories [18% from fat] per serving).

FAT 4.0g (SAT 0.9g, MONO 1.2g, POLY 1.2g)
PROTEIN 23.3g   CARBOHYDRATE 17.1g
FIBER 3.1g   CHOLESTEROL 54mg   SODIUM 247mg

SPICY CHICKEN CASSEROLE

Vegetable cooking spray
1 teaspoon vegetable oil
4 (4-ounce) skinned, boned chicken breast halves, cut into ½-inch strips
1 cup frozen whole kernel corn, thawed and drained
½ cup thinly sliced onion
⅓ cup chopped green pepper
½ cup no-salt-added tomato sauce
2½ tablespoons reduced-calorie chili sauce
2 tablespoons water
1½ teaspoons minced fresh cilantro
1 teaspoon chili powder
1 teaspoon finely chopped jalapeño pepper
½ cup (2 ounces) shredded reduced-fat Monterey Jack cheese

Coat a large nonstick skillet with cooking spray; add oil. Place skillet over medium-high heat until hot. Add chicken; cook 5 minutes or until lightly browned. Drain chicken, and pat dry with paper towels. Wipe drippings from skillet with a paper towel.

Combine chicken, corn, and next 8 ingredients in a large bowl; stir well. Spoon mixture into a 1½-quart casserole coated with cooking spray. Cover and bake at 350° for 30 to 35 minutes or until thoroughly heated. Uncover, and sprinkle with cheese. Bake an additional 5 minutes or until cheese melts. Yield: 4 servings (265 calories [26% from fat] per serving).

FAT 7.7g (SAT 2.8g, MONO 1.6g, POLY 1.7g)
PROTEIN 32.7g   CARBOHYDRATE 16.4g
FIBER 2.0g   CHOLESTEROL 82mg   SODIUM 177mg

CREAMY CHICKEN-BASIL PASTA

½ cup nonfat mayonnaise
¼ cup nonfat sour cream
  alternative
2 tablespoons chopped fresh basil
2 tablespoons skim milk
1 tablespoon lemon juice
½ teaspoon salt
¼ teaspoon garlic powder
¼ teaspoon dry mustard
1 cup fresh broccoli flowerets
½ cup frozen English peas,
  thawed
4 cups cooked fettuccine (cooked
  without salt or fat)
3 cups cubed, cooked chicken
  breast (skinned before cooking
  and cooked without salt)
4 ounces reduced-fat Cheddar
  cheese, cut into thin strips
1 cup chopped tomato
½ medium-size sweet red pepper,
  cut into julienne strips
¼ cup sliced green onions

Combine first 8 ingredients in a small bowl; stir well, and set aside.

Arrange broccoli and peas in a vegetable steamer over boiling water. Cover and steam 3 minutes or until crisp-tender; drain. Rinse under cold water until cool; drain.

Combine mayonnaise mixture, broccoli and peas, and remaining ingredients in a large bowl; toss gently. Cover and chill thoroughly. Yield: 8 servings (282 calories [18% from fat] per 1¼-cup serving).

FAT 5.5g (SAT 2.3g, MONO 0.8g, POLY 0.8g)
PROTEIN 28.1g CARBOHYDRATE 28.2g
FIBER 2.4g CHOLESTEROL 60mg SODIUM 510mg

PHYLLO CHICKEN POT PIE

Vegetable cooking spray
¼ cup reduced-calorie margarine
1 cup chopped onion
1 cup chopped celery
1 cup chopped carrot
1 cup frozen English peas
¼ cup plus 2 tablespoons
  all-purpose flour
2 cups canned no-salt-added
  chicken broth, undiluted
1 cup skim milk
4 cups chopped, cooked chicken
  breast (skinned before cooking
  and cooked without salt)
½ teaspoon salt
¼ teaspoon dried whole thyme
¼ teaspoon pepper
8 sheets commercial frozen phyllo
  pastry, thawed

Coat a large nonstick skillet with cooking spray; add margarine. Place over medium heat until margarine melts. Add onion, celery, and carrot; sauté until tender. Stir in peas and flour; cook 1 minute, stirring constantly. Gradually add chicken broth and milk; cook, stirring constantly, until thickened and bubbly. Remove from heat, and stir in chicken, salt, thyme, and pepper. Spoon mixture into a 2-quart casserole coated with cooking spray; set aside.

Place 1 sheet of phyllo on a damp towel (keep remaining phyllo covered). Lightly coat phyllo with cooking spray. Layer remaining 7 sheets phyllo on first sheet, lightly coating each sheet with cooking spray.

Place stack of phyllo over casserole; trim to ½ inch larger than rim of dish, discarding excess phyllo. Gently press phyllo to edge of dish to seal. Cut slits in top of phyllo to allow steam to escape. Coat surface of phyllo with cooking spray. Bake at 350° for 35 minutes or until phyllo is golden. Let stand 5 minutes before serving. Yield: 8 servings (303 calories [23% from fat] per serving).

FAT 7.8g (SAT 1.6g, MONO 2.5g, POLY 2.4g)
PROTEIN 31.9g CARBOHYDRATE 24.5g
FIBER 2.2g CHOLESTEROL 73mg SODIUM 359mg

CHICKEN CACCIATORE

1 (27½-ounce) jar low-fat pasta
  sauce
½ cup Burgundy or other dry red
  wine
1 medium-size green pepper, cut
  into 1-inch pieces
1 small onion, cut into 1-inch
  pieces
2 pounds chicken thighs, skinned
1 teaspoon dried Italian seasoning
½ teaspoon salt
¼ teaspoon pepper
6 cups cooked fettuccine (cooked
  without salt or fat)

Combine first 4 ingredients in a large Dutch oven, stirring well; add chicken. Bring to a boil; cover, reduce heat, and simmer 1 hour or until chicken is tender.

Remove chicken from sauce; let cool. Bone and cut chicken into bite-size pieces; set aside. Add Italian seasoning, salt, and pepper to sauce; cook, uncovered, over medium heat 15 minutes, stirring frequently.

Add chicken to sauce mixture, and cook until heated. Serve over fettuccine. Yield: 6 servings (397 calories [14% from fat] per serving).

FAT 6.3g (SAT 1.3g, MONO 1.5g, POLY 1.6g)
PROTEIN 30.0g CARBOHYDRATE 52.9g
FIBER 3.1g CHOLESTEROL 86mg SODIUM 721mg

Cornish Hens

For an entrée that will add diversity to your menus, try Cornish hens. These miniature chickens weigh up to two and one-half pounds and range in age from four to six weeks. They have a delicate flavor much like that of chicken and turkey.

You may think Cornish hens are only for special occasions, but they are perfect for casual entertaining and cookouts, too.

BAKED CORNISH HENS IN MUSHROOM GRAVY

2 (1-pound) Cornish hens, skinned
Vegetable cooking spray
¼ teaspoon salt
¼ teaspoon pepper
½ teaspoon paprika
½ pound fresh mushrooms, sliced
½ cup chopped onion
1 (10½-ounce) can low-sodium chicken broth
¼ cup all-purpose flour
¼ cup water
3 tablespoons instant nonfat dry milk powder
½ teaspoon chicken-flavored bouillon granules
½ teaspoon browning-and-seasoning sauce

Remove giblets from hens; reserve for another use. Rinse hens under cold water, and pat dry. Split each hen in half lengthwise, using an electric knife. Place hens, cut side down, on a rack in a roasting pan coated with cooking spray. Sprinkle hens with salt and pepper; coat with cooking spray, and sprinkle with paprika. Broil 5½ inches from heat 6 to 8 minutes on each side or until golden. Transfer to a 13- x 9- x 2-inch baking dish coated with cooking spray. Set aside.

Coat a large nonstick skillet with cooking spray; place over medium-high heat until hot. Add mushrooms; sauté 3 to 4 minutes or until mushrooms are tender. Drain well, and set aside. Wipe drippings from skillet with a paper towel.

Coat skillet with cooking spray; place over medium-high heat until hot. Add onion; sauté 3 to 4 minutes or until tender. Combine onion, broth, and remaining ingredients in container of an electric blender; top with cover, and process until mixture is smooth. Transfer broth mixture to skillet. Cook over medium heat, stirring constantly, until thickened and bubbly. Stir in mushrooms; cook just until heated.

Spoon mushroom mixture evenly over hens. Cover and bake at 350° for 40 to 45 minutes or until done. Yield: 4 servings (259 calories [29% from fat] per serving).

FAT 8.4g (SAT 2.7g, MONO 2.8g, POLY 2.1g)
PROTEIN 31.0g   CARBOHYDRATE 14.3g
FIBER 1.4g   CHOLESTEROL 81mg   SODIUM 387mg

Using an electric knife to cut Cornish hens or chickens in half is easier than using a regular knife.

Lean Tips for Poultry
• Trim away any visible fat.
• Remove and discard skin either before cooking or before eating.
• White meat generally contains less fat than dark meat.
• The smaller a chicken is, the leaner the meat.
• Save duck and goose for special occasions. They are higher in fat than other birds.

CORNISH HENS WITH ROSEMARY-WINE SAUCE

2 (1-pound) Cornish hens, skinned
Vegetable cooking spray
1 cup Chablis or other dry white wine
⅓ cup white wine vinegar
2 tablespoons low-sodium soy sauce
1 teaspoon dried whole rosemary, crushed
¼ teaspoon dried whole thyme
4 cloves garlic, minced

Remove giblets from hens; reserve for another use. Rinse hens under cold water, and pat dry. Split each hen in half lengthwise, using an electric knife. Place hens, cut side down, in a 13- x 9- x 2-inch baking dish coated with cooking spray.

Combine wine and remaining ingredients; pour over hens. Bake, uncovered, at 350° for 1 hour or until done, basting occasionally with wine mixture. Yield: 4 servings (185 calories [33% from fat] per serving).

FAT 6.8g (SAT 1.8g, MONO 2.4g, POLY 1.5g)
PROTEIN 26.2g   CARBOHYDRATE 2.0g
FIBER 0.1g   CHOLESTEROL 80mg   SODIUM 279mg

A fruity marinade enhances the delicate flavor of Grilled Apricot-Ginger Cornish Hens. Brush jam on near the end of cooking to add even more flavor.

GRILLED APRICOT-GINGER CORNISH HENS

3 (1-pound) Cornish hens, skinned
½ cup apricot nectar
2 tablespoons minced onion
2 tablespoons low-sodium soy sauce
2 tablespoons Chablis or other dry white wine
2 tablespoons lemon juice
3 large cloves garlic, minced
1 teaspoon ground ginger
¼ teaspoon pepper
Vegetable cooking spray
3 tablespoons apricot jam, melted

Remove giblets from hens; reserve for another use. Rinse hens under cold water, and pat dry. Split each hen in half lengthwise, using an electric knife. Place hens in a 13- x 9- x 2-inch baking dish.

Combine apricot nectar and next 7 ingredients in a medium bowl, stirring well. Pour mixture over hens, turning to coat. Cover hens, and marinate in refrigerator 2 hours, turning occasionally.

Remove hens from marinade; reserve marinade. Coat grill rack with vegetable cooking spray; place on grill over medium-hot coals. Place hens on rack, and cook 20 to 25 minutes or until hens are done, turning and basting frequently with marinade. Brush hens evenly with melted apricot jam; cook an additional 5 minutes. Yield: 6 servings (217 calories [28% from fat] per serving).

FAT 6.8g (SAT 1.8g, MONO 2.4g, POLY 1.5g)
PROTEIN 26.1g CARBOHYDRATE 11.6g
FIBER 0.4g CHOLESTEROL 79mg SODIUM 209mg

GARLIC-SAGE CORNISH HENS WITH WILD RICE

4 (1-pound) Cornish hens, skinned
Vegetable cooking spray
3 cloves garlic, crushed
2 teaspoons minced fresh sage or
  ½ teaspoon dried whole sage
2 teaspoons olive oil
¼ teaspoon salt
¼ teaspoon pepper
4 cups cooked wild rice (cooked without salt or fat)

Remove giblets from hens; reserve for another use. Rinse hens under cold water, and pat dry. Split each hen in half lengthwise, using an electric knife. Place hens, cut sides down, on a rack in a roasting pan coated with cooking spray.

Combine garlic and next 4 ingredients; rub hens with garlic mixture. Bake, uncovered, at 350° for 1 hour or until done. Serve hens with wild rice. Yield: 8 servings (250 calories [27% from fat] per serving).

FAT 7.5g (SAT 1.9g, MONO 3.0g, POLY 1.7g)
PROTEIN 26.9g CARBOHYDRATE 17.9g
FIBER 0.3g CHOLESTEROL 73mg SODIUM 146mg

Turkey

Turkey was once a twice-a-year holiday entrée. But because it fits so well into a low-fat eating plan, turkey is now served all year. It is an excellent source of protein that is low in cholesterol and saturated fat.

To help trim fat from your diet, use turkey as a substitute for red meat in your favorite recipes. For example, use ground turkey instead of ground beef or ground chuck in chili or spaghetti sauce. But beware! Commercially packaged ground turkey is usually a combination of light and dark meat and may even contain skin. If possible, have the butcher grind skinless turkey breast for the leanest product.

Supermarkets are selling a wide assortment of fresh turkey cuts, including breasts, tenderloins, cutlets, and ground. Turkey sausage, turkey bacon, and turkey cold cuts are also popular choices found in the deli case or the processed meats section of the meat counter.

TURKEY BREAST WITH CORNBREAD DRESSING

1 (4-pound) turkey breast, skinned
1 medium onion, halved
2 stalks celery, halved
Vegetable cooking spray
1½ tablespoons salt-free lemon-pepper seasoning
1½ teaspoons onion powder
1½ teaspoons garlic powder
1 teaspoon poultry seasoning
½ teaspoon paprika
Cornbread Dressing

Trim fat from turkey. Rinse turkey under cold water, and pat dry. Stuff turkey cavity with onion and celery; spray turkey with cooking spray.

Combine lemon-pepper seasoning and next 4 ingredients; sprinkle evenly over turkey.

Place turkey in an oven cooking bag prepared according to package directions; place in a shallow baking pan. Insert meat thermometer into meaty part of breast, making sure it does not touch bone. Bake at 325° for 1 hour. Cut a slit in top of bag; bake an additional 30 minutes or until meat thermometer registers 170°.

Transfer turkey to a serving platter; remove and discard onion and celery. Let turkey stand 15 minutes; cut into thin slices. Serve with Cornbread Dressing. Yield: 10 servings (375 calories [21% from fat] per serving).

Cornbread Dressing

2 cups yellow cornmeal
2½ teaspoons baking powder
½ teaspoon baking soda
½ teaspoon salt
1¾ cups nonfat buttermilk
¼ cup frozen egg substitute, thawed
2 tablespoons vegetable oil
Vegetable cooking spray
3 tablespoons reduced-calorie margarine
1 cup chopped celery
1 cup chopped onion
4 (1-ounce) slices white bread, torn into small pieces
4 cups canned no-salt-added chicken broth, undiluted
½ cup frozen egg substitute, thawed
2 teaspoons poultry seasoning
1 teaspoon rubbed sage
¾ teaspoon salt
½ teaspoon pepper

Combine cornmeal, baking powder, baking soda, and salt in a bowl; make a well in center of mixture.

Combine buttermilk, ¼ cup egg substitute, and oil; add to cornmeal mixture, stirring just until dry ingredients are moistened. Pour batter into a 9-inch cast-iron skillet coated with cooking spray. Bake at 450° for 20 to 25 minutes or until golden. Remove cornbread from skillet; cool completely on a wire rack.

Coat a large nonstick skillet with vegetable cooking spray; add margarine. Place over medium-high heat until margarine melts. Add celery and onion; sauté 4 to 5 minutes or until tender. Crumble cornbread into a large bowl; stir in vegetable mixture, white bread, and remaining ingredients. Spoon cornbread mixture into a 13- x 9- x 2-inch baking dish coated with cooking spray. Bake at 325° for 55 to 60 minutes or until golden. Yield: 10 servings.

FAT 8.9g (SAT 2.0g, MONO 2.8g, POLY 3.4g)
PROTEIN 38.0g CARBOHYDRATE 33.3g
FIBER 2.6g CHOLESTEROL 78mg SODIUM 721mg

Bag It!
Oven cooking bags offer a convenient and delicious way to cook poultry. No basting is required, and cleanup is minimal. When baked in an oven cooking bag, large cuts of chicken or turkey will be tender and juicy inside with a moist exterior. Follow the directions on the package for conventional or microwave cooking.

Risotto Turkey Breast

2½ cups canned no-salt-added
  chicken broth, undiluted and
  divided
Vegetable cooking spray
¾ cup Arborio rice, uncooked
½ teaspoon ground turmeric
½ cup diced onion
½ cup diced green pepper
½ cup diced sweet red pepper
2 cloves garlic, minced
½ teaspoon dried Italian
  seasoning
¼ teaspoon salt
¼ teaspoon pepper
1 (3-pound) boneless turkey breast,
  skinned
¼ cup commercial oil-free Italian
  dressing

Bring broth to a boil in a medium saucepan; cover, reduce heat to low, and keep warm.

Coat a large nonstick skillet with vegetable cooking spray; place over medium-high heat until hot. Add rice; sauté 2 to 3 minutes or until rice is translucent. Add 1 cup warm broth to rice. Bring to a boil; reduce heat, and simmer 5 minutes or until liquid is absorbed, stirring constantly. Repeat procedure 2 more times, adding ½ cup warm broth at a time (the entire process should take about 15 minutes).

Combine turmeric and remaining ½ cup warm broth, stirring until well blended; add to rice mixture. Cook, stirring constantly, until rice is tender and liquid is absorbed. Remove from heat, and set aside.

Coat a nonstick skillet with cooking spray; place over medium-high heat until hot. Add onion and next 3 ingredients; sauté until tender. Add onion mixture, Italian seasoning, salt, and pepper to rice mixture; stir well, and set aside.

Trim fat from turkey; remove tendons. Place turkey, boned side up, on heavy-duty plastic wrap. From center, slice horizontally through thickest part of each side of breast almost to outer edge; flip each cut piece over to enlarge turkey breast. Place heavy-duty plastic wrap over turkey, and flatten to ½-inch thickness, using a meat mallet or rolling pin.

Spoon rice mixture in center of turkey, leaving a 2-inch border at sides; roll up, jellyroll fashion, starting with short side. Tie securely at 2-inch intervals with string. Place turkey, seam side down, on a rack in a roasting pan coated with cooking spray. Brush Italian dressing over turkey. Insert meat thermometer. Shield turkey with aluminum foil. Bake at 325° for 1 hour, basting occasionally with remaining dressing. Uncover and bake an additional 30 minutes or until meat thermometer registers 170°. Transfer turkey to a large serving platter; let stand 10 minutes. Remove string; cut turkey into 12 slices. Yield: 12 servings (196 calories [16% from fat] per serving).

FAT 3.5g (SAT 1.1g, MONO 0.8g, POLY 1.0g)
PROTEIN 26.7g CARBOHYDRATE 12.1g
FIBER 0.6g CHOLESTEROL 59mg SODIUM 186mg

Saucy Italian Turkey Cutlets

Vegetable cooking spray
1 pound turkey breast cutlets
¾ pound small fresh mushrooms
2 medium shallots, thinly sliced
1 clove garlic, minced
1 (8-ounce) can no-salt-added
  tomato sauce
½ cup Chablis or other dry white
  wine
¼ teaspoon salt
¼ teaspoon pepper
1 large tomato, peeled, seeded,
  and chopped
1 tablespoon minced fresh parsley

Coat a large nonstick skillet with vegetable cooking spray; place over medium-high heat until hot. Add turkey, and cook 3 to 4 minutes on each side or until lightly browned. Drain turkey, and pat dry with paper towels. Wipe drippings from skillet with a paper towel.

Remove stems from mushrooms; reserve mushroom stems for another use. Coat skillet with vegetable cooking spray; place over medium-high heat until hot. Add mushroom caps, shallots, and garlic to skillet; sauté 3 to 4 minutes or until tender.

Combine tomato sauce, wine, salt, and pepper in a small bowl, stirring well. Add to mixture in skillet. Return turkey to skillet, and add chopped tomato. Cover, reduce heat, and simmer 12 minutes; uncover, and simmer an additional 2 to 3 minutes or until turkey is tender.

Transfer turkey mixture to a serving platter, and sprinkle evenly with minced fresh parsley. Yield: 4 servings (210 calories [17% from fat] per serving).

FAT 3.9g (SAT 1.0g, MONO 0.6g, POLY 1.0g)
PROTEIN 30.3g CARBOHYDRATE 13.0g
FIBER 1.7g CHOLESTEROL 64mg SODIUM 229mg

TURKEY CUTLETS MILANESE

¼ cup frozen egg substitute, thawed
2 teaspoons vegetable oil
½ cup fine, dry breadcrumbs
2 tablespoons grated Parmesan cheese
¾ teaspoon dried Italian seasoning
¼ teaspoon garlic powder
1 pound turkey breast cutlets
Vegetable cooking spray
½ cup commercial marinara sauce

Combine egg substitute and oil in a small shallow dish; stir well. Combine breadcrumbs and next 3 ingredients in a shallow dish, stirring well. Dip turkey cutlets in egg mixture; dredge in breadcrumb mixture.

Place turkey cutlets on a large baking sheet coated with vegetable cooking spray; coat each cutlet lightly with vegetable cooking spray. Bake at 350° for 20 to 25 minutes or until cutlets are lightly browned.

Heat marinara sauce in a small saucepan over medium heat just until warm. Spoon marinara sauce evenly over cutlets. Yield: 4 servings (248 calories [25% from fat] per serving).

FAT 7.0g (SAT 1.9g, MONO 2.1g, POLY 2.3g)
PROTEIN 31.4g CARBOHYDRATE 13.4g
FIBER 0.8g CHOLESTEROL 71mg SODIUM 448mg

TURKEY TETRAZZINI

1 (7-ounce) package spaghetti, uncooked
Vegetable cooking spray
1 tablespoon reduced-calorie margarine
3 cups sliced fresh mushrooms
⅓ cup minced onion
¼ cup diced celery
½ cup all-purpose flour
1½ cups skim milk
1 (13¾-ounce) can no-salt-added chicken broth
¼ cup light process cream cheese product
¼ cup grated Parmesan cheese, divided
¼ cup dry sherry
½ teaspoon salt
½ teaspoon garlic powder
¼ teaspoon pepper
1 (2-ounce) jar diced pimiento, drained
2 cups chopped cooked turkey breast (skinned before cooking and cooked without salt)

Break spaghetti in half, and cook according to package directions, omitting salt and fat. Drain spaghetti well, and set aside.

Coat a large saucepan with cooking spray; add margarine. Place over medium-high heat until margarine melts. Add mushrooms, onion, and celery; sauté until tender. Combine flour and milk; stir until smooth. Add flour mixture and broth to vegetable mixture. Bring to a boil over medium heat; reduce heat, and simmer 5 minutes, stirring constantly. Remove from heat; add cream cheese, stirring until cheese melts. Stir in spaghetti, 2 tablespoons Parmesan cheese, and remaining ingredients.

Spoon turkey mixture into a shallow 2-quart baking dish coated with vegetable cooking spray; sprinkle evenly with remaining 2 tablespoons Parmesan cheese. Bake at 350° for 25 to 30 minutes or until thoroughly heated. Yield: 6 servings (336 calories [18% from fat] per serving).

FAT 6.9g (SAT 2.6g, MONO 1.4g, POLY 1.5g)
PROTEIN 25.8g CARBOHYDRATE 41.2g
FIBER 1.9g CHOLESTEROL 41mg SODIUM 449mg

Creamy dishes such as Turkey Tetrazzini can be part of a healthy eating plan. Our version of this family favorite replaces the high-fat ingredients with lower fat substitutes.

TURKEY AND RICE CASSEROLE

1 (6-ounce) package long-grain and wild rice mix
Vegetable cooking spray
2 tablespoons reduced-calorie margarine
1 cup sliced fresh mushrooms
½ cup sliced celery
2 tablespoons all-purpose flour
1 cup skim milk
1 teaspoon low-sodium Worcestershire sauce
4 cups chopped cooked turkey breast (skinned before cooking and cooked without salt)

Prepare rice mix according to package directions, omitting salt and fat; set aside.

Coat a medium nonstick skillet with cooking spray; add margarine. Place over medium heat until margarine melts. Add mushrooms and celery; sauté until tender. Add flour, stirring until smooth. Cook 1 minute, stirring constantly. Gradually stir in milk and Worcestershire sauce; cook over medium heat, stirring constantly, until mixture is thickened and bubbly. Remove from heat, and stir in rice and turkey.

Spoon mixture into an 11- x 7- x 2-inch baking dish coated with cooking spray. Bake at 350° for 25 to 30 minutes or until thoroughly heated. Yield: 6 servings (308 calories [19% from fat] per serving).

FAT 6.4g (SAT 1.5g, MONO 1.5g, POLY 2.0g)
PROTEIN 35.8g CARBOHYDRATE 25.9g
FIBER 1.3g CHOLESTEROL 73mg SODIUM 620mg

ROSEMARY TURKEY TENDERLOINS

3 (½-pound) turkey tenderloins
1½ tablespoons finely chopped fresh rosemary
1 tablespoon olive oil
1 large clove garlic, minced
¼ teaspoon coarsely ground black pepper
¼ teaspoon salt
Vegetable cooking spray
3 tablespoons dry vermouth
2 tablespoons water
1 teaspoon cornstarch
Fresh rosemary sprigs (optional)

Trim fat from turkey; remove tendons. Combine rosemary and next 4 ingredients, stirring well. Rub mixture evenly over both sides of turkey. Coat a nonstick skillet with cooking spray; place over medium-high heat until hot. Add turkey; cook 7 to 8 minutes on each side or until done. Slice turkey diagonally across grain into thin slices. Arrange turkey slices on a serving platter; keep warm.

Combine vermouth, water, and cornstarch, stirring well; add to skillet. Bring to a boil; reduce heat, and simmer 1 minute or until thickened, stirring constantly. Pour sauce evenly over turkey slices. Garnish with fresh rosemary sprigs, if desired. Yield: 6 servings (332 calories [18% from fat] per serving).

FAT 6.5g (SAT 1.6g, MONO 2.4g, POLY 1.3g)
PROTEIN 62.3g CARBOHYDRATE 1.6g
FIBER 0.1g CHOLESTEROL 159mg SODIUM 265mg

SESAME TURKEY TENDERLOINS

4 (½-pound) turkey tenderloins
1 cup white grape juice
½ cup Chablis or other dry white
    wine
½ cup low-sodium soy sauce
2 tablespoons sesame seeds, toasted
1 tablespoon vegetable oil
1 tablespoon dark sesame oil
½ teaspoon garlic powder
½ teaspoon ground ginger
Vegetable cooking spray

Trim fat from turkey; remove tendons. Place turkey in a shallow dish. Combine grape juice and next 7 ingredients. Reserve ½ cup grape juice mixture; set aside. Pour remaining mixture over turkey, turning to coat. Cover and marinate in refrigerator 2 to 4 hours, turning occasionally.

Remove turkey from marinade; discard marinade. Coat grill rack with vegetable cooking spray; place on grill over medium-hot coals. Place turkey on rack, and cook 7 to 8 minutes on each side or until done, basting frequently with reserved grape juice mixture. Yield: 8 servings (190 calories [23% from fat] per serving).

FAT 4.5g (SAT 1.3g, MONO 1.1g, POLY 1.5g)
PROTEIN 31.8g CARBOHYDRATE 2.0g
FIBER 0.0g CHOLESTEROL 73mg SODIUM 190mg

Marinate poultry in a zip-top plastic bag in the refrigerator, turning occasionally to keep the poultry coated with marinade.

SANTA FE-STYLE GRILLED TURKEY TENDERLOINS

2 (½-pound) turkey tenderloins
¼ teaspoon salt
¼ teaspoon pepper
⅓ cup lime juice
2 teaspoons olive oil
¾ cup chopped yellow tomato
¾ cup chopped red tomato
¼ cup finely chopped purple
    onion
2½ tablespoons minced fresh
    cilantro
2 tablespoons red wine vinegar
1 tablespoon seeded, minced
    jalapeño pepper
Vegetable cooking spray
Fresh cilantro sprigs (optional)

Trim fat from turkey; remove tendons. Place turkey in a shallow baking dish; sprinkle evenly with salt and pepper. Combine lime juice and olive oil; pour evenly over turkey. Cover and marinate in refrigerator 2 to 4 hours, turning once.

Combine yellow tomato and next 5 ingredients in a small bowl; stir well. Cover and chill thoroughly.

Remove turkey from marinade; discard marinade. Coat grill rack with vegetable cooking spray; place on grill over medium-hot coals. Place turkey on rack, and cook 5 to 6 minutes on each side or until done. Slice turkey diagonally across grain into thin slices. Serve with tomato mixture. Garnish with fresh cilantro sprigs, if desired. Yield: 4 servings (173 calories [28% from fat] per serving).

FAT 5.3g (SAT 1.2g, MONO 2.2g, POLY 1.0g)
PROTEIN 25.0g CARBOHYDRATE 5.8g
FIBER 1.0g CHOLESTEROL 56mg SODIUM 205mg

TURKEY YAKITORI

¾ cup rice wine
½ cup Chablis or other dry white
    wine
3 tablespoons brown sugar
3 tablespoons low-sodium soy sauce
1½ pounds turkey tenderloins, cut
    into 1-inch cubes
1 large sweet red pepper, cut into
    1-inch pieces
1 large green pepper, cut into
    1-inch pieces
Vegetable cooking spray

Combine first 4 ingredients in a saucepan; bring to a boil. Reduce heat; simmer 5 minutes. Let cool.

Place turkey cubes in a zip-top heavy-duty plastic bag. Pour wine mixture over turkey; seal bag, and shake until turkey is well coated. Marinate in refrigerator 6 to 8 hours, turning bag occasionally.

Remove turkey from marinade, reserving marinade. Thread turkey and pepper pieces alternately on 6 (12-inch) skewers. Coat grill rack with vegetable cooking spray; place on grill over medium-hot coals. Place kabobs on rack, and cook 7 to 8 minutes or until done, turning and basting with marinade. Yield: 6 servings (172 calories [16% from fat] per serving).

FAT 3.0g (SAT 0.9g, MONO 0.5g, POLY 0.8g)
PROTEIN 24.4g CARBOHYDRATE 10.0g
FIBER 0.8g CHOLESTEROL 55mg SODIUM 254mg

Saucy Turkey Loaf

1½ pounds freshly ground raw
    turkey breast
⅔ cup soft breadcrumbs
½ cup chopped onion
½ teaspoon salt
⅛ teaspoon pepper
½ cup frozen egg substitute,
    thawed
Vegetable cooking spray
½ cup firmly packed brown sugar
⅓ cup reduced-calorie catsup
¾ teaspoon dry mustard
½ teaspoon low-sodium
    Worcestershire sauce

Combine turkey, breadcrumbs, onion, salt, pepper, and egg substitute in a large bowl; stir well. Shape turkey mixture into a loaf. Place turkey loaf on rack of a broiler pan coated with vegetable cooking spray. Bake at 350° for 1 hour.

Combine brown sugar, catsup, mustard, and Worcestershire sauce in a small bowl, stirring well. Pour brown sugar mixture over turkey loaf, and bake an additional 10 minutes or until meat is no longer pink. Yield: 8 servings (196 calories [12% from fat] per serving).

FAT 2.6g (SAT 0.8g, MONO 0.5g, POLY 0.7g)
PROTEIN 23.4g   CARBOHYDRATE 17.9g
FIBER 0.3g   CHOLESTEROL 50mg   SODIUM 250mg

Stuffed Cabbage Rolls

6 large cabbage leaves
½ pound freshly ground raw turkey
½ pound lean ground pork
1 cup cooked brown rice (cooked
    without salt or fat)
½ cup chopped onion
1 teaspoon dried Italian seasoning
⅛ teaspoon garlic powder
⅛ teaspoon salt
⅛ teaspoon pepper
2 (8-ounce) cans no-salt-added
    tomato sauce
1 teaspoon dried Italian seasoning
½ teaspoon salt
½ teaspoon pepper
¼ teaspoon garlic powder

Cook cabbage leaves in boiling water 5 to 7 minutes or until wilted; drain. Set aside.

Combine ground turkey and next 7 ingredients in a large bowl; stir well. Place ½ cup turkey mixture in center of each cabbage leaf; fold ends of leaf over, and roll up. Place cabbage rolls, seam side down, in a 13- x 9- x 2-inch baking dish.

Combine tomato sauce, Italian seasoning, salt, pepper, and garlic powder in a medium bowl, stirring well; pour evenly over cabbage rolls. Cover and bake at 350° for 1 hour or until done, basting rolls occasionally with tomato sauce mixture. Yield: 6 servings (190 calories [21% from fat] per serving).

FAT 4.4g (SAT 1.4g, MONO 1.7g, POLY 0.8g)
PROTEIN 18.7g   CARBOHYDRATE 18.7g
FIBER 3.6g   CHOLESTEROL 47mg   SODIUM 325mg

Turkey Talk

Turkey is available in many forms. Here are the varieties seen most often:

Whole. Although whole turkeys are most often available frozen, whole fresh turkeys are also available in some supermarkets. Avoid purchasing self-basting turkeys because the basting solution contains mostly fat.

Breasts. Sold either fresh or frozen, these large pieces of breast meat may be purchased with or without the bone.

Roasts. Although most commonly found as a combination of white and dark meat rolled together and tied with a net, roasts may be all white or all dark meat. They are sold boneless and usually weigh 2½ to 6 pounds.

Steaks. Slices of turkey breast that measure ½ to 1 inch thick are referred to as steaks.

Cutlets. Slices of turkey breast that measure ⅛ to ⅜ inch thick are referred to as cutlets.

Tenderloins. Usually about ½ inch thick, these fillets are cut from the tenderloin of the turkey.

Ground. Usually a combination of white and dark meat, ground turkey may also contain skin unless the label indicates otherwise. Some large supermarkets sell 100% ground turkey breast, but you may have to request it from the butcher.

Wild Birds

If there's a hunter in your family, chances are you've experimented with cooking dove and quail. Both can be prepared using many of the same cooking methods used for lean poultry, such as roasting, braising, and grilling.

Be careful not to overcook game birds or they will become tough and dry. Because these birds are so small, they tend to cook and cool quickly, so serve the prepared dish as quickly as possible.

You won't find any recipes in this section for duck or goose because they are extremely high in fat. Save these birds for a holiday dinner or other special occasion.

DOVE WITH MUSHROOM SAUCE

12 dove breasts, skinned
¾ cup Chablis or other dry
  white wine
2 tablespoons white wine
  Worcestershire sauce
¼ teaspoon salt
¼ teaspoon cracked pepper
Vegetable cooking spray
2 cloves garlic, minced
2 medium onions, sliced and
  separated into rings
½ pound fresh mushrooms, sliced
2 teaspoons chicken-flavored
  bouillon granules
1¼ cups hot water, divided
2½ tablespoons all-purpose flour
6 cups cooked medium egg noodles
  (cooked without salt or fat)
2 tablespoons chopped fresh
  parsley
Fresh parsley sprigs (optional)

Place dove in a zip-top heavy-duty plastic bag. Combine wine and next 3 ingredients in a small bowl, stirring well. Pour over dove; seal bag, and shake until dove is well coated. Marinate in refrigerator 2 to 4 hours, turning bag occasionally.

Remove dove from marinade, reserving marinade. Coat a large nonstick skillet with vegetable cooking spray; place over medium-high heat until hot. Add garlic; sauté until garlic is very lightly browned. Add dove; cook 2 to 3 minutes or until browned on all sides. Remove dove from skillet. Drain dove, and pat dry with paper towels. Wipe drippings from skillet with a paper towel.

Coat skillet with vegetable cooking spray; place over medium-high heat until hot. Add onion and mushrooms; sauté 3 to 4 minutes or until onion is crisp-tender. Stir in marinade, bouillon granules, and 1 cup hot water. Add dove to skillet. Bring to a boil; cover, reduce heat, and simmer 20 minutes or until dove is done, stirring occasionally. Remove dove from skillet, using a slotted spoon. Set aside, and keep warm.

Combine flour and remaining ¼ cup water in a small bowl, stirring until smooth. Add flour mixture to mixture in skillet. Cook, stirring constantly, about 10 minutes or until mixture is slightly thickened.

Combine cooked noodles and parsley; toss gently. Place noodle mixture on a large serving platter; arrange dove breasts over noodle mixture. Spoon sauce mixture evenly over dove breasts and noodle mixture. Garnish with fresh parsley sprigs, if desired. Yield: 6 servings (402 calories [15% from fat] per serving).

FAT 6.6g (SAT 1.7g, MONO 1.7g, POLY 1.7g)
PROTEIN 35.1g   CARBOHYDRATE 49.2g
FIBER 4.9g   CHOLESTEROL 62mg   SODIUM 499mg

HEARTY BRAISED QUAIL

6 quail, skinned
½ teaspoon salt
¼ teaspoon pepper
Vegetable cooking spray
1 cup sliced fresh mushrooms
4 green onions, sliced
1 clove garlic, minced
½ cup Chablis or other dry
  white wine
¼ teaspoon dried whole thyme
2 medium tomatoes, cut into
  wedges
1 tablespoon chopped fresh
  parsley

Rinse quail under cold water, and pat dry; sprinkle with salt and pepper. Coat a nonstick skillet with cooking spray; place over medium-high heat until hot. Add quail; cook until lightly browned on all sides. Drain quail, and pat dry with paper towels. Wipe drippings from skillet.

Coat skillet with cooking spray; place over medium-high heat until hot. Add mushrooms; sauté 2 minutes. Remove mushrooms; set aside. Wipe drippings from skillet.

Coat skillet with cooking spray; place over medium-high heat until hot. Add green onions and garlic; sauté 1 minute. Stir in wine and thyme. Add quail to skillet. Bring to a boil; cover, reduce heat, and simmer 25 minutes. Add mushrooms and tomato wedges; cover and simmer 2 to 3 minutes or just until thoroughly heated. Transfer quail mixture to a serving dish; sprinkle with parsley. Yield: 6 servings (172 calories [29% from fat] per serving).

FAT 5.6g (SAT 1.5g, MONO 1.5g, POLY 1.5g)
PROTEIN 25.6g   CARBOHYDRATE 3.8g
FIBER 1.0g   CHOLESTEROL 91mg   SODIUM 261mg

SALADS AND DRESSINGS

Salads are one of the most versatile menu items. They can be sweet or savory, light or hearty, and can be served as an appetizer, a side dish, or a main dish. Some are even served as palate cleansers between courses. The salads and dressings featured in this chapter have been developed to be low in fat and cholesterol while retaining all the flavor and texture we expect from a salad.

SALADS

Modern agriculture helps make a wide variety of fresh fruits and vegetables available to consumers year-round. With such an assortment, the possibilities for creating salads are unlimited.

Selecting Salad Greens

For optimum flavor, nutrition, and eye-appeal, use the freshest, highest quality ingredients for your salads. As a rule, the most colorful salad ingredients also contain the most vitamins and minerals.

Select fresh, crisp greens that have firm, unblemished leaves and good color. Avoid greens that are oversized, limp, spotty, or yellow. Check the stem end for freshness; if it's brown, slimy, or dry, make another selection.

Preparing and Storing Greens

To clean tight heads of greens such as red cabbage or iceberg lettuce, begin by removing the core. Then run cool water into the core end of the head and over the leaves; invert the head to drain.

To clean leafy greens such as leaf lettuce or spinach, remove the leaves from the stems and place in a sink full of cool water. Gently swish the greens before removing them from the water to drain.

A salad spinner quickly removes excess water from leafy greens. When using a salad spinner, dry the tender leaves in small batches to avoid bruising them. To dry leafy greens with a cotton towel or paper towel, put the leaves on the towel, gather the ends of the towel together, and shake gently.

Tear, rather than cut, large leaves into bite-size pieces, and leave small leaves whole. Wrap whole heads or torn greens loosely in several paper towels; do not pack the greens. Store the loosely wrapped greens in an airtight container. The paper towels pull excess moisture away from the greens, while the airtight container keeps the moisture in the paper towels from evaporating. This small amount of moisture in the paper towels helps keep the greens fresh longer.

Fresh Pears with Tangy Blue Cheese Dressing (page 169) fits right in at a salad luncheon. You can also serve it as a light, refreshing dessert after a filling meal.

167

Fruit Salads

These recipes combine a variety of luscious fruits and low-fat dressings for salads that are as flavorful as they are nutritious. The natural sweetness of the fruit makes some of these recipes sweet enough to serve as a light dessert.

CARROT-PINEAPPLE CONGEALED SALADS

1 (8-ounce) can crushed pineapple in juice, undrained
1¾ cups unsweetened orange juice
2 envelopes unflavored gelatin
2 tablespoons sugar
2 cups shredded carrot
Vegetable cooking spray
Green leaf lettuce (optional)
¼ cup plus 2 tablespoons pineapple low-fat yogurt

Drain pineapple, reserving juice. Set pineapple aside. Combine reserved pineapple juice and orange juice in a small saucepan. Sprinkle gelatin over juice mixture; let stand 1 minute. Add sugar; cook over low heat, stirring constantly, until gelatin and sugar dissolve. Chill gelatin mixture until the consistency of unbeaten egg white.

Gently fold pineapple and carrot into gelatin mixture. Spoon mixture evenly into 6 (½-cup) molds coated with cooking spray. Cover and chill until firm.

Unmold salads onto lettuce-lined salad plates, if desired; top each serving with 1 tablespoon yogurt. Yield: 6 servings (108 calories [4% from fat] per serving).

FAT 0.5g (SAT 0.2g, MONO 0.1g, POLY 0.2g)
PROTEIN 3.6g CARBOHYDRATE 23.4g
FIBER 1.3g CHOLESTEROL 1mg SODIUM 21mg

FOUR-BERRY SALAD

2 cups fresh blackberries
2 cups fresh blueberries
2 cups fresh raspberries
2 cups fresh strawberries
1 (8-ounce) carton vanilla low-fat yogurt
½ cup nonfat sour cream alternative
2 tablespoons cream sherry
2 tablespoons lemon juice
1½ tablespoons honey
3 tablespoons slivered almonds, toasted

Place berries in a large bowl; toss gently to combine. Combine yogurt and next 4 ingredients in a small bowl; stir well.

Spoon berry mixture evenly into each of 8 individual serving bowls. Top each serving evenly with yogurt mixture, and sprinkle evenly with toasted almonds. Yield: 8 servings (137 calories [17% from fat] per 1-cup serving).

FAT 2.6g (SAT 0.4g, MONO 1.2g, POLY 0.7g)
PROTEIN 4.1g CARBOHYDRATE 25.5g
FIBER 7.9g CHOLESTEROL 1mg SODIUM 33mg

FESTIVE CRANBERRY SALAD

2 cups fresh cranberries
1 orange, unpeeled, quartered, and seeded
½ cup sugar
2 (3-ounce) packages raspberry-flavored gelatin
2 cups boiling water
½ cup cold water
1½ cups diced apple
1 cup diced celery
Vegetable cooking spray
Green leaf lettuce (optional)

Position knife blade in food processor bowl; add cranberries and orange. Process until finely chopped. Transfer mixture to a bowl; stir in sugar. Cover; let stand at room temperature 1 hour, stirring occasionally.

Dissolve gelatin in boiling water. Stir in cold water. Chill until the consistency of unbeaten egg white.

Gently fold cranberry mixture, apple, and celery into gelatin mixture. Spoon mixture into a 2-quart mold coated with cooking spray. Cover and chill until firm.

Unmold salad onto a lettuce-lined serving plate, if desired. Yield: 8 servings (170 calories [2% from fat] per serving).

FAT 0.3g (SAT 0.0g, MONO 0.0g, POLY 0.1g)
PROTEIN 2.1g CARBOHYDRATE 41.0g
FIBER 2.3g CHOLESTEROL 0mg SODIUM 94mg

CRANBERRY WALDORF SALAD

1½ cups chopped fresh cranberries
1 cup chopped Red Delicious apple
1 cup chopped celery
1 cup seedless green grapes, halved
⅓ cup raisins
¼ cup chopped walnuts
2 tablespoons sugar
¼ teaspoon ground cinnamon
1 (8-ounce) carton vanilla low-fat yogurt

Combine all ingredients; toss well. Cover and chill at least 2 hours. Toss gently just before serving. Yield: 9 servings (103 calories [20% from fat] per ½-cup serving).

FAT 2.3g (SAT 0.4g, MONO 0.5g, POLY 1.3g)
PROTEIN 2.5g CARBOHYDRATE 19.9g
FIBER 1.7g CHOLESTEROL 1mg SODIUM 31mg

SIMPLE FRUIT SALAD

¼ cup unsweetened pineapple juice
1½ tablespoons honey
1 teaspoon grated orange rind
¼ teaspoon ground ginger
1 cup coarsely chopped apple
1 cup coarsely chopped fresh pear
1 cup sliced fresh plums
1 cup sliced banana
1 tablespoon lemon juice

Combine first 4 ingredients in a small jar; cover tightly, and shake vigorously. Cover and chill thoroughly.

Combine apple, pear, plums, banana, and lemon juice in a bowl; toss gently. Pour dressing over fruit mixture, and toss gently. Serve immediately. Yield: 7 servings (70 calories [5% from fat] per ½-cup serving).

FAT 0.4g (SAT 0.1g, MONO 0.1g, POLY 0.1g)
PROTEIN 0.5g CARBOHYDRATE 18.0g
FIBER 2.0g CHOLESTEROL 0mg SODIUM 1mg

ORANGE-JICAMA AVOCADO SALAD

¼ teaspoon unflavored gelatin
½ cup unsweetened orange juice
1 teaspoon sugar
2 teaspoons lemon juice
¼ teaspoon grated orange rind
⅛ teaspoon dried whole tarragon
Romaine lettuce leaves (optional)
1½ teaspoons unsweetened orange juice
1 small avocado, peeled and thinly sliced
¼ pound jicama, peeled, thinly sliced, and cut into wedges
3 large oranges, peeled and sectioned

Sprinkle gelatin over ½ cup orange juice in a saucepan; let stand 1 minute. Add sugar; cook over low heat, stirring until gelatin and sugar

dissolve. Stir in lemon juice, orange rind, and tarragon. Cover and chill.

Line a serving platter with romaine lettuce leaves, if desired. Sprinkle 1½ teaspoons orange juice evenly over avocado. Arrange avocado, jicama, and orange sections on platter; pour dressing evenly over salad. Serve immediately. Yield: 6 servings (73 calories [36% from fat] per serving).

FAT 3.0g (SAT 0.5g, MONO 1.8g, POLY 0.4g)
PROTEIN 1.2g CARBOHYDRATE 11.7g
FIBER 2.8g CHOLESTEROL 0mg SODIUM 3mg

FRESH PEARS WITH TANGY BLUE CHEESE DRESSING

½ cup 1% low-fat cottage cheese
3 tablespoons skim milk
1 teaspoon Dijon mustard
½ teaspoon lime juice
¼ cup crumbled blue cheese
4 large fresh ripe pears
1 tablespoon lime juice
Romaine lettuce leaves (optional)
2 tablespoons chopped walnuts

Combine first 4 ingredients in container of an electric blender; top with cover, and process until smooth. Transfer mixture to a bowl; stir in blue cheese. Cover and chill.

Slice each pear in half lengthwise; remove core. Slice each half lengthwise into ¼-inch slices, leaving slices attached at stem end. Brush pear slices with 1 tablespoon lime juice.

Arrange lettuce leaves on 8 salad plates, if desired. Arrange pear halves on lettuce, letting slices fan out. Spoon dressing evenly over pear halves; sprinkle with walnuts. Serve immediately. Yield: 8 servings (108 calories [23% from fat] per serving).

FAT 2.7g (SAT 0.9g, MONO 0.7g, POLY 0.8g)
PROTEIN 3.6g CARBOHYDRATE 19.4g
FIBER 3.2g CHOLESTEROL 3mg SODIUM 128mg

MEDITERRANEAN SPRING SALAD

2 cups tightly packed torn Boston lettuce
2 cups tightly packed torn Bibb lettuce
1 cup fresh strawberries, halved
1 kiwifruit, peeled and sliced lengthwise
½ small purple onion, peeled and separated into rings
⅓ cup unsweetened orange juice
1 tablespoon lemon juice
1 tablespoon Dijon mustard
2 teaspoons peeled, grated gingerroot
2 teaspoons vegetable oil
½ teaspoon honey
¼ teaspoon grated orange rind
Dash of pepper
¼ cup crumbled feta cheese

Combine Boston and Bibb lettuce, strawberries, kiwifruit, and onion in a large bowl; toss gently.

Combine orange juice and next 7 ingredients in a small jar; cover tightly, and shake vigorously to blend. Pour dressing over salad; toss gently. Sprinkle evenly with cheese. Serve immediately. Yield: 6 servings (62 calories [44% from fat] per 1-cup serving).

FAT 3.0g (SAT 1.0g, MONO 0.8g, POLY 0.9g)
PROTEIN 1.7g CARBOHYDRATE 7.7g
FIBER 1.6g CHOLESTEROL 4mg SODIUM 130mg

Vegetable Salads

Vegetable salads are simple to toss together, and they add filling complex carbohydrates and fiber to a meal. The recipes in this section vary from marinated vegetables to tossed green salads served with dressings. A food processor can make quick work of most slicing or chopping that may be required to prepare these salads.

SUPREME BEAN SALAD

1 (16-ounce) can no-salt-added cut green beans, drained
1 (16-ounce) can cut wax beans, drained
1 (15-ounce) can kidney beans, drained
1 (15-ounce) can garbanzo beans, drained
1 cup chopped green pepper
1 cup chopped purple onion
1 (2-ounce) jar diced pimiento, drained
1 teaspoon minced garlic
¾ cup cider vinegar
¼ cup sugar
1 tablespoon vegetable oil
½ teaspoon salt
½ teaspoon pepper

Combine first 8 ingredients in a large bowl; toss well.

Combine vinegar, sugar, oil, salt, and pepper in a small saucepan; bring to a boil, stirring constantly. Pour vinegar mixture over bean mixture; toss gently. Cover and chill at least 3 hours, stirring occasionally. Serve with a slotted spoon. Yield: 8 servings (141 calories [15% from fat] per 1-cup serving).

FAT 2.3g (SAT 0.4g, MONO 0.6g, POLY 1.2g)
PROTEIN 5.3g CARBOHYDRATE 26.7g
FIBER 3.5g CHOLESTEROL 0mg SODIUM 379mg

BLACK AND WHITE BEAN SALAD

1 (15.8-ounce) can Great Northern beans, rinsed and drained
1 (15-ounce) can black beans, rinsed and drained
1¼ cups peeled, seeded, and chopped tomato
¾ cup diced sweet red pepper
¾ cup diced sweet yellow pepper
¾ cup thinly sliced green onions
½ cup commercial salsa
¼ cup red wine vinegar
2 tablespoons chopped fresh cilantro
¼ teaspoon salt
⅛ teaspoon freshly ground pepper
10 cups shredded romaine lettuce

Combine first 6 ingredients in a large bowl; stir gently to combine.

Combine salsa, vinegar, cilantro, salt, and pepper in a small bowl, stirring well. Pour salsa mixture over bean mixture, and toss gently to combine. Divide shredded lettuce evenly among 10 salad plates; spoon bean mixture evenly over lettuce. Yield: 10 servings (74 calories [6% from fat] per serving).

FAT 0.5g (SAT 0.1g, MONO 0.0g, POLY 0.2g)
PROTEIN 5.1g CARBOHYDRATE 13.8g
FIBER 3.2g CHOLESTEROL 0mg SODIUM 187mg

MARINATED LEGUMES

½ (16-ounce) package 16-bean soup mix (about 1 cup)
4 cups water
½ cup peeled, seeded, and chopped tomato
⅓ cup diced sweet red pepper
⅓ cup diced sweet yellow pepper
⅓ cup thinly sliced green onions
¼ cup commercial salsa
2 tablespoons red wine vinegar
1 tablespoon chopped fresh cilantro
¼ teaspoon salt
⅛ teaspoon freshly ground pepper
4 cups finely shredded romaine lettuce

Remove seasoning packet from beans; reserve for another use. Sort and wash beans; place in a Dutch oven. Add water; bring to a boil. Cover, reduce heat, and simmer 50 to 60 minutes or until beans are tender. Drain beans; let cool.

Combine beans, tomato, red pepper, yellow pepper, and green onions in a large bowl; toss gently. Combine salsa and next 4 ingredients in a small bowl; stir well. Pour salsa mixture over bean mixture, and toss gently to combine. Cover and marinate in refrigerator at least 4 hours, tossing occasionally.

Line a serving platter with lettuce; top lettuce with bean mixture. Yield: 4 servings (241 calories [17% from fat] per 1-cup serving).

FAT 4.6g (SAT 1.1g, MONO 1.5g, POLY 1.4g)
PROTEIN 12.2g CARBOHYDRATE 35g
FIBER 5.1g CHOLESTEROL 6mg SODIUM 158mg

SPICY GAZPACHO MOLD

1 cup reduced-sodium tangy
   vegetable juice
½ cup canned no-salt-added beef
   broth, undiluted
3 envelopes unflavored gelatin
¼ cup white wine vinegar
2 tablespoons lemon juice
2 teaspoons low-sodium
   Worcestershire sauce
½ teaspoon salt
¼ teaspoon hot sauce
3 cups chopped tomato
1 cup finely chopped green pepper
½ cup finely chopped cucumber
½ cup finely chopped celery
¼ cup finely chopped onion
1 clove garlic, minced
Vegetable cooking spray
Green leaf lettuce (optional)
Cucumber slices (optional)
Lemon slices (optional)
Fresh parsley sprigs (optional)

Combine vegetable juice and broth in a medium saucepan; stir well.

Sprinkle gelatin over vegetable juice mixture; let stand 1 minute. Cook mixture over low heat, stirring constantly, until gelatin dissolves. Remove from heat; add vinegar and next 4 ingredients to gelatin mixture; stir well. Chill until the consistency of unbeaten egg white.

Combine tomato, green pepper, cucumber, celery, onion, and garlic in a large bowl, tossing well. Gently fold tomato mixture into gelatin mixture. Spoon gelatin mixture into a 5-cup mold coated with vegetable cooking spray. Cover and chill until firm.

Unmold salad onto a lettuce-lined serving plate, if desired. If desired, garnish with cucumber slices, lemon slices, and fresh parsley sprigs. Yield: 10 servings (34 calories [8% from fat] per serving).

FAT 0.3g (SAT 0.0g, MONO 0.0g, POLY 0.1g)
PROTEIN 2.7g   CARBOHYDRATE 5.6g
FIBER 1.3g   CHOLESTEROL 0mg   SODIUM 169mg

Sprinkle the gelatin over the cold liquid ingredients; let stand 1 minute. This allows the gelatin granules to soften so that they will dissolve smoothly when heated.

Chill the gelatin mixture until slightly thickened or the consistency of unbeaten egg white. If the mixture becomes too thick, "melt" it over low heat and chill again.

Fold the vegetables into the gelatin mixture. The gentle over-and-under motion of folding turns the two mixtures over on top of each other, combining them in the process.

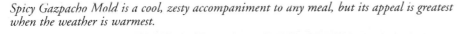

Spicy Gazpacho Mold is a cool, zesty accompaniment to any meal, but its appeal is greatest when the weather is warmest.

Cabbage and Pear Slaw

2 cups chopped fresh pear
2 tablespoons lemon juice
4½ cups coarsely shredded cabbage
½ cup coarsely shredded carrot
½ cup vanilla low-fat yogurt
¼ cup nonfat mayonnaise
¼ teaspoon celery seeds
¼ teaspoon onion salt

Combine pear and lemon juice in a large bowl; toss well. Add cabbage and carrot; toss well to combine.

Combine yogurt and remaining ingredients; add to slaw mixture, tossing well. Yield: 10 servings (40 calories [7% from fat] per ½-cup serving).

FAT 0.3g (SAT 0.1g, MONO 0.1g, POLY 0.1g)
PROTEIN 1.0g CARBOHYDRATE 9.2g
FIBER 1.4g CHOLESTEROL 1mg SODIUM 141mg

Overnight Coleslaw

6 cups coarsely shredded cabbage
3 cups coarsely shredded carrot
1 cup sliced green onions
1 cup cider vinegar
1 cup unsweetened apple juice
1½ tablespoons prepared mustard
1½ teaspoons paprika
1 teaspoon mustard seeds
½ teaspoon pepper
¼ teaspoon garlic powder
¼ teaspoon salt

Combine cabbage, carrot, and green onions in a large bowl. Combine vinegar and remaining ingredients; pour over cabbage mixture, tossing well. Cover and refrigerate at least 8 hours. Serve with a slotted spoon. Yield: 12 servings (35 calories [8% from fat] per ½-cup serving).

FAT 0.3g (SAT 0.0g, MONO 0.1g, POLY 0.1g)
PROTEIN 0.9g CARBOHYDRATE 8.3g
FIBER 1.7g CHOLESTEROL 0mg SODIUM 88mg

Tropical Carrot-Raisin Salad

2 cups coarsely shredded carrot
¼ cup plus 2 tablespoons raisins
1 (8-ounce) can crushed pineapple in juice, drained
¼ cup vanilla low-fat yogurt
2 tablespoons nonfat mayonnaise
1½ teaspoons creamy peanut butter
⅛ teaspoon ground cinnamon

Combine carrot, raisins, and pineapple in a medium bowl; toss well.

Combine yogurt and remaining ingredients in a small bowl; stir well. Add to carrot mixture, stirring well. Cover and chill thoroughly. Yield: 6 servings (85 calories [10% from fat] per ½-cup serving).

FAT 0.9g (SAT 0.2g, MONO 0.4g, POLY 0.3g)
PROTEIN 1.7g CARBOHYDRATE 19.1g
FIBER 2.1g CHOLESTEROL 0mg SODIUM 91mg

Dilled Cucumber Salad

2 small cucumbers, thinly sliced
1 small onion, thinly sliced and separated into rings
½ cup white wine vinegar
3 tablespoons sugar
2 tablespoons minced fresh dillweed
¼ teaspoon salt
⅛ teaspoon pepper

Place cucumber and onion in a shallow baking dish. Combine vinegar and remaining ingredients; pour over cucumber mixture, tossing well. Cover and marinate in refrigerator 8 hours, stirring occasionally. Yield: 6 servings (41 calories [2% from fat] per ½-cup serving).

FAT 0.1g (SAT 0.0g, MONO 0.0g, POLY 0.0g)
PROTEIN 0.6g CARBOHYDRATE 10.5g
FIBER 0.9g CHOLESTEROL 0mg SODIUM 100mg

Green Bean-Potato Salad

1 (8-ounce) carton plain nonfat yogurt
1½ cups canned low-sodium chicken broth, undiluted
6 medium-size round red potatoes (about 1 pound), unpeeled and cut into wedges
1 pound fresh green beans
¼ cup coarsely chopped purple onion
1 tablespoon white vinegar
¼ teaspoon freshly ground pepper
2 tablespoons nonfat mayonnaise

Spoon yogurt onto several layers of heavy-duty paper towels; spread to ½-inch thickness. Cover yogurt with additional paper towels; let stand 5 minutes. Scrape yogurt into a bowl, using a rubber spatula; cover and chill thoroughly.

Bring broth to a boil in a medium saucepan. Add potato; cover, reduce heat, and simmer 10 minutes or until potato is slightly tender. Drain, reserving ¼ cup broth. Set broth and potato aside.

Wash beans; trim ends, and remove strings. Cut beans into 1½-inch pieces. Arrange beans in a vegetable steamer over boiling water. Cover and steam 3 to 5 minutes or until crisp-tender. Combine potato, beans, and onion in a large bowl. Sprinkle with vinegar and pepper; toss gently.

Combine reserved broth, yogurt, and mayonnaise in a small bowl, stirring well. Pour mayonnaise mixture over vegetable mixture; toss gently. Cover and chill thoroughly. Yield: 6 servings (111 calories [5% from fat] per 1-cup serving).

FAT 0.6g (SAT 0.2g, MONO 0.2g, POLY 0.1g)
PROTEIN 5.7g CARBOHYDRATE 22.3g
FIBER 2.8g CHOLESTEROL 1mg SODIUM 121mg

Spicy Green Beans and Tomatoes

1 pound fresh green beans
8 cherry tomatoes, halved
⅓ cup water
⅓ cup cider vinegar
¾ teaspoon dill seeds
½ teaspoon sugar
¼ teaspoon salt
¼ teaspoon ground red pepper
2 cloves garlic, sliced

Wash beans; trim ends, and remove strings from beans. Cut beans into 1½-inch pieces. Arrange beans in a vegetable steamer over boiling water. Cover and steam 3 to 5 minutes or until beans are crisp-tender. Plunge steamed beans into ice water; drain well.

Place beans and cherry tomato halves in a shallow baking dish. Combine water and remaining ingredients in a small saucepan; bring mixture to a boil. Pour vinegar mixture over bean mixture; toss gently. Cover and marinate in refrigerator at least 8 hours, stirring occasionally. Serve with a slotted spoon. Yield: 8 servings (25 calories [7% from fat] per ½-cup serving).

Fat 0.2g (Sat 0.0g, Mono 0.0g, Poly 0.1g)
Protein 1.2g   Carbohydrate 5.9g
Fiber 1.4g   Cholesterol 0mg   Sodium 78mg

Marinated Tomato Slices

4 large tomatoes, cut into ¼-inch slices
¼ cup lemon juice
2 tablespoons minced onion
2 tablespoons red wine vinegar
1 teaspoon dried whole basil
¼ teaspoon garlic powder
¼ teaspoon pepper
Green leaf lettuce (optional)

Place tomato slices in a large shallow baking dish. Combine lemon juice and next 5 ingredients in a small bowl; pour over tomato slices, turning to coat. Cover and marinate in refrigerator at least 1 hour.

Arrange tomato slices on a lettuce-lined serving platter, if desired. Spoon marinade evenly over tomato slices. Yield: 8 servings (26 calories [10% from fat] per serving).

Fat 0.3g (Sat 0.1g, Mono 0.1g, Poly 0.1g)
Protein 1.0g   Carbohydrate 6.0g
Fiber 1.4g   Cholesterol 0mg   Sodium 9mg

Creamy Potato Salad

3 cups cooked, peeled, and cubed red potato (about 1 pound)
2 tablespoons chopped green onions
1 (2-ounce) jar diced pimiento, drained
¼ cup nonfat mayonnaise
¼ cup plain nonfat yogurt
1 tablespoon prepared mustard
1½ teaspoons sugar
1½ teaspoons white wine vinegar
¼ teaspoon salt
¼ teaspoon celery seeds
⅛ teaspoon garlic powder
⅛ teaspoon pepper

Combine potato, green onions, and pimiento in a large bowl, tossing gently to combine.

Combine mayonnaise and remaining ingredients in a small bowl; stir well. Add mayonnaise mixture to potato mixture; toss gently. Cover and chill thoroughly. Yield: 6 servings (85 calories [3% from fat] per ½-cup serving).

Fat 0.3g (Sat 0.0g, Mono 0.1g, Poly 0.1g)
Protein 2.0g   Carbohydrate 19.1g
Fiber 1.2g   Cholesterol 0mg   Sodium 269mg

Tabbouleh Salad

2 cups boiling water
1 cup bulgur wheat, uncooked
1½ cups seeded, chopped tomato
1 cup minced fresh parsley
½ cup finely chopped celery
½ cup chopped green onions
¼ cup chopped fresh mint
¼ cup lemon juice
2 cloves garlic, minced
2 tablespoons olive oil
¼ teaspoon salt
¼ teaspoon pepper

Pour water over bulgur in a large bowl; cover and let stand 1 hour. Drain thoroughly.

Combine bulgur, tomato, and remaining ingredients in a large bowl; stir well. Cover and chill at least 2 hours, stirring occasionally. Yield: 12 servings (70 calories [32% from fat] per ½-cup serving).

Fat 2.5g (Sat 0.4g, Mono 1.7g, Poly 0.3g)
Protein 1.9g   Carbohydrate 11.1g
Fiber 2.8g   Cholesterol 0mg   Sodium 61mg

Root Vegetables Are Great in Salads

Jicama, turnips, Jerusalem artichokes or sunchokes, and celery root or celeriac are four root vegetables that will add interesting textures and flavors to a salad. Simply peel away the outer skin to reveal the white, crunchy interior. Slice, grate, or cube the root; then toss it into a salad.

ITALIAN VEGETABLE SALAD

2 cups fresh broccoli flowerets
1 cup sliced fresh mushrooms
1 cup cherry tomato halves
¾ cup thinly sliced green pepper
¾ cup thinly sliced sweet red
    pepper
½ cup coarsely chopped purple
    onion
1 (14-ounce) can hearts of palm,
    drained and cut into ¼-inch
    slices
1 (14-ounce) can artichoke hearts,
    drained and quartered
1 (2¼-ounce) can sliced ripe olives,
    drained
⅔ cup commercial oil-free Italian
    dressing
1 teaspoon freshly ground pepper
Green leaf lettuce (optional)

Combine first 11 ingredients in a large bowl; toss gently. Cover and marinate in refrigerator at least 4 hours, tossing occasionally. Serve with a slotted spoon on individual lettuce-lined salad plates, if desired. Yield: 8 cups (86 calories [16% from fat] per 1-cup serving).

FAT 1.5g (SAT 0.3g, MONO 0.8g, POLY 0.4g)
PROTEIN 2.8g CARBOHYDRATE 18.3g
FIBER 2.5g CHOLESTEROL 0mg SODIUM 332mg

Hearts of palm and artichoke hearts are special treats found in Italian Vegetable Salad.

Where Should I Store Salad Greens?

The crisper drawer in the refrigerator maintains the ideal humidity for storing salad greens. When prepared and stored as directed on page 167, tender greens such as spinach and leaf lettuce will stay fresh for four to five days. Firmer greens such as iceberg lettuce and green cabbage will stay fresh for up to three weeks.

SPINACH-ORANGE SALAD

½ pound fresh spinach, washed
    and trimmed
3 large oranges, peeled and
    sectioned
1 (6-ounce) can sliced water
    chestnuts, drained
1 cup sliced fresh mushrooms
¼ cup thinly sliced green onions
Yogurt-Poppy Seed Dressing

Combine spinach and next 4 ingredients in a large bowl; toss gently. Serve with Yogurt-Poppy Seed Dressing. Yield: 8 servings (58 calories [6% from fat] per serving).

Yogurt-Poppy Seed Dressing
¼ cup plain nonfat yogurt
3 tablespoons nonfat mayonnaise
1 tablespoon honey
1 tablespoon skim milk
1 teaspoon poppy seeds
½ teaspoon grated orange rind

Combine all ingredients in a small bowl; stir well. Cover and chill thoroughly. Yield: ½ cup.

FAT 0.4g (SAT 0.1g, MONO 0.1g, POLY 0.2g)
PROTEIN 2.0g CARBOHYDRATE 13.1g
FIBER 3.0g CHOLESTEROL 0mg SODIUM 96mg

CONFETTI-STUFFED LETTUCE

1 large head iceberg lettuce
1 cup shredded carrot
¾ cup chopped radishes
⅓ cup thinly sliced green onions
3 ounces nonfat process cream
   cheese product
3 tablespoons nonfat mayonnaise
2 tablespoons sweet pickle relish
¼ teaspoon hot sauce

Core and wash lettuce, discarding outer leaves. Let drain. Remove heart of lettuce to enlarge the center cavity; reserve heart for other uses.

Combine carrot and remaining ingredients in a medium bowl; stir well. Spoon carrot mixture into cavity of lettuce. Cover and chill thoroughly. Cut lettuce into 6 wedges. Yield: 6 servings (46 calories [6% from fat] per serving).

FAT 0.3g (SAT 0.0g, MONO 0.0g, POLY 0.1g)
PROTEIN 3.1g CARBOHYDRATE 7.9g
FIBER 1.4g CHOLESTEROL 3mg SODIUM 240mg

EASY ENSALADA

3 cups torn iceberg lettuce
2 cups torn red leaf lettuce
½ cup chopped zucchini
½ cup frozen whole kernel corn,
   thawed and drained
½ cup diced sweet red pepper
½ cup peeled, diced jicama
¼ cup sliced green onions
½ cup commercial nonfat
   cucumber dressing
¼ cup commercial picante sauce

Combine first 7 ingredients in a large bowl, tossing gently. Cover and chill thoroughly. Combine cucumber dressing and picante sauce in a small bowl, stirring well. Cover and chill thoroughly.

To serve, pour dressing over salad mixture; toss gently. Serve immediately. Yield: 6 servings (40 calories [7% from fat] per 1-cup serving).

FAT 0.3g (SAT 0.1g, MONO 0.0g, POLY 0.2g)
PROTEIN 1.3g CARBOHYDRATE 9.1g
FIBER 1.1g CHOLESTEROL 0mg SODIUM 252mg

CAESAR SALAD

2 (1-ounce) slices white bread
Olive oil-flavored vegetable cooking
   spray
½ teaspoon garlic powder
1 clove garlic, halved
4 cups shredded romaine lettuce
⅓ cup canned no-salt-added
   chicken broth, undiluted
3 tablespoons lemon juice
2 teaspoons low-sodium
   Worcestershire sauce
1 teaspoon anchovy paste
¼ teaspoon dry mustard
3 tablespoons freshly grated
   Parmesan cheese
½ teaspoon cracked pepper

Coat one side of each slice of bread lightly with vegetable cooking spray; sprinkle evenly with garlic powder. Place bread on an ungreased baking sheet. Bake at 300° for 18 to 20 minutes or until golden. Cut bread into cubes; set aside.

Rub inside of a large salad bowl with garlic; discard garlic. Place lettuce in bowl. Combine chicken broth and next 4 ingredients in a small bowl; stirring well. Drizzle over lettuce. Sprinkle salad mixture with Parmesan cheese and pepper; toss well. Top with bread cubes. Serve immediately. Yield: 4 servings (82 calories [27% from fat] per 1-cup serving).

FAT 2.5g (SAT 1.0g, MONO 0.6g, POLY 0.2g)
PROTEIN 4.5g CARBOHYDRATE 10.4g
FIBER 1.1g CHOLESTEROL 4mg SODIUM 353mg

To remove the core from a head of iceberg lettuce, tap the core on a hard surface; gently twist out and discard the core.

GARLICKY GREEN SALAD

1 cup nonfat buttermilk
2 tablespoons minced fresh parsley
2 tablespoons nonfat mayonnaise
3 cloves garlic, minced
1 teaspoon cracked pepper
1 (14-ounce) can artichoke hearts,
   drained and quartered
1 (14-ounce) can hearts of palm,
   drained and sliced
3 cups tightly packed torn Boston
   lettuce
2 cups tightly packed torn fresh
   spinach
1 cup tightly packed torn curly
   endive
1 cup tightly packed torn fresh
   watercress
½ cup chopped celery
1 tablespoon chopped fresh chives

Combine first 5 ingredients in a jar; cover tightly, and shake vigorously. Cover and chill.

Combine artichoke hearts and remaining ingredients in a large serving bowl. Shake dressing mixture, and pour over salad; toss well. Yield: 10 servings (53 calories [5% from fat] per 1-cup serving).

FAT 0.3g (SAT 0.1g, MONO 0.0g, POLY 0.1g)
PROTEIN 2.9g CARBOHYDRATE 11.6g
FIBER 1.6g CHOLESTEROL 1mg SODIUM 101mg

Main-Dish Salads

Serve one of these main-dish salads as the entrée for a meal. They're full of flavor but low in fat, and they can easily satisfy large appetites. Add crusty bread and possibly a side dish of fruit for a complete meal.

MEXICAN SHRIMP AND PASTA SALAD

¾ **pound unpeeled medium-size fresh shrimp**
1 **teaspoon ground cumin**
¼ **teaspoon chili powder**
Vegetable cooking spray
1 **teaspoon olive oil**
½ **cup canned no-salt-added chicken broth, undiluted**
1 **small avocado, peeled and coarsely chopped**
1 **cup chopped fresh cilantro**
¼ **cup chopped green onions**
3 **tablespoons lime juice**
1 **large jalapeño pepper, seeded and chopped**
1 **clove garlic**
6 **ounces fettuccine, uncooked**
¼ **cup sliced ripe olives**
¼ **cup shredded zucchini**
2 **tablespoons chopped tomato**
Avocado slices (optional)
Fresh cilantro sprigs (optional)

Peel and devein shrimp. Sprinkle shrimp evenly with cumin and chili powder. Coat a large nonstick skillet with cooking spray; add oil. Place over medium heat until hot. Add shrimp; sauté 3 to 5 minutes or until done. Drain shrimp, and pat dry with paper towels; cover and chill. Wipe skillet dry with a paper towel.

Add broth to skillet; bring to a boil, and cook until reduced to ¼ cup. Remove from heat; let cool. Pour broth into container of an electric blender. Add avocado and next 5 ingredients; top with cover, and process until smooth.

Cook fettuccine according to package directions, omitting salt and fat; drain. Rinse under cold water; drain well. Combine fettuccine and one-third of avocado mixture; toss well. Place fettuccine in center of a serving platter. Top with shrimp, olives, zucchini, tomato, and remaining avocado mixture. If desired, garnish with avocado slices and fresh cilantro sprigs. Yield: 4 servings (322 calories [28% from fat] per serving).

FAT 10.0g (SAT 1.6g, MONO 5.5g, POLY 1.9g)
PROTEIN 21.7g CARBOHYDRATE 36.9g
FIBER 3.3g CHOLESTEROL 112mg SODIUM 199mg

Fat Facts About Avocados

Most fruits and vegetables are virtually fat-free — except avocados. A medium avocado contains about 300 calories, with a whopping 88 percent of those calories from fat. Although this fat is monounsaturated (the kind that may help lower blood cholesterol levels), you can't ignore the fact that avocados are mostly fat.

But you don't have to eliminate avocados from your diet completely. Use them in reduced amounts or as a garnish — perhaps a couple of thin slices to top a salad or soup.

Mexican Shrimp and Pasta Salad is a nutritious work of art. Beauty and taste aside, dieters will delight in this main-dish salad's calorie count — only 322 calories per serving.

SPICY CRABMEAT SALAD IN TOMATO CUPS

¾ pound fresh lump crabmeat,
 drained
⅓ cup thinly sliced celery
2 tablespoons thinly sliced green
 onions
2 tablespoons plain nonfat
 yogurt
2 tablespoons nonfat mayonnaise
2 tablespoons no-salt-added
 tomato sauce
1 tablespoon white wine vinegar
1 large clove garlic, minced
¼ teaspoon cracked black pepper
¼ teaspoon hot sauce
⅛ teaspoon salt
⅛ teaspoon ground white pepper
4 medium tomatoes
4 Bibb lettuce leaves

Combine crabmeat, celery, and green onions in a medium bowl; toss gently, and set aside. Combine yogurt and next 8 ingredients; stir well. Add to crabmeat mixture; stir well. Cover and chill 2 hours.

With stem end up, cut each tomato into 4 wedges, cutting to, but not through, base of tomato. Spread edges slightly apart. Spoon ½ cup crabmeat mixture into each tomato cup. Serve on individual lettuce-lined salad plates. Yield: 4 servings (156 calories [14% from fat] per serving).

FAT 2.4g (SAT 0.3g, MONO 0.4g, POLY 0.9g)
PROTEIN 19.5g CARBOHYDRATE 15.7g
FIBER 3.7g CHOLESTEROL 82mg SODIUM 439mg

CRABMEAT AND SHRIMP LOUIS

⅓ cup plain nonfat yogurt
¼ cup nonfat mayonnaise
3 tablespoons reduced-calorie
 chili sauce
1 tablespoon water
1 teaspoon paprika
¼ teaspoon dry mustard
⅛ teaspoon low-sodium
 Worcestershire sauce
2¼ cups water
¾ pound unpeeled medium-size
 fresh shrimp
½ pound fresh asparagus spears
4 cups torn green leaf lettuce
3 small tomatoes, cut into wedges
 and chilled
1½ cups thinly sliced, peeled
 cucumber, chilled
1 hard-cooked egg, thinly sliced and
 chilled
½ pound fresh lump crabmeat,
 drained
Lemon wedges (optional)

Combine first 7 ingredients, stirring well. Cover and chill.

Bring water to a boil; add shrimp. Cook 3 to 5 minutes or until shrimp are done. Drain shrimp, and rinse with cold water. Peel and devein shrimp. Set aside.

Snap off tough ends of asparagus. Remove scales from spears with a knife or vegetable peeler, if desired. Arrange asparagus spears in a vegetable steamer over boiling water. Cover and steam 4 to 5 minutes or until asparagus is crisp-tender. Remove asparagus, and set aside.

Divide lettuce evenly among 4 individual salad plates. Arrange shrimp, asparagus, tomato, cucumber, and egg over lettuce; top each serving evenly with crabmeat. Garnish with lemon wedges, if desired. Serve with chilled yogurt mixture. Yield: 4 servings (213 calories [16% from fat] per serving).

FAT 3.7g (SAT 0.8g, MONO 0.9g, POLY 1.1g)
PROTEIN 29.6g CARBOHYDRATE 16.2g
FIBER 3.0g CHOLESTEROL 228mg SODIUM 537mg

SALADE NIÇOISE

½ cup commercial oil-free Italian
 salad dressing
2 teaspoons dried whole tarragon
4 small round red potatoes
2 tablespoons Chablis or other dry
 white wine
1 clove garlic, crushed
½ pound fresh green beans
4 cups torn Bibb lettuce
½ small purple onion, thinly sliced
 and separated into rings
1 large tomato, cut into 12 wedges
1 (16½-ounce) can white tuna in
 spring water, drained
1 hard-cooked egg, sliced
8 pitted ripe olives, halved

Combine salad dressing and tarragon; stir well, and set aside.

Arrange potatoes in a vegetable steamer over boiling water; cover and steam 15 minutes or until tender. Let cool; slice crosswise into ¼-inch slices. Combine potato, wine, and garlic; cover and chill 2 hours.

Wash beans; trim ends, and remove strings. Arrange beans in a vegetable steamer over boiling water. Cover and steam 5 minutes or until crisp-tender. Combine beans and ¼ cup dressing mixture; toss gently. Cover and chill 30 minutes.

Divide lettuce evenly among 4 individual serving plates. Arrange onion rings evenly over lettuce. Drain potato mixture, discarding liquid; arrange potato slices evenly over onion slices. Drain bean mixture, discarding cooking liquid. Arrange beans, tomato wedges, tuna, egg slices, and olives over potato slices. Spoon remaining dressing mixture evenly over salads. Yield: 4 servings (244 calories [15% from fat] per serving).

FAT 4.2g (SAT 1.0g, MONO 1.9g, POLY 1.0g)
PROTEIN 15.9g CARBOHYDRATE 37.5g
FIBER 5.7g CHOLESTEROL 67mg SODIUM 488mg

Beef and Bean Salad Olé

¼ cup plus 2 tablespoons
  commercial mild salsa, divided
¼ cup white vinegar, divided
2 tablespoons water
4 (6-inch) corn tortillas
Vegetable cooking spray
½ pound ground round
½ teaspoon chili powder
¼ teaspoon dried whole oregano
1 (15-ounce) can dark red kidney
  beans, drained
½ cup chopped sweet yellow
  pepper
⅓ cup thinly sliced green onions
8 cherry tomatoes, quartered
3 cups torn iceberg lettuce
3 cups torn curly endive
¼ cup (1 ounce) shredded reduced-
  fat sharp Cheddar cheese

Combine 3 tablespoons salsa, 2 tablespoons vinegar, and water in a small jar; cover tightly, and shake vigorously to blend. Set aside.

Place tortillas on a baking sheet. Bake at 350° for 15 minutes or until crisp. Set aside.

Coat a nonstick skillet with cooking spray; place over medium heat until hot. Add beef, chili powder, and oregano; cook until meat is browned, stirring until it crumbles. Drain beef mixture; pat dry on paper towels.

Combine beef mixture, beans, and next 3 ingredients; toss gently. Stir in remaining 3 tablespoons salsa and remaining 2 tablespoons vinegar.

Place one tortilla on each of 4 salad plates. Divide lettuce and endive evenly among tortillas; spoon beef mixture evenly over lettuce. Top each with 1 tablespoon cheese; drizzle with salsa mixture. Yield: 4 servings (254 calories [23% from fat] per serving).

FAT 6.6g (SAT 2.2g, MONO 2.1g, POLY 1.0g)
PROTEIN 21.0g CARBOHYDRATE 29.2g
FIBER 3.5g CHOLESTEROL 40mg SODIUM 358mg

A salad is no longer just a plate of greens and fresh vegetables served before the entrée. High in protein and fiber, Beef and Bean Salad Olé is a satisfying meal in itself.

Chicken Waldorf Salad

2 cups chopped cooked chicken
  breast (skinned before cooking
  and cooked without salt)
1½ cups cubed Red Delicious apple
½ cup sliced celery
½ cup seedless red grape halves
3 tablespoons raisins
2 tablespoons chopped walnuts
¼ cup nonfat sour cream
  alternative
¼ cup vanilla low-fat yogurt
¼ teaspoon salt
5 cups loosely packed torn
  romaine lettuce

Combine first 6 ingredients in a medium bowl; toss gently. Combine sour cream, yogurt, and salt in a small bowl, stirring well. Add sour cream mixture to chicken mixture, tossing well. Place 1 cup lettuce on each of 5 individual salad plates; top each with 1 cup chicken mixture. Yield: 5 servings (218 calories [29% from fat] per serving).

FAT 7.0g (SAT 1.6g, MONO 2.2g, POLY 2.4g)
PROTEIN 21.1g CARBOHYDRATE 18.4g
FIBER 2.6g CHOLESTEROL 56mg SODIUM 202mg

TARRAGON CHICKEN SALAD

½ cup Chablis or other dry
  white wine
2 tablespoons minced shallots
1 tablespoon chopped fresh
  tarragon or 1 teaspoon dried
  whole tarragon
¼ teaspoon salt
⅛ teaspoon pepper
4 cups chopped cooked chicken
  breast (skinned before cooking
  and cooked without salt)
1½ cups plain low-fat yogurt
½ small purple onion, cut into thin
  strips
2 cups water
¾ pound small round red potatoes,
  quartered
1 pound fresh green beans
1½ teaspoons vegetable oil
¼ teaspoon salt
⅛ teaspoon pepper

Combine first 5 ingredients in a
small saucepan; cook over medium
heat until liquid is absorbed, stirring
constantly. Combine herb mixture,
chicken, yogurt, and onion in a medium bowl; stir well. Cover and chill
thoroughly.

Bring water to a boil in a medium
saucepan. Add potato; cover, reduce
heat, and simmer 10 minutes or until
tender. Remove potato from liquid,
reserving liquid. Set potato aside.

Wash beans; trim ends, and remove strings. Cut beans in half. Bring
reserved liquid to a boil. Add beans;
cover, reduce heat, and simmer 10
minutes or until crisp-tender. Drain.

Combine potato, beans, oil, ¼ teaspoon salt, and ⅛ teaspoon pepper in
a large bowl; toss gently. Cover and
chill thoroughly.

Spoon chicken mixture into center
of a serving platter. Arrange bean
mixture around chicken mixture.
Yield: 8 servings (195 calories [27%
from fat] per serving).

FAT 5.8g (SAT 1.8g, MONO 2.0g, POLY 1.4g)
PROTEIN 20.7g CARBOHYDRATE 15.0g
FIBER 2.0g CHOLESTEROL 53mg SODIUM 233mg

TURKEY CHOW MEIN SALAD

⅓ cup lemon low-fat yogurt
1 teaspoon low-sodium soy sauce
½ teaspoon ground ginger
8 large cabbage leaves
4 cups torn fresh spinach
2 (10¼-ounce) cans mandarin
  oranges in water, drained
1 cup chopped cooked turkey breast
  (skinned before cooking and
  cooked without salt)
¼ cup sliced water chestnuts
¼ cup sliced bamboo shoots
¼ cup shredded carrot
1 cup chow mein noodles

Combine yogurt, soy sauce, and
ginger; stir well. Cover and chill.

Arrange cabbage leaves on a large
serving platter. Combine spinach and
next 5 ingredients; toss gently. Spoon
spinach mixture evenly onto cabbage
leaves. Spoon yogurt mixture evenly
over salad, and top evenly with chow
mein noodles. Yield: 4 servings (226
calories [25% from fat] per serving).

FAT 6.2g (SAT 1.2g, MONO 1.4g, POLY 2.9g)
PROTEIN 16.5g CARBOHYDRATE 26.2g
FIBER 3.5g CHOLESTEROL 30mg SODIUM 182mg

DILLED TURKEY PASTA SALAD

6 ounces seashell macaroni,
  uncooked
¾ pound cooked turkey breast
  (skinned before cooking and
  cooked without salt), cut into
  strips
2 cups chopped tomato
½ cup diced celery
¼ cup minced red onion
¼ chopped fresh parsley
1 tablespoon plus 2 teaspoons red
  wine vinegar
1 tablespoon vegetable oil
2 teaspoons grated Parmesan cheese
1½ teaspoons dried whole dillweed
2 cloves garlic, minced
½ teaspoon pepper
¼ teaspoon salt

Cook pasta according to package
directions, omitting salt and fat.
Drain well. Rinse pasta under cold
water; drain.

Combine cooked pasta, turkey, tomato, celery, onion, and parsley in a
large bowl; toss well. Combine vinegar and remaining ingredients in a
small bowl, stirring well. Pour vinegar mixture over pasta mixture; toss
gently to combine. Cover and chill at
least 2 hours. Yield: 8 servings (285
calories [12% from fat] per 1-cup
serving).

FAT 3.9g (SAT 0.9g, MONO 0.9g, POLY 1.4g)
PROTEIN 15.8g CARBOHYDRATE 43.3g
FIBER 1.2g CHOLESTEROL 0mg SODIUM 443mg

*If cooked pasta is to be used in a chilled
salad, rinse it under cold running water to
prevent it from sticking together. For best
results, do not rinse pasta to be served hot.*

Each of the following salad dressing recipes is either fat-free or contains less than two grams of fat per serving. But because these dressings are low in calories, the percent of calories from fat may be more than 30 percent per serving. Keep in mind that this percentage drops when the dressing is combined with fruits, vegetables, or salad greens. A dressing should enhance, not overpower, a salad, so use it sparingly.

ORANGE-BASIL VINAIGRETTE

½ cup canned no-salt-added chicken broth, undiluted
½ cup unsweetened orange juice
2 tablespoons white wine vinegar
1 tablespoon Dijon mustard
1 teaspoon cornstarch
¼ teaspoon minced garlic
⅛ teaspoon salt
1 teaspoon minced fresh basil
¼ teaspoon grated orange rind

Combine first 5 ingredients in a small saucepan; stir well. Bring to a boil over medium heat, stirring constantly. Cook 1 minute; remove from heat, and set aside.
Combine garlic and salt in a small bowl; mash to a paste using the back of a spoon. Add orange juice mixture, basil, and orange rind; stir well. Cover and chill thoroughly. Serve vinaigrette with salad greens. Yield: 1¼ cups (5 calories [18% from fat] per tablespoon).

FAT 0.1g (SAT 0.0g, MONO 0.0g, POLY 0.0g)
PROTEIN 0.1g   CARBOHYDRATE 0.9g
FIBER 0.0g   CHOLESTEROL 0mg   SODIUM 41mg

BLUE CHEESE VINAIGRETTE

⅓ cup canned no-salt-added chicken broth, undiluted
⅓ cup crumbled blue cheese
2 tablespoons white wine vinegar
2 tablespoons lemon juice
1 teaspoon dried whole oregano
2 teaspoons Dijon mustard
½ teaspoon sugar
½ teaspoon freshly ground pepper

Combine all ingredients in a small jar; cover tightly, and shake vigorously to blend. Cover and chill thoroughly. Serve vinaigrette with salad greens. Yield: ¾ cup (17 calories [58% from fat] per tablespoon).

FAT 1.1g (SAT 0.7g, MONO 0.3g, POLY 0.0g)
PROTEIN 0.8g   CARBOHYDRATE 0.7g
FIBER 0.0g   CHOLESTEROL 3mg   SODIUM 78mg

RASPBERRY VINAIGRETTE

½ cup plus 1 tablespoon raspberry vinegar
½ cup plus 1 tablespoon canned low-sodium chicken broth, undiluted
2 teaspoons sugar
1½ teaspoons olive oil
⅛ teaspoon salt
⅛ teaspoon pepper

Combine all ingredients in a small jar; cover tightly, and shake vigorously to blend. Cover and chill thoroughly. Serve vinaigrette with salad greens. Yield: 1 cup (8 calories [54% from fat] per tablespoon).

FAT 0.5g (SAT 0.1g, MONO 0.3g, POLY 0.0g)
PROTEIN 0.1g   CARBOHYDRATE 1.1g
FIBER 0.0g   CHOLESTEROL 0mg   SODIUM 21mg

SESAME VINAIGRETTE

½ cup rice vinegar
¼ cup water
1 tablespoon low-sodium soy sauce
1 tablespoon sesame oil
2 teaspoons sugar
1½ teaspoons Dijon mustard
1 clove garlic, minced

Combine all ingredients in a small jar; cover tightly, and shake vigorously to blend. Cover and chill thoroughly. Serve vinaigrette with salad greens. Yield: 1 cup (12 calories [68% from fat] per tablespoon).

FAT 0.9g (SAT 0.1g, MONO 0.3g, POLY 0.4g)
PROTEIN 0.0g   CARBOHYDRATE 0.6g
FIBER 0.0g   CHOLESTEROL 0mg   SODIUM 39mg

GARLIC-HERB BUTTERMILK DRESSING

½ cup nonfat buttermilk
¼ cup instant nonfat dry milk powder
2 tablespoons nonfat mayonnaise
2 tablespoons white wine vinegar
1 small clove garlic, crushed
2 teaspoons dried Italian seasoning
½ teaspoon salt
Dash of ground red pepper

Combine all ingredients in a small bowl, stirring well with a wire whisk. Cover and chill thoroughly. Serve dressing with salad greens or fresh raw vegetables. Yield: ¾ cup (17 calories [5% from fat] per tablespoon).

FAT 0.1g (SAT 0.1g, MONO 0.0g, POLY 0.0g)
PROTEIN 1.3g   CARBOHYDRATE 2.6g
FIBER 0.1g   CHOLESTEROL 1mg   SODIUM 154mg

CREAMY YOGURT-MINT DRESSING

½ cup plain nonfat yogurt
¼ cup chopped fresh mint
¼ cup nonfat mayonnaise
1 teaspoon sugar
2 teaspoons white wine vinegar
2 teaspoons lemon juice
⅛ teaspoon ground white pepper

Combine all ingredients in a small bowl, stirring well with a wire whisk. Cover and chill thoroughly. Serve dressing with salad greens or fresh fruit. Yield: ¾ cup (11 calories [0% from fat] per tablespoon).

FAT 0.0g (SAT 0.0g, MONO 0.0g, POLY 0.0g)
PROTEIN 0.6g CARBOHYDRATE 2.2g
FIBER 0.0g CHOLESTEROL 0mg SODIUM 71mg

SWEET-AND-SOUR DRESSING

¾ cup plain nonfat yogurt
¼ cup nonfat mayonnaise
3 tablespoons cider vinegar
2 tablespoons sugar
1 teaspoon grated onion
½ teaspoon celery seeds
½ teaspoon paprika
¼ teaspoon dry mustard

Combine all ingredients in a small bowl, stirring well with a wire whisk. Cover and chill thoroughly. Serve dressing with salad greens. Yield: 1 cup plus 2 tablespoons (14 calories [0% from fat] per tablespoon).

FAT 0.0g (SAT 0.0g, MONO 0.0g, POLY 0.0g)
PROTEIN 0.6g CARBOHYDRATE 3.0g
FIBER 0.0g CHOLESTEROL 0mg SODIUM 50mg

HONEY MUSTARD DRESSING

1 (8-ounce) carton plain nonfat yogurt
⅓ cup nonfat mayonnaise
⅓ cup honey
2½ tablespoons Dijon mustard
2½ tablespoons coarse-grained mustard
1½ tablespoons rice vinegar

Combine all ingredients in a small bowl, stirring well with a wire whisk. Cover and chill yogurt mixture thoroughly. Serve as a dressing with salad greens or assorted sliced fresh fruits, or as a dipping sauce for broiled, roasted, or grilled poultry. Yield: 1¾ cups (22 calories [8% from fat] per tablespoon).

FAT 0.2g (SAT 0.0g, MONO 0.0g, POLY 0.0g)
PROTEIN 0.6g CARBOHYDRATE 4.7g
FIBER 0.0g CHOLESTEROL 0mg SODIUM 101mg

SAUCES AND CONDIMENTS

Many sauces and condiments are notorious for being high in fat, thus turning healthful foods into fat-laden fare. Yet these items are a welcome complement to many foods, and they can make an otherwise plain dish special. The recipes in this section offer a wide variety of menu accompaniments — without all the usual fat.

SAUCES

A good sauce should enhance the natural flavor of food, not cover it up. And who says it has to be high in fat to have flavor? The recipes in this section are full of flavor yet contain little or no fat.

Along with an assortment of savory sauces that can be served with vegetables, fish, poultry, and meats, this section includes a variety of marinades and a traditional barbecue sauce. The dessert sauces are perfect for serving over nonfat frozen yogurt or ice milk as well as angel food cake or fat-free pound cake.

Stirring Up the Sauce

The base for most traditional sauces and gravies is a mixture of flour and butter or margarine. Many of the sauces in this chapter and throughout the book call for this flour-and-fat blend, but they either use less regular margarine or replace it with reduced-calorie margarine. Once the margarine melts, the flour is added and the mixture is stirred

over medium heat until a paste is formed, about one minute. This short cooking time is just long enough to release the starch from the flour, which will eliminate a pasty flavor in the sauce or gravy.

Liquid is gradually stirred into the flour mixture to prevent lumps. If lumps do appear, the mixture should be stirred briskly with a wire whisk. The sauce mixture is then cooked over medium heat, while being stirred constantly, until it is thickened and bubbly. This process should not be rushed by cooking at a higher temperature; it's the longer cooking time at a lower temperature that keeps the sauce from scorching.

Even though the previous method is considered traditional for white sauces, we have featured a different method in our recipe for Basic White Sauce. This recipe contains so little margarine that our test kitchens came up with a better method for incorporating the flour. The flour and a small amount of the liquid are stirred

Raspberry-Peach Sauce and Kahlúa-Pecan Sauce (page 189) taste as luscious as they look. But don't let appearances fool you — both sauces contain less than one gram of fat per tablespoon.

together until smooth. This mixture, the remaining liquid, margarine, and any flavoring ingredients are combined in the saucepan prior to cooking. This method is easy to follow and is used throughout this book to create low-fat sauces and gravies.

Cornstarch is another thickening agent commonly used for sauces, puddings, and soups. Its thickening strength is twice that of flour, so half the amount will achieve the same effect. Sauces thickened with cornstarch are more transparent than those thickened with flour. To prevent lumps, cornstarch should be mixed with a little cold liquid until smooth before being added to a hot mixture. Stir the cornstarch mixture into the hot mixture, and cook until it reaches a full boil; boil one minute to allow the starch granules to swell and absorb liquid, which creates a thickening action. And don't cook cornstarch-thickened sauces too long or over heat that is too high; this can cause them to break down.

Problem Solving for Sauces

If your sauce develops lumps, don't panic. Lumps can sometimes be removed by pouring the sauce through a sieve or piece of cheesecloth or by whirling the sauce in the blender. If the sauce becomes too thick, thin it by stirring in more liquid, one tablespoon at a time, as the sauce cooks. If the sauce is too thin, stir together a small amount of flour or cornstarch and water. Add the mixture to the sauce, cooking and stirring constantly until the sauce is properly thickened.

Sauces containing an acidic ingredient such as vinegar or lemon juice may not thicken if that ingredient is added during the cooking process. For best results, remove the saucepan from the heat before stirring in the acidic ingredient.

Savory Sauces

With this assortment of savory sauces, it's easy to add richness and flavor to foods without adding extra fat and calories. In this section are sauces you can mix and match to serve with many foods.

BASIC WHITE SAUCE

1½ tablespoons all-purpose flour
1 cup skim milk, divided
¼ cup instant nonfat dry milk powder
1 tablespoon reduced-calorie margarine
¼ teaspoon salt

Combine flour and ¼ cup milk; stir until smooth. Combine flour mixture, remaining ¾ cup milk, milk powder, and margarine in a small saucepan; stir well. Cook over medium heat, stirring constantly, until mixture is thickened and bubbly. Remove from heat; stir in salt. Yield: 1 cup (19 calories [24% from fat] per tablespoon).

FAT 0.5g (SAT 0.1g, MONO 0.0g, POLY 0.0g)
PROTEIN 1.3g CARBOHYDRATE 2.3g
FIBER 0.0g CHOLESTEROL 1mg SODIUM 61mg

Creamy Dill Sauce: Add 1 tablespoon chopped fresh dillweed and 1 teaspoon lemon juice to Basic White Sauce. Serve with fish. Yield: 1 cup plus 1 tablespoon (18 calories [25% from fat] per tablespoon).

FAT 0.5g (SAT 0.1g, MONO 0.2g, POLY 0.2g)
PROTEIN 1.2g CARBOHYDRATE 2.2g
FIBER 0.0g CHOLESTEROL 1mg SODIUM 58mg

Mustard-Horseradish Sauce: Add 1 tablespoon spicy brown mustard and 1 tablespoon prepared horseradish to

Basic White Sauce. Serve with beef or poultry. Yield: 1 cup plus 1 tablespoon (19 calories [24% from fat] per tablespoon).

FAT 0.5g (SAT 0.1g, MONO 0.2g, POLY 0.2g)
PROTEIN 1.3g CARBOHYDRATE 2.3g
FIBER 0.0g CHOLESTEROL 1mg SODIUM 71mg

Sherried Mushroom Sauce: Coat a small nonstick skillet with vegetable cooking spray; place over medium-high heat until hot. Add ⅓ cup chopped fresh mushrooms; sauté 3 to 4 minutes or until mushrooms are tender. Add cooked mushrooms, 1 tablespoon dry sherry, and ¼ teaspoon dried whole tarragon to Basic White Sauce. Serve with beef or poultry. Yield: 1¼ cups (17 calories [21% from fat] per tablespoon).

FAT 0.4g (SAT 0.1g, MONO 0.1g, POLY 0.2g)
PROTEIN 1.1g CARBOHYDRATE 2.0g
FIBER 0.0g CHOLESTEROL 1mg SODIUM 49mg

HORSERADISH SAUCE

¾ cup plain nonfat yogurt
¾ cup nonfat mayonnaise
3 tablespoons grated fresh horseradish
2 tablespoons lemon juice
1 tablespoon Dijon mustard
½ teaspoon sugar
½ teaspoon ground red pepper

Combine all ingredients in a small bowl, stirring well. Cover and chill thoroughly. Serve with beef. Yield: 1½ cups (18 calories [5% from fat] per tablespoon).

FAT 0.1g (SAT 0.0g, MONO 0.0g, POLY 0.0g)
PROTEIN 0.4g CARBOHYDRATE 3.9g
FIBER 0.0g CHOLESTEROL 0mg SODIUM 214mg

CREAMY GRAVY

1½ tablespoons reduced-calorie
  margarine
2 tablespoons all-purpose flour
1 cup evaporated skimmed milk
½ cup canned no-salt-added
  chicken broth, undiluted
¼ teaspoon salt
⅛ teaspoon pepper

Melt margarine in a small saucepan over medium heat; add flour, and stir until smooth. Cook 1 minute, stirring constantly. Gradually add milk and broth; cook over medium heat, stirring constantly, until mixture is thickened. Remove from heat; stir in salt and pepper. Serve gravy immediately over roasted poultry. Yield: 1½ cups (15 calories [30% from fat] per tablespoon).

FAT 0.5g (SAT 0.1g, MONO 0.2g, POLY 0.2g)
PROTEIN 0.9g CARBOHYDRATE 1.8g
FIBER 0.0g CHOLESTEROL 0mg SODIUM 44mg

ENCHILADA SAUCE

Vegetable cooking spray
1½ tablespoons reduced-calorie
  margarine
2 cloves garlic, minced
2 tablespoons all-purpose flour
2 cups water
½ cup no-salt-added tomato sauce
1 tablespoon chili powder
1 tablespoon hot chili powder
¼ teaspoon salt
⅛ teaspoon dried whole oregano
⅛ teaspoon ground cumin

Coat a medium saucepan with cooking spray; add margarine. Place over medium heat until margarine melts. Add garlic; sauté until tender. Add flour, stirring until smooth. Cook 1 minute, stirring constantly.

Combine water and remaining ingredients; add to flour mixture, stirring constantly. Bring to a boil; reduce heat, and simmer 15 minutes, stirring occasionally. Serve warm with enchiladas. Yield: 2 cups (8 calories [45% from fat] per tablespoon).

FAT 0.4g (SAT 0.1g, MONO 0.1g, POLY 0.2g)
PROTEIN 0.2g CARBOHYDRATE 1.0g
FIBER 0.2g CHOLESTEROL 0mg SODIUM 29mg

SPICY JALAPEÑO-FRUIT SAUCE

Vegetable cooking spray
1½ teaspoons vegetable oil
⅓ cup chopped purple onion
2 tablespoons minced garlic
2 tablespoons minced jalapeño
  pepper
2 cups chopped fresh apricots
2 cups chopped fresh plums
⅓ cup lemon juice
⅓ cup honey
3 tablespoons low-sodium soy sauce
2 teaspoons curry powder
2 teaspoons ground allspice

Coat a saucepan with cooking spray; add oil. Place over medium heat until hot. Add onion, garlic, and pepper; sauté until tender. Stir in apricot and remaining ingredients; bring to a boil. Reduce heat; simmer 35 minutes, stirring occasionally. Serve with pork. Yield: 3 cups (19 calories [14% from fat] per tablespoon).

FAT 0.3g (SAT 0.0g, MONO 0.1g, POLY 0.1g)
PROTEIN 0.2g CARBOHYDRATE 4.2g
FIBER 0.4g CHOLESTEROL 0mg SODIUM 25mg

TANGY LEMON SAUCE

1 tablespoon cornstarch
½ teaspoon sugar
Dash of ground white pepper
1 cup canned no-salt-added
  chicken broth, undiluted
2 tablespoons water
½ teaspoon grated lemon rind
⅓ cup fresh lemon juice
2 teaspoons chopped fresh
  parsley

Combine first 3 ingredients in a small saucepan; stir well. Gradually stir in chicken broth and water. Cook over medium heat, stirring constantly, until mixture comes to a boil. Reduce heat, and simmer 1 minute or until mixture is thickened, stirring constantly. Remove from heat; stir in lemon rind, lemon juice, and parsley. Serve warm over fish or steamed vegetables. Yield: 1¼ cups plus 2 tablespoons (4 calories [23% from fat] per tablespoon).

FAT 0.1g (SAT 0.0g, MONO 0.0g, POLY 0.0g)
PROTEIN 0.1g CARBOHYDRATE 0.8g
FIBER 0.0g CHOLESTEROL 0mg SODIUM 6mg

MUSTARD SAUCE

⅓ cup plain nonfat yogurt
¼ cup nonfat mayonnaise
3 tablespoons Dijon mustard
2 tablespoons sweet pickle relish
1 tablespoon minced onion
2 teaspoons white wine vinegar

Combine all ingredients; stirring well. Cover and chill thoroughly. Serve with fish or shellfish. Yield: ¾ cup plus 2 tablespoons (14 calories [13% from fat] per tablespoon).

FAT 0.2g (SAT 0.0g, MONO 0.2g, POLY 0.0g)
PROTEIN 0.3g CARBOHYDRATE 2.3g
FIBER 0.0g CHOLESTEROL 0mg SODIUM 172mg

RÉMOULADE SAUCE

1 cup nonfat mayonnaise
3 tablespoons sliced green onions
3 tablespoons diced celery
3 tablespoons Dijon mustard
2 tablespoons lemon juice
1 tablespoon prepared horseradish
2 small cloves garlic, crushed
½ teaspoon paprika
¼ teaspoon salt
¼ teaspoon ground white
   pepper
4 drops hot sauce

Combine all ingredients in container of an electric blender or food processor; top with cover, and process until smooth. Transfer mixture to a small bowl. Cover and chill thoroughly. Serve with fish or shellfish. Yield: 1½ cups (12 calories [8% from fat] per tablespoon).

FAT 0.1g (SAT 0.0g, MONO 0.1g, POLY 0.0g)
PROTEIN 0.1g   CARBOHYDRATE 2.6g
FIBER 0.1g   CHOLESTEROL 0mg   SODIUM 209mg

FRESH SPINACH SAUCE

1 cup water
1½ cups torn fresh spinach
½ cup loosely packed fresh basil
   leaves
½ cup nonfat buttermilk
¼ cup chopped green onions
1 tablespoon nonfat mayonnaise
2 cloves garlic, minced

Bring water to a boil in a medium saucepan. Add spinach; cook 3 to 4 minutes or until tender. Drain spinach; press between paper towels until barely moist.

Combine cooked spinach, basil, and remaining ingredients in container of an electric blender or food processor; top with cover, and process until mixture is smooth. Transfer mixture to a small bowl; cover and chill thoroughly. Serve chilled sauce with sliced fresh tomatoes. Yield: 1 cup (5 calories [0% from fat] per tablespoon).

FAT 0.0g (SAT 0.0g, MONO 0.0g, POLY 0.0g)
PROTEIN 0.4g   CARBOHYDRATE 0.9g
FIBER 0.1g   CHOLESTEROL 0mg   SODIUM 22mg

Sauces in the Microwave

It's easy to prepare sauces in the microwave oven because you don't have to contend with problems such as lumping, scorching, and constant stirring.

Prepare microwave sauces in a glass measuring cup or casserole dish that is large enough to prevent the sauce from bubbling over. To be safe, use a container that will hold twice the volume of the sauce.

As the sauce cooks, stir occasionally to combine the cooked portion along the sides of the container with the uncooked portion in the center. Stirring the sauce at 1- to 2-minute intervals is usually sufficient.

Most sauces can be reheated on HIGH, stirring every 30 seconds. The amount of cooking time will vary depending on the amount and temperature of the sauce.

Marinades and Barbecue Sauces ——————

A marinade is a seasoned liquid in which cuts of meat, poultry, fish, and shellfish are soaked (or marinated) to add flavor and help tenderize the cut.

Most marinades (and some barbecue sauces) are based on the combination of an acidic ingredient such as lemon juice, wine, or vinegar, herbs and spices, and sometimes oil. The acidic ingredient helps tenderize tough cuts of meat. Because of the high acid content in a marinade, you should marinate only in a glass or ceramic baking dish or a large zip-top heavy-duty plastic bag. Never marinate in an aluminum dish. Foods should be covered and refrigerated while they're marinating.

In general, the more a meat is basted with a marinade or sauce, the more tender and juicy it will be. Basting every five to 10 minutes is a good rule of thumb for most meats. When basting with a barbecue sauce or other sauce that may have a high sugar content, wait until the last 30 minutes of cooking time to begin applying the sauce to larger cuts of meat or poultry; the sugar in the sauce may burn on the meat if it is brushed on too soon.

Following are several recipes for low-fat marinades that contain little, if any, oil. You will also find a low-fat version of traditional tomato-based barbecue sauce and a spicy dry seasoning mix for rubbing on fish, meats, or poultry before grilling to add lots of flavor.

DIJON-LEMON MARINADE

2 teaspoons grated lemon rind
⅔ cup fresh lemon juice
3 tablespoons Dijon mustard
2 tablespoons water
1 teaspoon pepper
1 clove garlic, minced
½ teaspoon sugar
¼ teaspoon paprika

Combine all ingredients in a small bowl; stir well. Use to marinate fish or poultry before cooking. Baste with remaining marinade while cooking. Yield: 1 cup (7 calories [26% from fat] per tablespoon).

FAT 0.2g (SAT 0.0g, MONO 0.1g, POLY 0.0g)
PROTEIN 0.1g CARBOHYDRATE 1.4g
FIBER 0.0g CHOLESTEROL 0mg SODIUM 84mg

SHERRIED BEEF MARINADE

¼ cup low-sodium Worcestershire
  sauce
3 tablespoons dry sherry
2 tablespoons water
2 tablespoons lemon juice
1½ tablespoons low-sodium
  soy sauce
1½ teaspoons dry mustard
1 teaspoon pepper
½ teaspoon minced fresh
  parsley
1 clove garlic, minced

Combine all ingredients in a small bowl; stir well. Use to marinate beef or veal before cooking. Baste with remaining marinade while cooking. Yield: ¾ cup (8 calories [11% from fat] per tablespoon).

FAT 0.1g (SAT 0.0g, MONO 0.0g, POLY 0.0g)
PROTEIN 0.2g CARBOHYDRATE 1.8g
FIBER 0.1g CHOLESTEROL 0mg SODIUM 80mg

SPICY BARBECUE SAUCE

1 (8-ounce) can no-salt-added
  tomato sauce
½ cup reduced-calorie catsup
¼ cup red wine vinegar
¼ cup low-sodium Worcestershire
  sauce
2 tablespoons grated onion
1 tablespoon dark brown sugar
1 tablespoon liquid smoke
1 teaspoon chili powder
1 teaspoon pepper
1 clove garlic, minced
1 bay leaf

Combine all ingredients in a medium saucepan, stirring well. Bring mixture to a boil over medium heat, stirring frequently. Reduce heat, and simmer 10 minutes, stirring occasionally. Remove and discard bay leaf. Use for basting meat or poultry while cooking. Yield: 2 cups (8 calories [0% from fat] per tablespoon).

FAT 0.0g (SAT 0.0g, MONO 0.0g, POLY 0.0g)
PROTEIN 0.1g CARBOHYDRATE 1.8g
FIBER 0.2g CHOLESTEROL 0mg SODIUM 10mg

If the secret to great barbecue really is in the sauce, Spicy Barbecue Sauce is sure to be a winner. It can be prepared in about 15 minutes — just enough time to heat up the grill.

Teriyaki Marinade

1¼ cups unsweetened pineapple
   juice
⅓ cup low-sodium soy sauce
¼ cup white wine Worcestershire
   sauce
1 tablespoon vegetable oil
1 teaspoon ground ginger
½ teaspoon onion powder
1 clove garlic, crushed

Combine all ingredients. Use for
marinating poultry. Baste with marinade while cooking. Yield: 1¾ cups
plus 2 tablespoons (13 calories [35%
from fat] per tablespoon).

FAT 0.5g (SAT 0.1g, MONO 0.1g, POLY 0.2g)
PROTEIN 0.1g CARBOHYDRATE 1.9g
FIBER 0.0g CHOLESTEROL 0mg SODIUM 89mg

Cajun Seasoning

1 tablespoon black peppercorns,
   crushed
1 tablespoon dried whole basil
1 tablespoon paprika
1 teaspoon cumin seeds, crushed
1 teaspoon caraway seeds, crushed
1 teaspoon fennel seeds, crushed
1 teaspoon dried whole thyme
1 teaspoon dried whole oregano
1 teaspoon ground white pepper
½ teaspoon crushed red pepper

Combine all ingredients in a skillet; place over medium-high heat.
Cook 3 to 4 minutes or until lightly
toasted, stirring constantly. Let cool
completely. Store in an airtight container. Use to coat fish or poultry before grilling. Yield: ¼ cup plus 1
tablespoon (16 calories [28% from
fat] per tablespoon).

FAT 0.5g (SAT 0.1g, MONO 0.2g, POLY 0.2g)
PROTEIN 0.8g CARBOHYDRATE 3.2g
FIBER 0.9g CHOLESTEROL 0mg SODIUM 3mg

Dessert Sauces

Rich and gooey — yes; high in fat
and calories — no. These dessert
sauces use fresh fruits, spices, spirits,
and other ingredients to add flavor
without extra fat and calories. All are
thickened with cornstarch to keep
them translucent. Some of the sauces
can be served either warm or chilled,
depending on your preference and
what type of food the sauce will
accompany.

Fresh Blueberry Sauce

1¾ cups unsweetened grape juice,
   divided
2 cups fresh blueberries, divided
1 tablespoon frozen orange juice
   concentrate, thawed and
   undiluted
⅛ teaspoon ground ginger
⅛ teaspoon ground cinnamon
2 tablespoons cornstarch

Combine 1 cup grape juice, 1 cup
blueberries, and next 3 ingredients in
a medium saucepan. Bring mixture to
a boil; reduce heat, and simmer 3 to 5
minutes or until blueberry skins pop,
stirring occasionally.
Combine cornstarch and remaining ¾ cup grape juice, stirring until
smooth; add to blueberry mixture.
Cook over medium heat, stirring
constantly, until thickened. Remove
from heat; let cool completely. Stir in
remaining 1 cup blueberries. Serve
chilled over ice milk, nonfat frozen
yogurt, or angel food cake. Yield: 2¾
cups (13 calories [0% from fat] per
tablespoon).

FAT 0.0g (SAT 0.0g, MONO 0.0g, POLY 0.0g)
PROTEIN 0.1g CARBOHYDRATE 3.3g
FIBER 0.3g CHOLESTEROL 0mg SODIUM 1mg

Sweet Cherry Sauce

½ cup water
⅓ cup grenadine syrup
2 tablespoons cornstarch
1 (16-ounce) package frozen sweet
   cherries, thawed
½ teaspoon almond extract

Combine first 3 ingredients in a
saucepan. Cook over medium heat,
stirring constantly, until thickened.
Stir in cherries; cook until heated. Remove from heat; stir in extract. Serve
warm or chilled over ice milk, nonfat
frozen yogurt, or angel food cake.
Yield: 2¾ cups (12 calories [0% from
fat] per tablespoon).

FAT 0.0g (SAT 0.0g, MONO 0.0g, POLY 0.0g)
PROTEIN 0.1g CARBOHYDRATE 3.0g
FIBER 0.0g CHOLESTEROL 0mg SODIUM 0mg

Lemon Dessert Sauce

½ cup sugar
2 tablespoons cornstarch
1 cup water
2 teaspoons grated lemon rind
⅓ cup fresh lemon juice

Combine sugar and cornstarch in
a small saucepan. Gradually stir in
water. Cook over medium heat, stirring constantly, until mixture comes
to a boil. Reduce heat, and simmer 1
minute. Remove from heat; stir in
lemon rind and lemon juice. Serve
warm or chilled over angel food cake,
fat-free pound cake, or fresh fruit.
Yield: 1½ cups (19 calories [0% from
fat] per tablespoon).

FAT 0.0g (SAT 0.0g, MONO 0.0g, POLY 0.0g)
PROTEIN 0.0g CARBOHYDRATE 5.1g
FIBER 0.0g CHOLESTEROL 0mg SODIUM 0mg

Brandied Peach Sauce

3 tablespoons sugar
2 teaspoons cornstarch
½ cup peach nectar
¼ cup unsweetened orange juice
2 tablespoons brandy
½ teaspoon vanilla extract
⅛ teaspoon almond extract

Combine sugar and cornstarch in a small saucepan. Gradually stir in peach nectar and orange juice. Cook over medium heat, stirring constantly, until mixture comes to a boil. Reduce heat, and simmer 1 minute, stirring constantly.

Remove pan from heat; add brandy and flavorings, stirring well. Serve warm or chilled over ice milk, nonfat frozen yogurt, angel food cake, or fat-free pound cake. Yield: ¾ cup plus 3 tablespoons (18 calories [0% from fat] per tablespoon).

FAT 0.0g (SAT 0.0g, MONO 0.0g, POLY 0.0g)
PROTEIN 0.1g CARBOHYDRATE 4.5g
FIBER 0.0g CHOLESTEROL 0mg SODIUM 1mg

When exposed to air, a sauce or custard will develop a skin on the surface. To prevent this, cover the mixture with plastic wrap, pressing it directly onto the surface of the mixture to completely seal it.

Raspberry-Peach Sauce

1 cup peeled, sliced fresh peaches
¾ cup peach nectar
¼ cup water
1 tablespoon cornstarch
⅛ teaspoon almond extract
½ cup fresh raspberries

Combine peaches and peach nectar in a medium saucepan. Bring to a boil; reduce heat to medium, and cook 5 minutes or until peaches are tender, stirring occasionally.

Combine water and cornstarch in a small bowl, stirring until smooth. Add cornstarch mixture to peach mixture. Cook, stirring constantly, until thickened and bubbly. Remove from heat; stir in almond extract. Let cool completely.

Stir in raspberries. Serve chilled over ice milk, nonfat frozen yogurt, angel food cake, or fat-free pound cake. Yield: 2 cups (8 calories [0% from fat] per tablespoon).

FAT 0.0g (SAT 0.0g, MONO 0.0g, POLY 0.0g)
PROTEIN 0.1g CARBOHYDRATE 1.9g
FIBER 0.3g CHOLESTEROL 0mg SODIUM 0mg

Dark Chocolate Sauce

⅓ cup unsweetened cocoa
3 tablespoons sifted powdered sugar
1 tablespoon cornstarch
⅔ cup light-colored corn syrup
⅓ cup water
1 teaspoon vanilla extract

Combine first 3 ingredients in a small saucepan. Gradually stir in corn syrup and water. Cook over medium heat, stirring constantly, until thickened. Remove from heat; stir in vanilla. Serve warm or chilled over ice milk, nonfat frozen yogurt, or angel food cake. Yield: 1 cup (56 calories [3% from fat] per tablespoon).

FAT 0.2g (SAT 0.2g, MONO 0.0g, POLY 0.0g)
PROTEIN 0.5g CARBOHYDRATE 12.8g
FIBER 0.0g CHOLESTEROL 0mg SODIUM 17mg

Kahlúa-Pecan Sauce

¼ cup sugar
1 tablespoon cornstarch
⅔ cup water
¼ cup Kahlúa or other coffee-flavored liqueur
¼ cup chopped pecans, toasted

Combine sugar and cornstarch in a small saucepan. Gradually stir in water. Cook over medium heat, stirring constantly, until mixture comes to a boil. Reduce heat, and simmer 2 minutes or until mixture is thickened, stirring constantly. Remove from heat; stir in Kahlúa and pecans. Serve warm or chilled over ice milk, nonfat frozen yogurt, angel food cake, or fat-free pound cake. Yield: 1 cup plus 2 tablespoons (30 calories [27% from fat] per tablespoon).

FAT 0.9g (SAT 0.1g, MONO 0.5g, POLY 0.2g)
PROTEIN 0.1g CARBOHYDRATE 4.2g
FIBER 0.1g CHOLESTEROL 0mg SODIUM 0mg

CONDIMENTS

Condiments, or accompaniments to foods, can be savory, spicy, or piquant. They include chutneys, relishes, salsas, and spreads. For the most part, these items contain little, if any, fat and add a lot of flavor and color to foods. For convenience, many of these condiments can be prepared ahead of time and stored in the refrigerator. They can then be served at a moment's notice to add a special touch to a meal.

CARROT AND JICAMA RELISH WITH CILANTRO

1 cup peeled, cubed jicama
⅔ cup sliced carrot
¼ cup loosely packed fresh cilantro
2 tablespoons sliced green onions
2 teaspoons chopped fresh green chile pepper
½ teaspoon peeled, minced gingerroot
1 small clove garlic, halved
⅓ cup water
⅓ cup lime juice
2 tablespoons sugar
¼ teaspoon salt

Position knife blade in food processor bowl. Add first 7 ingredients; process 5 seconds or until ingredients are coarsely chopped. Transfer mixture to a small bowl.

Add water and remaining ingredients to chopped mixture; toss well. Cover and chill. Serve with a slotted spoon. Serve with chicken or seafood. Yield: 2 cups (7 calories [0% from fat] per tablespoon).

FAT 0.0g (SAT 0.0g, MONO 0.0g, POLY 0.0g)
PROTEIN 0.1g CARBOHYDRATE 1.8g
FIBER 0.2g CHOLESTEROL 0mg SODIUM 20mg

RED PEPPER SALSA

2 medium-size sweet red peppers
1 Anaheim chile
1½ cups peeled, seeded, and chopped tomato
2 jalapeño peppers, seeded and chopped
1 clove garlic, minced
2 teaspoons red wine vinegar
½ teaspoon ground cumin
¼ teaspoon salt

Cut red peppers and chile in half lengthwise; remove and discard seeds and membrane. Place peppers, skin side up, on a baking sheet; flatten with palm of hand. Broil 5½ inches from heat 15 minutes or until peppers are charred. Place in ice water; chill 5 minutes. Remove peppers from water; peel and discard skins.

Chop peppers; place in a bowl. Stir in tomato and remaining ingredients. Cover and chill. Serve with chicken or fish. Yield: 2¾ cups (4 calories [23% from fat] per tablespoon).

FAT 0.1g (SAT 0.0g, MONO 0.0g, POLY 0.0g)
PROTEIN 0.2g CARBOHYDRATE 1.0g
FIBER 0.3g CHOLESTEROL 0mg SODIUM 14mg

SANTA FE SALSA

3 cups chopped tomato
1 (4-ounce) can chopped green chiles, drained
½ cup finely chopped purple onion
¼ cup chopped fresh cilantro
2 tablespoons lime juice
1 large clove garlic, minced
1 teaspoon dried whole oregano
¼ teaspoon ground cumin
⅛ teaspoon salt

Combine all ingredients in a small bowl; stir well. Cover and chill thoroughly. Serve with fish or poultry. Yield: 3½ cups (3 calories [0% from fat] per tablespoon).

FAT 0.0g (SAT 0.0g, MONO 0.0g, POLY 0.0g)
PROTEIN 0.1g CARBOHYDRATE 0.7g
FIBER 0.2g CHOLESTEROL 0mg SODIUM 8mg

HORSERADISH SPREAD

1 (3-ounce) package lemon-flavored gelatin
1 cup water
⅛ teaspoon salt
½ cup prepared horseradish
⅓ cup nonfat sour cream alternative
⅓ cup nonfat mayonnaise
Dash of hot sauce
Vegetable cooking spray

Sprinkle gelatin over water in a small saucepan; let stand 1 minute. Cook mixture over low heat, stirring constantly, until gelatin dissolves. Remove pan from heat, and stir in salt. Chill mixture until the consistency of unbeaten egg white.

Combine horseradish and next 3 ingredients; gently fold into gelatin mixture. Spoon mixture into a 2¼-cup mold coated with cooking spray. Cover and chill until firm. Serve with beef. Yield: 2¼ cups (19 calories [0% from fat] per tablespoon).

FAT 0.0g (SAT 0.0g, MONO 0.0g, POLY 0.0g)
PROTEIN 2.6g CARBOHYDRATE 1.4g
FIBER 0.0g CHOLESTEROL 0mg SODIUM 75mg

MANGO CHUTNEY

12 whole cloves
8 whole allspice
8 whole cardamom seeds
2 (3-inch) sticks cinnamon, broken
3 cups peeled, chopped fresh mango
1 cup coarsely chopped onion
⅔ cup firmly packed brown sugar
½ cup golden raisins
1 tablespoon peeled, minced gingerroot
2 jalapeño peppers
2 cloves garlic, minced
1½ cups cider vinegar

Place cloves, allspice, cardamom, and cinnamon sticks on a piece of cheesecloth. Bring edges of cheesecloth together, and tie securely.

Combine mango and remaining ingredients in a large nonaluminum saucepan; stir well. Add spice bag. Bring mixture to a boil. Reduce heat, and simmer, uncovered, 1½ hours or until mixture is thickened, stirring occasionally.

Remove and discard spice bag and peppers. Transfer mixture to a bowl; cover and chill. Serve with pork or poultry. Yield: 2¼ cups (34 calories [3% from fat] per tablespoon).

FAT 0.1g (SAT 0.0g, MONO 0.0g, POLY 0.0g)
PROTEIN 0.2g CARBOHYDRATE 9.1g
FIBER 0.4g CHOLESTEROL 0mg SODIUM 2mg

Use cheesecloth to make a spice bag for simmering. Place the spices on the cheesecloth, and gather the ends to form a bag; tie the ends securely with cotton string.

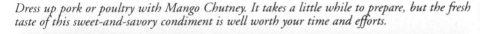

Dress up pork or poultry with Mango Chutney. It takes a little while to prepare, but the fresh taste of this sweet-and-savory condiment is well worth your time and efforts.

Cook the chutney mixture over low heat until very thick. Toward the end of cooking time when the mixture becomes thick, stir frequently to prevent it from scorching.

Remove the spice bag and jalapeño peppers from the mixture using tongs. Discard the spice bag and peppers; cover and chill the chutney before serving.

MANGO CHUTNEY

12 whole cloves
8 whole allspice
8 whole cardamom seeds
2 (3-inch) sticks cinnamon, broken
3 cups peeled, chopped fresh mango
1 cup coarsely chopped onion
⅔ cup firmly packed brown sugar
½ cup golden raisins
1 tablespoon peeled, minced gingerroot
2 jalapeño peppers
2 cloves garlic, minced
1½ cups cider vinegar

Place cloves, allspice, cardamom, and cinnamon sticks on a piece of cheesecloth. Bring edges of cheesecloth together, and tie securely.

Combine mango and remaining ingredients in a large nonaluminum saucepan; stir well. Add spice bag. Bring mixture to a boil. Reduce heat, and simmer, uncovered, 1½ hours or until mixture is thickened, stirring occasionally.

Remove and discard spice bag and peppers. Transfer mixture to a bowl; cover and chill. Serve with pork or poultry. Yield: 2¼ cups (34 calories [3% from fat] per tablespoon).

FAT 0.1g (SAT 0.0g, MONO 0.0g, POLY 0.0g)
PROTEIN 0.2g   CARBOHYDRATE 9.1g
FIBER 0.4g   CHOLESTEROL 0mg   SODIUM 2mg

Use cheesecloth to make a spice bag for simmering. Place the spices on the cheesecloth, and gather the ends to form a bag; tie the ends securely with cotton string.

Cook the chutney mixture over low heat until very thick. Toward the end of cooking time when the mixture becomes thick, stir frequently to prevent it from scorching.

Dress up pork or poultry with Mango Chutney. It takes a little while to prepare, but the fresh taste of this sweet-and-savory condiment is well worth your time and efforts.

Remove the spice bag and jalapeño peppers from the mixture using tongs. Discard the spice bag and peppers; cover and chill the chutney before serving.

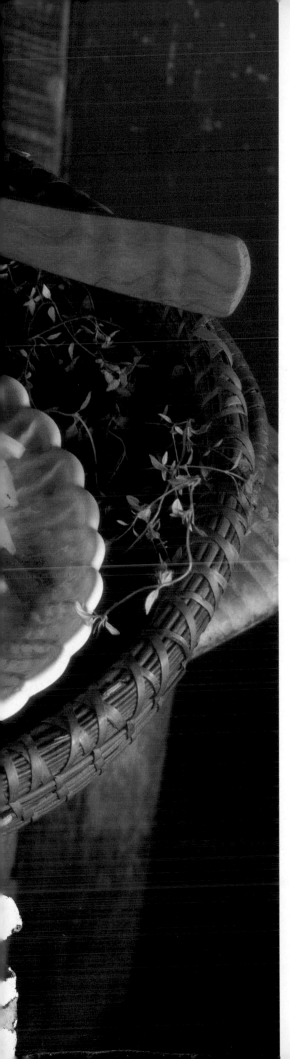

SIDE DISHES

The quality and variety of fresh, frozen, and canned produce has increased in recent years. Consumers know they can count on these food items for healthy, low-fat side dishes that provide abundant nutrients and few calories.

Featuring produce from apples to zucchini, the recipes in this section boast fresh flavors that are sure to add sparkle to your meals. According to the current U.S. Dietary Guidelines, adults should eat at least five servings of vegetables and fruits each day. You will have no trouble working those servings into your daily diet with these simple, fresh-tasting recipes.

Selecting Vegetables and Fruits

Fresh. For the freshest, most nutritious vegetables and fruits, choose those that are in season and are locally grown. They will not only be at their peak quality but will also be significantly lower in cost. Local produce is often available at roadside stands, farmer's markets, and supermarkets. Purchase fresh vegetables as close as possible to the time you plan to use them — the quality of the produce and the nutrient content will decrease with every day of storage.

When selecting vegetables and fruits, look for those with richly colored skins. The produce should have a slight resistance when lightly pressed.

Frozen. Fresh vegetables and fruits that are frozen can have a higher nutritional value than fresh produce that has been shipped a long distance. When buying frozen produce, make sure the package is frozen solid. Avoid packages that have ice crystals on the outside, which indicates that the package has been thawed and refrozen.

Canned. Although canned vegetables and fruits are somewhat lower in nutrients than their fresh or frozen counterparts, they still make a valuable contribution to healthy eating. Select no-salt-added canned vegetables when possible, and make sure the can is free of dents or bulges. A bulge in the can could indicate that the product inside is spoiled, which could cause food poisoning.

Cooking Vegetables

The tastiest, most nutritious vegetables are those that aren't overcooked or laden with heavy sauces. Cook vegetables in as little water as possible and only until they are tender — that is, until they are soft enough to yield a slight resistance when pierced with a fork. Steaming, stir-frying, grilling, and sautéing are excellent ways to cook vegetables and bring out their natural flavors.

When possible, cook vegetables whole to help retain nutrients. Vegetables that are cut into small pieces lose more nutrients during the cooking process than if left whole.

Herbed Vegetable Medley (page 204) brings all the goodness of the garden to your dinner table. This distinctive side dish is flavored with thyme, dillweed, and garlic.

GRECIAN STUFFED ARTICHOKES

4 small artichokes
Lemon wedge
Vegetable cooking spray
½ cup minced shallots
1 cup soft breadcrumbs
1 (2-ounce) jar diced pimiento,
  drained
3 tablespoons crumbled feta cheese
2 tablespoons sliced ripe olives
1 teaspoon dried whole basil
½ teaspoon dried whole thyme
¼ teaspoon cracked pepper

Wash artichokes by plunging up and down in cold water. Cut off stem ends; trim ½ inch from top of each artichoke. Remove any loose bottom leaves from artichokes. With scissors, trim away about one-fourth of each outer leaf. Rub tops and edges of each artichoke with lemon wedge to prevent discoloration.

Place artichokes in a Dutch oven; add water to a depth of 1 inch. Bring to a boil; cover, reduce heat, and simmer 22 to 25 minutes or until almost tender. Drain; let cool. Spread leaves apart; scrape out the fuzzy thistle center (choke) with a spoon, and discard. Set artichokes aside.

Coat a large nonstick skillet with cooking spray. Place over medium-high heat until hot. Add shallots; sauté until tender. Remove from heat. Add breadcrumbs and remaining ingredients; toss gently. Spoon breadcrumb mixture evenly into artichoke cavities. Place artichokes in a shallow baking dish. Bake at 350° for 15 to 20 minutes or until thoroughly heated. Serve immediately. Yield: 4 servings (193 calories [19% from fat] per serving).

FAT 4.0g (SAT 1.9g, MONO 1.2g, POLY 0.5g)
PROTEIN 8.9g CARBOHYDRATE 36.1g
FIBER 11.8g CHOLESTEROL 10mg SODIUM 411mg

Snap off the tough, stalky ends of fresh asparagus spears (about 1 to 2 inches). When buying asparagus, choose firm, bright green or pale ivory spears with tightly closed tips.

ASPARAGUS-LEEK BUNDLES

2 medium leeks
2 pounds fresh asparagus spears
2 tablespoons lemon juice
½ teaspoon salt
¼ teaspoon ground white pepper

Remove roots, tough outer leaves, and tops from leeks, leaving 2 inches of dark leaves attached to white part of leeks. Reserve 2 (9-inch) dark leaves from tops that were removed. Set reserved leaves aside. Wash leeks; cut each leek lengthwise into 8 sections. Set aside.

Cook reserved leaves in boiling water 30 seconds or until crisp-tender; drain. Rinse under cold water until cool; drain. Cut each leaf, lengthwise, into 4 equal strips. Set strips aside.

Snap off tough ends of asparagus. Remove scales from spears with a knife or vegetable peeler, if desired. Trim asparagus to same length as leek sections (about 6 inches). Arrange leek sections and asparagus pieces in a vegetable steamer over boiling water. Cover and steam 4 to 5 minutes or until vegetables are crisp-tender.

Divide leek and asparagus evenly into 8 bundles. Tie each bundle with a strip of leek leaf, and snip ends to trim. Brush bundles with lemon juice, and sprinkle with salt and pepper. Serve immediately. Yield: 8 servings (45 calories [6% from fat] per serving).

FAT 0.3g (SAT 0.1g, MONO 0.0g, POLY 0.1g)
PROTEIN 2.1g CARBOHYDRATE 10.1g
FIBER 1.8g CHOLESTEROL 0mg SODIUM 158mg

HERBED ASPARAGUS SAUTÉ

1 pound fresh asparagus spears
Vegetable cooking spray
1 clove garlic, minced
10 cherry tomatoes, halved
½ teaspoon dried whole oregano
⅛ teaspoon dried whole thyme
Dash of pepper
1 tablespoon grated Parmesan
  cheese

Snap off tough ends of asparagus spears. Remove scales from spears with a knife or vegetable peeler, if desired. Cut asparagus spears diagonally into 1-inch pieces. Arrange asparagus pieces in a vegetable steamer over boiling water. Cover and steam 4 to 5 minutes or until asparagus is crisp-tender.

Coat a large nonstick skillet with cooking spray; place over medium-high heat until hot. Add asparagus and garlic; sauté 4 to 5 minutes or until tender. Stir in tomato halves, oregano, thyme, and pepper. Cook 1 minute or until thoroughly heated, stirring constantly. Transfer mixture to a serving dish; sprinkle evenly with Parmesan cheese. Yield: 4 servings (35 calories [23% from fat] per ¾-cup serving).

FAT 0.9g (SAT 0.3g, MONO 0.1g, POLY 0.2g)
PROTEIN 2.6g CARBOHYDRATE 5.9g
FIBER 2.1g CHOLESTEROL 1mg SODIUM 30mg

Fresh Beets in Orange Sauce

1½ pounds medium-size fresh beets
1½ tablespoons reduced-calorie
  margarine
½ cup unsweetened orange juice
2 teaspoons cornstarch
1 teaspoon sugar
1 teaspoon grated orange rind
1 teaspoon cider vinegar
¼ teaspoon salt

Leave root and 1 inch of stem on beets; scrub with a vegetable brush. Place beets in a large saucepan; add water to cover. Bring to a boil; cover, reduce heat, and simmer 35 to 40 minutes or until beets are tender. Drain. Pour cold water over beets; drain. Trim stems and roots from beets; rub off skins. Slice beets into ¼-inch slices.

Melt margarine in a heavy saucepan over medium heat; stir in orange juice and remaining ingredients. Cook, stirring constantly, until mixture is thickened. Add beets; reduce heat to low, and cook 3 to 4 minutes or until thoroughly heated, stirring occasionally. Yield: 5 servings (61 calories [38% from fat] per ½-cup serving).

FAT 2.6g (SAT 0.3g, MONO 0.8g, POLY 1.0g)
PROTEIN 1.0g   CARBOHYDRATE 10.0g
FIBER 0.9g   CHOLESTEROL 0mg   SODIUM 189mg

Easy Citrus Broccoli

1½ pounds fresh broccoli
1 tablespoon reduced-calorie
  margarine
1 tablespoon all-purpose flour
1 teaspoon grated orange rind
¾ cup fresh orange juice

Trim off large leaves of broccoli, and remove tough ends of lower stalks. Wash broccoli thoroughly, and cut into flowerets. Arrange flowerets in a vegetable steamer over boiling water. Cover and steam 3 to 5 minutes or until crisp-tender. Transfer to a serving bowl, and keep warm.

Melt margarine in a small heavy saucepan over medium heat. Add flour, stirring until smooth. Cook 1 minute, stirring constantly. Combine orange rind and orange juice. Gradually add orange juice mixture to flour mixture; cook, stirring constantly, until mixture is thickened and bubbly. Pour sauce evenly over broccoli. Yield: 6 servings (58 calories [22% from fat] per serving).

FAT 1.4g (SAT 0.2g, MONO 0.5g, POLY 0.6g)
PROTEIN 3.6g   CARBOHYDRATE 10.0g
FIBER 2.8g   CHOLESTEROL 0mg   SODIUM 44mg

Steamed fresh broccoli tastes great on its own, but a simple sauce can magnify its appeal. The sauce for Easy Citrus Broccoli is naturally sweetened with fresh orange juice.

Broccoli with Parmesan Sauce

1 pound fresh broccoli
Vegetable cooking spray
¼ cup chopped sweet red pepper
¼ cup chopped onion
2 teaspoons reduced-calorie
  margarine
1 teaspoon all-purpose flour
½ cup skim milk
1 ounce light process cream cheese
  product
3 tablespoons freshly grated
  Parmesan cheese
⅛ teaspoon garlic powder

Trim off large leaves of broccoli; remove tough ends of lower stalks. Wash broccoli; cut into spears. Arrange spears in a vegetable steamer over boiling water. Cover and steam 3 to 5 minutes or until crisp-tender. Transfer broccoli to a serving platter; keep warm.

Coat a small heavy saucepan with cooking spray; place over medium-high heat until hot. Add pepper and onion; sauté 3 to 4 minutes or until tender. Remove vegetables from pan; set aside.

Melt margarine in pan over medium heat. Add flour, stirring until smooth. Cook 1 minute, stirring constantly. Gradually add milk; cook, stirring constantly, until mixture is slightly thickened. Add vegetable mixture, cream cheese, Parmesan cheese, and garlic powder; cook over low heat, stirring constantly, until cheese melts. Spoon sauce evenly over broccoli. Yield: 4 servings (85 calories [43% from fat] per serving).

FAT 4.1g (SAT 1.7g, MONO 0.8g, POLY 0.7g)
PROTEIN 5.9g CARBOHYDRATE 7.8g
FIBER 2.4g CHOLESTEROL 8mg SODIUM 165mg

Herbed Brussels Sprouts

1½ pounds fresh brussels sprouts
Vegetable cooking spray
½ teaspoon reduced-calorie
  margarine
1 shallot, minced
1¼ cups skim milk
1 teaspoon chicken-flavored
  bouillon granules
½ teaspoon dried whole marjoram
⅛ teaspoon pepper
1 bay leaf
1 tablespoon plus 1 teaspoon
  cornstarch
3 tablespoons skim milk

Wash brussels sprouts thoroughly, and remove discolored leaves. Cut off stem ends, and cut a shallow X in bottom of each sprout using a sharp knife. Arrange sprouts in a vegetable steamer over boiling water. Cover and steam 10 minutes or until tender.

Transfer sprouts to a serving bowl, and keep warm.

Coat a medium saucepan with cooking spray; add margarine. Place over medium heat until margarine melts. Add shallot; sauté until tender. Stir in 1¼ cups milk, bouillon granules, marjoram, pepper, and bay leaf. Cook over medium heat 10 minutes, stirring occasionally.

Combine cornstarch and 3 tablespoons milk; add to shallot mixture. Cook over low heat, stirring constantly, until thickened. Remove and discard bay leaf. Pour sauce over sprouts, tossing gently. Serve immediately. Yield: 6 servings (83 calories [10% from fat] per serving).

FAT 0.9g (SAT 0.2g, MONO 0.1g, POLY 0.2g)
PROTEIN 6.0g CARBOHYDRATE 15.3g
FIBER 4.8g CHOLESTEROL 1mg SODIUM 199mg

Confetti Cabbage

6 cups shredded cabbage
1 cup diced celery
1 cup seeded, chopped tomato
½ cup chopped sweet red pepper
½ cup chopped onion
½ cup water
¼ cup cider vinegar
¾ teaspoon caraway seeds
½ teaspoon salt

Combine all ingredients in a large Dutch oven; bring to a boil. Cover, reduce heat to medium, and cook 5 minutes or until vegetables are crisp-tender, stirring frequently. Serve with a slotted spoon. Yield: 6 servings (29 calories [9% from fat] per serving).

FAT 0.3g (SAT 0.0g, MONO 0.1g, POLY 0.1g)
PROTEIN 1.2g CARBOHYDRATE 6.7g
FIBER 2.2g CHOLESTEROL 0mg SODIUM 227mg

Lemon-Basil Carrot Bundles

6 medium carrots, scraped and cut
  into 3-inch julienne strips
½ cup water
2 tablespoons lemon juice
2 teaspoons sugar
2 cloves garlic, minced
1 tablespoon minced fresh basil or
  1 teaspoon dried whole basil
½ teaspoon grated lemon rind
1 tablespoon olive oil
2 green onions

Combine first 5 ingredients in a medium saucepan; bring to a boil over medium heat. Cover, reduce heat, and simmer 8 minutes or until carrot strips are crisp-tender. Remove from heat. Transfer carrot strips to a shallow bowl, reserving liquid in saucepan. Add basil, lemon rind, and olive oil to cooking liquid; stir well, and set aside.

Trim white portion from green onions; reserve for another use. Place green onion tops in a small bowl; add boiling water to cover. Drain immediately. Rinse in cold water; drain well. Cut tops into 8 narrow strips.

Divide carrot strips into 8 equal bundles; tie each bundle with a green onion strip. Place bundles in a shallow bowl; pour basil mixture over bundles. Cover; chill at least 2 hours.

Remove bundles from basil mixture using a slotted spoon; arrange on a serving platter. Yield: 8 servings (28 calories [19% from fat] per serving).

FAT 0.6g (SAT 0.1g, MONO 0.4g, POLY 0.1g)
PROTEIN 0.5g CARBOHYDRATE 5.7g
FIBER 1.3g CHOLESTEROL 0mg SODIUM 14mg

SPICED CARROTS POLYNESIAN

2 tablespoons reduced-calorie margarine
½ cup unsweetened pineapple juice
1 tablespoon brown sugar
½ teaspoon ground nutmeg
⅛ teaspoon salt
⅛ teaspoon ground white pepper
4 cups sliced carrot
1 medium onion, thinly sliced and separated into rings
2 tablespoons chopped fresh parsley

Melt margarine in a Dutch oven over medium heat. Add pineapple juice and next 6 ingredients; bring to a boil. Cover, reduce heat, and simmer 10 to 12 minutes or until carrot is crisp-tender. Transfer mixture to a serving bowl using a slotted spoon, and sprinkle evenly with parsley. Yield: 8 servings (71 calories [27% from fat] per ½-cup serving).

FAT 2.1g (SAT 0.3g, MONO 0.7g, POLY 0.9g)
PROTEIN 1.1g CARBOHYDRATE 13.1g
FIBER 2.9g CHOLESTEROL 0mg SODIUM 92mg

CAULIFLOWER MEDLEY

8 cups cauliflower flowerets
½ cup commercial oil-free Italian dressing
1 (4-ounce) jar diced pimiento, drained
2 tablespoons sliced ripe olives
2 tablespoons capers
¼ teaspoon cracked pepper

Arrange cauliflower in a vegetable steamer over boiling water. Cover and steam 10 to 12 minutes or until cauliflower is crisp-tender.

Place cauliflower in a large zip-top plastic bag. Combine dressing and remaining ingredients; pour over cauliflower. Seal bag, and shake gently until cauliflower is well coated. Marinate in refrigerator at least 8 hours. Serve with a slotted spoon. Yield: 8 servings (51 calories [11% from fat] per 1-cup serving).

FAT 0.6g (SAT 0.1g, MONO 0.2g, POLY 0.2g)
PROTEIN 3.4g CARBOHYDRATE 10.2g
FIBER 3.8g CHOLESTEROL 0mg SODIUM 432mg

SAUCY CELERY BAKE

Vegetable cooking spray
1 tablespoon reduced-calorie margarine
3 cups thinly sliced celery
1 cup sliced fresh mushrooms
¼ cup chopped onion
2 tablespoons all-purpose flour
1 cup evaporated skimmed milk
¼ teaspoon salt
⅛ teaspoon ground white pepper
1 (2-ounce) jar diced pimiento, drained
½ cup (2 ounces) shredded reduced-fat Cheddar cheese

Coat a large nonstick skillet with cooking spray; add margarine. Place over medium-high heat until margarine melts. Add celery, mushrooms, and onion; sauté until tender. Add flour; cook 1 minute, stirring constantly. Gradually add milk; cook, stirring constantly, until mixture is thickened. Remove from heat; stir in salt, pepper, and pimiento.

Spoon mixture into a 1-quart casserole coated with vegetable cooking spray. Bake, covered, at 350° for 15 to 20 minutes or until thoroughly heated. Sprinkle with cheese; bake, uncovered, an additional 5 minutes or until cheese melts. Yield: 6 servings (101 calories [31% from fat] per serving).

FAT 3.5g (SAT 1.3g, MONO 0.6g, POLY 0.8g)
PROTEIN 7.2g CARBOHYDRATE 11.0g
FIBER 1.4g CHOLESTEROL 8mg SODIUM 289mg

Fresh Corn Pudding is a colorful way to serve this summer favorite, and it's an appealing alternative to potatoes or pasta.

HERB-ROASTED CORN-ON-THE-COB

12 ears fresh corn
3 tablespoons reduced-calorie margarine, melted
2 tablespoons minced fresh chives
2 tablespoons minced fresh parsley
2 tablespoons lemon juice
¾ teaspoon salt
½ teaspoon pepper
Vegetable cooking spray

Remove husks and silk from corn. Combine margarine and next 5 ingredients in a small bowl, stirring well. Rub margarine mixture evenly over corn. Place each ear on a piece of heavy-duty aluminum foil. Roll foil lengthwise around each ear; twist at each end to seal.

Coat grill rack with vegetable cooking spray; place on grill over medium-hot coals. Place corn on rack, and cook 15 to 20 minutes or until tender, turning every 5 minutes. Yield: 12 servings (97 calories [26% from fat] per serving).

FAT 2.8g (SAT 0.4g, MONO 1.0g, POLY 1.2g)
PROTEIN 2.4g CARBOHYDRATE 19.1g
FIBER 2.8g CHOLESTEROL 0mg SODIUM 187mg

FRESH CORN PUDDING

4 cups fresh corn cut from cob (about 3 large ears)
2 cups (8 ounces) shredded reduced-fat sharp Cheddar cheese
1 cup frozen egg substitute, thawed
1 (4-ounce) jar diced pimiento, drained
2 cups evaporated skimmed milk, divided
½ cup all-purpose flour
2 tablespoons sugar
½ teaspoon salt
½ teaspoon ground red pepper
½ teaspoon ground mace
Vegetable cooking spray
¼ cup chopped green pepper
¼ cup chopped sweet red pepper

Combine corn, cheese, egg substitute, and pimiento in a large bowl, stirring well. Combine 1 cup milk and flour in a small bowl, stirring until smooth. Add remaining 1 cup milk, sugar, and next 3 ingredients; stir well. Add flour mixture to corn mixture, stirring well.

Pour corn mixture into a shallow 2-quart casserole coated with cooking spray; place in a 13- x 9- x 2-inch baking pan. Add hot water to pan to a depth of 1 inch. Bake, uncovered, at 325° for 35 minutes. Sprinkle chopped green and red pepper evenly over corn mixture. Bake an additional 45 to 50 minutes or until a knife inserted in center comes out clean. Remove pan from oven. Remove casserole from pan, and let stand 5 minutes. Yield: 12 servings (181 calories [22% from fat] per serving).

FAT 4.5g (SAT 2.3g, MONO 1.2g, POLY 0.5g)
PROTEIN 13.3g CARBOHYDRATE 23.6g
FIBER 2.1g CHOLESTEROL 14mg SODIUM 323mg

Preserving the Sweet Taste of Vegetables

The sweet taste of fresh corn, green beans, and peas diminishes with storage because their sugar turns to starch. These vegetables should be stored, unwashed, in plastic bags for only short periods of time.

GRILLED EGGPLANT WITH FRESH HERBS

1 large eggplant
¼ cup plus 2 tablespoons lemon
 juice
1 tablespoon plus 1 teaspoon
 minced fresh thyme
1 tablespoon plus 1 teaspoon
 minced fresh rosemary
1 tablespoon olive oil
4 cloves garlic, crushed
½ teaspoon salt
½ teaspoon pepper
Vegetable cooking spray

Cut eggplant lengthwise into ½-inch slices. Place eggplant in a large shallow baking dish. Combine lemon juice and next 6 ingredients; stir well. Pour over eggplant, turning to coat. Cover and marinate in refrigerator 1 to 2 hours, turning once.

Remove eggplant from marinade, reserving marinade. Coat grill rack with cooking spray; place on grill over medium-hot coals. Place eggplant on rack, and cook 3 to 5 minutes on each side or until done, basting frequently with marinade. Yield: 6 servings (59 calories [38% from fat] per serving).

FAT 2.5g (SAT 0.3g, MONO 1.7g, POLY 0.3g)
PROTEIN 1.5g CARBOHYDRATE 9.8g
FIBER 1.9g CHOLESTEROL 0mg SODIUM 201mg

SEASONED GREEN BEANS

1 pound fresh green beans
1 cup canned no-salt-added beef
 broth, undiluted
1 medium onion, chopped
⅓ cup chopped lean cooked ham
¾ teaspoon salt
¼ teaspoon freshly ground pepper

Wash beans; trim ends, and remove strings. Cut beans into 1½-inch pieces. Combine beans, broth, and remaining ingredients in a saucepan. Bring to a boil; cover, reduce heat, and simmer 25 minutes or until beans are tender, stirring occasionally. Yield: 6 servings (56 calories [14% from fat] per ½-cup serving).

FAT 0.9g (SAT 0.3g, MONO 0.4g, POLY 0.1g)
PROTEIN 4.8g CARBOHYDRATE 7.6g
FIBER 1.9g CHOLESTEROL 8mg SODIUM 535mg

SWEET-AND-SOUR GREEN BEANS

1½ pounds fresh green beans
Vegetable cooking spray
⅓ cup chopped onion
1½ teaspoons cornstarch
1 cup water, divided
⅓ cup white vinegar
1½ tablespoons sugar
3 whole cloves
1 bay leaf
¼ teaspoon salt
Dash of pepper

Wash beans; trim ends, and remove strings. Cut beans into 1½-inch pieces; arrange in vegetable steamer over boiling water. Cover and steam 10 minutes or until crisp-tender.

Coat a nonstick skillet with cooking spray; place over medium heat until hot. Add onion; sauté until tender.

Combine cornstarch and ⅓ cup water, stirring well; add to onion mixture. Cook 1 minute, stirring constantly. Stir in beans, remaining ⅔ cup water, vinegar, and remaining ingredients; bring to a boil. Cover, reduce heat, and simmer 15 minutes or until beans are crisp-tender. Remove and discard cloves and bay leaf. Yield: 8 servings (43 calories [4% from fat] per ½-cup serving).

FAT 0.2g (SAT 0.0g, MONO 0.0g, POLY 0.1g)
PROTEIN 1.7g CARBOHYDRATE 10.1g
FIBER 2.0g CHOLESTEROL 0mg SODIUM 79mg

CRISPY OVEN-FRIED OKRA

1¾ pounds fresh okra
1½ cups yellow cornmeal
½ teaspoon salt
⅛ teaspoon pepper
½ cup nonfat buttermilk
1 egg, lightly beaten
Vegetable cooking spray

Wash okra; trim ends, and cut into ½-inch pieces. Combine cornmeal, salt, and pepper in a medium bowl; stir well, and set aside.

Combine buttermilk and egg in a large bowl; stir in okra. Let stand 10 minutes. Dredge okra in cornmeal mixture. Place okra on a baking sheet coated with cooking spray. Bake at 450° for 40 minutes or until crisp, stirring occasionally. Yield: 12 servings (84 calories [12% from fat] per ½-cup serving).

FAT 1.1g (SAT 0.3g, MONO 0.3g, POLY 0.3g)
PROTEIN 3.1g CARBOHYDRATE 15.9g
FIBER 2.1g CHOLESTEROL 19mg SODIUM 123mg

Parsnips au Gratin

1 pound parsnips, peeled and sliced
Vegetable cooking spray
1 cup chopped sweet red pepper
1 tablespoon reduced-calorie
  margarine
1½ tablespoons all-purpose flour
1 cup skim milk
¼ teaspoon salt
¼ teaspoon ground nutmeg
⅛ teaspoon ground red pepper
¾ cup (3 ounces) shredded
  reduced-fat Swiss cheese
1 tablespoon fine, dry breadcrumbs
¼ teaspoon paprika

Place parsnips in a medium saucepan; add water to cover. Bring to a boil; cover, reduce heat, and simmer 8 minutes or until crisp-tender. Drain well, and set aside.

Coat a small nonstick skillet with cooking spray; place over medium-high heat until hot. Add sweet red pepper; sauté until tender. Set aside.

Melt margarine in a small heavy saucepan over medium heat; add flour, stirring until smooth. Cook 1 minute, stirring constantly. Gradually add milk; cook, stirring constantly, until thickened and bubbly. Remove from heat; add salt, nutmeg, ground red pepper, and cheese, stirring until cheese melts.

Arrange half of parsnips in a 1-quart casserole coated with cooking spray. Top with half of peppers and half of sauce mixture; repeat layers.

Combine breadcrumbs and paprika; sprinkle breadcrumb mixture evenly over parsnips mixture. Bake, uncovered, at 350° for 25 to 30 minutes or until thoroughly heated. Yield: 8 servings (96 calories [24% from fat] per serving).

FAT 2.6g (SAT 0.9g, MONO 0.4g, POLY 0.5g)
PROTEIN 4.5g CARBOHYDRATE 14.5g
FIBER 1.5g CHOLESTEROL 5mg SODIUM 126mg

Sesame Snow Peas and Red Peppers

¾ pound fresh snow pea pods
Vegetable cooking spray
2 large sweet red peppers, cut into
  thin strips
½ cup chopped onion
1 tablespoon sesame seeds, toasted
½ teaspoon salt-free herb-and-spice
  blend

Wash snow peas; trim ends, and remove strings. Coat a large nonstick skillet with cooking spray; place over medium-high heat until hot. Add snow peas, pepper, and onion; sauté until tender. Add sesame seeds and herb-and-spice blend, stirring well. Yield: 10 servings (25 calories [22% from fat] per ½-cup serving).

FAT 0.6g (SAT 0.1g, MONO 0.2g, POLY 0.2g)
PROTEIN 1.3g CARBOHYDRATE 3.9g
FIBER 1.2g CHOLESTEROL 0mg SODIUM 2mg

Serve Sesame Snow Peas and Red Peppers for a change of pace from ordinary vegetables. This side dish goes especially well with beef and poultry.

MINTED ENGLISH PEAS

2½ cups frozen English peas,
  thawed
2 teaspoons minced fresh mint
1 teaspoon reduced-calorie
  margarine
¼ teaspoon salt

Place peas in a saucepan; add water
to cover. Bring to a boil; reduce heat,
and simmer 4 to 5 minutes or until
peas are tender; drain well. Add mint,
margarine, and salt, stirring until
margarine melts. Yield: 4 servings (60
calories [12% from fat] per ½-cup
serving).

FAT 0.8g (SAT 0.1g, MONO 0.2g, POLY 0.3g)
PROTEIN 3.7g CARBOHYDRATE 10.1g
FIBER 3.1g CHOLESTEROL 0mg SODIUM 217mg

THREE-PEPPER STIR-FRY

Vegetable cooking spray
2 medium-size green peppers, cut
  into julienne strips
2 medium-size sweet red peppers,
  cut into julienne strips
2 medium-size sweet yellow
  peppers, cut into julienne strips
½ cup sliced green onions
¼ cup Chablis or other dry white
  wine
1 tablespoon minced fresh basil
1 tablespoon minced fresh oregano

Coat a wok or a large nonstick skillet with cooking spray; place over
medium-high heat (375°) until hot.
Add green pepper and remaining ingredients; stir-fry 2 to 3 minutes or
until pepper is crisp-tender. Yield: 10
servings (21 calories [21% from fat]
per serving).

FAT 0.5g (SAT 0.1g, MONO 0.0g, POLY 0.2g)
PROTEIN 0.7g CARBOHYDRATE 4.3g
FIBER 1.3g CHOLESTEROL 0mg SODIUM 3mg

CREAMY GARLIC POTATOES

4 cups peeled, cubed baking potato
½ cup skim milk
½ cup plain nonfat yogurt
4 cloves garlic, minced
½ teaspoon salt
2 tablespoons minced fresh chives

Cook potato in boiling water to
cover 30 minutes or until tender.
Drain potato, and mash. Add milk,
yogurt, garlic, and salt; beat at medium speed of an electric mixer until
mixture is smooth. Stir in chives.
Yield: 8 servings (83 calories [1%
from fat] per ½-cup serving).

Microwave Directions: Combine
potato and ½ cup water in a 2-quart
casserole. Cover and microwave at
HIGH 13 to 15 minutes or until tender, stirring every 5 minutes. Drain
potato, and mash. Add milk, yogurt,
garlic, and salt; beat at medium speed
of an electric mixer until mixture is
smooth. Stir in chives.

FAT 0.1g (SAT 0.1g, MONO 0.0g, POLY 0.0g)
PROTEIN 3.2g CARBOHYDRATE 17.6g
FIBER 1.4g CHOLESTEROL 1mg SODIUM 171mg

LEMON POTATO WEDGES

6 medium baking potatoes (about 3
  pounds)
2 tablespoons reduced-calorie
  margarine, melted
1½ teaspoons grated lemon rind
2 tablespoons fresh lemon juice
1½ teaspoons dried whole dillweed
Vegetable cooking spray
¼ cup grated Parmesan cheese

Scrub potatoes; cut each lengthwise into 8 wedges. Place wedges in a
bowl, and cover with cold water. Let
stand 30 minutes. Drain and pat dry
with paper towels.

Combine margarine and next 3 ingredients in a small bowl; stir well.
Brush margarine mixture evenly over
potato wedges. Place potato wedges,
skin side down, in a single layer on a
baking sheet coated with cooking
spray. Sprinkle Parmesan cheese
evenly over potato wedges. Bake at
400° for 45 to 50 minutes or until
tender and lightly browned. Yield: 8
servings (183 calories [14% from fat]
per serving).

FAT 2.8g (SAT 0.8g, MONO 0.9g, POLY 0.9g)
PROTEIN 4.2g CARBOHYDRATE 36.3g
FIBER 2.6g CHOLESTEROL 2mg SODIUM 86mg

ROASTED ROSEMARY
POTATOES

24 small round red potatoes (about
  2 pounds)
1 tablespoon olive oil
Vegetable cooking spray
1¼ teaspoons dried whole
  rosemary, crushed
¼ teaspoon dried whole thyme
¼ teaspoon salt
⅛ teaspoon pepper

Scrub potatoes; cut in half, and
brush with olive oil. Place potato
halves, skin side down, in a single
layer on a baking sheet coated with
cooking spray. Combine rosemary,
thyme, salt, and pepper; sprinkle
evenly over potato halves. Bake at
375° for 55 to 60 minutes or until
tender and lightly browned. Yield: 6
servings (143 calories [16% from fat]
per serving).

FAT 2.6g (SAT 0.4g, MONO 1.7g, POLY 0.3g)
PROTEIN 3.6g CARBOHYDRATE 27.3g
FIBER 3.0g CHOLESTEROL 0mg SODIUM 109mg

Scalloped Potatoes

3 tablespoons reduced-calorie
  margarine
3 tablespoons all-purpose flour
1½ cups skim milk
½ teaspoon salt
¼ teaspoon pepper
1 (2-ounce) jar diced pimiento,
  drained
1½ pounds baking potatoes, peeled
  and thinly sliced
1 small onion, thinly sliced and
  separated into rings
Vegetable cooking spray
½ cup soft whole wheat breadcrumbs

Melt margarine in a saucepan over
medium heat. Add flour; cook 1
minute, stirring constantly. Gradually
add milk; cook, stirring constantly,
until thickened. Remove from heat;
stir in salt, pepper, and pimiento.

Layer half each of potato and onion in the bottom of an 8-inch square
baking dish coated with cooking
spray. Top with half of sauce mixture;
repeat layers. Sprinkle evenly with
breadcrumbs. Bake, uncovered, at
350° for 55 minutes or until potato is
tender. Yield: 6 servings (134 calories
[28% from fat] per serving).

FAT 4.2g (SAT 0.6g, MONO 1.4g, POLY 1.7g)
PROTEIN 5.3g CARBOHYDRATE 20.1g
FIBER 2.0g CHOLESTEROL 1mg SODIUM 317mg

Candied Sweet Potatoes

2½ pounds sweet potatoes
⅓ cup firmly packed brown sugar
2 tablespoons reduced-calorie
  margarine
2 tablespoons unsweetened orange
  juice

Place potatoes in a Dutch oven;
add water to cover. Bring to a boil;
cover, reduce heat, and simmer 20 to
25 minutes or until tender. Drain; let
cool slightly. Peel potatoes, and cut
into 1½-inch pieces; place potato in a
large bowl, and set aside.

Combine brown sugar, margarine,
and orange juice in a saucepan. Cook
over medium heat until margarine
melts, stirring occasionally. Pour mixture over potato; toss gently. Yield: 6
servings (194 calories [10% from fat]
per ¾-cup serving).

FAT 2.2g (SAT 0.3g, MONO 0.7g, POLY 1.0g)
PROTEIN 2.3g CARBOHYDRATE 42.4g
FIBER 4.1g CHOLESTEROL 0mg SODIUM 48mg

Sweet Potatoes in Orange Cups

4 small oranges
2 cups cooked, mashed sweet
  potato
¼ cup firmly packed brown sugar
1 teaspoon grated orange rind
¼ cup plus 2 tablespoons fresh
  orange juice
1 teaspoon butter flavoring
¾ teaspoon ground cinnamon
¼ teaspoon salt
½ cup miniature marshmallows

Cut oranges in half crosswise. Clip
membranes, and carefully remove
pulp (do not puncture bottom). Reserve orange pulp for other uses.

Combine sweet potato and next 6
ingredients; spoon mixture evenly
into orange cups. Place cups in a
9-inch square baking pan. Cover and
bake at 350° for 20 minutes or until
thoroughly heated. Sprinkle with
marshmallows; bake an additional 5
minutes or until marshmallows melt.
Yield: 8 servings (110 calories [2%
from fat] per serving).

FAT 0.2g (SAT 0.0g, MONO 0.0g, POLY 0.1g)
PROTEIN 1.1g CARBOHYDRATE 26.6g
FIBER 1.8g CHOLESTEROL 0mg SODIUM 85mg

Mashed Rutabaga

4 cups peeled, diced rutabaga
¾ cup water
¾ cup unsweetened apple juice
¼ cup evaporated skimmed milk
2 tablespoons brown sugar
2 tablespoons unsweetened apple
  juice
¼ teaspoon salt

Combine first 3 ingredients in a
saucepan; bring to a boil. Cover, reduce heat, and simmer 25 to 30 minutes or until tender. Drain, and place
in a medium bowl.

Combine milk and remaining ingredients; add to rutabaga. Mash until soft, but chunky. Yield: 7 servings
(80 calories [3% from fat] per ½-cup
serving).

FAT 0.3g (SAT 0.1g, MONO 0.0g, POLY 0.1g)
PROTEIN 2.2g CARBOHYDRATE 18.3g
FIBER 1.4g CHOLESTEROL 0mg SODIUM 121mg

Simple Sesame Spinach

1 pound fresh spinach
Vegetable cooking spray
1 tablespoon sesame seeds, toasted
1 teaspoon lemon juice
¼ teaspoon salt

Remove and discard stems from
spinach. Wash spinach, and pat dry
with paper towels.

Coat a Dutch oven with cooking
spray; place over medium heat until
hot. Add spinach; cover and cook until spinach wilts, stirring occasionally.
Remove from heat, and stir in sesame
seeds, lemon juice, and salt. Toss
gently. Yield: 4 servings (46 calories
[49% from fat] per ½-cup serving).

FAT 2.5g (SAT 0.3g, MONO 0.7g, POLY 1.0g)
PROTEIN 3.9g CARBOHYDRATE 4.0g
FIBER 4.2g CHOLESTEROL 0mg SODIUM 229mg

STIR-FRIED SPINACH AND VEGETABLES

1 pound fresh spinach
2 tablespoons low-sodium soy
  sauce, divided
1 teaspoon cornstarch
Vegetable cooking spray
2 teaspoons vegetable oil
1½ cups thinly sliced carrot
1 medium onion, thinly sliced and
  separated into rings
1 clove garlic, minced
1 teaspoon peeled, minced
  gingerroot
1 (8-ounce) can sliced water
  chestnuts, drained
6 ounces fresh snow pea pods,
  trimmed

Remove and discard stems from spinach. Wash spinach leaves, and gently pat dry with paper towels. Set spinach aside.

Combine 1 tablespoon soy sauce and cornstarch in a small bowl; stir well, and set aside.

Coat a wok or a large Dutch oven with cooking spray; add oil. Place over medium-high heat (375°) until hot. Add carrot, onion, garlic, and gingerroot; stir-fry 2 minutes. Add spinach, water chestnuts, snow peas, and remaining 1 tablespoon soy sauce; stir-fry 5 to 6 minutes or until snow peas are crisp-tender. Add cornstarch mixture to vegetable mixture; cook, stirring constantly, 1 minute or until thickened. Yield: 8 servings (57 calories [24% from fat] per ½-cup serving).

FAT 1.5g (SAT 0.3g, MONO 0.4g, POLY 0.7g)
PROTEIN 2.3g CARBOHYDRATE 9.5g
FIBER 3.3g CHOLESTEROL 0mg SODIUM 140mg

CHEESY SQUASH CASSEROLE

2 pounds yellow squash, sliced
¾ cup chopped onion
1 tablespoon reduced-calorie
  margarine
2 tablespoons all-purpose flour
1 cup skim milk
¾ cup (3 ounces) shredded
  reduced-fat mild Cheddar cheese
½ teaspoon salt
¼ teaspoon pepper
Vegetable cooking spray
½ cup soft breadcrumbs, toasted

Cook squash and onion in a small amount of boiling water 10 to 12 minutes or until vegetables are tender. Drain; set aside.

Melt margarine in a medium heavy saucepan over medium heat. Add flour; cook 1 minute, stirring constantly. Gradually add milk; cook, stirring constantly, until mixture is thickened and bubbly. Remove from heat; add cheese, salt, and pepper, stirring until cheese melts. Add squash mixture; stir well.

Spoon squash mixture into a shallow 1½-quart casserole coated with cooking spray. Sprinkle squash mixture evenly with breadcrumbs. Bake at 350° for 20 to 25 minutes or until mixture is thoroughly heated. Yield: 8 servings (95 calories [32% from fat] per serving).

FAT 3.4g (SAT 1.4g, MONO 0.4g, POLY 0.6g)
PROTEIN 6.2g CARBOHYDRATE 11.0g
FIBER 2.2g CHOLESTEROL 8mg SODIUM 277mg

MEXICAN SPAGHETTI SQUASH

1 (3-pound) spaghetti squash
Vegetable cooking spray
½ cup chopped onion
1 small clove garlic, minced
1 cup chopped tomato
2 tablespoons canned chopped
  green chiles
¼ teaspoon chili powder
⅛ teaspoon ground cumin
⅛ teaspoon ground red pepper

Wash squash; cut in half lengthwise. Remove and discard seeds. Place squash, cut sides down, in a Dutch oven; add water to pan to a depth of 2 inches. Bring to a boil; cover, reduce heat, and simmer 20 to 25 minutes or until squash is tender. Drain squash, and let cool.

Using a fork, remove spaghetti-like strands from squash; discard shells. Set squash aside.

Coat a large nonstick skillet with cooking spray; place over medium-high heat until hot. Add onion and garlic; sauté 3 to 4 minutes or until tender. Stir in tomato and remaining ingredients; cook until thoroughly heated. Add squash; cook until thoroughly heated, tossing gently to combine. Yield: 8 servings (38 calories [9% from fat] per ½-cup serving).

FAT 0.4g (SAT 0.1g, MONO 0.0g, POLY 0.2g)
PROTEIN 1.0g CARBOHYDRATE 8.3g
FIBER 1.8g CHOLESTEROL 0mg SODIUM 25mg

Tomatoes Provençal

Olive oil-flavored vegetable cooking
  spray
2 cloves garlic, minced
¼ cup fine dry breadcrumbs
2 tablespoons chopped fresh parsley
½ teaspoon chopped fresh basil
½ teaspoon chopped fresh thyme
¼ teaspoon salt
¼ teaspoon pepper
3 medium tomatoes (about
  1½ pounds)

Coat a small nonstick skillet with
cooking spray; place over medium-
high heat until hot. Add garlic; sauté
3 to 4 minutes or until tender. Remove from heat; stir in breadcrumbs
and next 5 ingredients.

Cut tomatoes in half crosswise.
Place tomato halves, cut side up, on
rack of a broiler pan. Sprinkle breadcrumb mixture evenly over tomato
halves. Broil 5½ inches from heat 3
to 4 minutes or until lightly browned.
Yield: 6 servings (39 calories [16%
from fat] per serving).

FAT 0.7g (SAT 0.1g, MONO 0.1g, POLY 0.2g)
PROTEIN 1.5g CARBOHYDRATE 8.1g
FIBER 1.8g CHOLESTEROL 0mg SODIUM 127mg

Herbed Tomato Slices

36 tomato slices (½ inch thick)
Vegetable cooking spray
¾ cup Italian-seasoned
  breadcrumbs
3 tablespoons grated Parmesan
  cheese
1½ tablespoons reduced-calorie
  margarine, melted
2 teaspoons chopped fresh basil
Fresh basil sprigs (optional)

Arrange tomato slices in 2 (15- x
10- x 1-inch) jellyroll pans coated
with cooking spray; set aside.

Combine breadcrumbs and next 3
ingredients; sprinkle mixture evenly
over tomato slices. Bake at 350° for
10 to 12 minutes or until tomato
slices are thoroughly heated. Garnish
with fresh basil sprigs, if desired.
Yield: 12 servings (69 calories [26%
from fat] per serving).

FAT 2.0g (SAT 0.5g, MONO 0.5g, POLY 0.6g)
PROTEIN 2.7g CARBOHYDRATE 11.5g
FIBER 1.8g CHOLESTEROL 1mg SODIUM 248mg

Herbed Vegetable Medley

2 cups water
1 teaspoon chicken-flavored
  bouillon granules
½ teaspoon dried whole thyme
½ teaspoon dried whole dillweed
1 clove garlic, minced
2 medium carrots, scraped and cut
  into julienne strips
3 small zucchini, cut into julienne
  strips
3 small yellow squash, cut into
  julienne strips
1 medium-size sweet red pepper,
  cut into julienne strips
⅓ cup chopped green onions
Fresh thyme sprigs (optional)

Combine first 5 ingredients in a
skillet; bring to a boil. Add carrot; reduce heat, and simmer 1 minute, stirring occasionally. Add zucchini,
yellow squash, pepper, and green onions; simmer 2 to 3 minutes or until
vegetables are crisp-tender, tossing
frequently. Drain well.

Transfer mixture to a serving dish;
garnish with fresh thyme sprigs, if desired. Yield: 8 servings (29 calories
[12% from fat] per ¾-cup serving).

FAT 0.4g (SAT 0.1g, MONO 0.0g, POLY 0.1g)
PROTEIN 1.4g CARBOHYDRATE 6.1g
FIBER 1.8g CHOLESTEROL 0mg SODIUM 112mg

Cookout Vegetable Packets

1½ cups sliced yellow squash
1½ cups sliced zucchini
1½ cups cauliflower flowerets
1½ cups broccoli flowerets
1 cup thinly sliced carrot
1 medium onion, thinly sliced
½ teaspoon dried whole basil
¼ teaspoon salt
¼ teaspoon pepper
⅔ cup commercial oil-free Italian
  dressing
Vegetable cooking spray

Combine first 6 ingredients in a
large bowl, tossing gently. Combine
basil, salt, pepper, and Italian dressing in a small bowl, stirring well. Pour
basil mixture over vegetable mixture,
and toss gently to combine.

Divide vegetable mixture evenly
among 6 large squares of heavy-duty
aluminum foil. Wrap vegetables securely, sealing edges of foil packets.

Coat grill rack with vegetable
cooking spray; place on grill over
medium-hot coals. Place vegetable
packets on grill rack, and cook 4 to 5
minutes or until vegetables are crisp-
tender, turning packets once. Yield: 6
servings (56 calories [5% from fat]
per serving).

FAT 0.3g (SAT 0.1g, MONO 0.0g, POLY 0.1g)
PROTEIN 2.5g CARBOHYDRATE 12.2g
FIBER 3.3g CHOLESTEROL 0mg SODIUM 358mg

STUFFED ZUCCHINI

3 medium zucchini
Vegetable cooking spray
¾ cup sliced fresh mushrooms
¼ cup chopped onion
¾ cup chopped tomato
1¼ teaspoons dried Italian
  seasoning
⅛ teaspoon pepper
1 tablespoon grated Parmesan
  cheese
Fresh thyme sprigs (optional)

Arrange zucchini in a vegetable steamer over boiling water. Cover and steam 10 to 12 minutes or until crisp-tender. Cut zucchini in half lengthwise, leaving stems intact. Carefully remove pulp, leaving ¼-inch-thick shells. Dice pulp, and set aside; reserve zucchini shells.

Coat a nonstick skillet with cooking spray; place over medium heat until hot. Add mushrooms and onion; sauté until tender. Stir in zucchini pulp, tomato, Italian seasoning, and pepper. Cook, stirring frequently, until thoroughly heated.

Spoon zucchini mixture evenly into reserved shells; sprinkle with cheese. Arrange stuffed shells in a 13- x 9- x 2-inch baking dish. Bake at 350° for 25 minutes or until thoroughly heated. Transfer to a serving platter; garnish with fresh thyme sprigs, if desired. Yield: 6 servings (30 calories [21% from fat] per serving).

FAT 0.7g (SAT 0.2g, MONO 0.1g, POLY 0.1g)
PROTEIN 2.0g   CARBOHYDRATE 5.3g
FIBER 1.1g   CHOLESTEROL 1mg   SODIUM 22mg

Use a small spoon to carefully scoop out the pulp from the steamed zucchini halves. Be sure to leave a ¼-inch-thick rim — this will add support to the shells once they are filled.

Sauté the vegetable mixture in a nonstick skillet coated with cooking spray. The cooking spray prevents the food from sticking without adding a lot of fat and calories.

For less mess, place the shells on a cutting board or other surface, fill with the vegetable mixture, and sprinkle with cheese. Then transfer the filled shells to the baking dish.

Stuffed Zucchini is a winner with anyone looking for a different way to serve squash. The filling contains mushrooms, onion, and tomato and is topped with Parmesan cheese.

205

Family members might expect apple pie for dessert when they smell Cinnamon-Crusted Baked Apples, but they won't be disappointed in the taste of this low-fat treat. Serve it as a side dish or as a light dessert.

GRILLED MAPLE APPLE RINGS

4 medium cooking apples
3 tablespoons reduced-calorie
 maple syrup
2 teaspoons reduced-calorie
 margarine, melted
½ teaspoon ground cinnamon
⅛ teaspoon ground nutmeg
Vegetable cooking spray
2 tablespoons sliced almonds,
 toasted

Core apples, and slice each crosswise into thin rings. Arrange apple rings evenly on 4 large squares of heavy-duty aluminum foil. Combine syrup, margarine, cinnamon, and nutmeg in a small bowl; stir well. Spoon syrup mixture evenly over apple rings. Wrap securely, sealing edges of foil packets well.

Coat grill rack with cooking spray; place on grill over medium coals. Place packets on grill, and cook 13 to 15 minutes or until apple is tender, turning packets once. Place packets on individual serving plates; cut an opening in the top of each packet, and fold foil back. Sprinkle apple mixture evenly with almonds. Yield: 4 servings (150 calories [26% from fat] per serving).

FAT 4.3g (SAT 0.5g, MONO 2.1g, POLY 1.2g)
PROTEIN 1.3g   CARBOHYDRATE 30.3g
FIBER 6.2g   CHOLESTEROL 0mg   SODIUM 22mg

CINNAMON-CRUSTED BAKED APPLES

Butter-flavored vegetable cooking
 spray
⅓ cup water
5 medium cooking apples
⅓ cup firmly packed brown sugar
¼ cup all-purpose flour
½ teaspoon ground cinnamon
¼ teaspoon ground nutmeg
2 tablespoons reduced-calorie
 margarine, softened

Coat an 11- x 7- x 2-inch baking dish with cooking spray; pour water into dish. Peel, core, and slice apples. Arrange apple slices in prepared dish; coat apple slices lightly with vegetable cooking spray.

Combine brown sugar, flour, cinnamon, and nutmeg; cut in margarine with a pastry blender until mixture resembles coarse meal. Sprinkle mixture evenly over apple. Bake, uncovered, at 350° for 30 minutes or until apple is tender. Yield: 8 servings (127 calories [16% from fat] per serving).

FAT 2.3g (SAT 0.3g, MONO 0.7g, POLY 0.9g)
PROTEIN 0.5g   CARBOHYDRATE 28.4g
FIBER 3.2g   CHOLESTEROL 0mg   SODIUM 30mg

BROILED BRANDIED APRICOTS

1 (16-ounce) can apricot halves in juice, undrained
¼ cup brandy
1 (3-inch) stick cinnamon
Vegetable cooking spray
2½ tablespoons no-sugar-added apricot spread
½ teaspoon brandy
Ground nutmeg (optional)

Drain apricot halves, reserving ½ cup juice. Place apricot halves in a small baking dish; set aside.

Combine reserved apricot juice, ¼ cup brandy, and cinnamon stick in a small saucepan. Bring to a boil; reduce heat, and simmer, uncovered, 10 minutes. Remove and discard cinnamon stick. Pour mixture over apricot halves; cover and chill thoroughly.

Drain apricot halves, and arrange in an 8-inch square baking dish coated with cooking spray. Combine apricot spread and ½ teaspoon brandy, stirring well. Spoon ½ teaspoon mixture into each apricot half; sprinkle with nutmeg, if desired. Broil 5½ inches from heat 5 minutes or until bubbly and lightly browned. Serve warm. Yield: 4 servings (74 calories [2% from fat] per serving).

FAT 0.2g (SAT 0.0g, MONO 0.0g, POLY 0.0g)
PROTEIN 0.7g CARBOHYDRATE 18.4g
FIBER 0.5g CHOLESTEROL 0mg SODIUM 6mg

BAKED DIJON PEARS

3 medium-size ripe pears (about 1¼ pounds)
1 tablespoon honey
1 tablespoon reduced-calorie margarine, softened
2 teaspoons Dijon mustard
1 tablespoon water
Vegetable cooking spray

Slice pears in half lengthwise; core pear halves. Combine honey, margarine, mustard, and water in a small bowl, stirring until smooth; brush honey mixture evenly over entire surface of each pear half.

Place pear halves, cut side down, in a 10- x 6- x 2-inch baking dish coated with cooking spray. Cover and bake at 350° for 40 to 45 minutes or until pear halves are tender. Serve warm. Yield: 6 servings (81 calories [19% from fat] per serving).

FAT 1.7g (SAT 0.0g, MONO 0.1g, POLY 0.1g)
PROTEIN 0.4g CARBOHYDRATE 18.0g
FIBER 2.6g CHOLESTEROL 0mg SODIUM 68mg

SPICED PINEAPPLE STICKS

1 medium-size fresh pineapple
1½ teaspoons whole cloves
1 teaspoon whole allspice
1 (3-inch) stick cinnamon
1 cup fresh orange juice
1 medium orange, sliced
2 tablespoons sugar
2 tablespoons white vinegar

Peel and core pineapple, discarding top. Cut pineapple lengthwise into 16 sticks; cut each stick in half crosswise. Set pineapple sticks aside.

Place cloves, allspice, and cinnamon stick on a small cheesecloth square. Bring edges of cheesecloth together, and tie securely. Combine spice bag, orange juice, orange slices, sugar, and vinegar in a nonaluminum Dutch oven; bring mixture to a boil. Add pineapple sticks. Reduce heat, and simmer, uncovered, 30 to 35 minutes or until pineapple is done, stirring occasionally.

Remove and discard spice bag and orange slices. Transfer pineapple sticks and cooking liquid to a large bowl; cover and chill 8 hours. Drain pineapple sticks, and serve chilled. Yield: 8 servings (85 calories [5% from fat] per serving).

FAT 0.5g (SAT 0.0g, MONO 0.1g, POLY 0.2g)
PROTEIN 0.7g CARBOHYDRATE 21.5g
FIBER 1.9g CHOLESTEROL 0mg SODIUM 2mg

HOT FRUIT COMPOTE

4 medium-size fresh peaches, peeled, pitted, and sliced
30 fresh sweet cherries, pitted and halved (about ½ pound)
2 medium-size fresh pears, peeled, cored, and thinly sliced
2 tablespoons brown sugar
½ teaspoon ground cinnamon
2 tablespoons peach-flavored brandy or apricot nectar
Vegetable cooking spray

Combine first 3 ingredients in a large bowl; toss gently.

Combine brown sugar, cinnamon, and brandy in a small bowl, stirring well. Add brown sugar mixture to fruit mixture; toss gently to combine. Spoon mixture into a 2-quart casserole coated with vegetable cooking spray. Cover and bake at 350° for 35 minutes or until fruit is tender, stirring once. Serve immediately. Yield: 8 servings (79 calories [5% from fat] per ½-cup serving).

FAT 0.4g (SAT 0.1g, MONO 0.1g, POLY 0.1g)
PROTEIN 0.9g CARBOHYDRATE 20.1g
FIBER 2.8g CHOLESTEROL 0mg SODIUM 1mg

SOUPS AND SANDWICHES

Few foods are quite as comforting as a bowl of homemade soup or stew. Both can be healthy and flavorful menu items, as this chapter will prove. Add a hearty, low-fat sandwich, and you have a full meal. We hope these recipes will inspire you to create simple meals your family will request again and again.

SOUPS

Some of the most versatile menu items are soups and stews. As a first course, light soups can take the edge off your appetite so you won't overeat. As an entrée, hearty soups, chowders, and stews can offer a one-dish meal with minimal fat and calories. And some fruit soups can be served as an appetizer or dessert.

On the Menu

The yields for our soups and stews are given in cup amounts, with the actual serving size and its calorie and fat count given in parentheses. Allow three-fourths to one cup of soup for an appetizer or dessert course. For a main-dish soup, allow one to one and one-half cups per serving.

Getting the Fat Out

To keep soups virtually free of fat, start with fat-free broth or stock. If you don't have time to prepare it yourself, canned broth will work nicely. But beware — some brands of canned broth contain fat. To defat commercial broth, simply place the unopened can in the refrigerator an hour or so before using. When you open the can, skim off the layer of solidified fat.

When preparing broths, stocks, and soups, chill the strained broth thoroughly. Then skim and discard the layer of solidified fat that forms on top. What's left behind is the flavor of the broth but minimal fat.

Storing and Freezing Soups

Many soups, stews, chilies, and gumbos taste even better when refrigerated a day or so to allow the flavors to blend. This trait helps make soups ideal make-ahead items for entertaining or working into a hectic schedule.

Most soups freeze well, which is an added plus because many soup recipes yield large amounts. When freezing soups, use airtight plastic freezer containers or zip-top freezer bags, and label the bags with the date the item was frozen. Use the frozen soup within three or four months for optimum flavor.

Pair Hearty Vegetable-Barley Soup (page 216) with Garden Turkey Pockets (page 225) for a satisfying meal that has less than 300 calories and only three grams of fat.

Broths and Stocks _____

Broths and stocks should be simmered, uncovered, for a long period of time to draw all the flavor from the meat and vegetables. As water evaporates during cooking, the flavor intensifies. Strain the mixture, and chill thoroughly to allow fat to solidify on the surface of the broth. Then skim and discard the fat.

Refrigerate homemade broths and stocks up to three days or freeze up to three months for best flavor. Ice-cube trays offer a convenient way to freeze broths and stocks. Each cube is equivalent to about two tablespoons. When the broth is frozen, transfer the cubes to zip-top freezer bags.

BEEF BROTH

4 pounds cut-up beef shanks
12 cups water
3 stalks celery with leaves, cut into 1-inch pieces
2 carrots, scraped and cut into 1-inch pieces
2 medium onions, quartered
3 cloves garlic
2 bay leaves
¾ teaspoon salt
¾ teaspoon pepper

Place beef shanks in a 13- x 9- x 2-inch baking pan; bake at 400° for 20 to 25 minutes or until beef shanks are browned.

Place browned beef shanks and drippings in a large Dutch oven; add water and remaining ingredients. Bring mixture to a boil; cover, reduce heat, and simmer 2 hours. Strain broth through a cheesecloth- or paper towel-lined sieve. Reserve beef shanks and vegetables for other uses; discard bay leaves. Cover and chill thoroughly.

Skim and discard solidified fat from top of broth. Refrigerate broth in a tightly covered container up to 3 days, or freeze in a labeled airtight container up to 3 months. Use as directed in recipes calling for beef broth. Yield: 3 quarts (22 calories [0% from fat] per 1-cup serving).

FAT 0.0g (SAT 0.0g, MONO 0.0g, POLY 0.0g)
PROTEIN 0.5g CARBOHYDRATE 2.0g
FIBER 0.0g CHOLESTEROL 0mg SODIUM 154mg

CHICKEN BROTH

6 pounds chicken pieces
12 cups water
3 stalks celery with leaves, cut into 1-inch pieces
2 carrots, scraped and cut into 1-inch pieces
2 medium onions, quartered
1 bay leaf
¾ teaspoon salt
¾ teaspoon pepper
¾ teaspoon dried whole thyme

Combine all ingredients in a large Dutch oven. Bring to a boil; cover, reduce heat, and simmer 2 hours. Strain broth through a cheesecloth- or paper-towel lined sieve. Reserve chicken and vegetables for other uses; discard bay leaf. Cover and chill.

Skim and discard solidified fat from top of broth. Refrigerate broth in a tightly covered container up to 3 days, or freeze in a labeled airtight container up to 3 months. Use as directed in recipes calling for chicken broth. Yield: 3 quarts (22 calories [0% from fat] per 1-cup serving).

FAT 0.0g (SAT 0.0g, MONO 0.0g, POLY 0.0g)
PROTEIN 0.5g CARBOHYDRATE 2.1g
FIBER 0.0g CHOLESTEROL 0mg SODIUM 151mg

FISH STOCK

3 pounds fish bones
2 medium carrots, scraped and sliced
2 medium stalks celery with leaves, sliced
2 medium onions, sliced
4 cups water
3 (8-ounce) bottles clam juice
2 cups Chablis or other dry white wine
8 black peppercorns
6 sprigs fresh parsley
4 whole cloves
1 lemon, halved
1 bay leaf

Combine all ingredients in a large Dutch oven. Bring to a boil; cover, reduce heat, and simmer 30 minutes. Strain stock through a cheesecloth- or paper-towel lined sieve. Cover and chill thoroughly.

Skim and discard solidified fat from top of stock. Refrigerate stock in a tightly covered container up to 3 days, or freeze in a labeled airtight container up to 3 months. Use as directed in recipes calling for fish stock. Yield: 2 quarts (10 calories [18% from fat] per 1-cup serving).

FAT 0.2g (SAT 0.0g, MONO 0.0g, POLY 0.0g)
PROTEIN 1.0g CARBOHYDRATE 1.3g
FIBER 0.0g CHOLESTEROL 0mg SODIUM 250mg

Chilled Soups

These recipes take advantage of naturally low-fat fruits and vegetables. Many call for low-fat or nonfat dairy products such as skim milk and yogurt to give the soup a creamy consistency without adding much fat. These soups are perfect as appetizers or desserts.

CARROT VICHYSSOISE

Vegetable cooking spray
1½ teaspoons reduced-calorie margarine
⅓ cup chopped leek
¼ cup chopped onion
¼ cup chopped celery
2 (10½-ounce) cans low-sodium chicken broth, undiluted
1¼ cups diced carrot
1 cup diced potato
¼ teaspoon salt
1 tablespoon chopped fresh dillweed
Fresh dillweed sprigs (optional)

Coat a saucepan with vegetable cooking spray; add margarine. Place over medium-high heat until margarine melts. Add leek, onion, and celery; sauté until tender. Stir in broth and next 3 ingredients; bring to a boil. Cover, reduce heat, and simmer 20 minutes or until vegetables are tender.

Position knife blade in food processor bowl; add vegetable mixture. Process until smooth. Pour mixture into a medium bowl, and stir in chopped dillweed. Cover and chill.

Ladle soup into individual bowls. Garnish with fresh dillweed sprigs, if desired. Yield: 4 cups (91 calories [23% from fat] per 1-cup serving).

FAT 2.3g (SAT 0.5g, MONO 0.9g, POLY 0.7g)
PROTEIN 3.7g CARBOHYDRATE 15.3g
FIBER 2.9g CHOLESTEROL 0mg SODIUM 244mg

CHILLED CUCUMBER SOUP

½ cup plain nonfat yogurt
Vegetable cooking spray
1 tablespoon reduced-calorie margarine
1 cup peeled, seeded, and chopped cucumber
2 tablespoons chopped green onions
2 teaspoons cornstarch
1¼ cups skim milk, divided
½ teaspoon chicken-flavored bouillon granules
¼ teaspoon dried whole dillweed
Thin cucumber slices (optional)
Chopped green onions (optional)

Spoon yogurt onto several layers of heavy-duty paper towels; spread to ½-inch thickness. Cover with additional paper towels; let stand 5 minutes. Scrape yogurt into a small bowl, using a rubber spatula. Set aside.

Coat a small saucepan with cooking spray; add margarine. Place over medium heat until margarine melts. Add cucumber and green onions; sauté until tender. Combine cornstarch and ¼ cup milk; stir well. Add cornstarch mixture, remaining 1 cup milk, bouillon granules, and dillweed to cucumber mixture. Cook, stirring constantly, until mixture comes to a boil. Reduce heat, and simmer 1 minute, stirring constantly. Remove from heat; let cool slightly.

Pour cucumber mixture into container of an electric blender; top with cover, and process until smooth. Pour mixture into a small bowl; stir in yogurt. Cover and chill thoroughly.

Ladle soup into individual bowls. If desired, garnish with cucumber slices and green onions. Yield: 2 cups (139 calories [28% from fat] per 1-cup serving).

FAT 4.4g (SAT 0.9g, MONO 1.5g, POLY 1.6g)
PROTEIN 9.1g CARBOHYDRATE 16.8g
FIBER 0.9g CHOLESTEROL 4mg SODIUM 385mg

COOL GAZPACHO

2¼ cups peeled, coarsely chopped tomato
1½ cups no-salt-added tomato juice
¾ cup peeled, seeded, and diced cucumber
3 tablespoons chopped fresh parsley
2 tablespoons chopped onion
1 tablespoon balsamic vinegar
1 small clove garlic, minced
½ teaspoon ground cumin
½ teaspoon minced jalapeño pepper
⅛ teaspoon salt
⅛ teaspoon coarsely ground pepper
Sliced green onions (optional)

Combine first 11 ingredients in container of an electric blender; top with cover, and process until mixture is chunky. Pour tomato mixture into a medium bowl; cover and chill mixture thoroughly.

Ladle soup into individual bowls. Garnish with sliced green onions, if desired. Yield: 4 cups (46 calories [8% from fat] per 1-cup serving).

FAT 0.4g (SAT 0.1g, MONO 0.1g, POLY 0.2g)
PROTEIN 2.1g CARBOHYDRATE 10.7g
FIBER 1.9g CHOLESTEROL 0mg SODIUM 96mg

Whether served before or after the entrée, Minted Peach and Champagne Soup or Fresh Raspberry Soup will make a lasting impression on your guests.

MINTED PEACH AND CHAMPAGNE SOUP

3 pounds fresh peaches, peeled, pitted, and coarsely chopped
½ cup peach nectar
¼ cup water
1 tablespoon sugar
1½ tablespoons lemon juice
¼ teaspoon ground cinnamon
⅛ teaspoon ground ginger
¼ cup loosely packed fresh mint leaves
1¼ cups champagne, chilled
Fresh peach slices (optional)
Fresh mint sprigs (optional)

Combine first 7 ingredients in a medium saucepan. Bring to a boil; cover, reduce heat, and simmer 10 to 15 minutes or until peaches are tender. Remove from heat; let mixture cool slightly.

Transfer peach mixture to container of an electric blender; add mint. Top with cover, and process until smooth. Transfer mixture to a large bowl. Cover and chill thoroughly.

To serve, add champagne to peach mixture; stir gently. Ladle soup into individual bowls. If desired, garnish with fresh peach slices and fresh mint sprigs. Yield: 6 cups (136 calories [1% from fat] per 1-cup serving).

FAT 0.2g (SAT 0.0g, MONO 0.1g, POLY 0.1g)
PROTEIN 1.5g CARBOHYDRATE 26.2g
FIBER 3.0g CHOLESTEROL 0mg SODIUM 4mg

FRESH RASPBERRY SOUP

7 cups fresh raspberries (about 2 pounds)
¼ cup plus 2 tablespoons sugar
2 tablespoons cornstarch
½ teaspoon grated orange rind
2 cups fresh orange juice
⅔ cup water
⅔ cup plus 2 tablespoons vanilla low-fat yogurt, divided

Place raspberries in container of an electric blender or food processor; top with cover, and process until smooth. Strain raspberries, and discard seeds.

Combine raspberry puree, sugar, and next 4 ingredients in a medium nonaluminum saucepan; stir well. Cook over medium heat, stirring constantly, until mixture comes to a boil. Reduce heat, and simmer 1 minute, stirring constantly. Remove from heat; let cool. Pour mixture into a large bowl; cover and chill.

Add ⅔ cup yogurt to raspberry mixture, stirring well. Ladle soup into individual bowls; top evenly with remaining 2 tablespoons yogurt, swirling yogurt to form a design, if desired. Yield: 6 cups (195 calories [6% from fat] per 1-cup serving).

FAT 1.3g (SAT 0.3g, MONO 0.2g, POLY 0.5g)
PROTEIN 3.4g CARBOHYDRATE 45.5g
FIBER 11.4g CHOLESTEROL 1mg SODIUM 21mg

Vegetable Soups

Vegetable soups are a nutritious menu addition. Fresh produce is, of course, a good choice for rich flavor, but soups made with canned or frozen items can be just as delicious and often more convenient to prepare.

Keep in mind that not all vegetables cook in the same length of time. Those that take the longest to cook should be cut into uniform pieces; add the cut vegetables to the soup mixture at the beginning to ensure that they are done.

GARBANZO BEAN SOUP

2 (14½-ounce) cans no-salt-added
   whole tomatoes, undrained and
   coarsely chopped
1¾ cups canned no-salt-added beef
   broth, undiluted
1 cup chopped onion
½ cup chopped carrot
⅓ cup chopped celery
½ teaspoon ground cumin
½ teaspoon caraway seeds, crushed
¼ teaspoon ground red pepper
1 bay leaf
1 (15-ounce) can garbanzo beans,
   drained
1 medium-size yellow squash, sliced
1 medium zucchini, sliced

Combine first 9 ingredients in a Dutch oven; bring to a boil. Cover, reduce heat, and simmer 30 minutes.

Add beans, yellow squash, and zucchini; cover and simmer 30 minutes or until squash is tender, stirring occasionally. Remove and discard bay leaf. Yield: 2 quarts (90 calories [9% from fat] per 1-cup serving).

FAT 0.9g (SAT 0.1g, MONO 0.2g, POLY 0.4g)
PROTEIN 4.4g   CARBOHYDRATE 16.9g
FIBER 2.8g   CHOLESTEROL 0mg   SODIUM 89mg

OLD-FASHIONED WHITE BEAN SOUP

1 pound dried Great Northern
   beans
4 cups water
1 (13¾-ounce) can no-salt-added
   beef broth, undiluted
1 teaspoon beef-flavored bouillon
   granules
¾ teaspoon dried whole thyme
2 medium-size dried red chiles
1 bay leaf
4 cups water
2½ cups sliced carrot
2 cups coarsely chopped lean
   cooked ham
1 cup chopped onion
3 cups peeled, diced red potato
¼ teaspoon freshly ground pepper

Sort and wash beans; place in a Dutch oven. Cover with water to a depth of 2 inches above beans; let soak 8 hours. Drain beans; return to pan. Add 4 cups water and next 5 ingredients. Bring to a boil; cover, reduce heat, and simmer 1 hour.

Add 4 cups water, carrot, ham, and onion to bean mixture. Bring to a boil; cover, reduce heat, and simmer 15 minutes, stirring occasionally. Add potato; bring to a boil. Cover, reduce heat, and simmer 20 minutes or until beans and vegetables are tender, stirring occasionally. Stir in pepper. Remove and discard bay leaf. Yield: 13½ cups (292 calories [9% from fat] per 1½-cup serving).

FAT 2.8g (SAT 0.9g, MONO 1.0g, POLY 0.5g)
PROTEIN 20.3g   CARBOHYDRATE 46.9g
FIBER 22.7g   CHOLESTEROL 19mg   SODIUM 568mg

CREAM OF BROCCOLI SOUP

1 (10-ounce) package frozen
   chopped broccoli
Vegetable cooking spray
2 tablespoons reduced-calorie
   margarine
⅔ cup sliced fresh mushrooms
⅔ cup chopped onion
3 tablespoons all-purpose flour
1 (12-ounce) can evaporated
   skimmed milk
¾ cup canned no-salt-added
   chicken broth, undiluted
½ teaspoon salt
¼ teaspoon dried whole thyme
¼ teaspoon pepper

Cook broccoli according to package directions; drain well. Set aside.

Coat a large saucepan with cooking spray; add margarine. Place over medium heat until margarine melts. Add mushrooms and onion; sauté until tender. Add flour; cook 1 minute, stirring constantly. Gradually add milk and chicken broth; cook, stirring constantly, until mixture is thickened and bubbly. Add broccoli, salt, thyme, and pepper; cook, stirring frequently, until mixture is thoroughly heated. Yield: 4 cups (155 calories [27% from fat] per 1-cup serving).

FAT 4.6g (SAT 0.8g, MONO 1.4g, POLY 1.7g)
PROTEIN 10.0g   CARBOHYDRATE 20.2g
FIBER 2.7g   CHOLESTEROL 3mg   SODIUM 489mg

MUSHROOM AND RICE SOUP

Vegetable cooking spray
2 tablespoons reduced-calorie
    margarine
3 cups finely chopped celery
1 cup chopped onion
½ pound fresh mushrooms, sliced
2½ tablespoons all-purpose flour
3½ cups skim milk, divided
¾ teaspoon salt
1½ cups cooked long-grain rice
    (cooked without salt or fat)

Coat a Dutch oven with cooking spray; add margarine. Place over medium heat until margarine melts. Add celery, onion, and mushrooms; sauté until tender.

Combine flour and ½ cup milk, stirring until smooth; add to vegetable mixture. Add remaining 3 cups milk and salt; cook, stirring constantly, until mixture is thickened. Stir in rice; reduce heat to low, and simmer 15 minutes. Yield: 2 quarts (124 calories [17% from fat] per 1-cup serving).

FAT 2.3g (SAT 0.4g, MONO 0.8g, POLY 0.9g)
PROTEIN 5.8g CARBOHYDRATE 20.6g
FIBER 1.7g CHOLESTEROL 2mg SODIUM 345mg

ROASTED RED PEPPER SOUP

4 medium-size sweet red peppers
1 medium leek
Vegetable cooking spray
¾ teaspoon dried whole thyme
¼ teaspoon salt
¼ teaspoon pepper
2 cloves garlic, minced
1¼ cups canned no-salt-added
    chicken broth, undiluted and
    divided
1 tablespoon reduced-calorie
    margarine
1 tablespoon all-purpose flour
½ cup skim milk
¼ cup plus 1 teaspoon nonfat sour
    cream alternative, divided

Cut peppers in half lengthwise; remove and discard seeds and membranes. Place peppers, skin side up, on a baking sheet; flatten peppers with palm of hand. Broil peppers 5½ inches from heat 15 to 20 minutes or until charred. Place peppers in ice water until cool. Remove from water; peel and discard skins. Coarsely chop peppers, and set aside.

Remove root, tough outer leaves, and top from leek. Cut white part of leek into thin slices. Coat a nonstick skillet with cooking spray; place over medium heat until hot. Add leek; sauté until tender.

Combine roasted peppers, leek, thyme, salt, pepper, garlic, and ¼ cup chicken broth in container of an electric blender; top with cover, and process until mixture is smooth. Add remaining 1 cup chicken broth; process until smooth.

Melt margarine in a medium heavy saucepan over medium heat; add flour, stirring until smooth. Cook 1 minute, stirring constantly. Gradually add milk; cook, stirring constantly, until mixture is thickened and bubbly. Stir in pepper mixture and 3 tablespoons sour cream; cook just until mixture is thoroughly heated, stirring constantly.

Ladle soup into individual bowls; top each with 1 teaspoon sour cream. Yield: 4 cups (102 calories [29% from fat] per 1-cup serving).

FAT 3.3g (SAT 0.6g, MONO 1.0g, POLY 1.3g)
PROTEIN 4.5g CARBOHYDRATE 14.4g
FIBER 2.6g CHOLESTEROL 1mg SODIUM 251mg

DILLED POTATO SOUP

5 cups peeled and diced red potato
    (about 2 pounds)
⅔ cup chopped onion
⅔ cup chopped celery
½ teaspoon salt
¼ teaspoon freshly ground pepper
3 cups canned no-salt-added
    chicken broth, undiluted
½ cup evaporated skimmed milk
1 teaspoon dried whole dillweed

Combine first 6 ingredients in a large saucepan; bring to a boil. Cover, reduce heat, and simmer 15 to 20 minutes or until vegetables are tender. Stir in milk and dillweed.

Place half of potato mixture in container of an electric blender or food processor; top with cover, and process until smooth. Add pureed potato mixture to mixture in pan. Cook over medium heat, stirring frequently, until mixture is thoroughly heated (do not boil). Yield: 7 cups (127 calories [7% from fat] per 1-cup serving).

FAT 1.0g (SAT 0.4g, MONO 0.4g, POLY 0.3g)
PROTEIN 4.8g CARBOHYDRATE 24.6g
FIBER 2.3g CHOLESTEROL 1mg SODIUM 264mg

PUMPKIN-CUMIN SOUP

Vegetable cooking spray
1 tablespoon reduced-calorie
    margarine
1 cup chopped onion
2 (10½-ounce) cans low-sodium
    chicken broth, undiluted and
    divided
2 tablespoons all-purpose flour
1 (16-ounce) can cooked, mashed
    pumpkin
1½ teaspoons ground cumin
½ teaspoon salt
1 cup skim milk
Fresh chives (optional)

Coat a large saucepan with cooking spray; add margarine. Place over medium heat until margarine melts. Add onion; sauté until tender. Stir in 1 can chicken broth; bring to a boil. Cover, reduce heat, and simmer 15 minutes.

Transfer mixture to container of an electric blender; add flour. Top with cover, and process until smooth. Return mixture to pan; add remaining 1 can chicken broth, pumpkin, cumin, and salt, stirring well. Bring to a boil; cover, reduce heat, and simmer 10 minutes, stirring occasionally. Stir in milk; cook just until thoroughly heated (do not boil).

Ladle soup into individual bowls. Garnish with fresh chives, if desired. Yield: 6 cups (74 calories [28% from fat] per 1-cup serving).

FAT 2.3g (SAT 0.5g, MONO 0.9g, POLY 0.7g)
PROTEIN 3.6g CARBOHYDRATE 10.9g
FIBER 1.2g CHOLESTEROL 1mg SODIUM 270mg

HERBED SPLIT PEA SOUP

½ pound dried split peas
3 (10½-ounce) cans low-sodium chicken broth, undiluted
¾ cup chopped onion
½ cup chopped carrot
½ cup chopped lean cooked ham
½ teaspoon ground celery seeds
¼ teaspoon salt
¼ teaspoon dried whole marjoram, crushed
¼ teaspoon freshly ground pepper
⅛ teaspoon dried whole thyme
Fresh thyme sprigs (optional)

Sort and wash peas; place in a Dutch oven. Add broth and next 8 ingredients. Bring to a boil; cover, reduce heat, and simmer 1 hour or until peas are tender.

Transfer mixture in batches to container of an electric blender or food processor; top with cover, and process until smooth. Return puree to pan. Cook over medium heat just until thoroughly heated (do not boil).

Ladle soup into individual bowls. Garnish with fresh thyme sprigs, if desired. Yield: 5 cups (221 calories [11% from fat] per 1-cup serving).

FAT 2.8g (SAT 0.8g, MONO 1.2g, POLY 0.6g)
PROTEIN 17.3g CARBOHYDRATE 33.2g
FIBER 3.6g CHOLESTEROL 9mg SODIUM 475mg

SUMMER SQUASH SOUP

Vegetable cooking spray
2 teaspoons reduced-calorie margarine
1 cup chopped onion
2 tablespoons chopped fresh parsley
1½ teaspoons minced fresh basil
1¾ pounds yellow squash, cut into ¼-inch slices
1 medium zucchini, cut into ¼-inch slices
1 cup canned no-salt-added chicken broth, undiluted
½ teaspoon salt
⅛ teaspoon ground white pepper
1 cup skim milk
Chopped fresh chives (optional)

Coat a Dutch oven with vegetable cooking spray; add margarine. Place over medium-high heat until margarine melts. Add onion, parsley, and basil; sauté until onion is tender. Add yellow squash and next 4 ingredients; cover and cook over medium heat 15 to 20 minutes or until squash is tender, stirring occasionally. Add milk; cook until mixture is thoroughly heated, stirring constantly.

Transfer mixture in batches to container of an electric blender or food processor; top with cover, and process until smooth. Return puree to pan. Cook over medium heat just until thoroughly heated (do not boil).

Ladle soup into individual bowls. Garnish with chopped fresh chives, if desired. Yield: 5 cups (77 calories [23% from fat] per 1-cup serving).

FAT 2.0g (SAT 0.4g, MONO 0.6g, POLY 0.7g)
PROTEIN 4.5g CARBOHYDRATE 11.9g
FIBER 3.2g CHOLESTEROL 1mg SODIUM 307mg

TOMATO-BASIL SOUP

4 cups peeled, seeded, and chopped tomato
2½ cups no-salt-added tomato juice
1 cup coarsely chopped onion
¼ cup chopped fresh basil
2 cloves garlic, halved
½ teaspoon salt
¼ teaspoon ground white pepper
2 tablespoons reduced-calorie margarine
3 tablespoons all-purpose flour
1½ cups skim milk
Fresh basil sprigs (optional)

Combine first 7 ingredients in container of an electric blender or food processor. Top with cover; process until smooth. Transfer mixture to a saucepan; bring to a boil. Cover, reduce heat, and simmer 10 minutes, stirring occasionally.

Melt margarine in a small heavy saucepan over medium heat; add flour, stirring until smooth. Cook 1 minute, stirring constantly. Gradually add milk; cook, stirring constantly, until thickened and bubbly. Gradually stir sauce mixture into tomato mixture. Cook over medium heat just until thoroughly heated (do not boil).

Ladle soup into individual bowls. Garnish with fresh basil sprigs, if desired. Yield: 6 cups (114 calories [24% from fat] per 1-cup serving).

FAT 3.1g (SAT 0.5g, MONO 1.0g, POLY 1.3g)
PROTEIN 5.0g CARBOHYDRATE 19.3g
FIBER 2.6g CHOLESTEROL 1mg SODIUM 287mg

Hearty Vegetable-Barley Soup

Vegetable cooking spray
1 cup chopped onion
½ cup chopped celery
2 tablespoons chopped fresh parsley
1 clove garlic, minced
4 (13¾-ounce) cans no-salt-added beef broth, undiluted
2 (14½-ounce) cans no-salt-added whole tomatoes, undrained and chopped
1 cup thinly sliced carrot
½ cup pearl barley, uncooked
½ teaspoon salt
¼ teaspoon pepper
¼ teaspoon dried whole oregano
¼ teaspoon dried whole basil
¼ teaspoon dried whole thyme
1 bay leaf
1 cup thinly sliced leek
1 cup sliced fresh okra
½ cup peeled, diced turnip

Coat a large Dutch oven with cooking spray; place over medium-high heat until hot. Add onion, celery, parsley, and garlic; sauté 3 to 4 minutes or until vegetables are tender. Add broth and next 9 ingredients to vegetable mixture; bring mixture to a boil, stirring occasionally. Cover, reduce heat, and simmer 20 minutes, stirring occasionally.

Add leek, okra, and turnip to broth mixture; stir well. Cover and simmer an additional 15 to 20 minutes or until vegetables are tender, stirring occasionally. Remove and discard bay leaf. Yield: 3 quarts (113 calories [3% from fat] per 1½-cup serving).

FAT 0.4g (SAT 0.1g, MONO 0.1g, POLY 0.1g)
PROTEIN 3.5g CARBOHYDRATE 23.0g
FIBER 4.2g CHOLESTEROL 0mg SODIUM 190mg

Homemade Vegetable Soup

1¾ cups peeled, cubed potato
1½ cups chopped onion
1 cup sliced carrot
1 cup sliced celery
½ teaspoon dried whole basil
¼ teaspoon dried whole thyme
2 bay leaves
2 (13¾-ounce) cans no-salt-added beef broth, undiluted
1 cup water
¼ cup no-salt-added tomato paste
3 (14½-ounce) cans no-salt-added whole tomatoes, undrained
1 (10-ounce) package frozen whole kernel corn, thawed
1 (10-ounce) package frozen baby lima beans, thawed
1 (10-ounce) package frozen sliced okra, thawed

Combine first 10 ingredients in a large Dutch oven. Place tomatoes, in batches, in container of an electric blender. Top with cover, and process until smooth; add to broth mixture. Bring to a boil; cover, reduce heat, and simmer 30 minutes.

Add corn and lima beans to tomato mixture; bring to a boil. Cover, reduce heat, and simmer 20 minutes, stirring occasionally. Add okra. Bring to a boil; reduce heat and simmer 5 minutes. Remove and discard bay leaves. Yield: 15 cups (145 calories [3% from fat] per 1½-cup serving).

FAT 0.5g (SAT 0.1g, MONO 0.1g, POLY 0.2g)
PROTEIN 6.0g CARBOHYDRATE 31.1g
FIBER 4.2g CHOLESTEROL 0mg SODIUM 84mg

Zucchini and Tomato Soup

2 cups coarsely shredded zucchini
2 (8-ounce) cans no-salt-added tomato sauce
1½ cups sliced fresh mushrooms
1 cup canned no-salt-added chicken broth, undiluted
⅓ cup finely chopped onion
1 small clove garlic, minced
½ teaspoon dried whole basil
½ teaspoon dried whole oregano
1 (14½-ounce) can no-salt-added whole tomatoes, undrained and chopped
1½ teaspoons lemon juice
¼ teaspoon salt
⅛ teaspoon pepper
1½ tablespoons freshly grated Parmesan cheese

Combine first 8 ingredients in a large saucepan; bring to a boil. Reduce heat, and simmer, uncovered, 25 minutes or until zucchini and mushrooms are tender, stirring occasionally. Add tomato, lemon juice, salt, and pepper; cook until thoroughly heated.

Ladle soup into individual bowls; sprinkle evenly with cheese. Yield: 6 cups (68 calories [13% from fat] per 1-cup serving).

Microwave Directions: Combine first 8 ingredients in a 3-quart casserole; cover with heavy-duty plastic wrap, and vent. Microwave at HIGH 18 minutes or until zucchini is tender, stirring after 9 minutes. Stir in tomato, lemon juice, salt, and pepper. Microwave at HIGH 1 to 2 minutes or until mixture is thoroughly heated. Ladle soup into individual bowls; sprinkle evenly with cheese.

FAT 1.3g (SAT 0.6g, MONO 0.5g, POLY 0.2g)
PROTEIN 3.4g CARBOHYDRATE 12.6g
FIBER 2.3g CHOLESTEROL 1mg SODIUM 177mg

Meat and Seafood Soups

Pair a hearty meat or seafood soup with crusty bread, and you have a satisfying meal. For convenience, prepare the soup ahead of time and store in the refrigerator or freezer. You can have dinner on the table in a flash.

BEEF TACO SOUP

3 (6-inch) corn tortillas
Vegetable cooking spray
1 pound ground round
1 cup chopped onion
2 cloves garlic, minced
2 teaspoons chili powder
1 teaspoon ground cumin
¾ teaspoon dried whole oregano
¾ teaspoon salt
¼ teaspoon pepper
1 (14½-ounce) can no-salt-added whole tomatoes, undrained and chopped
1 (16-ounce) can dark red kidney beans, drained
1 (13¾-ounce) can no-salt-added beef broth, undiluted
1 (8-ounce) can no-salt-added tomato sauce
1 (4-ounce) can chopped green chiles
1½ tablespoons seeded and minced jalapeño pepper
½ cup finely shredded iceberg lettuce
½ cup chopped tomato
½ cup (2 ounces) shredded reduced-fat sharp Cheddar cheese

Cut tortillas into ½-inch-wide strips; cut strips in half crosswise. Place tortilla strips on an ungreased baking sheet. Bake at 350° for 12 to 15 minutes or until crisp. Set aside.

Coat a Dutch oven with cooking spray; place over medium heat until hot. Add ground round, onion, and garlic; cook until beef is browned, stirring until it crumbles. Drain beef mixture; pat dry with paper towels. Wipe drippings from pan with a paper towel.

Return beef mixture to pan; add chili powder, cumin, oregano, salt, and pepper, stirring well. Stir in tomato and next 5 ingredients. Bring to a boil; cover, reduce heat, and simmer 30 minutes, stirring occasionally.

Ladle soup into individual bowls; top evenly with lettuce, tomato, cheese, and tortilla strips. Yield: 8 servings (200 calories [23% from fat] per 1-cup serving).

FAT 5.2g (SAT 2.0g, MONO 1.8g, POLY 0.5g)
PROTEIN 17.9g CARBOHYDRATE 20.5g
FIBER 3.4g CHOLESTEROL 36mg SODIUM 400mg

GROUND BEEF-MUSHROOM SOUP

Vegetable cooking spray
1 pound ground round
¾ cup chopped onion
¾ cup chopped celery
¾ cup sliced carrot
3 cloves garlic, minced
6 cups sliced fresh mushrooms
3 tablespoons all-purpose flour
4¼ cups canned no-salt-added beef broth, undiluted and divided
¾ teaspoon salt
½ teaspoon dried whole thyme
½ teaspoon dried whole marjoram
½ cup cooked long-grain rice (cooked without salt or fat)
⅓ cup skim milk
1½ tablespoons diced pimiento
1½ tablespoons dry sherry

Coat a large Dutch oven with cooking spray; place over medium heat until hot. Add ground round, onion, celery, carrot, and garlic; cook until beef is browned, stirring until it crumbles. Drain beef mixture; pat dry with paper towels. Wipe drippings from pan with a paper towel. Return mixture to pan; add mushrooms. Cook 4 minutes or until vegetables are tender, stirring frequently.

Combine flour and ½ cup broth; stir until smooth. Add flour mixture, remaining 3¾ cups broth, salt, thyme, and marjoram to beef mixture; stir well. Cook, uncovered, over medium heat 30 minutes, stirring occasionally. Stir in rice, milk, pimiento, and sherry; cook just until mixture is thoroughly heated (do not boil). Yield: 2 quarts (149 calories [27% from fat] per 1-cup serving).

Microwave Directions: Crumble beef into a deep 5-quart casserole; add onion, celery, carrot, and garlic. Microwave, uncovered, at HIGH 6 to 7 minutes or until beef is no longer pink, stirring every 2 minutes. Drain beef mixture, and pat dry with paper towels. Wipe drippings from casserole with a paper towel. Return mixture to casserole; add mushrooms. Microwave, uncovered, at HIGH 3 minutes or until vegetables are tender.

Combine flour and ½ cup broth; stir until smooth. Add flour mixture, remaining 3¾ cups broth, salt, thyme, and marjoram to beef mixture; stir well. Cover and microwave at HIGH 14 to 16 minutes or until mixture is slightly thickened, stirring every 5 minutes. Stir in rice, milk, pimiento, and sherry; cover and microwave at HIGH 2 minutes or until mixture is thoroughly heated.

FAT 4.5g (SAT 1.5g, MONO 1.8g, POLY 0.5g)
PROTEIN 14.4g CARBOHYDRATE 12.0g
FIBER 1.8g CHOLESTEROL 31mg SODIUM 339mg

CURRIED CHICKEN AND APPLE SOUP

Vegetable cooking spray
½ cup chopped onion
½ cup chopped celery
½ cup shredded carrot
1 cup chopped cooking apple
2½ tablespoons all-purpose flour
⅔ cup canned no-salt-added
   chicken broth, undiluted
1 cup water
½ teaspoon curry powder
¼ teaspoon salt
⅛ teaspoon pepper
¾ cup skim milk
1 cup chopped cooked chicken
   breast (skinned before cooking
   and cooked without salt)

Coat a large saucepan with vegetable cooking spray; place pan over medium-high heat until hot. Add onion, celery, and carrot; sauté until tender. Stir in apple.

Combine flour and broth in a small bowl; stir until smooth. Add flour mixture, water, and next 3 ingredients to vegetable mixture; stir well. Bring to a boil; cover, reduce heat, and simmer 5 to 7 minutes or until mixture is slightly thickened. Stir in milk and chicken; cook just until mixture is thoroughly heated, stirring occasionally. Yield: 4 cups (161 calories [22% from fat] per 1-cup serving).

FAT 4.0g (SAT 1.0g, MONO 1.3g, POLY 0.9g)
PROTEIN 15.4g CARBOHYDRATE 15.7g
FIBER 2.6g CHOLESTEROL 39mg SODIUM 255mg

CREAMY CHICKEN AND MUSHROOM SOUP

Vegetable cooking spray
1 tablespoon reduced-calorie
   margarine
1 cup sliced fresh mushrooms
½ cup sliced green onions
1½ tablespoons all-purpose flour
1 cup skim milk
3 tablespoons water
1 teaspoon chicken-flavored
   bouillon granules
¾ cup diced, cooked chicken breast
   (skinned before cooking and
   cooked without salt)

Coat a large saucepan with vegetable cooking spray; add margarine. Place over medium-high heat until margarine melts. Add mushrooms and green onions; sauté 3 to 4 minutes or until tender.

Add flour; cook 1 minute, stirring constantly. Gradually add milk, water, and bouillon granules; cook over medium heat, stirring constantly, until mixture is thickened. Stir in chicken, and cook until thoroughly heated. Yield: 2 cups (234 calories [29% from fat] per 1-cup serving).

FAT 7.5g (SAT 1.5g, MONO 2.3g, POLY 2.2g)
PROTEIN 27.8g CARBOHYDRATE 14.2g
FIBER 1.2g CHOLESTEROL 61mg SODIUM 585mg

HOT-AND-SOUR SOUP

½ ounce dried shiitake mushrooms
2 cups water
1 (4-ounce) skinned, boned chicken
   breast half
4½ cups canned no-salt-added
   chicken broth, undiluted
½ cup bamboo shoots, cut into strips
½ cup canned shrimp
¼ cup rice vinegar
1 tablespoon sugar
1 tablespoon dry sherry
1 tablespoon low-sodium soy sauce
1½ teaspoons peeled, grated
   gingerroot
1 teaspoon dark sesame oil
½ teaspoon pepper
¼ teaspoon dry mustard
2½ tablespoons cornstarch
2 tablespoons water
1 egg, beaten
2 tablespoons sliced green onion tops

Combine mushrooms and 2 cups water in a small saucepan. Bring to a boil; remove from heat. Cover and let stand 30 minutes. Drain mushrooms, and cut into thin strips. Set aside.

Place chicken between 2 sheets of heavy-duty plastic wrap; flatten to ¼-inch thickness, using a meat mallet or rolling pin. Cut into thin strips.

Combine mushrooms, chicken strips, broth, and next 10 ingredients in a large saucepan. Bring to a boil; cover, reduce heat, and simmer 10 minutes. Combine cornstarch and 2 tablespoons water; add to chicken mixture. Cook 1 minute, stirring constantly. Slowly drizzle egg into soup, stirring constantly with the handle of a wooden spoon. Ladle soup into bowls; sprinkle with green onions. Yield: 6 cups (109 calories [18% from fat] per 1-cup serving).

FAT 2.2g (SAT 0.5g, MONO 0.7g, POLY 0.6g)
PROTEIN 8.8g CARBOHYDRATE 9.4g
FIBER 0.7g CHOLESTEROL 66mg SODIUM 112mg

CHICKEN NOODLE SOUP

1 (3-pound) broiler-fryer, skinned
   and cut in half
1 large onion, cut into 8 wedges
6 sprigs fresh parsley
3 bay leaves
1 clove garlic, halved
8 whole black peppercorns
2 quarts water
Vegetable cooking spray
1 cup sliced carrot
¾ cup chopped celery
½ cup chopped onion
4 ounces medium egg noodles,
   uncooked
½ cup frozen English peas, thawed
¾ teaspoon salt
½ teaspoon pepper
⅛ teaspoon rubbed sage

Combine first 7 ingredients in a Dutch oven. Bring mixture to a boil; cover, reduce heat, and simmer 45 to 50 minutes or until chicken is tender.

Remove chicken from broth, reserving broth. Let chicken cool to touch.

Bone chicken, and coarsely chop; set aside. Strain broth through a cheesecloth- or paper towel-lined sieve; discard onion and seasonings. Cover broth, and chill thoroughly. Skim and discard solidified fat from top of broth. Set aside.

Coat pan with cooking spray; place over medium-high heat until hot. Add carrot, celery, and onion; sauté until tender. Add chicken, broth, noodles, peas, salt, pepper, and sage; bring to a boil. Reduce heat, and simmer, uncovered, 10 minutes or until noodles are tender. Yield: 2½ quarts (122 calories [22% from fat] per 1-cup serving).

FAT 3.0g (SAT 0.6g, MONO 0.8g, POLY 0.7g)
PROTEIN 11.9g CARBOHYDRATE 11.4g
FIBER 1.1g CHOLESTEROL 40mg SODIUM 223mg

Place the first 7 ingredients in a Dutch oven to cook until the chicken is tender. As it simmers, this mixture will create a savory broth that will be the base for the soup.

Chill the strained broth mixture for several hours to allow the fat to condense on the surface. Defat the broth by skimming off the layer of fat that forms.

Sauté the vegetables until tender. This assures the vegetables will be done; the soup does not cook much longer once the other ingredients are added.

You'll welcome cold, rainy days if it means savoring a steaming cup of Chicken Noodle Soup. This healthy version of an old favorite uses skinned poultry to keep fat to a minimum.

CIOPPINO

½ pound unpeeled large fresh
 shrimp
10 littleneck clams
Vegetable cooking spray
1 teaspoon olive oil
1½ cups chopped onion
½ cup chopped green pepper
2½ tablespoons chopped fresh
 parsley
1 large clove garlic, minced
2 (8-ounce) cans no-salt-added
 tomato sauce
1⅔ cups canned tomato puree
1¼ cups canned no-salt-added
 chicken broth, undiluted
½ cup Burgundy or other dry
 red wine
1 bay leaf
½ teaspoon dried whole thyme
½ teaspoon dried whole oregano
¼ teaspoon pepper
¼ teaspoon hot sauce
½ pound red snapper fillets, cut
 into 2-inch pieces
¼ pound fresh sea scallops

Peel and devein shrimp; set aside.
Scrub clam shells; discard any that are
open or cracked. Set aside.

Coat a Dutch oven with cooking
spray; add oil. Place over medium-
high heat until hot. Add onion, green
pepper, parsley, and garlic; sauté until
tender. Add tomato sauce and next 8
ingredients; bring to a boil. Cover, reduce heat, and simmer 20 minutes.

Add shrimp, clams, fish, and scallops to sauce; bring to a boil. Reduce
heat, and simmer 8 to 10 minutes or
until clam shells open wide and fish
flakes easily when tested with a fork.
Remove and discard bay leaf. Yield: 9
cups (189 calories [13% from fat] per
1½-cup serving).

FAT 2.8g (SAT 0.5g, MONO 0.9g, POLY 0.7g)
PROTEIN 22.9g CARBOHYDRATE 18.5g
FIBER 3.7g CHOLESTEROL 77mg SODIUM 441mg

A bowl of Louisiana Gumbo will satisfy even the heartiest appetites.

LOUISIANA GUMBO

¾ cup all-purpose flour
Vegetable cooking spray
1½ cups chopped onion
1½ cups chopped green pepper
¾ cup chopped celery
3 cloves garlic, minced
6½ cups water
2 (14½-ounce) cans no-salt-added
 stewed tomatoes, undrained and
 chopped
2 (10-ounce) packages frozen sliced
 okra, thawed
¾ pound fully cooked smoked
 turkey sausage, sliced
1 (6-ounce) can no-salt-added
 tomato paste
3 bay leaves
1½ teaspoons dried whole thyme
¾ teaspoon Creole seasoning
¾ teaspoon black pepper
1½ pounds unpeeled medium-size
 fresh shrimp
¾ pound fresh lump crabmeat,
 drained
1 (12-ounce) container Select
 oysters, undrained
13½ cups cooked long-grain rice
 (cooked without salt or fat)

Spread flour evenly in a 15- x 10- x
1-inch jellyroll pan. Bake at 350° for
10 to 12 minutes or until browned,
stirring occasionally. Remove from
oven, and set aside.

Coat a large Dutch oven with
cooking spray; place over medium-
high heat until hot. Add onion, green
pepper, celery, and garlic; sauté 3 to 4
minutes or until vegetables are tender. Stir in browned flour, water, and
next 8 ingredients. Bring mixture to a
boil; cover, reduce heat, and simmer
1½ hours, stirring occasionally. Remove and discard bay leaves.

Peel and devein shrimp. Add
shrimp, crabmeat, and oysters to vegetable mixture; cook 5 to 10 minutes
or until shrimp are done and oyster
edges begin to curl. For each serving,
place ¾ cup rice in individual bowls.
Ladle 1 cup gumbo over each serving.
Yield: 18 servings (324 calories [12%
from fat] per serving).

FAT 4.3g (SAT 1.2g, MONO 1.3g, POLY 1.3g)
PROTEIN 20.6g CARBOHYDRATE 50.0g
FIBER 2.2g CHOLESTEROL 90mg SODIUM 338mg

Chowders, Stews, and Chilies

Cool weather just seems to call for the stick-to-your-ribs goodness of chowders, stews, and chilies. Like many long-simmered dishes, these recipes taste even better the second day, and most of them are suitable for freezing.

New England Clam Chowder

Vegetable cooking spray
1 tablespoon reduced-calorie margarine
½ cup chopped onion
½ cup chopped celery
4 (1-ounce) slices Canadian bacon, cut into ½-inch pieces
2 (6½-ounce) cans minced clams, undrained
1 (10½-ounce) can low-sodium chicken broth, undiluted
3 cups peeled, chopped red potato
¼ cup plus 3 tablespoons all-purpose flour
4 cups skim milk, divided
⅛ teaspoon ground white pepper
⅛ teaspoon hot sauce
Chopped fresh parsley (optional)

Coat a Dutch oven with cooking spray; add margarine. Place over medium heat until margarine melts. Add onion, celery, and bacon; sauté until vegetables are tender and bacon is browned.

Drain clams, reserving juice; set clams aside. Add reserved clam juice, broth, and potato to pan. Bring to a boil; cover, reduce heat, and simmer 20 minutes or until potato is tender.

Combine flour and 1½ cups milk; stir until smooth. Add flour mixture, remaining 2½ cups milk, clams, pepper, and hot sauce to potato mixture. Cook over medium heat, stirring constantly, about 10 minutes or until mixture is thickened (do not boil).

Ladle chowder into individual bowls. Garnish with chopped fresh parsley, if desired. Yield: 9 cups (149 calories [13% from fat] per 1-cup serving).

FAT 2.2g (SAT 0.6g, MONO 0.8g, POLY 0.5g)
PROTEIN 10.6g CARBOHYDRATE 21.5g
FIBER 1.2g CHOLESTEROL 19mg SODIUM 431mg

Cheesy Corn Chowder

Vegetable cooking spray
¾ cup sliced green onions
½ cup chopped celery
½ cup chopped sweet red pepper
3½ tablespoons all-purpose flour
4½ cups skim milk, divided
2 cups frozen whole kernel corn, thawed
2½ teaspoons chicken-flavored bouillon granules
⅛ teaspoon ground white pepper
¾ cup (3 ounces) shredded reduced-fat sharp Cheddar cheese

Coat a large saucepan with cooking spray; place over medium heat until hot. Add green onions, celery, and sweet red pepper; sauté until tender.

Combine flour and ½ cup milk; stir until smooth. Add flour mixture, remaining 4 cups milk, corn, bouillon granules, and ground pepper to vegetable mixture. Bring to a boil; reduce heat, and simmer, uncovered, 15 minutes. Add cheese; cook, stirring constantly, until cheese melts. Yield: 6 cups (181 calories [20% from fat] per 1-cup serving).

FAT 4.1g (SAT 2.0g, MONO 1.0g, POLY 0.3g)
PROTEIN 12.9g CARBOHYDRATE 25.2g
FIBER 2.0g CHOLESTEROL 13mg SODIUM 553mg

Oven-Baked Beef Stew

1½ pounds lean boneless round steak
Vegetable cooking spray
¼ cup all-purpose flour
¾ cup canned no-salt-added beef broth, undiluted
1 (12-ounce) can light beer
2 tablespoons prepared mustard
1½ teaspoons low-sodium Worcestershire sauce
1 teaspoon sugar
½ teaspoon pepper
¼ teaspoon salt
3 cups peeled, diced baking potato
2 cups sliced fresh mushrooms
2 medium carrots, scraped and cut into 1-inch julienne strips
¾ cup frozen pearl onions
¾ cup frozen English peas

Trim fat from steak; cut steak into 1-inch pieces. Place steak in a 3-quart casserole or Dutch oven coated with vegetable cooking spray.

Combine flour and broth in a medium bowl; stir until smooth. Add beer and next 5 ingredients to flour mixture; stir well. Pour flour mixture over steak, stirring gently to combine. Cover and bake at 350° for 1 hour, stirring occasionally.

Add potato, mushrooms, carrot, and onion to steak mixture, stirring well. Cover and bake 50 minutes. Stir in peas; cover and bake an additional 10 minutes or until steak and vegetables are tender. Yield: 9 cups (310 calories [18% from fat] per 1½-cup serving).

FAT 6.1g (SAT 2.0g, MONO 2.6g, POLY 0.4g)
PROTEIN 28.9g CARBOHYDRATE 30.5g
FIBER 3.0g CHOLESTEROL 63mg SODIUM 274mg

VEAL RAGOÛT

1½ pounds lean boneless veal
¼ cup plus 3 tablespoons
    all-purpose flour
½ teaspoon pepper
Vegetable cooking spray
1 tablespoon vegetable oil
3 cups water
1 (13¾-ounce) can no-salt-added
    beef broth, undiluted
¼ cup tomato puree
1 teaspoon dried whole thyme
1 teaspoon dried parsley flakes
½ teaspoon salt
1 clove garlic, crushed
1 small bay leaf
4 cups peeled, cubed red potato
4 carrots, scraped and cut into
    1-inch pieces
1 cup frozen English peas

Trim fat from veal; cut veal into 1-inch pieces. Combine flour and pepper; dredge veal in flour mixture. Coat a large Dutch oven with vegetable cooking spray; add oil. Place over medium-high heat until hot. Add veal; cook until browned on all sides, stirring frequently. Drain and pat dry with paper towels. Wipe drippings from skillet with a paper towel.

Return veal to pan. Combine any remaining flour mixture, water, and next 6 ingredients, stirring well. Add flour mixture and bay leaf to veal. Bring to a boil; cover, reduce heat, and simmer 1 hour. Add potato and carrot; cover and simmer 45 minutes or until veal is tender. Stir in peas; cover and cook 10 minutes or until peas are tender. Remove and discard bay leaf. Yield: 9 cups (200 calories [14% from fat] per 1-cup serving).

FAT 3.1g (SAT 0.7g, MONO 0.9g, POLY 1.0g)
PROTEIN 18.5g CARBOHYDRATE 23.7g
FIBER 3.2g CHOLESTEROL 55mg SODIUM 238mg

Invite a few friends or neighbors to share a pot of Veal Ragoût. Begin the meal with a tossed salad, and make sure guests have plenty of crusty French bread to accompany the chunky stew.

EASY VEGETABLE CHILI

Vegetable cooking spray
1 cup chopped onion
1 cup chopped green pepper
¾ cup chopped carrot
3 cloves garlic, minced
4 cups canned no-salt-added beef
    broth, undiluted
1 (15-ounce) can kidney beans,
    drained
1 (15-ounce) can pinto beans,
    drained
1 (14½-ounce) can no-salt-added
    whole tomatoes, undrained and
    chopped
1 (6-ounce) can no-salt-added
    tomato paste
2 tablespoons chili powder
¾ teaspoon ground cumin
¾ teaspoon dried whole oregano
½ teaspoon ground cinnamon
⅛ teaspoon hot sauce
1 jalapeño pepper, seeded and
    chopped
1 bay leaf
¾ cup (3 ounces) shredded
    reduced-fat sharp Cheddar cheese
¼ cup plus 2 tablespoons nonfat
    sour cream alternative

Coat a nonstick skillet with cooking spray; place over medium-high heat until hot. Add onion and next 3 ingredients; sauté until crisp-tender.

Combine vegetable mixture, beef broth, and next 11 ingredients in a Dutch oven; bring to a boil. Reduce heat, and simmer, uncovered, 45 minutes, stirring occasionally. Remove and discard bay leaf.

Ladle chili into individual bowls; top each serving with 2 tablespoons cheese and 1 tablespoon sour cream. Yield: 9 cups (253 calories [13% from fat] per 1½-cup serving).

FAT 3.8g (SAT 1.8g, MONO 0.9g, POLY 0.6g)
PROTEIN 15.5g CARBOHYDRATE 39.7g
FIBER 7.2g CHOLESTEROL 9mg SODIUM 377mg

SANDWICHES

Making sandwiches part of a low-fat eating plan calls for wise selections when choosing ingredients. Condiments, especially mayonnaise, can add a significant amount of fat to a sandwich. But you can substitute nonfat mayonnaise for regular and not give up any of the flavor.

Other low-fat condiments include mustards, nonfat salad dressings, horseradish, and relishes. Some of those items are, however, high in sodium, so use them in moderation if you are on a sodium-restricted diet. The selection of lean meats, poultry, and low-fat or nonfat cheeses goes a long way toward keeping calories and fat to a minimum in sandwiches. We've applied that principle to these recipes — some contain less than 300 calories and all have less than 30 percent of calories from fat.

CRABMEAT SALAD ON ENGLISH MUFFINS

1 (2-ounce) jar diced pimiento, drained
¼ cup finely chopped celery
2 tablespoons chopped green onions
1½ tablespoons nonfat mayonnaise
1½ teaspoons prepared mustard
½ teaspoon lemon juice
1 cup fresh lump crabmeat, drained
2 English muffins, split and toasted
4 tomato slices (¼ inch thick)
3 tablespoons (¾ ounce) shredded reduced-fat sharp Cheddar cheese
Freshly ground pepper

Combine first 6 ingredients in a medium bowl; stir in crabmeat. Place English muffin halves on an ungreased baking sheet. Spoon crabmeat mixture evenly over muffin halves. Top each serving with 1 tomato slice; sprinkle evenly with cheese and pepper. Broil 5½ inches from heat 3 to 4 minutes or until cheese melts. Yield: 4 servings (157 calories [15% from fat] per serving).

FAT 2.6g (SAT 1.2g, MONO 0.7g, POLY 0.5g)
PROTEIN 12.0g   CARBOHYDRATE 21.5g
FIBER 0.6g   CHOLESTEROL 39mg   SODIUM 412mg

TANGY GROUPER SANDWICHES

2 tablespoons lemon juice
1 teaspoon low-sodium Worcestershire sauce
1 teaspoon olive oil
½ teaspoon freshly ground pepper
⅛ teaspoon paprika
Vegetable cooking spray
1 (1-pound) grouper fillet, cut into 4 pieces
3 tablespoons nonfat mayonnaise
1 tablespoon minced onion
2 teaspoons dill pickle relish
½ teaspoon prepared mustard
4 hamburger buns, split and toasted
4 green leaf lettuce leaves
4 tomato slices (¼ inch thick)

Combine lemon juice, Worcestershire sauce, oil, pepper, and paprika; stir well. Coat grill rack with cooking spray; place on grill over medium-hot coals. Place fish on rack, and grill 5 minutes on each side or until fish flakes easily when tested with a fork, basting frequently with lemon juice mixture.

Combine mayonnaise and next 3 ingredients, stirring well; spread mixture evenly over both sides of hamburger buns. Place a piece of fish on bottom half of each bun. Top each with a lettuce leaf, tomato slice, and top half of bun. Yield: 4 servings (273 calories [20% from fat] per serving).

FAT 6.0g (SAT 1.0g, MONO 1.8g, POLY 1.1g)
PROTEIN 25.0g   CARBOHYDRATE 28.5g
FIBER 1.0g   CHOLESTEROL 53mg   SODIUM 352mg

GRILLED MUSHROOM BURGERS

1½ pounds ground round
1½ cups finely chopped fresh mushrooms
¼ cup finely chopped onion
1 tablespoon chili powder
½ teaspoon salt
Vegetable cooking spray
¼ cup plus 2 tablespoons reduced-calorie catsup
6 whole wheat hamburger buns
6 green leaf lettuce leaves
6 tomato slices (¼ inch thick)
6 purple onion slices (¼ inch thick)

Combine first 5 ingredients in a large bowl; stir well. Shape mixture into 6 (½-inch-thick) patties. Coat grill rack with cooking spray; place on grill over medium-hot coals. Place patties on rack, and cook 5 to 7 minutes on each side or to desired degree of doneness.

Spread 1 tablespoon catsup over bottom half of each bun; top each with 1 beef patty. Top each patty with a lettuce leaf, tomato slice, onion slice, and top half of bun. Yield: 6 servings (344 calories [29% from fat] per serving).

FAT 11.0g (SAT 3.6g, MONO 4.3g, POLY 1.3g)
PROTEIN 30.0g   CARBOHYDRATE 30.5g
FIBER 3.2g   CHOLESTEROL 87mg   SODIUM 575mg

Savory Mock Gyros

1 pound lean ground lamb
1 clove garlic, minced
1 teaspoon dried whole oregano
½ teaspoon dried whole marjoram
⅛ teaspoon salt
⅛ teaspoon pepper
Vegetable cooking spray
2 (8-inch) whole wheat pita bread
    rounds, cut in half crosswise
1 cup finely shredded leaf lettuce
Yogurt-Cucumber Sauce
1 small purple onion, thinly sliced
    and separated into rings
¾ cup chopped tomato

Combine first 6 ingredients in a large bowl; stir well. Shape mixture into 16 (1-inch) meatballs. Place meatballs on rack of a broiler pan coated with cooking spray. Broil 5½ inches from heat 12 to 13 minutes or to desired degree of doneness.

Line each pita half with ¼ cup lettuce; place 4 meatballs in each pita half. Top each serving evenly with Yogurt-Cucumber Sauce, onion, and tomato. Yield: 4 servings (331 calories [26% from fat] per serving).

Yogurt-Cucumber Sauce
½ cup plain nonfat yogurt
⅓ cup finely chopped cucumber
1 clove garlic, minced
¾ teaspoon dried whole dillweed

Combine all ingredients in a small bowl; stir well. Cover and chill thoroughly. Yield: ⅔ cup.

FAT 9.5g (SAT 3.0g, MONO 3.7g, POLY 0.6g)
PROTEIN 30.1g CARBOHYDRATE 27.8g
FIBER 5.0g CHOLESTEROL 81mg SODIUM 171mg

Monte Cristo Sandwiches

½ cup skim milk
1 egg, lightly beaten
2 egg whites, lightly beaten
⅓ cup nonfat sour cream
    alternative
3 tablespoons low-sugar strawberry
    spread
4 (1-ounce) slices reduced-fat Swiss
    cheese
4 (1-ounce) slices roasted turkey
    breast
8 (1-ounce) slices French bread
⅔ cup finely crushed shredded
    whole wheat cereal biscuits
Butter-flavored vegetable cooking
    spray

Combine milk, egg, and egg whites in a shallow bowl; stir well, and set aside. Combine sour cream and strawberry spread in a small bowl; stir well, and set aside.

Place 1 cheese slice and 1 turkey slice on each of 4 bread slices; top with remaining 4 bread slices. Carefully dip sandwiches in egg mixture, allowing excess to drip off. Sprinkle each sandwich with crushed cereal.

Place sandwiches on a baking sheet coated with cooking spray. Bake at 400° for 3 minutes; turn sandwiches, and bake an additional 4 to 6 minutes or until crisp and golden. Serve immediately with strawberry spread mixture. Yield: 4 servings (411 calories [19% from fat] per serving).

FAT 8.8g (SAT 3.9g, MONO 1.3g, POLY 1.3g)
PROTEIN 30.2g CARBOHYDRATE 49.9g
FIBER 2.6g CHOLESTEROL 95mg SODIUM 454mg

Hot Turkey Sandwiches

Vegetable cooking spray
1 medium onion, thinly sliced
1 tablespoon reduced-calorie
    margarine
1½ tablespoons all-purpose flour
¼ cup canned low-sodium chicken
    broth, undiluted
¼ cup skim milk
¼ cup (1 ounce) shredded reduced-
    fat Monterey Jack cheese
⅛ teaspoon ground red pepper
6 (¾-ounce) slices Italian bread,
    toasted
12 (½-ounce) slices cooked turkey
    breast
12 tomato slices (¼ inch thick)
Freshly ground black pepper
    (optional)

Coat a saucepan with cooking spray; place over medium-high heat until hot. Add onion; sauté until tender. Remove from pan; set aside.

Melt margarine in pan over medium heat; add flour, stirring until smooth. Cook 1 minute, stirring constantly. Gradually add broth and milk; cook, stirring constantly, until thickened and bubbly. Remove from heat; add cheese and red pepper, stirring until cheese melts. Set aside.

Arrange bread slices on an ungreased baking sheet. Top each bread slice with 2 turkey slices and 2 tomato slices. Spoon sauce mixture evenly over tomato slices; top evenly with onion slices. Sprinkle with freshly ground black pepper, if desired. Broil 5½ inches from heat 4 to 5 minutes or until thoroughly heated. Yield: 6 servings (169 calories [18% from fat] per serving).

FAT 3.4g (SAT 1.0g, MONO 0.8g, POLY 0.8g)
PROTEIN 10.8g CARBOHYDRATE 22.8g
FIBER 2.0g CHOLESTEROL 27mg SODIUM 458mg

The taste of Turkey Barbecue Sandwiches will earn top honors at a family picnic.

TURKEY BARBECUE SANDWICHES

1 (3-pound) boneless turkey breast, skinned
Tangy Barbecue Sauce
12 whole wheat hamburger buns
Sliced dill pickles (optional)

Trim fat from turkey. Rinse turkey under cold water, and pat dry. Place turkey in an oven cooking bag prepared according to package directions; place in a shallow baking dish. Pour 1 cup Tangy Barbecue Sauce over turkey. Insert meat thermometer. Bake at 325° for 1 hour. Cut a slit in top of bag; bake an additional 30 minutes or until thermometer registers 170°.

Carefully remove turkey from bag; let cool to touch. Chop turkey, and return to baking dish; stir in remaining 3 cups Tangy Barbecue Sauce. Cover and bake 15 minutes or until turkey is thoroughly heated, stirring occasionally.

Place bottom halves of buns on a serving platter. Divide turkey mixture evenly among bottom halves. Top with remaining halves of buns. Serve with sliced dill pickles, if desired. Yield: 12 servings (342 calories [13% from fat] per serving).

Tangy Barbecue Sauce
Vegetable cooking spray
2 teaspoons reduced-calorie margarine
1½ cups finely chopped onion
1¾ cups reduced-calorie catsup
⅔ cup water
⅔ cup white vinegar
½ cup firmly packed dark brown sugar
1 tablespoon plus 1 teaspoon chili powder
1 tablespoon cracked pepper
3 tablespoons low-sodium Worcestershire sauce
¾ teaspoon salt

Coat a large saucepan with vegetable cooking spray; add margarine. Place over medium-high heat until margarine melts. Add onion; sauté 3 to 4 minutes or until crisp-tender. Add catsup and remaining ingredients; stir well. Bring catsup mixture to a boil; cover, reduce heat, and simmer 30 minutes, stirring occasionally. Yield: 4 cups.

FAT 5.0g (SAT 1.3g, MONO 1.5g, POLY 1.2g)
PROTEIN 32.6g CARBOHYDRATE 40.2g
FIBER 2.5g CHOLESTEROL 93mg SODIUM 540mg

GARDEN TURKEY POCKETS

1½ cups cubed cooked turkey breast (skinned before cooking and cooked without salt)
½ cup coarsely shredded carrot
½ cup diced celery
2½ tablespoons plain nonfat yogurt
2 tablespoons commercial oil-free Italian dressing
2 (6-inch) whole wheat pita bread rounds, cut in half crosswise
Green leaf lettuce leaves (optional)

Combine first 5 ingredients; stir well. Cover and chill.

Line pita halves with lettuce, if desired. Spoon ½ cup turkey mixture into each half. Yield: 4 servings (184 calories [13% from fat] per serving).

FAT 2.6g (SAT 0.6g, MONO 0.7g, POLY 0.5g)
PROTEIN 19.8g CARBOHYDRATE 17.5g
FIBER 3.3g CHOLESTEROL 48mg SODIUM 148mg

VEGETABLE MELTS

½ cup thinly sliced cucumber
¼ cup shredded carrot
2 tablespoons sliced green onions
1½ tablespoons commercial oil-free Italian dressing
¼ cup (1 ounce) shredded part-skim mozzarella cheese
2 English muffins, split and toasted
¼ cup alfalfa sprouts

Combine first 4 ingredients; set aside. Sprinkle cheese over English muffin halves. Broil 5½ inches from heat 1 minute or until cheese melts. Top each half with vegetable mixture and sprouts. Serve immediately. Yield: 2 servings (231 calories [14% from fat] per serving).

FAT 3.7g (SAT 1.8g, MONO 1.0g, POLY 0.3g)
PROTEIN 9.5g CARBOHYDRATE 39.8g
FIBER 1.6g CHOLESTEROL 8mg SODIUM 529mg

MENUS FOR ALL OCCASIONS

The following pages are filled with a colorful assortment of menus for everyday meals, holidays, and special occasions. These appetizing selections are made up of recipes from every chapter in this book; they even include commercial items for added convenience. And all will easily fit into a healthy, low-fat lifestyle.

In this chapter, you will find 30 taste-tempting menus designed to meet current dietary guidelines for healthy eating. They meet these guidelines with no more than 30 percent of the total menu calories from fat and less than 10 percent of calories from saturated fat. At least 50 percent of the menu calories are derived from carbohydrate, while the remaining calories (about 20 percent) are from protein. Each menu lists the total number of calories per serving and the percent of those calories that come from fat.

From a quick and easy breakfast to a lavish cocktail supper, these menus can be relied on to meet your everyday and entertaining needs. Use them exactly as presented or simply as a guide for creating your own low-fat menus that incorporate other recipes in the book.

Menus for Every Day

Day-to-day meals don't have to be monotonous. Featured in this section is an array of flavorful menus perfect for serving to your family or a casual gathering of friends. Most of the recipes are quick and easy to fix, and several of them can be prepared ahead to save time.

Quick Menus

If the menus in this section interest you, chances are you don't have a lot of time to cook, and yet you are concerned about good nutrition. Cooking mouth-watering, low-fat meals doesn't have to take a lot of time. Nor should you be frustrated trying to locate hard-to-find ingredients. Our menus are made up of simple recipes that incorporate common items found in most supermarkets.

Menus for Entertaining

Whether entertaining two or 25, use these menu themes help take the panic out of entertaining. You'll find that some of these menus are slightly lengthier than others, but with a little planning and advance preparation, they can be accomplished with skill and artistry.

Beef Tenderloin au Poivre (page 130) is the highlight of this French Fall Supper menu (page 233). Tomatoes Provençal (page 204) and steamed baby carrots offer a subtle flavor contrast to the peppery entrée.

Menus for Every Day

CARTOON BREAKFAST
Serves 12

362 CALORIES (18% FROM FAT) PER SERVING

Even die-hard cartoon fans will come running when this fun menu is served. Menu calories reflect 2 sweet rolls, 1 ounce of bacon, and ½ cup of fresh melon per person.

Cinnamon-Almond Sweet Rolls
(page 54)

Canadian bacon

Fresh melon

Orange Juicy (page 34)

CASUAL WEEKEND LUNCH
Serves 6

664 CALORIES (19% FROM FAT) PER SERVING

A casual Saturday lunch with friends is a nice way to catch up on the week's events. So why not serve a soup-and-sandwich combo that's quick to prepare? Each person has ½ cup carrot and celery sticks to enjoy with the soup and sandwich — a light but hearty meal that still leaves room for dessert.

Hot Turkey Sandwiches (page 224)

Cheesy Corn Chowder (page 221)

Carrot and celery sticks

Old-Fashioned Banana Pudding
(page 68)

TV TRAY DINING
Serves 4

705 CALORIES (22% FROM FAT) PER SERVING

Here's a quick menu that lends itself to dining in front of the television. Let the dessert bake while you eat dinner, and it will be ready to take out of the oven just as the evening movie begins.

Monte Cristo Sandwiches
(page 224)

Cream of Broccoli Soup (page 213)

Apple-Berry Crisp (page 71)

FRIDAY NIGHT PIZZA
Serves 4

710 CALORIES (21% FROM FAT) PER SERVING

The end of a busy week at work and school calls for a celebration. Each person enjoys 2 hefty slices of pizza accompanied by 1 cup tossed green salad with 2 tablespoons commercial fat-free dressing. Top each serving of frozen yogurt with 2 tablespoons chocolate syrup for an extra-special treat.

Crispy Snack Mix (page 33)

Hearty Vegetable Pizza with
Oatmeal Crust (page 126)

Tossed green salad

Vanilla Frozen Yogurt (page 68)
with chocolate syrup

COZY WINTER SUPPER
Serves 4

577 CALORIES (17% FROM FAT) PER SERVING

Distinct flavors are showcased in this hearty menu. The calories reflect 1 cup salad and 2 tablespoons salad dressing per serving. For dessert, serve each person 1 ounce of commercial angel food cake with ½ cup ice milk and 3 tablespoons peach sauce.

Spicy Lamb with Couscous (page 140)

Mixed salad greens with Creamy
Yogurt-Mint Dressing (page 181)

Angel food cake with
vanilla ice milk and
Brandied Peach Sauce (page 189)

ASIAN DINNER
Serves 4

340 CALORIES (9% FROM FAT) PER SERVING

Bring home the flavors of Asian cooking with this menu. Serve each person ½ cup cellophane noodles cooked in fat-free beef broth and 1 cup salad with 2 tablespoons dressing.

Vietnamese-Style Steamed
Halibut (page 88)

Cellophane noodles

Mixed salad greens with
Sweet-and-Sour Dressing (page 171)

Refreshing Pineapple Sherbet
(page 67)

CHILI SUPPER

Serves 6

706 CALORIES (17% FROM FAT) PER SERVING

Nothing warms like a bowl of chili. Especially Easy Vegetable Chili, a healthy alternative to the meaty, high-fat varieties. Sugar-and-Spice Baked Apples is the perfect dessert to enjoy by the fireplace; at only 206 calories per serving, you won't feel guilty for your indulgence.

Easy Vegetable Chili (page 223)

Confetti-Stuffed Lettuce (page 175)

Buttermilk Corn Muffins (page 43)

Sugar-and-Spice Baked Apples (page 65)

FAMILY FIESTA

Serves 6

697 CALORIES (9% FROM FAT) PER SERVING

Turn an ordinary dinner into a flavor fiesta with a menu centered around Jalisco-Style Pork Tenderloins, named after a state in Mexico. Along with the side dishes, serve each person a 6-inch corn tortilla.

Jalisco-Style Pork Tenderloins (page 144)

Spicy Mexican Rice (page 107)

Southwestern Black Beans (page 110)

Corn tortillas

Pumpkin Flan (page 69)

ISLAND SAMPLER

Serves 6

705 CALORIES (5% FROM FAT) PER SERVING

Perfect for poolside entertaining, this Caribbean menu features grilled mahimahi, black beans and rice, and 1 commercial dinner roll per guest. The piña coladas set the mood for a fun evening, while the dessert ends the meal on a sweet note.

Creamy Piña Coladas (page 37)

Ginger-Lime Mahimahi (page 88)

Cuban Black Beans and Rice (page 109)

Hard dinner rolls

Tropical Fruit in Custard Sauce (page 66)

SOUTHERN SUNDAY DINNER

Serves 8

720 CALORIES (23% FROM FAT) PER SERVING

Sunday dinner is a special time when families and friends gather to visit and enjoy favorite foods. This menu features traditional recipes prepared in a low-fat manner. Menu calories reflect a ½-cup serving of steamed fresh green beans per person.

Savory Pot Roast (page 132)

Lemon Potato Wedges (page 201)

Steamed green beans

Summer Blackberry Cobbler (page 72)

DOWN-HOME SUPPER

Serves 8

690 CALORIES (20% FROM FAT) PER SERVING

Dish up home-style cooking with this menu. Phyllo pastry replaces high-fat pastry in the pot pie, while tomato slices and 1 commercial roll per person complete the meal.

Phyllo Chicken Pot Pie (page 156)

Marinated Tomato Slices (page 173)

Whole wheat dinner rolls

Old-Fashioned Gingerbread (page 59)

NEIGHBORLY DINNER

Serves 8

547 CALORIES (11% FROM FAT) PER SERVING

If you haven't visited with the neighbors lately, now's the time to renew friendships over dinner. And the more casual the meal, the better. The calories in this informal menu reflect ½ cup peas and carrots and 1 biscuit per serving. Cinnamon-Raisin Apple Turnovers completes a meal that will receive compliments for months to come.

Saucy Turkey Loaf (page 164)

Creamy Garlic Potatoes (page 201)

Steamed peas and carrots

Easy Drop Biscuits (page 40)

Cinnamon-Raisin Apple Turnovers (page 65)

Quick Menus

RUSH-HOUR BREAKFAST

Serves 4

466 CALORIES (14% FROM FAT) PER SERVING

If you are tempted to skip breakfast to save time in the mornings, try this quick menu. The calories reflect 2 muffins per serving. If you don't have time to eat ½ cup of apple wedges for breakfast, carry a medium apple with you to enjoy as a snack.

Three-Bran Muffins (page 42)

Apple wedges

Banana Split Smoothie (page 35)

LUNCH IN A FLASH

Serves 2

465 CALORIES (19% FROM FAT) PER SERVING

This simple but filling menu can be on the table in about 30 minutes. For dessert, serve each person ½ cup commercial strawberry sorbet.

Creamy Chicken-Mushroom Soup (page 218)

Vegetable Melts (page 225)

Strawberry sorbet

Burgers on the Grill is a family-pleasing menu that's easy on the chef. Creamy Potato Salad can be prepared ahead of time, and Grilled Mushroom Burgers and Cookout Vegetable Packets are ready in no time.

LUNCH FOR THE LADIES

Serves 8

623 CALORIES (12% FROM FAT) PER SERVING

Ideal for midday entertaining, this menu features items that can be prepared ahead of time. Accompany each serving of pasta with 1 commercial roll. For dessert, delight everyone with Peach Frozen Yogurt.

Ruby Refresher (page 34)

Creamy Chicken-Basil Pasta (page 156)

Whole wheat dinner rolls

Peach Frozen Yogurt (page 68)

ALFRESCO SUMMER SUPPER

Serves 4

559 CALORIES (14% FROM FAT) PER SERVING

A warm-weather dinner under the stars can be yours with this menu. The entrée teams tender chicken with fresh asparagus, while a creamy pasta side dish and 1 commercial roll per guest serve as accompaniments.

Chicken and Asparagus en Papillote (page 152)

Linguine in Sour Cream-Wine Sauce (page 114)

Whole wheat dinner rolls

Summer Fruit in Sparkling Cider (page 65)

EASY ELEGANT DINNER

Serves 4

588 CALORIES (12% FROM FAT) PER SERVING

Casual entertaining can be fun with these quick and easy recipes. Menu calories reflect a 1-inch slice of commercial French bread and ¾ cup sparkling grape juice per person.

Veal Cutlets in Green Peppercorn Sauce (page 139)

Saffron Rice (page 107)

Herbed Asparagus Sauté (page 194)

French bread

Strawberries à l'Orange (page 66)

Sparkling grape juice

BURGERS ON THE GRILL

Serves 6

668 CALORIES (21% FROM FAT) PER SERVING

If you've been reluctant to enjoy a hamburger lately, take heart. Our burger uses lean ground round to keep fat to a minimum while retaining all the flavor you expect.

Grilled Mushroom Burgers (page 223)

Creamy Potato Salad (page 173)

Cookout Vegetable Packets (page 204)

Frosted Chocolate Brownies (page 64)

Menus for Entertaining

BRUNCH OLÉ
Serves 8

447 CALORIES (22% FROM FAT) PER SERVING

Spice up a brunch with this menu. A cup of coffee punch can be enjoyed while the casserole and muffins bake. The menu calories include 1 muffin and ½ cup fresh fruit per guest.

Chilled Coffee Punch (page 36)

Mexican Breakfast Casserole (page 78)

Granola Muffins (page 43)

Fresh fruit tray

ROMANTIC REPAST
Serves 2

790 CALORIES (16% FROM FAT) PER SERVING

Light some candles and begin this special dinner with 1-cup servings of romaine lettuce topped with 1 tablespoon commercial fat-free dressing. Serve each person 6 ounces of dry red wine with the main course.

Romaine salad

Grilled Pesto Lamb Chops (page 141)

Pasta and Red Peppers (page 115)

Red wine

Raspberry-Champagne Sorbet (page 67)

SAMURAI SAMPLER
Serves 6

443 CALORIES (16% FROM FAT) PER SERVING

Bring out the chopsticks and paper lanterns for this supper. Serve each guest 1 cup fresh spinach with 2 tablespoons vinaigrette. A ¾-cup serving of fresh berries topped with 3 tablespoons lemon sauce is a sweet ending to this low-calorie meal.

Steak Sukiyaki (page 133)

Fresh spinach with Sesame Vinaigrette (page 180)

Fresh berries with Lemon Dessert Sauce (page 188)

MARDI GRAS CELEBRATION
Serves 6

558 CALORIES (12% FROM FAT) PER SERVING

A fun evening is guaranteed when you serve New Orleans-Style Barbecue Shrimp over hot rice (¾ cup rice per serving). Accompaniments include 1 cup salad, 2 tablespoons dressing, and 1 slice bread per serving.

New Orleans-Style Barbecue Shrimp (page 99) with hot rice

Mixed salad greens with Garlic-Herb Buttermilk Dressing (page 180)

French Bread (page 52)

Raspberry Custard Brûlée (page 68)

CHESAPEAKE FEAST
Serves 6

519 CALORIES (19% FROM FAT) PER SERVING

Traditional crabmeat cake recipes use mayonnaise to add moistness before the cakes are deep fat-fried. Our version uses nonfat mayonnaise, and the cakes are browned, not fried, to further reduce the fat content. Serve each guest ½ cup of broccoli.

East Coast Crabmeat Cakes (page 93)

Roasted Rosemary Potatoes (page 201)

Steamed broccoli flowerets

Creamy Vanilla Mousse with Blueberry Sauce (page 73)

CHINESE NEW YEAR'S DINNER
Serves 6

544 CALORIES (22% FROM FAT) PER SERVING

Whether you're celebrating Chinese New Year or another occasion, this meal is sure to please with only 6 percent saturated fat per serving. Instead of fortune cookies, offer 2 lemon wafers per person.

Hot-and-Sour Soup (page 218)

Beef and Broccoli Stir-Fry (page 133)

Oriental Rice (page 107)

Chewy Lemon Wafers (page 62)

FRENCH FALL SUPPER

Serves 6

638 CALORIES (23% FROM FAT) PER SERVING

Bring the flavors of a French country inn to your table with this pleasing menu. Menu calories reflect ½ cup of carrots and a 1-inch slice of commercial French bread per person.

Mushroom-Almond Pastry Cups (page 28)

Beef Tenderloin au Poivre (page 130)

Steamed baby carrots

Tomatoes Provençal (page 204)

French bread

Grand Marnier Soufflés (page 75)

HOLIDAY DINNER

Serves 8

878 CALORIES (14% FROM FAT) PER SERVING

The menu calories for this traditional dinner include ½ cup green beans and 1 roll per person.

Turkey Breast with Cornbread Dressing (page 159)

Sweet Potatoes in Orange Cups (page 202)

Steamed green beans

Festive Cranberry Salad (page 168)

Overnight Crescent Rolls (page 51)

Fresh Fruit Ambrosia (page 66)

BARBECUE BUFFET

Serves 12

719 CALORIES (17% FROM FAT) PER SERVING

You'll jump at the chance to entertain with this fun menu. Each guest may enjoy 2 cookies.

Lemon-Mint Tea (page 36)

Turkey Barbecue Sandwiches (page 225)

Herb-Roasted Corn-on-the-Cob (page 198)

Herbed Tomato Slices (page 204)

Overnight Coleslaw (page 172)

Applesauce-Date Oatmeal Cookies (page 62)

EASTER BUFFET

Serves 8

782 CALORIES (20% FROM FAT) PER SERVING

A lovely centerpiece of fresh-cut flowers will set the mood for this spring feast. Serve each guest 1 commercial dinner roll.

Crabmeat-Stuffed Cherry Tomatoes (page 28)

Apricot-Glazed Ham (page 145)

Candied Sweet Potatoes (page 202)

Asparagus-Leek Bundles (page 194)

Whole wheat dinner rolls

Chocolate Cream Pie (page 71)

CELEBRATION FEAST

Serves 8

706 CALORIES (21% FROM FAT) PER SERVING

Make any occasion an event to remember with this menu. Serve each guest 6 ounces of grape juice.

Hot Artichoke and Parmesan Spread (page 26)

Garlic-Sage Cornish Hens With Wild Rice (page 158)

Lemon-Basil Carrot Bundles (page 196)

Whole Wheat Rolls (page 50)

Chocolate Swirl Cheesecake (page 62)

Sparkling grape juice

COCKTAIL DINNER PARTY

Serves 24

469 CALORIES (21% FROM FAT) PER SERVING

This menu contains all the nutrients needed for a complete meal. The calories reflect ¾ cup fresh fruit and 2 tablespoons dip per serving.

Herb-Crusted Beef Tenderloin Appetizers (page 30)

Appetizer Crabmeat Cakes (page 30)

Spinach-Ricotta Phyllo Triangles (page 31)

Party Antipasto (page 29)

Fresh fruit with Creamy Amaretto Dip (page 26)

Calorie and Nutrient Chart

FOOD	APPROXIMATE MEASURE	FOOD ENERGY (CALORIES)	FAT (GRAMS)	SATURATED FAT (GRAMS)	MONOUNSATURATED FAT (GRAMS)	POLYUNSATURATED FAT (GRAMS)	PROTEIN (GRAMS)	CARBOHYDRATE (GRAMS)	FIBER (GRAMS)	CHOLESTEROL (MILLIGRAMS)	SODIUM (MILLIGRAMS)
Apple											
Fresh, with skin	1 medium	81	0.5	0.08	0.02	0.14	0.2	21.0	4.3	0	0
Juice, unsweetened	½ cup	58	0.1	0.02	0.00	0.04	0.1	14.5	0.2	0	4
Applesauce, unsweetened	½ cup	52	0.1	0.01	0.00	0.02	0.2	13.8	1.8	0	2
Apricot											
Fresh	1 each	18	0.1	0.01	0.01	0.03	0.4	4.1	0.8	0	0
Canned, in juice	½ cup	58	0.0	0.00	0.02	0.01	0.8	15.0	0.5	0	5
Canned, in light syrup	½ cup	75	0.1	—	—	—	0.7	19.0	0.5	—	1
Canned, peeled, in water	½ cup	25	0.0	0.00	0.01	0.01	0.8	6.2	1.7	0	12
Dried, uncooked	1 each	17	0.0	0.00	0.01	0.01	0.3	4.3	0.5	0	1
Nectar	½ cup	70	0.1	0.01	0.05	0.02	0.5	18.0	0.8	0	4
Artichoke											
Whole, cooked	1 each	53	0.2	0.04	0.00	0.09	2.6	12.4	1.1	0	79
Hearts, cooked	½ cup	37	0.1	0.03	0.00	0.06	1.8	8.7	0.8	0	55
Arugula	3 ounces	21	0.5	—	—	—	2.2	3.1		0	23
Asparagus, fresh, cooked	½ cup	23	0.3	0.06	0.01	0.12	2.3	4.0	0.9	0	4
Avocado	1 medium	322	30.6	4.88	19.20	3.92	3.9	14.8	4.2	0	20
Bacon											
Canadian-style	1 ounce	45	2.0	0.63	0.89	0.18	5.8	0.5	0.0	14	399
Cured, broiled	1 ounce	163	14.0	4.93	6.72	1.65	8.6	0.2	0.0	24	452
Turkey, cooked	1 ounce	60	4.0	—	—	—	4.0	8.0	—	20	400
Bamboo shoots, cooked	½ cup	7	0.1	0.03	0.00	0.06	0.9	1.1	0.4	0	2
Banana, whole	1 medium	109	0.5	0.22	0.05	0.11	1.2	27.6	3.5	0	1
Barley, cooked	½ cup	97	0.3	0.07	0.04	0.17	1.8	22.2	—	0	2
Basil, fresh, raw	¼ cup	1	0.0	—	—	—	0.1	0.1	—	0	0
Bean sprouts, raw	½ cup	16	0.1	0.01	0.01	0.01	1.6	3.1	0.6	0	3
Beans, cooked and drained											
Black	½ cup	114	0.5	0.12	0.04	0.20	7.6	20.4	3.6	0	1
Cannellini	½ cup	112	0.4	0.06	0.03	0.24	7.7	20.2	3.2	0	2
Garbanzo	½ cup	134	2.1	0.22	0.48	0.95	7.3	22.5	2.9	0	6
Great Northern	½ cup	132	0.5	0.16	0.02	0.21	9.3	23.7	3.8	0	2
Green, fresh	½ cup	22	0.2	0.04	0.01	0.09	1.2	4.9	1.1	0	2
Green, canned, regular pack	½ cup	14	0.1	0.01	0.00	0.03	0.8	3.1	0.9	0	171
Kidney or red	½ cup	112	0.4	0.06	0.03	0.24	7.7	20.2	3.2	0	2
Lima, frozen, baby	½ cup	94	0.3	0.06	0.02	0.13	6.0	17.5	4.8	0	26
Pinto, canned	½ cup	94	0.4	0.08	0.08	0.14	5.5	17.5	2.6	0	184
Wax, canned	½ cup	14	0.1	0.01	0.00	0.03	0.8	3.1	0.8	0	171
White	½ cup	127	0.6	0.15	0.05	0.25	8.0	23.2	3.9	0	2
Beef, trimmed of fat											
Flank steak, broiled	3 ounces	207	12.7	5.43	5.34	0.39	21.6	0.0	0.0	60	71
Ground, extra-lean, broiled	3 ounces	218	13.9	5.46	6.08	0.52	21.5	0.0	0.0	71	60
Liver, braised	3 ounces	137	4.2	1.62	0.54	0.91	20.7	2.9	0.0	331	60
Round, bottom, braised	3 ounces	189	8.2	2.92	3.75	0.33	26.9	0.0	0.0	82	43
Round, eye of, cooked	3 ounces	156	5.5	2.12	2.43	0.20	24.7	0.0	0.0	59	53
Round, top, lean, broiled	3 ounces	162	5.3	1.84	2.07	0.25	27.0	0.0	0.0	71	52

Dash (—) indicates insufficient data available

FOOD	APPROXIMATE MEASURE	FOOD ENERGY (CALORIES)	FAT (GRAMS)	SATURATED FAT (GRAMS)	MONOUNSATURATED FAT (GRAMS)	POLYUNSATURATED FAT (GRAMS)	PROTEIN (GRAMS)	CARBOHYDRATE (GRAMS)	FIBER (GRAMS)	CHOLESTEROL (MILLIGRAMS)	SODIUM (MILLIGRAMS)
Beef *(continued)*											
Sirloin, broiled	3 ounces	177	7.4	3.03	3.27	0.31	25.8	0.0	0.0	76	56
Tenderloin, roasted	3 ounces	173	7.9	3.09	3.06	0.31	24.0	0.0	0.0	71	54
Beets											
Fresh, diced, cooked	½ cup	26	0.4	0.01	0.01	0.02	0.9	5.7	0.8	0	42
Canned, regular pack	½ cup	31	0.1	0.02	0.02	0.04	0.8	7.5	0.7	0	201
Beverages											
Beer	12 fluid ounces	146	0.0	0.00	0.00	0.00	1.1	13.1	0.7	0	18
Beer, light	12 fluid ounces	95	0.0	0.00	0.00	0.00	0.7	4.4	—	0	10
Brandy, bourbon, gin, rum, vodka, or whiskey, 80 proof	1 fluid ounce	65	0.0	0.00	0.00	0.00	0.0	0.0	0.0	0	0
Champagne	6 fluid ounces	135	0.0	0.00	0.00	0.00	0.5	2.1	0.0	0	7
Club soda	8 fluid ounces	0	0.0	0.00	0.00	0.00	0.0	0.0	0.0	0	48
Coffee liqueur	1 fluid ounce	99	0.1	0.03	0.01	0.03	0.0	13.9	—	0	2
Sherry, sweet	1 fluid ounce	39	0.0	—	—	—	0.1	2.0	0.0	0	4
Vermouth, dry	1 fluid ounce	35	0.0	0.00	0.00	0.00	0.0	1.6	0.0	0	5
Wine, red	6 fluid ounces	121	0.0	0.00	0.00	0.00	0.4	0.5	0.0	0	18
Wine, white, dry	6 fluid ounces	117	0.0	0.00	0.00	0.00	0.2	1.1	0.0	0	7
Blackberries, fresh	½ cup	37	0.3	0.01	0.03	0.16	0.5	9.2	5.3	0	0
Blueberries, fresh	½ cup	41	0.3	0.02	0.04	0.12	0.5	10.2	3.3	0	4
Bouillon, dry											
Beef-flavored cubes	1 cube	3	0.0	—	—	—	0.1	0.2	—	—	400
Beef-flavored granules	1 teaspoon	10	1.1	0.30	—	—	0.5	0.5	—	—	945
Chicken-flavored cubes	1 cube	10	0.2	—	—	—	0.7	1.1	—	1	1152
Chicken-flavored granules	1 teaspoon	10	1.1	0.30	—	—	0.5	0.5	—	—	819
Bran											
Oat, dry, uncooked	½ cup	153	3.0	0.28	0.64	0.72	8.0	23.5	6.0	0	1
Oat, unprocessed	½ cup	114	3.3	0.62	1.10	1.29	8.0	30.8	7.4	0	2
Wheat, crude	½ cup	65	1.3	0.19	0.19	0.66	4.7	19.4	12.7	0	1
Bread											
Bagel, plain	1 each	161	1.5	0.21	0.58	0.63	5.9	30.5	1.2	—	196
Biscuit, homemade	1 each	127	6.4	1.74	2.72	1.62	2.3	14.9	0.6	2	224
Bun, hamburger or hot dog	1 each	136	3.4	0.52	0.66	0.60	3.2	22.4	0.1	13	112
Cornbread	2-ounce square	154	6.0	3.36	1.80	0.41	3.5	21.1	1.2	56	273
English muffin	1 each	182	3.6	1.93	1.02	0.35	5.9	30.9	0.8	32	234
French	1 slice	73	0.5	0.16	0.25	0.25	2.3	13.9	0.6	1	145
Light, wheatberry or 7-grain	1 slice	40	1.0	—	—	—	2.0	7.0	2.8	0	105
Pita, whole wheat	1 medium	122	0.9	0.10	0.07	0.32	2.4	23.5	4.4	0	
Pumpernickel	1 slice	76	0.4	0.05	0.04	0.17	2.8	16.4	1.8	0	176
Rye	1 slice	61	0.3	0.04	0.03	0.12	2.3	13.0	1.5	0	139
White	1 slice	67	0.8	0.19	0.29	0.27	2.2	12.6	0.5	1	127
Whole wheat	1 slice	56	0.7	0.12	0.16	0.29	2.4	11.0	2.1	1	121
Breadcrumbs											
Fine, dry	½ cup	196	2.2	0.52	0.79	0.73	6.3	36.7	2.1	2	368
Seasoned	½ cup	214	1.5	—	—	—	8.4	41.5	0.3	—	1590
Breadstick, plain	1 each	17	0.5	—	—	—	0.4	2.7	—	—	20
Broccoli, fresh, chopped, cooked or raw	½ cup	12	0.1	0.02	0.01	0.07	1.3	2.3	1.4	0	12
Broth											
Beef, canned, diluted	1 cup	31	0.7	0.34	0.29	0.02	4.8	2.6	0.0	24	782
Beef, no-salt-added	1 cup	22	1.2	0.34	0.29	0.02	0.5	1.9	0.0	0	7
Chicken, low-sodium	1 cup	22	0.0	—	—	—	0.4	2.0	0.0	0	4
Chicken, no-salt-added	1 cup	16	1.0	—	—	—	1.0	0.0	—	—	67
Brussels sprouts, fresh, cooked	½ cup	30	0.4	0.08	0.03	0.19	2.0	6.8	3.4	0	16
Buffalo, roasted	3 ounces	111	1.5	0.51	0.47	0.31	22.8	0.0	—	52	48

FOOD	APPROXIMATE MEASURE	FOOD ENERGY (CALORIES)	FAT (GRAMS)	SATURATED FAT (GRAMS)	MONOUNSATURATED FAT (GRAMS)	POLYUNSATURATED FAT (GRAMS)	PROTEIN (GRAMS)	CARBOHYDRATE (GRAMS)	FIBER (GRAMS)	CHOLESTEROL (MILLIGRAMS)	SODIUM (MILLIGRAMS)
Bulgur, uncooked	½ cup	239	0.9	0.16	0.12	0.38	8.6	53.1	12.8	0	12
Butter											
Regular	1 tablespoon	102	11.5	7.17	3.33	0.43	0.1	0.0	0.0	31	117
Whipped	1 tablespoon	68	7.7	4.78	2.22	0.28	0.1	0.0	0.0	21	78
Cabbage											
Bok choy	1 cup	9	0.1	0.02	0.01	0.07	1.0	1.5	0.7	0	45
Common varieties, raw, shredded	½ cup	8	0.1	0.01	0.00	0.03	0.4	1.9	0.8	0	6
Cake, without frosting											
Angel food	2-ounce slice	147	0.1	—	—	—	3.2	33.7	0.0	0	83
Pound	1-ounce slice	305	17.5	10.19	5.22	0.89	3.6	33.7	0.4	134	245
Sponge, cut into 12 slices	1 slice	183	5.0	1.48	1.96	0.69	3.6	30.8	0.3	221	99
Candy											
Hard	1 each	27	0.0	0.00	0.00	0.00	0.0	6.8	0.0	0	2
Jelly beans	1 ounce	104	0.1	0.09	0.04	0.00	0.0	26.4	0.0	0	3
Milk chocolate	1 ounce	153	8.7	5.13	—	0.31	2.4	16.4	—	7	23
Cantaloupe, raw, diced	½ cup	28	0.2	0.12	0.03	0.02	0.7	6.7	0.9	0	7
Capers	1 tablespoon	4	0.0	—	—	—	0.4	0.6	—	0	670
Carambola (starfruit)	1 medium	42	0.4	—	—	—	0.7	9.9	1.5	0	3
Carrot											
Raw	1 medium	31	0.1	0.02	0.01	0.06	0.7	7.3	2.3	0	25
Cooked, sliced	½ cup	33	0.1	0.22	0.01	0.06	0.8	7.6	1.4	0	48
Catsup											
Regular	1 tablespoon	18	0.1	0.01	0.01	0.03	0.3	4.3	0.3	0	178
Reduced-calorie	1 tablespoon	7	0.0	—	—	—	0.0	1.2	—	—	3
Cauliflower, raw, flowerets	½ cup	12	0.1	0.01	0.01	0.04	1.0	2.5	1.2	0	7
Celery, raw, diced	½ cup	10	0.1	0.02	0.02	0.04	0.4	2.2	1.0	0	52
Cereal											
Bran flakes	½ cup	64	0.4	0.06	0.06	0.19	2.5	15.3	2.7	0	182
Corn flakes	½ cup	44	0.0	0.00	0.01	0.02	0.9	9.8	0.1	0	140
Crispy rice	½ cup	55	0.1	—	—	—	0.9	12.4	0.2	0	103
Granola, homemade	½ cup	297	16.6	2.92	4.68	8.60	7.5	33.7	0.7	0	6
Puffed wheat	½ cup	22	0.1	0.01	0.01	0.04	0.9	4.8	0.2	0	0
Raisin bran	½ cup	77	0.5	—	—	—	2.7	18.6	3.4	0	179
Shredded wheat miniatures	½ cup	76	0.5	0.08	0.08	0.25	2.3	17.0	2.0	0	2
Toasted oat	½ cup	44	0.7	0.13	0.26	0.30	1.7	7.8	0.4	0	123
Whole-grain wheat flakes	½ cup	79	0.2	0.04	0.02	0.10	1.9	18.6	1.4	0	150
Cheese											
American, processed	1 ounce	106	8.9	5.58	2.53	0.28	6.3	0.5	0.0	27	405
American, processed, light	1 ounce	50	2.0	—	—	—	6.9	1.0	0.0	—	407
American, processed, skim	1 ounce	69	4.0	—	—	—	6.0	2.0	0.0	15	407
Blue	1 ounce	100	8.1	5.30	2.21	0.23	6.1	0.7	0.0	21	395
Brie	1 ounce	95	7.8	4.94	2.27	0.24	5.9	0.1	0.0	28	178
Cheddar	1 ounce	114	9.4	5.98	2.66	0.26	7.0	0.4	0.0	30	176
Cheddar, 40% less-fat	1 ounce	71	4.1	2.40	1.20	0.10	5.0	6.0	—	15	195
Cheddar, light, processed	1 ounce	50	2.0	—	—	—	6.9	1.0	0.0	—	442
Cheddar, reduced-fat, sharp	1 ounce	86	5.4	3.15	1.50	0.17	8.3	1.2	—	19	205
Colby, reduced-fat	1 ounce	85	5.5	3.23	—	0.17	8.2	0.7	—	19	163
Cottage, nonfat	½ cup	70	0.0	0.00	0.00	0.00	15.0	3.0	—	5	419
Cottage, low-fat (1% milkfat)	½ cup	81	1.1	0.72	0.33	0.03	14.0	3.1	0.0	5	459
Cottage, low-fat (2% milkfat)	½ cup	102	2.2	1.38	0.62	0.06	15.5	4.1	0.0	9	459
Cottage (4% milkfat)	½ cup	108	4.7	2.99	1.34	0.15	13.1	2.8	0.0	16	425

Dash (—) indicates insufficient data available

FOOD	APPROXIMATE MEASURE	FOOD ENERGY (CALORIES)	FAT (GRAMS)	SATURATED FAT (GRAMS)	MONOUNSATURATED FAT (GRAMS)	POLYUNSATURATED FAT (GRAMS)	PROTEIN (GRAMS)	CARBOHYDRATE (GRAMS)	FIBER (GRAMS)	CHOLESTEROL (MILLIGRAMS)	SODIUM (MILLIGRAMS)
Cheese *(continued)*											
Cream, light	1 ounce	62	4.8	2.86	—	0.14	2.9	1.8	—	16	160
Cream, nonfat	1 ounce	24	0.0	—	—	—	4.0	1.0	0.0	5	170
Feta	1 ounce	75	6.0	4.24	1.31	0.17	4.0	1.2	0.0	25	316
Gruyère	1 ounce	117	9.2	5.36	2.84	0.49	8.4	0.1	0.0	31	95
Monterey Jack	1 ounce	106	8.6	5.41	2.48	0.26	6.9	0.2	0.0	22	152
Monterey Jack, reduced-fat	1 ounce	83	5.4	3.15	—	0.17	8.4	0.5	—	19	181
Mozzarella, part-skim	1 ounce	72	4.5	2.86	1.28	0.13	6.9	0.8	0.0	16	132
Mozzarella, whole milk	1 ounce	80	6.1	3.73	1.86	0.21	5.5	0.6	0.0	22	106
Muenster	1 ounce	104	8.5	5.42	2.47	0.19	6.6	0.3	0.0	27	178
Neufchâtel	1 ounce	74	6.6	4.20	1.92	0.18	2.8	0.8	0.0	22	113
Parmesan, grated	1 ounce	129	8.5	5.40	2.47	0.19	11.8	1.1	0.0	22	528
Ricotta, lite	1 ounce	20	1.0	0.60	0.30	0.03	3.0	1.0	—	4	20
Ricotta, nonfat	1 ounce	20	0.0	—	—	—	4.0	2.0	—	3	15
Ricotta, part-skim	1 ounce	39	2.2	1.39	0.65	0.07	3.2	1.5	0.0	9	35
Swiss	1 ounce	107	7.8	5.04	2.06	0.27	8.1	1.0	0.0	26	74
Swiss, reduced-fat	1 ounce	85	5.0	2.78	—	0.17	9.6	0.5	—	18	44
Cherries											
Fresh, sweet	½ cup	52	0.7	0.16	0.19	0.21	0.9	12.0	1.7	0	0
Sour, in light syrup	½ cup	94	0.1	0.03	0.03	0.04	0.9	24.3	0.1	0	9
Sour, unsweetened	½ cup	39	0.2	0.05	0.06	0.07	0.8	9.4	1.8	0	2
Chicken, skinned, boned, and roasted											
White meat	3 ounces	147	3.8	1.07	1.30	0.83	26.1	0.0	0.0	72	65
Dark meat	3 ounces	174	8.3	2.26	3.02	1.91	23.3	0.0	0.0	79	79
Liver	3 ounces	134	4.6	1.56	1.14	0.68	20.7	0.7	0.0	537	43
Chili sauce	1 tablespoon	18	0.1	0.03	0.01	0.00	0.4	4.2	0.1	0	228
Chives, raw, chopped	1 tablespoon	1	0.0	0.00	0.00	0.00	0.1	0.1	0.1	0	0
Chocolate											
Chips, semisweet	¼ cup	215	15.2	—	—	—	1.7	24.2	0.4	0	1
Sweet	1 ounce	150	9.9	—	—	—	1.2	16.4	0.1	0	9
Unsweetened, baking	1 ounce	141	14.7	8.79	4.86	0.45	3.1	8.5	0.7	0	1
Chutney, apple	1 tablespoon	41	0.0				0.2	10.5	—	—	34
Cilantro, fresh, minced	1 tablespoon	1	0.0	0.00	0.00	0.00	0.1	0.3	0.2	0	1
Clams											
Raw	½ cup	92	1.2	0.12	0.10	0.35	15.8	3.2	0.0	42	69
Canned, drained	½ cup	118	1.6	0.15	0.14	0.44	20.4	4.1	0.0	54	90
Cocoa powder, unsweetened	1 tablespoon	24	0.7	0.44	—	0.03	1.6	2.6	—	0	2
Coconut											
Dried, sweetened, shredded	1 cup	463	32.8	29.08	1.39	0.35	2.7	44.0	4.9	0	242
Dried, unsweetened, shredded	1 cup	526	51.4	45.62	2.18	0.56	5.5	18.8	4.2	0	30
Cookies											
Brownie	2-ounce bar	243	10.1	3.13	3.83	2.64	2.7	39.0	—	10	153
Chocolate	1 each	72	3.4	0.90	1.25	0.46	1.0	9.4	0.0	13	61
Chocolate chip	1 each	52	2.9	1.10	1.14	0.49	0.6	6.2	0.0	5	29
Fig bar	1 each	60	1.0	0.26	0.39	0.24	0.5	11.0	—	—	60
Fortune	1 each	23	0.2	—	—	—	0.3	5.0	0.1	—	—
Gingersnaps	1 each	36	1.3	0.33	0.57	0.34	0.5	5.4	0.0	3	11
Oatmeal, plain	1 each	57	2.7	0.68	1.17	0.72	0.9	7.2	0.4	9	46
Sugar wafers	1 each	47	2.4	0.48	1.03	0.73	0.6	5.9	0.0	7	61
Vanilla wafers	1 each	17	0.9	0.17	0.37	0.26	0.2	2.1	0.0	2	22
Corn											
Fresh, kernels, cooked	½ cup	89	1.0	0.16	0.31	0.49	2.6	20.6	3.0	0	14
Cream-style, regular pack	½ cup	92	0.5	0.08	0.16	0.25	2.2	23.2	1.5	0	365

FOOD	APPROXIMATE MEASURE	FOOD ENERGY (CALORIES)	FAT (GRAMS)	SATURATED FAT (GRAMS)	MONOUNSATURATED FAT (GRAMS)	POLYUNSATURATED FAT (GRAMS)	PROTEIN (GRAMS)	CARBOHYDRATE (GRAMS)	FIBER (GRAMS)	CHOLESTEROL (MILLIGRAMS)	SODIUM (MILLIGRAMS)
Cornmeal											
Degermed, yellow	1 cup	505	2.3	0.31	0.57	0.98	11.7	107.2	7.2	0	4
Self-rising	1 cup	407	4.1	0.58	1.09	1.89	10.1	85.7	—	0	1521
Cornstarch	1 tablespoon	31	0.0	0.00	0.00	0.00	0.0	7.3	0.1	0	1
Couscous, cooked	½ cup	100	0.1	0.03	0.02	0.06	3.4	20.8	—	0	4
Crab											
Blue, cooked	3 ounces	87	1.5	0.19	0.24	0.58	17.2	0.0	0.0	85	237
Imitation	3 ounces	87	1.1	—	—	—	10.2	8.7	0.0	17	715
King, cooked	3 ounces	82	1.3	0.11	0.16	0.46	16.5	0.0	0.0	45	912
Crackers											
Graham, plain	1 square	30	0.5	—	—	—	0.5	5.5	—	—	48
Melba rounds, plain	1 each	11	0.2	—	—	—	0.4	2.0	—	—	34
Saltine	1 each	13	0.4	—	—	—	0.3	2.1	—	—	43
Whole wheat	1 each	33	1.3	0.33	0.67	0.00	0.7	4.7	0.3	0	60
Cranberry											
Fresh, whole	½ cup	23	0.1	0.01	0.01	0.04	0.2	6.0	0.6	0	0
Juice cocktail, reduced-calorie	½ cup	22	0.0	0.00	0.00	0.00	0.0	5.6	—	0	4
Juice cocktail, regular	½ cup	75	0.1	0.00	0.01	0.03	0.0	19.2	—	0	5
Sauce, sweetened	¼ cup	105	0.1	0.01	0.01	0.05	0.1	26.9	0.2	0	20
Cream											
Half-and-half	1 tablespoon	20	1.7	1.08	0.50	0.07	0.4	0.7	0.0	6	6
Sour	1 tablespoon	31	3.0	1.88	0.87	0.11	0.5	0.6	0.0	6	8
Sour, nonfat	1 tablespoon	10	0.0	—	—	—	1.0	1.0	—	0	10
Sour, reduced-calorie	1 tablespoon	20	1.8	1.12	0.52	0.07	0.4	0.6	0.0	6	6
Whipping, unwhipped	1 tablespoon	51	5.5	3.43	1.59	0.20	0.3	0.4	0.0	20	6
Creamer, non-dairy, powder	1 teaspoon	11	0.7	0.64	0.02	0.00	0.1	1.1	0.0	0	4
Croutons, seasoned	1 ounce	139	5.0	—	—	—	3.0	18.9	—	—	—
Cucumbers, raw, whole	1 medium	32	0.3	0.08	0.01	0.12	1.3	7.1	2.4	0	5
Currants	1 tablespoon	25	0.0	0.00	0.00	0.02	0.4	6.7	0.1	0	1
Dates, pitted, unsweetened	5 each	114	0.2	0.08	0.07	0.00	0.8	30.5	3.6	0	1
Doughnut, plain, yeast	1 each	166	10.7	2.60	4.64	2.80	2.5	15.1	0.9	10	94
Egg											
White	1 each	16	0.0	0.00	0.00	0.00	3.4	0.3	0.0	0	52
Whole	1 each	77	5.2	1.61	2.00	0.71	6.5	0.6	0.0	213	66
Yolk	1 each	61	5.2	1.62	2.00	0.71	2.8	0.3	0.0	213	7
Substitute, frozen, thawed	¼ cup	30	0.0	0.00	0.00	0.00	6.0	1.0	—	0	90
Eggplant, cooked without salt	½ cup	13	0.1	0.02	0.00	0.04	0.4	3.2	0.5	0	1
Fennel, leaves, raw	½ cup	13	0.2	—	—	—	1.2	2.3	0.2	0	4
Figs											
Fresh	1 medium	37	0.2	0.03	0.03	0.07	0.4	9.9	1.9	0	1
Dried	1 each	48	0.2	0.04	0.05	0.10	0.6	12.2	3.2	0	2
Fish, cooked											
Flounder	3 ounces	100	1.3	0.31	0.26	0.35	20.5	0.0	0.0	58	89
Grouper	3 ounces	100	1.1	0.25	0.23	0.34	21.1	0.0	0.0	40	45
Haddock	3 ounces	95	0.8	0.14	0.13	0.26	20.6	0.0	0.0	63	74
Halibut	3 ounces	119	2.5	0.35	0.82	0.80	22.7	0.0	0.0	35	59
Mackerel, Spanish	3 ounces	134	5.4	1.53	1.82	1.54	20.1	0.0	0.0	62	56
Mahimahi	3 ounces	93	0.8	0.20	0.13	0.18	20.2	0.0	0.0	80	96
Perch	3 ounces	100	1.0	0.20	0.17	0.40	21.1	0.0	0.0	98	67

Dash (—) indicates insufficient data available

FOOD	APPROXIMATE MEASURE	FOOD ENERGY (CALORIES)	FAT (GRAMS)	SATURATED FAT (GRAMS)	MONOUNSATURATED FAT (GRAMS)	POLYUNSATURATED FAT (GRAMS)	PROTEIN (GRAMS)	CARBOHYDRATE (GRAMS)	FIBER (GRAMS)	CHOLESTEROL (MILLIGRAMS)	SODIUM (MILLIGRAMS)
Fish *(continued)*											
Pollock	3 ounces	100	1.1	0.14	0.12	0.53	21.2	0.0	0.0	77	94
Pompano	3 ounces	179	10.3	3.83	2.82	1.24	20.1	0.0	0.0	54	65
Salmon, sockeye	3 ounces	184	9.3	1.63	4.50	2.05	23.2	0.0	0.0	74	56
Scamp	3 ounces	100	1.1	0.25	0.23	0.34	21.1	0.0	0.0	40	45
Snapper	3 ounces	109	1.5	0.31	0.27	0.50	22.4	0.0	0.0	40	48
Sole	3 ounces	100	1.3	0.31	0.26	0.35	20.5	0.0	0.0	58	89
Swordfish	3 ounces	132	4.4	1.20	1.68	1.01	21.6	0.0	0.0	43	98
Trout, rainbow	3 ounces	128	3.7	0.71	1.13	1.31	22.4	0.0	0.0	62	29
Tuna, yellowfin	3 ounces	118	1.0	0.26	0.17	0.31	25.5	0.0	0.0	49	40
Tuna, canned in oil, drained	3 ounces	168	7.0	1.30	2.51	2.45	24.8	0.0	0.0	15	301
Tuna, white, canned in water	3 ounces	116	2.1	0.56	0.55	0.78	22.7	0.0	0.0	36	333
Flour											
All-purpose, unsifted	1 cup	455	1.2	0.19	0.11	0.52	12.9	95.4	3.4	0	2
Bread, sifted	1 cup	495	2.3	0.33	0.19	1.00	16.4	99.4	—	0	3
Cake, sifted	1 cup	395	0.9	0.14	0.08	0.41	8.9	85.1	—	0	2
Rye, light, sifted	1 cup	374	1.4	0.15	0.16	0.58	8.6	81.8	14.9	0	2
Whole wheat, unsifted	1 cup	407	2.2	0.39	0.28	0.93	16.4	87.1	15.1	0	6
Frankfurter											
Beef	1 each	139	12.6	5.30	5.99	0.60	5.3	0.7	0.0	27	451
Turkey	1 each	103	8.5	2.65	3.42	2.29	5.6	1.1	—	42	488
Fruit bar, frozen	1 each	41	0.0	0.01	0.00	0.01	0.9	9.7	0.0	0	5
Fruit cocktail, canned, packed in juice	½ cup	57	0.0	0.00	0.00	0.00	0.6	14.6	0.8	0	5
Garlic, raw	1 clove	4	0.0	0.00	0.00	0.01	0.2	1.0	0.0	0	1
Gelatin											
Flavored, prepared with water	½ cup	81	0.0	—	—	—	1.5	18.6	0.0	0	54
Unflavored	1 teaspoon	10	0.0	—	—	—	2.6	0.0	—	—	3
Ginger											
Fresh, grated	1 teaspoon	1	0.0	0.00	0.00	0.00	0.0	0.3	0.0	0	0
Crystallized	1 ounce	96	0.1	—	—	—	0.1	24.7	0.2	0	17
Grape juice, Concord	½ cup	60	0.0	—	—	—	0.0	14.9	—	—	11
Grapefruit											
Fresh	1 medium	77	0.2	0.03	0.03	0.06	1.5	19.3	1.5	0	0
Juice, unsweetened	½ cup	47	0.1	0.02	0.02	0.03	0.6	11.1	0.0	0	1
Grapes, green, seedless	1 cup	114	0.9	0.30	0.04	0.27	1.1	28.4	2.6	0	3
Grits, cooked	½ cup	73	0.2	0.04	0.06	0.10	1.7	15.7	—	0	0
Ham											
Cured, roasted, extra-lean	3 ounces	123	4.7	1.54	2.23	0.46	17.8	1.3	0.0	45	1023
Reduced-fat, low-salt	3 ounces	104	4.2	—	—	—	15.3	1.8	—	42	658
Hominy, white or yellow	½ cup	58	0.7	0.10	0.18	0.32	1.2	11.4	2.0	0	168
Honey	1 tablespoon	64	0.0	0.00	0.00	0.00	0.1	17.5	0.0	0	1
Honeydew, raw, diced	1 cup	59	0.2	0.08	0.02	0.02	0.8	15.6	1.5	0	17
Horseradish, prepared	1 tablespoon	6	0.0	0.01	0.00	0.01	0.2	1.4	0.1	0	14
Hot sauce, bottled	¼ teaspoon	0	0.0	—	—	—	0.0	0.0	—	0	9
Ice cream, vanilla, regular	½ cup	134	7.2	4.39	2.06	0.27	2.3	15.9	0.0	30	58
Ice milk, vanilla	½ cup	92	2.8	1.76	0.81	0.10	2.6	14.5	0.0	9	52
Jams and Jellies											
Regular	1 tablespoon	54	0.0	0.01	0.00	0.01	0.1	14.0	0.2	0	2
Reduced-calorie	1 tablespoon	29	0.0	—	—	—	0.1	7.4	—	0	16
Jicama	1 cup	49	0.2	0.07	0.01	0.16	1.6	10.5	0.7	0	7

FOOD	APPROXIMATE MEASURE	FOOD ENERGY (CALORIES)	FAT (GRAMS)	SATURATED FAT (GRAMS)	MONOUNSATURATED FAT (GRAMS)	POLYUNSATURATED FAT (GRAMS)	PROTEIN (GRAMS)	CARBOHYDRATE (GRAMS)	FIBER (GRAMS)	CHOLESTEROL (MILLIGRAMS)	SODIUM (MILLIGRAMS)
Kiwifruit	1 each	44	0.5	0.08	0.11	0.06	1.0	8.9	2.6	0	0
Kumquat	1 each	12	0.0	0.00	0.00	0.00	0.2	3.1	0.7	0	1
Lamb											
Ground, cooked	3 ounces	241	16.7	6.91	7.08	1.19	21.0	0.0	—	82	69
Leg, roasted	3 ounces	162	6.6	2.35	2.88	0.43	24.1	0.0	—	76	58
Loin or chop, broiled	3 ounces	184	8.3	2.96	3.62	0.54	25.5	0.0	—	81	71
Rib, broiled	3 ounces	200	11.0	3.95	4.43	1.00	23.6	0.0	—	77	72
Lard	1 tablespoon	116	12.8	5.03	5.77	1.44	0.0	0.0	0.0	12	0
Leeks, bulb, raw	½ cup	32	0.2	0.03	0.05	0.11	0.8	7.3	0.6	0	10
Lemon											
Fresh	1 each	22	0.3	0.04	0.01	0.10	1.3	11.4	0.4	0	3
Juice	1 tablespoon	3	0.0	0.01	0.00	0.01	0.1	1.0	—	0	3
Lentils, cooked	½ cup	115	0.4	0.05	0.06	0.17	8.9	19.9	4.0	0	2
Lettuce											
Belgian endive	1 cup	14	0.1	0.02	0.00	0.04	0.9	2.9	—	0	6
Boston or Bibb, shredded	1 cup	7	0.1	0.02	0.00	0.06	0.7	1.3	0.4	0	3
Curly endive or escarole	1 cup	8	0.1	0.02	0.00	0.04	0.6	1.7	0.4	0	11
Iceberg, chopped	1 cup	7	0.1	0.01	0.00	0.05	0.5	1.1	0.5	0	5
Radicchio, raw	1 ounce	7	0.1	—	—	—	0.4	1.3	—	0	6
Romaine, chopped	1 cup	9	0.1	0.01	0.00	0.06	0.9	1.3	1.0	0	4
Lime											
Fresh	1 each	20	0.1	0.01	0.01	0.04	0.4	6.8	0.3	0	1
Juice	1 tablespoon	4	0.0	0.00	0.00	0.00	0.1	1.4	—	0	0
Lobster, cooked, meat only	3 ounces	83	0.5	0.09	0.14	0.08	17.4	1.1	0.0	61	323
Luncheon meats											
Bologna, all meat	1 slice	90	8.0	3.01	3.80	0.68	3.3	0.8	0.0	16	289
Turkey ham	1 ounce	34	1.2	0.45	0.48	0.37	5.5	0.3	—	19	286
Mango, raw	½ cup	54	0.2	0.05	0.08	0.04	0.4	14.0	1.2	0	2
Margarine											
Regular	1 tablespoon	101	11.4	2.23	5.04	3.57	0.1	0.1	0.0	0	133
Reduced-calorie, stick	1 tablespoon	50	5.6	0.93	2.10	2.37	0.1	0.1	0.0	0	139
Marshmallows, miniature	½ cup	73	0.0	0.00	0.00	0.00	0.5	18.5	0.0	0	9
Mayonnaise											
Regular	1 tablespoon	99	10.9	1.62	3.12	5.68	0.2	0.4	0.0	8	78
Nonfat	1 tablespoon	12	0.0	—	—	—	0.0	3.0	—	0	190
Reduced-calorie	1 tablespoon	44	4.6	0.70	—	2.58	0.1	0.7	0.0	6	88
Milk											
Buttermilk	1 cup	98	2.1	1.35	0.61	0.07	7.8	11.7	0.0	10	257
Buttermilk, nonfat	1 cup	88	0.8	0.64	—	—	8.8	12.0	—	8	256
Chocolate, low-fat 1%	1 cup	158	2.5	1.55	0.75	0.10	8.1	26.1	0.1	8	153
Chocolate, low-fat 2%	1 cup	180	5.0	3.10	1.45	0.18	8.0	25.8	0.1	18	150
Condensed, sweetened	1 cup	982	26.3	16.77	7.44	1.04	24.2	166.5	0.0	104	389
Evaporated, skimmed, canned	1 cup	200	0.5	0.31	0.16	0.02	19.3	29.1	0.0	10	294
Low-fat, 1% fat	1 cup	102	2.5	1.61	0.76	0.07	8.0	11.6	0.0	10	122
Low-fat, 2% fat	1 cup	122	4.7	2.93	1.37	0.17	8.1	11.7	0.0	20	122
Nonfat dry	⅓ cup	145	0.3	0.20	0.08	0.01	14.5	20.8	0.0	8	214
Skim	1 cup	86	0.4	0.28	0.11	0.02	8.3	11.9	0.0	5	127
Whole	1 cup	149	8.1	5.05	2.32	0.27	8.0	11.3	0.0	34	120
Millet, cooked	½ cup	143	1.2	0.21	0.22	0.61	4.2	28.4	—	0	2
Molasses, cane, light	1 tablespoon	52	0.0	—	—	—	0.0	13.3	0.0	0	3

Dash (—) indicates insufficient data available

FOOD	APPROXIMATE MEASURE	FOOD ENERGY (CALORIES)	FAT (GRAMS)	SATURATED FAT (GRAMS)	MONOUNSATURATED FAT (GRAMS)	POLYUNSATURATED FAT (GRAMS)	PROTEIN (GRAMS)	CARBOHYDRATE (GRAMS)	FIBER (GRAMS)	CHOLESTEROL (MILLIGRAMS)	SODIUM (MILLIGRAMS)
Mushrooms											
Fresh	½ cup	9	0.1	0.02	0.00	0.06	0.7	1.6	0.5	0	1
Canned	½ cup	19	0.2	0.02	0.00	0.08	1.5	3.9	—	0	—
Shiitake, dried	1 each	14	0.0	0.01	0.01	0.00	0.3	2.6	0.4	0	0
Mussels, blue, cooked	3 ounces	146	3.8	0.72	0.86	1.03	20.2	6.3	0.0	48	314
Mustard											
Dijon	1 tablespoon	18	1.0	—	—	—	0.0	1.0	0.0	0	446
Prepared, yellow	1 tablespoon	12	0.7	0.03	0.53	0.13	0.7	1.0	0.2	0	196
Nectarine, fresh	1 each	67	0.6	0.07	0.23	0.30	1.3	16.1	2.2	0	0
Noodles, bean thread	½ cup	66	0.5	—	—	—	0.5	14.9	—	0	—
Nuts											
Almonds, chopped	1 tablespoon	48	4.2	0.40	2.76	0.89	1.6	1.7	0.9	0	1
Cashews, dry roasted, unsalted	1 tablespoon	49	4.0	0.78	2.34	0.67	1.3	2.8	0.5	0	1
Macadamia, roasted, unsalted	1 tablespoon	60	6.4	0.96	5.06	0.11	0.6	1.1	0.1	0	1
Peanuts, roasted, unsalted	1 tablespoon	53	4.5	0.62	2.22	4.67	2.4	1.7	0.8	0	1
Pecans, chopped	1 tablespoon	50	5.0	0.40	3.14	1.25	0.6	1.4	0.5	0	0
Pine	1 tablespoon	52	5.1	0.78	1.91	2.14	2.4	1.4	0.1	0	0
Walnuts, black	1 tablespoon	47	4.4	0.28	1.00	2.93	1.9	0.9	0.5	0	0
Oats											
Cooked	1 cup	145	2.3	0.42	0.75	0.87	6.1	25.3	2.1	0	374
Rolled, dry	½ cup	156	2.6	0.45	0.80	0.93	6.5	27.1	4.2	0	2
Oil											
Canola	1 tablespoon	117	13.6	0.97	8.76	3.89	0.0	0.0	0.0	0	0
Corn	1 tablespoon	121	13.6	1.73	3.30	8.00	0.0	0.0	0.0	0	0
Olive	1 tablespoon	119	13.5	1.82	9.96	1.13	0.0	0.0	0.0	0	0
Peanut	1 tablespoon	119	13.5	2.28	6.24	4.32	0.0	0.0	0.0	0	0
Safflower	1 tablespoon	121	13.6	1.24	1.65	10.16	0.0	0.0	0.0	0	0
Sesame	1 tablespoon	121	13.6	1.92	5.41	5.69	0.0	0.0	0.0	0	0
Okra, cooked	½ cup	26	0.1	0.04	0.02	0.04	1.5	5.8	0.6	0	4
Olives											
Green, stuffed	1 each	4	0.4	—	—	—	0.0	0.1	—	—	290
Ripe	1 medium	5	0.4	0.08	0.32	0.08	0.0	0.3	0.1	0	35
Onions											
Green, chopped	1 tablespoon	2	0.0	0.00	0.00	0.00	0.1	0.5	0.2	0	1
Raw, chopped	½ cup	32	0.1	0.02	0.02	0.05	1.0	7.3	1.6	0	3
Cooked, yellow or white	½ cup	23	0.1	0.02	0.01	0.04	0.7	5.3	—	0	2
Orange											
Fresh	1 medium	62	0.2	0.02	0.03	0.03	1.2	15.4	5.8	0	0
Juice	½ cup	56	0.1	0.01	0.01	0.01	0.8	13.4	0.2	0	1
Mandarin, canned, packed in juice	½ cup	46	0.0	0.00	0.01	0.01	0.7	12.0	0.1	0	6
Mandarin, canned, packed in light syrup	½ cup	77	0.1	0.02	0.02	0.03	0.6	20.4	0.1	0	8
Mandarin, canned, packed in water	½ cup	37	0.0	—	—	—	0.0	8.4	—	—	11
Oysters, raw	3 ounces	59	2.1	0.54	0.21	0.63	6.0	3.3	0.0	47	95
Papaya											
Fresh, cubed	½ cup	27	0.1	0.03	0.03	0.02	0.4	6.9	1.2	0	2
Nectar, canned	½ cup	71	0.3	0.06	0.05	0.04	0.3	18.1	—	0	6
Parsley, raw	1 tablespoon	1	0.0	0.00	0.00	0.00	0.1	0.3	0.2	0	1
Parsnips, cooked, diced	½ cup	63	0.2	0.04	0.09	0.04	1.0	15.1	2.1	0	8
Pasta, cooked											
Macaroni or lasagna noodles	½ cup	99	0.5	0.07	0.06	0.19	3.3	19.8	1.1	0	1

FOOD	APPROXIMATE MEASURE	FOOD ENERGY (CALORIES)	FAT (GRAMS)	SATURATED FAT (GRAMS)	MONOUNSATURATED FAT (GRAMS)	POLYUNSATURATED FAT (GRAMS)	PROTEIN (GRAMS)	CARBOHYDRATE (GRAMS)	FIBER (GRAMS)	CHOLESTEROL (MILLIGRAMS)	SODIUM (MILLIGRAMS)
Pasta, cooked *(continued)*											
Medium egg noodles	½ cup	106	1.2	0.25	0.34	0.33	3.8	19.9	1.8	26	6
Rice noodles	½ cup	138	1.3	—	—	—	3.1	28.6	—	0	—
Spaghetti or fettuccine	½ cup	99	0.5	0.07	0.06	0.19	3.3	19.8	1.1	0	1
Spinach noodles	½ cup	100	1.0	0.15	0.54	0.21	3.8	18.9	1.4	0	22
Whole wheat	½ cup	100	1.4	0.18	0.64	0.33	3.7	19.8	2.5	0	1
Peaches											
Fresh	1 medium	37	0.1	0.01	0.03	0.04	0.6	9.7	1.4	0	0
Canned, packed in juice	½ cup	55	0.0	0.00	0.01	0.02	0.8	14.3	0.6	0	5
Canned, packed in light syrup	½ cup	69	0.0	0.00	0.02	0.02	0.6	18.6	0.4	0	6
Canned, packed in water	½ cup	29	0.1	0.01	0.03	0.03	0.5	7.5	0.4	0	4
Juice	½ cup	57	0.0	—	—	—	0.0	13.6	—	0	5
Peanut butter, regular	1 tablespoon	95	8.3	1.38	3.99	2.47	4.6	2.6	1.0	0	79
Pear											
Fresh	1 medium	97	0.7	0.03	0.14	0.15	0.6	24.9	4.3	0	0
Canned, packed in juice	½ cup	62	0.1	0.00	0.02	0.02	0.4	16.0	1.1	0	5
Canned, packed in light syrup	½ cup	71	0.0	—	—	—	0.2	19.6	3.1	0	6
Nectar, canned	½ cup	64	0.2	—	—	—	0.4	16.1	0.4	—	1
Peas											
Black-eyed, cooked	½ cup	90	0.7	0.17	0.06	0.28	6.7	15.0	1.5	0	3
English, cooked	½ cup	62	0.2	0.04	0.02	0.10	4.1	11.4	3.5	0	70
Snow pea pods, cooked or raw	½ cup	34	0.2	0.03	0.02	0.08	2.6	5.6	2.2	0	3
Split, cooked	½ cup	116	0.4	0.05	0.08	0.16	8.2	20.7	2.3	0	2
Peppers											
Jalapeño, green	1 each	4	0.0	0.00	0.00	0.01	0.2	0.9	0.2	0	1
Sweet, raw, green, red, or yellow	1 medium	19	0.4	0.05	0.01	0.18	0.6	3.9	1.2	0	2
Phyllo strudel dough, raw	1 each	63	0.2	—	—	—	2.1	13.3	—	—	—
Pickle											
Dill, sliced	¼ cup	4	0.1	0.02	0.00	0.03	0.2	0.9	0.5	0	553
Sweet, sliced	¼ cup	57	0.2	0.04	0.00	0.06	0.2	14.1	0.4	0	276
Pie, baked, 9-inch diameter, cut into 8 slices											
Apple, fresh	1 slice	409	15.3	5.22	5.96	3.18	3.3	67.7	3.5	12	229
Chocolate meringue	1 slice	354	13.4	5.38	4.98	2.05	6.8	53.8	0.5	109	307
Pecan	1 slice	478	20.3	4.31	10.28	4.41	5.8	71.1	0.5	141	324
Pumpkin	1 slice	181	6.8	2.24	2.68	1.37	4.0	27.0	0.8	61	210
Pimiento, diced	1 tablespoon	4	0.1	0.01	0.01	0.05	0.2	1.0	—	0	3
Pineapple											
Fresh, diced	½ cup	38	0.3	0.02	0.04	0.11	0.3	9.6	1.2	0	1
Canned, packed in juice	½ cup	75	0.1	0.01	0.01	0.30	0.5	19.6	0.9	0	1
Canned, packed in light syrup	½ cup	66	0.2	0.01	0.02	0.05	0.5	16.9	0.6	0	1
Juice, unsweetened	½ cup	70	0.1	0.01	0.01	0.04	0.4	17.2	0.1	0	1
Plum, fresh	1 medium	35	0.4	0.03	0.26	0.09	0.5	8.3	1.3	0	0
Popcorn, hot-air popped	1 cup	23	0.3	0.04	0.07	0.16	0.8	4.6	0.9	0	0
Poppy seeds	1 tablespoon	47	3.9	0.43	0.56	2.70	1.6	2.1	0.5	0	2
Pork, cooked											
Chop, center-loin	3 ounces	204	11.1	—	—	—	24.2	0.0	0.0	77	59
Roast	3 ounces	204	11.7	4.07	5.30	1.42	22.7	0.0	0.0	77	59
Tenderloin	3 ounces	141	4.1	1.41	1.84	0.49	24.5	0.0	0.0	79	57
Potatoes											
Baked, with skin	1 medium	218	0.2	0.05	0.00	0.09	4.4	50.4	3.6	0	16
Boiled, diced	½ cup	67	0.1	0.02	0.00	0.03	1.3	15.6	1.2	0	4

Dash (—) indicates insufficient data available

FOOD	APPROXIMATE MEASURE	FOOD ENERGY (CALORIES)	FAT (GRAMS)	SATURATED FAT (GRAMS)	MONOUNSATURATED FAT (GRAMS)	POLYUNSATURATED FAT (GRAMS)	PROTEIN (GRAMS)	CARBOHYDRATE (GRAMS)	FIBER (GRAMS)	CHOLESTEROL (MILLIGRAMS)	SODIUM (MILLIGRAMS)
Potato chips, regular	10 each	105	7.1	1.81	1.25	3.63	1.3	10.4	1.0	0	94
Pretzel sticks, thin	10 each	25	0.5	—	—	—	0.5	4.4	0.0	—	83
Prunes											
Dried, pitted	1 each	20	0.0	0.00	0.03	0.01	0.2	5.3	0.6	0	0
Juice	½ cup	91	0.0	0.00	0.03	0.01	0.8	22.3	1.3	0	5
Pumpkin, canned	½ cup	42	0.3	0.18	0.05	0.18	1.3	9.9	2.0	0	6
Radish, fresh, sliced	½ cup	10	0.3	0.01	0.01	0.03	0.3	2.1	0.3	0	14
Raisins	1 tablespoon	27	0.0	0.01	0.00	0.01	0.3	7.2	0.5	0	1
Raspberries											
Black, fresh	½ cup	33	0.4	0.01	0.03	0.21	0.6	7.7	5.0	0	0
Red, fresh	½ cup	30	0.3	0.01	0.03	0.19	0.6	7.1	4.6	0	0
Rhubarb											
Raw, diced	½ cup	13	0.1	0.02	0.01	0.04	0.5	2.8	0.4	0	2
Cooked, with sugar	½ cup	157	0.1	0.01	0.00	0.03	0.5	42.1	—	0	1
Rice, cooked without salt or fat											
Brown	½ cup	110	0.9	—	—	—	2.5	23.2	0.3	1	1
White, long-grain	½ cup	108	0.1	0.06	0.07	0.06	2.0	24.0	0.5	0	0
Wild	½ cup	83	0.3	0.04	0.04	0.17	3.3	17.5	—	0	2
Rice cake, plain	1 each	36	0.2	0.00	0.00	0.01	0.7	7.7	0.1	0	1
Roll											
Croissant	1 each	272	17.3	10.67	4.96	0.78	4.6	24.6	0.8	47	384
Hard	1 each	156	1.6	0.35	0.50	0.55	4.9	29.8	0.1	2	312
Kaiser, small	1 each	92	1.8	—	—	—	3.0	16.0	0.1	—	192
Plain, brown-and-serve	1 each	82	2.0	0.34	0.54	0.43	2.2	13.7	0.1	2	141
Whole wheat	1 each	72	1.8	0.51	0.62	0.40	2.3	12.0	0.8	9	149
Rutabaga, cooked, cubed	½ cup	29	0.2	0.02	0.02	0.07	0.9	6.6	0.9	0	15
Salad dressing											
Blue cheese	1 tablespoon	84	9.2	—	—	—	0.4	0.3	0.0	0	216
Blue cheese, low-calorie	1 tablespoon	59	5.8	1.40	—	2.58	0.9	0.8	—	11	171
Catalina, fat-free	1 tablespoon	16	0.0	0.0	0.0	0.0	0.0	3.0	—	0	120
French	1 tablespoon	96	9.4	—	—	—	0.3	2.9	0.0	8	205
French, low-calorie	1 tablespoon	20	0.0	0.00	0.00	0.00	0.0	4.0	—	0	120
Italian	1 tablespoon	84	9.1	—	—	—	0.1	0.6	0.0	0	172
Italian, no-oil, low-calorie	1 tablespoon	8	0.0	—	—	—	0.1	1.8	0.0	0	161
Ranch, fat-free	1 tablespoon	16	0.0	0.00	0.00	0.00	0.0	3.0	—	0	150
Thousand Island	1 tablespoon	59	5.6	0.94	1.30	3.08	0.1	2.4	0.3	—	109
Thousand Island, fat-free	1 tablespoon	20	0.0	0.00	0.00	0.00	0.0	5.0	—	0	135
Thousand Island, low-calorie	1 tablespoon	24	1.6	0.25	0.37	0.93	0.1	2.5	0.2	2	153
Salsa, commercial	1 tablespoon	3	0.0	—	—	—	0.1	0.5	—	—	42
Scallops, raw, large	3 ounces	75	0.6	0.07	0.03	0.22	14.3	2.0	0.0	28	137
Sesame seeds, dry, whole	1 teaspoon	17	1.5	0.21	0.56	0.65	0.5	0.7	0.1	0	0
Sherbet											
Lime or raspberry	½ cup	104	0.9	—	—	—	0.9	23.8	0.0	0	67
Orange	½ cup	135	1.9	1.19	0.54	0.07	1.1	29.3	0.0	7	44
Shortening	1 tablespoon	115	12.8	5.17	5.17	1.46	0.0	0.0	0.0	0	0
Shrimp											
Fresh, cooked, peeled, and deveined	3 ounces	84	0.9	0.25	0.17	0.37	17.8	0.0	0.0	166	191
Canned, drained	3 ounces	102	1.7	0.32	0.25	0.64	19.6	0.9	0.0	147	144
Soup, condensed, made with water											
Chicken noodle	1 cup	75	2.4	0.65	1.11	0.55	4.0	9.3	0.2	7	1106
Cream of chicken	1 cup	117	7.3	2.07	3.27	1.49	2.9	9.0	0.1	10	986
Cream of mushroom	1 cup	129	9.0	2.44	1.46	4.22	2.3	9.0	0.4	2	1032

FOOD	APPROXIMATE MEASURE	FOOD ENERGY (CALORIES)	FAT (GRAMS)	SATURATED FAT (GRAMS)	MONOUNSATURATED FAT (GRAMS)	POLYUNSATURATED FAT (GRAMS)	PROTEIN (GRAMS)	CARBOHYDRATE (GRAMS)	FIBER (GRAMS)	CHOLESTEROL (MILLIGRAMS)	SODIUM (MILLIGRAMS)
Soup, condensed, made with water *(continued)*											
Cream of potato	1 cup	73	2.3	1.22	0.56	0.41	1.7	11.0	—	5	1000
Tomato	1 cup	85	1.9	0.37	0.44	0.93	2.0	16.6	0.5	0	871
Vegetable, beef	1 cup	78	2.0	0.83	0.81	0.12	5.4	9.8	0.2	5	956
Soy sauce											
Regular	1 tablespoon	8	0.0	0.00	0.00	0.01	0.8	1.2	0.0	0	829
Low-sodium	1 tablespoon	6	0.0	0.00	0.00	0.01	0.0	0.0	—	0	390
Reduced-sodium	1 tablespoon	8	0.0	0.00	0.00	0.01	0.8	1.2	0.0	0	484
Spinach											
Fresh	1 cup	12	0.2	0.03	0.01	0.08	1.6	2.0	2.2	0	44
Cooked	½ cup	21	0.2	0.04	0.01	0.10	2.7	3.4	2.4	0	63
Squash, cooked											
Acorn	½ cup	57	0.1	0.03	0.00	0.06	1.1	14.9	1.2	0	4
Butternut	½ cup	41	0.1	0.02	0.01	0.04	0.8	10.7	1.2	0	4
Spaghetti	½ cup	22	0.2	0.05	0.02	0.10	0.5	5.0	1.0	0	14
Summer	½ cup	18	0.3	0.06	0.02	0.12	0.8	3.9	1.4	0	1
Strawberries, fresh	1 cup	45	0.6	0.03	0.08	0.28	0.9	10.5	3.9	0	1
Sugar											
Granulated	1 tablespoon	48	0.0	0.00	0.00	0.00	0.0	12.4	0.0	0	0
Brown, packed	1 tablespoon	51	0.0	—	0.00	0.00	0.0	13.3	0.0	0	4
Powdered	1 tablespoon	29	0.0	0.00	0.00	0.00	0.0	7.5	0.0	0	0
Sunflower kernels	¼ cup	205	17.8	1.87	3.41	11.78	8.2	6.8	2.4	0	1
Sweet potatoes											
Whole, baked	½ cup	103	0.1	0.02	0.00	0.05	1.7	24.3	3.0	0	10
Mashed	½ cup	172	0.5	0.10	0.02	0.21	2.7	39.8	4.9	0	21
Syrup											
Chocolate-flavored	1 tablespoon	49	0.2	0.00	—	0.00	0.6	11.0	—	0	12
Corn, dark or light	1 tablespoon	60	0.0	0.00	—	—	0.0	15.4	0.0	0	14
Maple, reduced-calorie	1 tablespoon	30	0.2	0.00	0.00	0.00	0.0	7.8	0.0	0	41
Pancake	1 tablespoon	50	0.0	0.00	0.00	0.00	0.0	12.8	0.0	0	2
Tangerine, fresh	1 medium	38	0.1	0.02	0.03	0.03	0.5	9.6	1.6	0	1
Tapioca, dry	1 tablespoon	32	0.0	—	—	—	0.0	8.4	0.1	0	0
Tofu											
Firm	4 ounces	164	9.9	1.43	2.18	5.58	17.9	4.9	1.4	0	16
Soft	4 ounces	60	3.0	—	—	—	7.0	2.0	—	0	5
Tomato											
Fresh	1 medium	26	0.4	0.06	0.06	0.17	1.0	5.7	1.6	0	11
Cooked	½ cup	30	0.3	0.04	0.04	0.13	1.3	6.8	0.9	0	13
Juice, regular	1 cup	41	0.1	0.02	0.02	0.06	1.8	10.3	0.9	0	881
Juice, no-salt-added	1 cup	41	0.1	0.02	0.02	0.06	1.8	10.3	0.9	—	24
Paste, regular	1 tablespoon	14	0.1	0.02	0.02	0.06	0.6	3.1	0.7	0	129
Paste, no-salt-added	1 tablespoon	11	0.0	—	—	—	0.5	2.6	—	0	6
Sauce, regular	½ cup	37	0.2	0.03	0.03	0.08	1.6	8.8	1.8	0	741
Sauce, no-salt-added	½ cup	40	0.0	—	—	—	1.2	9.2	1.6	—	24
Stewed, canned	½ cup	30	1.1	0.20	0.35	0.22	0.9	5.2	0.2	0	187
Whole, canned, peeled	½ cup	22	0.0	—	—	—	0.9	5.2	0.8	—	424
Whole, canned, no-salt-added	½ cup	22	0.0	—	—	—	0.9	5.2	0.8	—	15
Tortilla											
Chips, plain	10 each	135	7.3	1.05	2.96	2.83	2.1	16.0	0.2	0	24
Corn, 6″ diameter	1 each	67	1.1	0.12	0.23	0.53	2.1	12.8	1.6	0	53
Flour, 6″ diameter	1 each	111	2.3	0.56	1.00	0.59	2.4	22.2	0.9	0	0

Dash (—) indicates insufficient data available

FOOD	APPROXIMATE MEASURE	FOOD ENERGY (CALORIES)	FAT (GRAMS)	SATURATED FAT (GRAMS)	MONOUNSATURATED FAT (GRAMS)	POLYUNSATURATED FAT (GRAMS)	PROTEIN (GRAMS)	CARBOHYDRATE (GRAMS)	FIBER (GRAMS)	CHOLESTEROL (MILLIGRAMS)	SODIUM (MILLIGRAMS)
Turkey, skinned, boned, and roasted											
White meat	3 ounces	134	2.7	0.87	0.48	0.73	25.3	0.0	0.0	59	54
Dark meat	3 ounces	159	6.1	2.06	1.39	1.84	24.3	0.0	0.0	72	67
Smoked	3 ounces	126	4.9	1.45	—	1.29	20.4	0.0	0.0	48	586
Turnip greens, cooked	½ cup	14	0.2	0.04	0.01	0.07	0.8	3.1	2.2	0	21
Turnips, cooked, cubed	½ cup	14	0.1	0.01	0.00	0.03	0.6	3.8	1.6	0	39
Veal, cooked											
Ground	3 ounces	146	6.4	2.59	2.42	0.47	20.7	0.0	—	88	71
Leg	3 ounces	128	2.9	1.04	1.01	0.25	23.9	0.0	—	88	58
Loin	3 ounces	149	5.9	2.19	2.12	0.48	22.4	0.0	—	90	82
Vegetable juice cocktail											
Regular	1 cup	46	0.2	0.03	0.03	0.09	1.5	11.0	0.5	0	883
Low-sodium	1 cup	48	0.2	—	—	—	2.4	9.7	—	—	48
Venison, roasted	3 ounces	134	2.7	1.06	0.75	0.53	25.7	0.0	—	95	46
Vinegar, distilled	1 tablespoon	2	0.0	0.00	0.00	0.00	0.0	0.8	0.0	0	0
Water chestnuts, canned, sliced	½ cup	35	0.0	0.01	0.01	0.01	0.6	8.7	0.4	0	6
Watermelon, raw, diced	1 cup	51	0.7	0.35	0.10	0.03	1.0	11.5	0.9	0	3
Wheat germ	1 tablespoon	26	0.7	0.12	0.10	0.43	1.7	3.7	1.1	0	1
Whipped cream	1 tablespoon	26	2.8	1.71	0.79	0.10	0.2	0.2	0.0	10	3
Whipped topping, non-dairy, frozen	1 tablespoon	15	1.2	1.02	0.08	0.02	0.1	1.1	0.0	0	1
Wonton wrappers	1 each	6	0.1	0.03	0.04	0.02	0.2	0.9	0.0	5	12
Worcestershire sauce											
Regular	1 tablespoon	12	0.0	0.00	0.00	0.00	0.3	2.7	0.0	0	147
Low-sodium	1 tablespoon	12	0.0	0.00	0.00	0.00	0.0	3.0	—	0	57
Yeast, active, dry	1 package	20	0.1	0.01	0.06	0.00	2.6	2.7	2.2	0	4
Yogurt											
Coffee and vanilla, low-fat	1 cup	193	2.8	1.84	0.77	0.07	11.2	31.3	0.0	11	150
Frozen, low-fat	½ cup	99	2.0	1.41	0.00	0.58	3.0	18.0	—	10	35
Frozen, nonfat	½ cup	82	0.0	0.00	0.00	0.00	3.4	18.1	—	0	60
Fruit varieties, low-fat	1 cup	225	2.6	1.68	0.70	0.05	9.0	42.3	0.2	9	120
Plain, low-fat	1 cup	143	3.5	2.27	0.98	0.07	11.9	16.0	0.0	14	159
Plain, nonfat	1 cup	127	0.4	0.26	0.11	0.01	13.0	17.4	0.0	5	173
Zucchini											
Raw	½ cup	9	0.1	0.02	0.01	0.03	0.7	1.9	0.3	0	2
Cooked, diced	½ cup	17	0.1	0.01	0.00	0.02	0.7	4.1	0.5	0	3

Source of Data:
Computrition, Inc., Chatsworth, California. Primarily comprised of *Composition of Foods: Raw, Processed, Prepared.* Agriculture Handbook No. 8 Series. United States Department of Agriculture, Human Nutrition Information Service, 1976–1990.

Recipe Index

SUBJECT INDEX

Labeling *(continued)*
  Nutrition and Labeling Education
      Act, 15
  regulations, 15, 16, 17
  serving sizes and, 17
Lamb, 140. *See also* Meats.
  nutritional content of, 147
Legumes, 18, 109
  cooking of dried, 109, 111
  nutritional content of, 109

Margarine, 20-21, 23
Marinades, 13, 186
Meatless main dishes, 117-18
  protein content of, 118
Meats, 20, 129. *See also* specific types.
  cooking of, 12, 14, 129
  nutritional comparison of, 147
  recommended servings of, 129
  selection of, 20, 129
Meat thermometers, use of, 11, 129
Menus, dietary guidelines for, 227
Meringues, preparation of baked, 74
Milk and milk products
  low-fat choices, 19, 23, 36
  recommended servings of, 19
Monounsaturated fat
  percentage in fats and oils, 21
  sources of, 8

Nutrients, computer analysis of, 7

Oils. *See also* Tropical oils and
      Vegetable oils.
  comparison of fatty acids in, 21
Omega-3 fatty acids, 85, 88
Oven cooking bags, use of, 159

Pastas, 18, 112
  cooked yield of, 113
  cooking of, 112
Polenta, preparation of, 121
Polyunsaturated fat
  percentage in fats and oils, 21
  sources of, 8
Pork, 142. *See also* Meats.
  internal temperature of cooked, 142
  nutritional content of, 147

Poultry, 20, 149. *See also* specific types.
  cooking of, 12, 14
  food safety and, 150
  lean tips for, 151, 157
  selection of, 149
  storage and handling of, 149
Protein, 117-18
  amino acids and, 117
  calories in, 8
  complementary, 117
  complete and incomplete, 117
  sources of, 117

Recipe modification, 22, 23
Rice, 103-4, 108. *See also* Grains.

Salad dressings, 21, 180
Salads, 167
  fruit, 168
  main-dish, 176
  preparing salad greens for, 167
  selecting and storing salad greens
      for, 167
  vegetable, 170
Salt, 117
Sandwiches, 223
Saturated fat, 7, 8
  labeling for, 16
  percentage in fats and oils, 21
  recommendations for, 8
  reducing intake of, 8
  sources of, 8, 21
Sauces, 183-84
  dessert, 188
  marinades and barbecue, 186
  savory, 184
Serving size. *See* Labeling.
Shellfish, 20, 93
  nutritional content of, 101
  purchasing of, 29, 93
  recommended servings of, 20
  selection and storage of, 93
Side dishes, 193. *See also* Fruits and
      Vegetables.
  cooking vegetables for, 193
  selecting vegetables and fruits for, 193
Sodium. *See* Salt.
Soups, 209
  broths and stocks, 210
  chilled, 211

  chowders, stews, and chilies, 221
  meat and seafood, 217
  removing fat from, 12, 209, 219
  vegetable, 213
Spices, cooking with, 13
Spinach, removing excess moisture from
      cooked, 31
Stir-frying, 14, 134
Substitutions, ingredient, 22-23
Sugar, 21

Tofu, 127
Techniques. *See* Cooking/techniques.
Tools, cooking. *See* Cooking/equipment.
Tropical oils, 8
Turkey, 20, 159. *See also* Poultry.
  forms of, 164

Unsaturated fat, 8. *See also* specific types.

Veal, 136. *See also* Meats.
  nutritional content of, 147
Vegetable cooking spray, cooking with,
      13, 31, 44, 205
Vegetable oils, 20-21
  comparison of fatty acids in, 21
Vegetables, 193
  cooking of, 193
  cutting terms, 9
  preserving the sweet taste of, 198
  recommended servings of, 18, 19, 193
  selection of, 193
  storage of, 199
Vitamins, 16, 18

Wild birds, 165. *See also* Poultry.
Wild game, 146. *See also* Meats.
  cooking of, 146
  nutritional content of, 147
Wine, cooking with, 13

Yeast, 49
Yogurt
  as a low-fat ingredient substitution,
      19, 23
  making yogurt cheese, 13, 83
  selection of, 19

Acknowledgments and Credits

Oxmoor House wishes to thank the following individuals and merchants:

Bromberg's, Birmingham, AL
Cassis & Co., New York, NY
Christine's, Birmingham, AL
Cutco Cutlery Corp., Olean, NY
Cyclamen Studio, Berkley, CA
Dansk International Designs Ltd.,
    Mount Kisco, NY
Deruta of Italy, New York, NY
Barbara Eigen Arts, Jersey City, NJ
Goldsmith/Corot, Inc., New York, NY
Gorham, Smithfield, RI
N.S. Gustin, Atlanta, GA
Haldon, Irving, TX
The Holly Tree, Inc., Birmingham, AL
Jacques Jugeat, Inc., New York, NY
The Loom Co., New York, NY
MacKenzie-Childs, Ltd., Aurora, NY
Monroe Salt Works, Inc., Monroe, ME
Palais Royal, Charlottesville, VA
Sasaki, Secaucus, NJ
Table Matters, Birmingham, AL
Vagabond, Atlanta, GA
Vietri, Hillsborough, NC
Villeroy & Boch Tableware Ltd.,
    New York, NY
Walker Zanger, Houston, TX
Yamazaki Tableware Inc., Teterboro, NJ

Photographers

Ralph Anderson: pages 2, 7, 22, 24, 27, 32, 35, 38, 41, 46, 50, 53, 56, 63, 69, 72, 84, 87, 94, 97, 98, 102, 106, 108, 111, 128, 132, 136, 139, 141, 143, 148, 151, 155, 158, 161, 162, 174, 176, 178, 181, 187, 192, 205, 206

Jim Bathie: front cover, pages 10, 15, 31, 44, 54, 74, 76, 79, 89, 91, 113, 116, 119, 121, 134, 153, 166, 171, 191, 198, 200, 219, 220

Colleen Duffley: pages 226, 230

Keith Harrelson: pages 182, 195, 208, 212, 222, 225

Photo Stylists

Kay E. Clarke: front cover, pages 10, 15, 31, 44, 54, 74, 76, 79, 89, 91, 111, 113, 116, 119, 121, 134, 151, 153, 166

Virginia R. Cravens: pages 2, 7, 24, 27, 32, 35, 38, 41, 46, 50, 53, 56, 63, 69, 72, 84, 97, 98, 102, 106, 108, 128, 132, 136, 139, 141, 143, 148, 155, 158, 161, 162, 171, 174, 176, 178, 181, 182, 187, 191, 192, 195, 198, 200, 205, 206, 208, 212, 219, 220, 222, 225, 226, 230

Angie Neskaug Sinclair: pages 22, 87, 94